THE ULTIMATE U.S. SCHOOL SHOOTING REFERENCE GUIDE

THE ULTIMATE U.S. SCHOOL SHOOTING REFERENCE GUIDE

LUIS D. APONTE

Copyright

Copyright © 2026 by Luis D. Aponte.
Book cover design by Luis D. Aponte.

eBooks distributed by Draft2Digital.com.
Physical books distributed by IngramSpark.com.

All rights reserved. No part of this book may be reproduced in any manner whatsoever without written permission except in the case of brief quotations embodied in critical articles and reviews.

Paperback ISBN-13: 979-8-9910989-6-0
eBook ISBN-13 (ePub): 979-8-9910989-1-5

Owl & Scroll Publishers ♦ Manassas, Virginia

Contents

Copyright — iv
Dedication — vi
Special Thank You — vii
Introduction — viii

1. U.S. School Shootings from 1990-1999 — 1
2. About the Author — 214
3. Connect With Me — 216
4. Other Titles by Luis D. Aponte — 217
5. Notes — 220

Dedication

This book is dedicated to my sister—a special education teacher, wife, mother and grandmother—who took her own life with a firearm on October 31, 2022. It also is written in honor of my alma mater, Marjory Stoneman Douglas High School, which suffered the worst school shooting in Florida's history on February 14, 2018. Lastly, the countless victims of gun violence in schools—those who are no longer with us, as well as the family members and friends who still suffer every day from the wake of its rippling effect—this book is dedicated to you.

My hope is that this reference book will help bring us together in order to help save lives.

Children and educators deserve to feel safe in schools without the threat of gun violence.

Special Thank You

The documentation featured within this book would not have been possible without the endless support and encouragement of my loving wife, Eileen; the tireless diligence of thousands of journalists and authors; the resourcefulness of dozens of research librarians across the country fulfilling my information requests; and the brilliant teams behind Newspapers.com, NewsBank, Gun Violence Archive, Everytown for Gun Safety, the Naval Postgraduate School Center for Homeland Defense and Security, GunMemorial.org, the National School Safety Center, Citizens Crime Commission of New York City, Ballotpedia, Eric Laurine of the School Shooting Database, several law enforcement agencies, coroner's offices, public court documents, the U.S. House of Representatives Subcommittee on Early Childhood, Youth and Families; as well as the Founding Fathers of the United States, who believed, "Our liberty depends on the freedom of the press, and that cannot be limited without being lost." ~ Thomas Jefferson, 1786

Special thanks to Emily Taffel-Cohen of Mugsy PR for your expert book launching advice; Research Librarian Michelle Quigley, who created data heat maps of my results; and my talented book cover designer, David Provolo. You are all worth your weight in gold!

Finally, heartfelt thanks to Lori Alhadeff and Kirk Smalley for generously sharing your stories with me and for your tireless, selfless work in saving lives every day. Your dedication is truly inspirational. As a token of my gratitude, fifty percent of all profits from this book will be donated to your nonprofit organizations, Make Our Schools Safe and Stand for the Silent.

Your collective efforts and expertise help made a positive impact in this world. Thank you!

Introduction

A single-stemmed red rose, a box of assorted chocolates, a stack of greeting cards for my classmates, and one special card set aside for the person who had captured my heart. Inside the card would be a bold question: "Do you like me? Check yes, no, or maybe." If they checked "Yes," I might even call their favorite radio station to dedicate a love song at a time I hoped they were listening. My parents called it "puppy love," yet the emotions, excitement, and anticipation of possibly having that attraction reciprocated sent my heart racing and made it very difficult to focus on schoolwork. That is what I remember about Valentine's Day as a child.

On February 14, 2018, Valentine's Day became a different and far more dangerous memory for many students at my alma mater, Marjory Stoneman Douglas High School in Parkland, Florida. At approximately 2:21 p.m., a 19-year-old former student entered the campus unchallenged with an AR-15 semiautomatic rifle and indiscriminately killed 17 students and staff, injuring 17 more within six and a half minutes. The devastation rippled through the entire South Florida community, and the survivors' bold response was heard around the world.

When the news of the mass shooting broke, I felt paralyzed, angry, and emotionally shredded for the children and families who had been affected so horribly and needlessly. Watching nearly a million people march peacefully in Washington, D.C., alongside solidarity demonstrations worldwide, I questioned my ability to make a meaningful impact to prevent the next school shooting: "Who am I compared to these giants? How can I make a positive difference? What will it take for us to be angry enough to create meaningful, enduring change so that school shootings never happen again?" The answer came when I realized my research skills as a librarian could gather fact-based data and reveal patterns that might help prevent future tragedies. My call to action is to simplify and make this information accessible, in the hope that it will save lives by fostering constructive dialogue and inspiring communities to take preventive action grounded in factual, nonpartisan data.

A Safe Place: How to Prevent the Next School Shooting and *The Ultimate U.S. School Shooting Reference Guide, Volumes 1–3* are the result of seven years of meticulous research into every reported school shooting in the United States during a thirty-year period, from 1990 to 2019. Each incident is cited and cross-referenced with multiple credible sources, including newspapers, books, paid news databases, police and government reports, court documents, nonprofit organizations dedicated to studying gun violence, and others. I hope the patterns and nonpartisan conclusions presented in these books will empower you and your community to help prevent the next school shooting and restore a sense of safety for children and educators.

Walk into any public or school library and search their collection for books on school shootings. Most titles cover between one and eighteen incidents. What makes these four companion volumes different is that they are the first and only books to offer insights into 1,204 U.S. school shooting cases. No community, school, or law enforcement agency can afford to be without these resources.

Please encourage your local schools, colleges, and public libraries to purchase multiple copies so parents, researchers, and community members can learn from the deadly lessons of the past. Children, teachers, and school resource officers deserve to feel safe from gun violence in their schools. Fifty percent of all profits from these books after publishing fees will be donated to the nonprofit organizations Make Our Schools Safe and Stand for the Silent. Thank you for your support!

1

U.S. School Shootings from 1990-1999

#1204

Location of shooting: Compton High School
Date: 1/9/1990
City, State: Compton, CA
Name of victim(s) killed: N/A.
Age of victim(s) killed: N/A.
Name of victim(s) injured: Unnamed high school student due to age.
Age of victim(s) injured: Unreported.
Name of suspect(s)/shooter(s): Two unknown male shooters in a red Chevrolet Blazer.
Age of suspect(s)/shooter(s): Unreported.
Weapon(s): Unreported.
High capacity magazine(s)?: Unreported.
Weapon(s) legally acquired by suspect(s)/shooter(s)?: Unreported.
# of people killed: 0
# of people injured: 1
Total # of victims: 1
Time suspect(s)/shooter(s) were apprehended or killed?: Unreported.
Suspect(s)' mental illness: Unreported.
Suspect(s)' medication or drug use: Unreported.
Suspect(s)' criminal history: Unreported.
Warning signs: Unreported.
Suspect(s)' country of citizenship: Unreported.
Suspect(s)' religious affiliation: Unreported.
Alleged reason for shooting: Gang-related. The gunman fired from a vehicle parked on the street after exchanging words with another student who stood near the victim.
Metal detectors present?: N/A. Victim was shot in the face as he stood inside the school fence.
Location & time of shooting: Unreported.
For more information, contact: Compton Police Disbanded in 2000. Compton Sheriff and L.A. County Sheriff.

Citations/sources: (Shots from car wound youth, 1990) (Fuetsch, 1990, p. J3)

#1203
Location of shooting: Central High School
Date: 1/16/1990
City, State: Providence, RI
Name of victim(s) killed: N/A.
Age of victim(s) killed: N/A.
Name of victim(s) injured: Unnamed girl and man.
Age of victim(s) injured: 16 & 19
Name of suspect(s)/shooter(s): Cambodian teenager.
Age of suspect(s)/shooter(s): 17
Weapon(s): Unreported.
High capacity magazine(s)?: Unreported.
Weapon(s) legally acquired by suspect(s)/shooter(s)?: No
# of people killed: 0
# of people injured: 2
Total # of victims: 2
Time suspect(s)/shooter(s) were apprehended or killed?: Unreported.
Suspect(s)' mental illness: Unreported.
Suspect(s)' medication or drug use: Unreported.
Suspect(s)' criminal history: Unreported.
Warning signs: Unreported.
Suspect(s)' country of citizenship: Cambodia
Suspect(s)' religious affiliation: Unreported.
Alleged reason for shooting: Bullying. Revenge. Racial Tensions.
Metal detectors present?: Unreported.
Location & time of shooting: Unreported.
For more information, contact: Police Capt. Lloyd Allen and Superintendent Joseph Almagno.
Citations/sources: (Middleton, 1990)

#1202
Location of shooting: Taft High School
Date: 2/20/1990
City, State: Cincinnati, OH
Name of victim(s) killed: Derrick Turnbow.
Age of victim(s) killed: 16
Name of victim(s) injured: N/A.
Age of victim(s) injured: N/A.
Name of suspect(s)/shooter(s): Edwin Orlando Swan.
Age of suspect(s)/shooter(s): 18

Weapon(s): Unreported.
High capacity magazine(s)?: Unreported.
Weapon(s) legally acquired by suspect(s)/shooter(s)?: No.
# of people killed: 1
# of people injured: 0
Total # of victims: 1
Time suspect(s)/shooter(s) were apprehended or killed?: Unreported.
Suspect(s)' mental illness: Unreported.
Suspect(s)' medication or drug use: Unreported.
Suspect(s)' criminal history: Unreported.
Warning signs: Unreported.
Suspect(s)' country of citizenship: Unreported.
Suspect(s)' religious affiliation: Unreported.
Alleged reason for shooting: Fight. Stray bullet.
Metal detectors present?: N/A. Fight occurred outside of the high school building. Victim was paralyzed from the shooting, but died 20 months later during routine care at the hospital on October 20, 1991.
Location & time of shooting: Unreported.
For more information, contact: Unreported.
Citations/sources: (Paralyzed for life, 1990, p. 29) (Noble, 2017)

#1201
Location of shooting: New Utrecht High School
Date: 3/27/1990
City, State: Brooklyn, NY
Name of victim(s) killed: N/A.
Age of victim(s) killed: N/A.
Name of victim(s) injured: Unnamed black student.
Age of victim(s) injured: 14
Name of suspect(s)/shooter(s): Three older Caucasian teenagers.
Age of suspect(s)/shooter(s): Unreported.
Weapon(s): .38-caliber handgun.
High capacity magazine(s)?: Unreported.
Weapon(s) legally acquired by suspect(s)/shooter(s)?: Unreported.
# of people killed: 0
# of people injured: 1
Total # of victims: 1
Time suspect(s)/shooter(s) were apprehended or killed?: Unreported.
Suspect(s)' mental illness: Unreported.
Suspect(s)' medication or drug use: Unreported.
Suspect(s)' criminal history: Unreported.

Warning signs: Unreported.
Suspect(s)' country of citizenship: Unreported.
Suspect(s)' religious affiliation: Unreported.
Alleged reason for shooting: Racial tensions. Victim tried to act as a peacemaker in a previous conflict with another black teen.
Metal detectors present?: Unreported.
Location & time of shooting: Shooting occurred at 8:40 A.M. on a school stairwell.
For more information, contact: Detective Joseph McConville, Sgt. Mary Wrensen, and Officer Joseph M. Gallagher, 62nd Precinct squad.
Citations/sources: (Black youth shot by whites, 1990, p. 6) (Hevesi, 1990)

#1200
Location of shooting: Skyline High School
Date: 4/3/1990
City, State: Dallas, TX
Name of victim(s) killed: N/A.
Age of victim(s) killed: N/A.
Name of victim(s) injured: Unnamed youth.
Age of victim(s) injured: 16
Name of suspect(s)/shooter(s): Unreported.
Age of suspect(s)/shooter(s): 17
Weapon(s): Unreported.
High capacity magazine(s)?: Unreported.
Weapon(s) legally acquired by suspect(s)/shooter(s)?: No.
# of people killed: 0
# of people injured: 1
Total # of victims: 1
Time suspect(s)/shooter(s) were apprehended or killed?: Unreported.
Suspect(s)' mental illness: Unreported.
Suspect(s)' medication or drug use: Unreported.
Suspect(s)' criminal history: Suspect had been suspended from school the day before the shooting for fighting.
Warning signs: Unreported.
Suspect(s)' country of citizenship: Unreported.
Suspect(s)' religious affiliation: Unreported.
Alleged reason for shooting: Dispute.
Metal detectors present?: Unreported.
Location & time of shooting: Unreported.
For more information, contact: Senior Cpl. Don Mashburm, Dallas Police Detective Joe Henderson and Skyline Principal Gene Golden.
Citations/sources: (Student is shot at Dallas campus, 1990) (Mittelstadt, 1990, p. 4A)

1199
Location of shooting: Manuel Arts High School
Date: 5/2/1990
City, State: Los Angeles, CA
Name of victim(s) killed: N/A.
Age of victim(s) killed: N/A.
Name of victim(s) injured: Freddy Tapia.
Age of victim(s) injured: 19
Name of suspect(s)/shooter(s): Male Hispanic who may have been a former student.
Age of suspect(s)/shooter(s): 17
Weapon(s): .22 revolver.
High capacity magazine(s)?: Unreported.
Weapon(s) legally acquired by suspect(s)/shooter(s)?: No.
# of people killed: 0
# of people injured: 1
Total # of victims: 1
Time suspect(s)/shooter(s) were apprehended or killed?: Unreported.
Suspect(s)' mental illness: Unreported.
Suspect(s)' medication or drug use: Unreported.
Suspect(s)' criminal history: Unreported.
Warning signs: Unreported.
Suspect(s)' country of citizenship: Unreported.
Suspect(s)' religious affiliation: Unreported.
Alleged reason for shooting: Gang-related.
Metal detectors present?: N/A.
Location & time of shooting: Shooting occurred at a crowded school outdoor volleyball court just after 10:30 a.m.
For more information, contact: Principal Marvin Starer and Los Angeles Police Sgt. Leonard Knight.
Citations/sources: (Adams, 1990) (Sahagun & Churm, 1990, p. A20) (Ethnic tensions start, 1990, p. 7)

#1198
Location of shooting: Mount Pleasant High School
Date: 5/4/1990
City, State: East San Jose, CA
Name of victim(s) killed: Larry Brown.
Age of victim(s) killed: 15
Name of victim(s) injured: N/A.
Age of victim(s) injured: N/A.

Name of suspect(s)/shooter(s): Thu Nguyen, Cang Binh Troung and a teenaged girl.
Age of suspect(s)/shooter(s): 18, 16 & 14
Weapon(s): Unreported.
High capacity magazine(s)?: Unreported.
Weapon(s) legally acquired by suspect(s)/shooter(s)?: No.
# of people killed: 1
# of people injured: 0
Total # of victims: 1
Time suspect(s)/shooter(s) were apprehended or killed?: Unreported.
Suspect(s)' mental illness: Unreported.
Suspect(s)' medication or drug use: Unreported.
Suspect(s)' criminal history: Unreported.
Warning signs: Unreported.
Suspect(s)' country of citizenship: Unreported.
Suspect(s)' religious affiliation: Unreported.
Alleged reason for shooting: Feud. Retaliation for an insult.
Metal detectors present?: Unreported.
Location & time of shooting: Unreported.
For more information, contact: Officer Bruce Toney, Sgt. Jeff Ouimet, Sgt. George Padilla and East Side Union High School District Trustee Richard Tanaka.
Citations/sources: (2 teens arrested, 1990, p. B-8) (Quintero, 1992) (Shooting suspect, 1990, p. A-19) (Boy, 15, fatally shot, p. A-2)

1197
Location of shooting: Waynesburg Elementary School
Date: 5/10/1990
City, State: Waynesburg, KY
Name of victim(s) killed: Glenda Kay Greer (School Secretary) & Shannon Greer (shooter).
Age of victim(s) killed: 42 & 46
Name of victim(s) injured: N/A.
Age of victim(s) injured: N/A.
Name of suspect(s)/shooter(s): Shannon Greer.
Age of suspect(s)/shooter(s): 46
Weapon(s): 12-gauge shotgun
High capacity magazine(s)?: N/A.
Weapon(s) legally acquired by suspect(s)/shooter(s)?: Unreported.
# of people killed: 2
# of people injured: 0
Total # of victims: 2
Time suspect(s)/shooter(s) were apprehended or killed?: Suspect committed suicide approximately two hours after suspect killed his wife.

Suspect(s)' mental illness: Unreported.
Suspect(s)' medication or drug use: Unreported.
Suspect(s)' criminal history: Unreported.
Warning signs: Unreported.
Suspect(s)' country of citizenship: U.S.A.
Suspect(s)' religious affiliation: Christian: Baptist.
Alleged reason for shooting: Rejection. Suspect had been served divorce papers and a restraining order a few days before the shooting.
Metal detectors present?: Unreported.
Location & time of shooting: Victim was in her school office at approximately 9:15 a.m.
For more information, contact: Kentucky State Police & Lincoln County Sheriff Earl Dean McWhorter, deputies J.D. Smoth and Tim Gambrel.
Citations/sources: (Joint services planned, 1990, p. A2) (Stevens, 1990, p. A1) (Kentucky man kills wife, 1990, p. 9A)

#1196
Location of shooting: Hickman County High School
Date: 5/20/1990
City, State: Centerville, TN
Name of victim(s) killed: Ron Wallace (Assistant School Principal).
Age of victim(s) killed: 41
Name of victim(s) injured: N/A.
Age of victim(s) injured: N/A.
Name of suspect(s)/shooter(s): Donald Givens.
Age of suspect(s)/shooter(s): 50
Weapon(s): .38-caliber revolver.
High capacity magazine(s)?: Unreported.
Weapon(s) legally acquired by suspect(s)/shooter(s)?: Unreported.
# of people killed: 1
# of people injured: 0
Total # of victims: 1
Time suspect(s)/shooter(s) were apprehended or killed?: Suspect was arrested during the evening of the shooting.
Suspect(s)' mental illness: Unreported.
Suspect(s)' medication or drug use: Unreported.
Suspect(s)' criminal history: Unreported.
Warning signs: Unreported.
Suspect(s)' country of citizenship: Unreported.
Suspect(s)' religious affiliation: Unreported.

Alleged reason for shooting: Protest authority. Suspect was a science teacher charged with "conduct unbecoming of a teacher," potentially facing dismissal. Principal was shot and killed when he discovered the suspect was attempting to blow up the school.

Metal detectors present?: N/A.

Location & time of shooting: Shooting occurred on a Sunday by a science teacher at the school.

For more information, contact: District Attorney General Joe Baugh.

Citations/sources: (Schoonover, 1990, p. 1-B) (Teacher charged in killing, 1990, p. A3) (Teacher charged in slaying, 1990)

1195
Location of shooting: Adams Elementary School

Date: 5/31/1990

City, State: San Antonio, TX

Name of victim(s) killed: John Moreno, Jr. & John Moreno (shooter).

Age of victim(s) killed: 1 & 22

Name of victim(s) injured: N/A.

Age of victim(s) injured: N/A.

Name of suspect(s)/shooter(s): John Moreno.

Age of suspect(s)/shooter(s): 22

Weapon(s): Unreported.

High capacity magazine(s)?: Unreported.

Weapon(s) legally acquired by suspect(s)/shooter(s)?: Unreported.

# of people killed: 2

# of people injured: 0

Total # of victims: 2

Time suspect(s)/shooter(s) were apprehended or killed?: Suicide.

Suspect(s)' mental illness: Unreported.

Suspect(s)' medication or drug use: Unreported.

Suspect(s)' criminal history: Unreported.

Warning signs: Unreported.

Suspect(s)' country of citizenship: Unreported.

Suspect(s)' religious affiliation: Unreported.

Alleged reason for shooting: Rejection. Suspect was reportedly upset over separation from his girlfriend.

Metal detectors present?: N/A.

Location & time of shooting: Shooting occurred at the elementary school yard around 7:00 a.m.

For more information, contact: Police Homicide Lt. Albert Ortiz.

Citations/sources: (Police say father shot toddler, 1990, p. 8-A) (San Antonian shoots baby, 1990, p. B3)

#1194
Location of shooting: Sunrise Elementary School
Date: 5/31/1990
City, State: Fort Worth, TX
Name of victim(s) killed: N/A.
Age of victim(s) killed: N/A.
Name of victim(s) injured: Crystal Treinece Dillon & Elton Lawrence.
Age of victim(s) injured: 9 & 10
Name of suspect(s)/shooter(s): Three teenagers.
Age of suspect(s)/shooter(s): 16, 15 & 15
Weapon(s): Unreported.
High capacity magazine(s)?: Unreported.
Weapon(s) legally acquired by suspect(s)/shooter(s)?: No.
# of people killed: 0
# of people injured: 2
Total # of victims: 2
Time suspect(s)/shooter(s) were apprehended or killed?: Suspects arrested about 45 minutes after shooting.
Suspect(s)' mental illness: Unreported.
Suspect(s)' medication or drug use: Unreported.
Suspect(s)' criminal history: Unreported.
Warning signs: Unreported.
Suspect(s)' country of citizenship: Unreported.
Suspect(s)' religious affiliation: Unreported.
Alleged reason for shooting: Unreported.
Metal detectors present?: N/A.
Location & time of shooting: Shooting was a drive-by toward a elementary school playground where children were playing.
For more information, contact: Fort Worth Police spokesman Doug Clark.
Citations/sources: (Two students hit in drive-by, 1990, p. 8-A) (2 Fort Worth students shot, 1990, p. B3) (2 schoolchildren hurt in drive-by, 1990, p. 4B)

#1193
Location of shooting: Myers Park High School
Date: 8/24/1990
City, State: Charlotte, NC
Name of victim(s) killed: Marcus Greer.
Age of victim(s) killed: 15
Name of victim(s) injured: Eric Henderson.
Age of victim(s) injured: 22
Name of suspect(s)/shooter(s): Nick Bianco Miller & Jaraun Ladaire Boyd.

Age of suspect(s)/shooter(s): 17 & 16

Weapon(s): Semi-automatic assault rifle & semi-automatic handgun.

High capacity magazine(s)?: Unreported.

Weapon(s) legally acquired by suspect(s)/shooter(s)?: No.

# of people killed: 1

# of people injured: 1

Total # of victims: 2

Time suspect(s)/shooter(s) were apprehended or killed?: Suspect was in custody the following day of the shooting.

Suspect(s)' mental illness: Unreported.

Suspect(s)' medication or drug use: Unreported.

Suspect(s)' criminal history: Boyd had three outstanding arrest warrants: two for resisting and obstructing police and a third for damage to property.

Warning signs: Unreported.

Suspect(s)' country of citizenship: Unreported.

Suspect(s)' religious affiliation: Unreported.

Alleged reason for shooting: Unreported.

Metal detectors present?: N/A.

Location & time of shooting: Shooting occurred at a high school football game at 10:15 p.m. from a vehicle.

For more information, contact: School principal Charles LaBorde, Charlotte Police Captain Tom Gaughan and Police Spokesman Ronnie Rash.

Citations/sources: (Shots kill teenager, 1990, p. D-10) (One dead, one injured, 1990, p. 33) (Charlotte schools move times, 1990, p. 13-A) (Youth shot, killed during football, 1990, p. 14A) (Police charge 2 teens, 1990, p. 4A)

#1192

Location of shooting: Eldorado High School

Date: 8/26/1990

City, State: Las Vegas, NV

Name of victim(s) killed: Donnie Lee Bolden.

Age of victim(s) killed: 16

Name of victim(s) injured: N/A.

Age of victim(s) injured: N/A.

Name of suspect(s)/shooter(s): Curtis Collins.

Age of suspect(s)/shooter(s): 15

Weapon(s): Pistol

High capacity magazine(s)?: Unreported.

Weapon(s) legally acquired by suspect(s)/shooter(s)?: No.

# of people killed: 1

# of people injured: 0

Total # of victims: 1
Time suspect(s)/shooter(s) were apprehended or killed?: Unreported.
Suspect(s)' mental illness: Unreported.
Suspect(s)' medication or drug use: Unreported.
Suspect(s)' criminal history: None.
Warning signs: Unreported.
Suspect(s)' country of citizenship: Unreported.
Suspect(s)' religious affiliation: Unreported.
Alleged reason for shooting: Gang related. Fight.
Metal detectors present?: Unreported.
Location & time of shooting: Shooting occurred in the school cafeteria about 7:15 a.m.
For more information, contact: Unreported.
Citations/sources: (Shoro & Delaney, 2018) (Smith, 2016) (Grove, 1998)

#1191
Location of shooting: Sam Houston High School
Date: 9/11/1990
City, State: San Antonio, TX
Name of victim(s) killed: N/A.
Age of victim(s) killed: N/A.
Name of victim(s) injured: John Campbell, Larry Johnson & unnamed male student.
Age of victim(s) injured: 17, 18 & 16
Name of suspect(s)/shooter(s): Kenneth Wolford and two other unnamed male students.
Age of suspect(s)/shooter(s): 18, ? & ?
Weapon(s): Unreported.
High capacity magazine(s)?: Unreported.
Weapon(s) legally acquired by suspect(s)/shooter(s)?: Unreported.
# of people killed: 0
# of people injured: 3
Total # of victims: 3
Time suspect(s)/shooter(s) were apprehended or killed?: Unreported.
Suspect(s)' mental illness: Unreported.
Suspect(s)' medication or drug use: Unreported.
Suspect(s)' criminal history: Unreported.
Warning signs: A student said he was afraid to go to school he heard there was going to be gang violence. "He said that they (the gangs) were going to finish it at the game."
Suspect(s)' country of citizenship: Unreported.
Suspect(s)' religious affiliation: Unreported.
Alleged reason for shooting: Gang-related.
Metal detectors present?: Unreported.

Location & time of shooting: Shooting occurred during the school lunch break at approximately 11:55 a.m.

For more information, contact: Police Sgt. Paul Buske, San Antonio School District Police Lt. William Maldonado and School Superintendent Victor Rodriguez.

Citations/sources: (3 San Antonio teens wounded, 1990, p. 3C) (School shooting part of a bigger, 1990, p. 6) (3 teens hurt in high school, 1990, p. 3B) (Shannon, 1990, p. 13A)

#1190
Location of shooting: William Hardin Adamson High School
Date: 10/2/1990
City, State: Dallas, TX
Name of victim(s) killed: N/A.
Age of victim(s) killed: N/A.
Name of victim(s) injured: Unnamed female student.
Age of victim(s) injured: 17
Name of suspect(s)/shooter(s): Two young women in a car.
Age of suspect(s)/shooter(s): Unreported.
Weapon(s): Unreported.
High capacity magazine(s)?: Unreported.
Weapon(s) legally acquired by suspect(s)/shooter(s)?: Unreported.
# of people killed: 0
# of people injured: 1
Total # of victims: 1
Time suspect(s)/shooter(s) were apprehended or killed?: Unreported.
Suspect(s)' mental illness: Unreported.
Suspect(s)' medication or drug use: Unreported.
Suspect(s)' criminal history: Unreported.
Warning signs: Unreported.
Suspect(s)' country of citizenship: Unreported.
Suspect(s)' religious affiliation: Unreported.
Alleged reason for shooting: Unreported.
Metal detectors present?: N/A.
Location & time of shooting: Drive-by shooting from outside the school toward students waiting for busses at approximately 4:50 p.m.; 50 minutes after classes were dismissed.

For more information, contact: Principal Edward Baca.
Citations/sources: (Nevins, 1990, p. 32A)

#1189
Location of shooting: Naaman Forest High School
Date: 10/30/1990
City, State: Garland, TX

Name of victim(s) killed: N/A.
Age of victim(s) killed: N/A.
Name of victim(s) injured: Steven Bake (Principal).
Age of victim(s) injured: 35
Name of suspect(s)/shooter(s): Manuela Chacon Reyes.
Age of suspect(s)/shooter(s): 32
Weapon(s): .25 caliber pistol
High capacity magazine(s)?: Unreported.
Weapon(s) legally acquired by suspect(s)/shooter(s)?: Unreported.
# of people killed: 0
# of people injured: 1
Total # of victims: 1
Time suspect(s)/shooter(s) were apprehended or killed?: Moments after the shooting. Assistant football coach Harvey Oaxacha saw the pair wrestling after the shot and grabbed the gun away from the suspect.
Suspect(s)' mental illness: Unreported.
Suspect(s)' medication or drug use: Unreported.
Suspect(s)' criminal history: Unreported.
Warning signs: Unreported.
Suspect(s)' country of citizenship: Unreported.
Suspect(s)' religious affiliation: Unreported.
Alleged reason for shooting: Protest authority. Parent was upset because her 8th grade son was suspended.
Metal detectors present?: Unreported.
Location & time of shooting: Unreported.
For more information, contact: Garland Independent School District Spokeswoman Mary Ellen Marnholtz and Assistant Football Coach Harvey Oaxacha.
Citations/sources: (Assistant principal shot, 1990, p. 14A) (Mother accused of shooting, 1990, p. 3B)

1188
Location of shooting: Richardson High School
Date: 1/8/1991
City, State: Richardson, TX
Name of victim(s) killed: Jeremy Wade Delle (shooter).
Age of victim(s) killed: 16
Name of victim(s) injured: N/A.
Age of victim(s) injured: N/A.
Name of suspect(s)/shooter(s): Jeremy Wade Delle.
Age of suspect(s)/shooter(s): 16
Weapon(s): .357 caliber Magnum revolver

High capacity magazine(s)?: Unreported.
Weapon(s) legally acquired by suspect(s)/shooter(s)?: No.
# of people killed: 1
# of people injured: 0
Total # of victims: 1
Time suspect(s)/shooter(s) were apprehended or killed?: Suicide.
Suspect(s)' mental illness: Student had been receiving counseling before his death.
Suspect(s)' medication or drug use: Unreported.
Suspect(s)' criminal history: Unreported.
Warning signs: Shooter left a suicide note with a classmate but did not immediately divulge its contents.
Suspect(s)' country of citizenship: Unreported.
Suspect(s)' religious affiliation: Unreported.
Alleged reason for shooting: Unreported.
Metal detectors present?: Unreported.
Location & time of shooting: Student shot himself in front of his classmates in a school classroom at around 10:00 a.m.
For more information, contact: Spokesman, Sgt. Ray Pennington.
Citations/sources: (Miller & Nevins, 1991) (H.S. students recovering after, 1991, p. 4A) (Student shoots, kills himself, 1991, p. 2B)

1187
Location of shooting: John B. Hood Middle School
Date: 1/17/1991
City, State: Dallas, TX
Name of victim(s) killed: N/A.
Age of victim(s) killed: N/A.
Name of victim(s) injured: Unnamed female student.
Age of victim(s) injured: 15
Name of suspect(s)/shooter(s): Unreported.
Age of suspect(s)/shooter(s): Unreported.
Weapon(s): Unreported.
High capacity magazine(s)?: Unreported.
Weapon(s) legally acquired by suspect(s)/shooter(s)?: Unreported.
# of people killed: 0
# of people injured: 1
Total # of victims: 1
Time suspect(s)/shooter(s) were apprehended or killed?: Unreported.
Suspect(s)' mental illness: Unreported.
Suspect(s)' medication or drug use: Unreported.
Suspect(s)' criminal history: Unreported.

Name of victim(s) injured: Crystal Scott, Craig Goston, Rodney Demond Pitts (Shooter shot by officer) & LeShawn Jones (Shooter shot by officer).
Age of victim(s) injured: 11, 20, 18 & 20
Name of suspect(s)/shooter(s): Rodney Demond Pitts & LeShawn Jones.
Age of suspect(s)/shooter(s): 18 & 20
Weapon(s): Revolver.
High capacity magazine(s)?: Unreported.
Weapon(s) legally acquired by suspect(s)/shooter(s)?: Unreported.
# of people killed: 0
# of people injured: 4
Total # of victims: 4
Time suspect(s)/shooter(s) were apprehended or killed?: Both suspects were sent to the hospital for injuries sustained on the night of the shooting and were arrested upon their release.
Suspect(s)' mental illness: Unreported.
Suspect(s)' medication or drug use: Unreported.
Suspect(s)' criminal history: Pitts was also convicted for two armed robberies during the fall before the shooting.
Warning signs: Unreported.
Suspect(s)' country of citizenship: Unreported.
Suspect(s)' religious affiliation: Unreported.
Alleged reason for shooting: Fight. Long-running feud between the two suspects.
Metal detectors present?: N/A.
Location & time of shooting: Shooting took place in the school parking lot after a school talent show.
For more information, contact: Greenville County Sheriff Capt. Eddie Candler and Lt. Sam Simmons.
Citations/sources: (Moore, 1991a, p. 1A & 6A) (Moore, 1991b, p. 2C) (4 injured at high school, 1991, p. 9) (Burns, 1992, p. 1C)

#1183
Location of shooting: Garinger High School
Date: 3/25/1991
City, State: Charlotte, NC
Name of victim(s) killed: Ronald Martin.
Age of victim(s) killed: 21
Name of victim(s) injured: N/A.
Age of victim(s) injured: N/A.
Name of suspect(s)/shooter(s): Marcus Anthony Belk.
Age of suspect(s)/shooter(s): 22
Weapon(s): Unreported.
High capacity magazine(s)?: Unreported.

Weapon(s) legally acquired by suspect(s)/shooter(s)?: Unreported.
# of people killed: 1
# of people injured: 0
Total # of victims: 1
Time suspect(s)/shooter(s) were apprehended or killed?: Unreported.
Suspect(s)' mental illness: Unreported.
Suspect(s)' medication or drug use: Unreported.
Suspect(s)' criminal history: Unreported.
Warning signs: Unreported.
Suspect(s)' country of citizenship: Unreported.
Suspect(s)' religious affiliation: Unreported.
Alleged reason for shooting: Feud. Retaliation for an incident a few weeks earlier in which a woman was injured in a neighborhood.
Metal detectors present?: N/A.
Location & time of shooting: Drive-by shooting in the school parking lot around 2:20 p.m.
For more information, contact: Charlotte Police Department.
Citations/sources: (Extra security at high school, 1991, p. 2B) (Previous dispute prompted, 1991, p. 3)

#1182
Location of shooting: Ralph J. Bunche Middle School
Date: 4/23/1991
City, State: Compton, CA
Name of victim(s) killed: Alejandro Vargas.
Age of victim(s) killed: 11
Name of victim(s) injured: N/A.
Age of victim(s) injured: N/A.
Name of suspect(s)/shooter(s): Two unnamed males.
Age of suspect(s)/shooter(s): 14 & 17
Weapon(s): Unreported.
High capacity magazine(s)?: Unreported.
Weapon(s) legally acquired by suspect(s)/shooter(s)?: Unreported.
# of people killed: 1
# of people injured: 0
Total # of victims: 1
Time suspect(s)/shooter(s) were apprehended or killed?: Unreported.
Suspect(s)' mental illness: Unreported.
Suspect(s)' medication or drug use: Unreported.
Suspect(s)' criminal history: Unreported.
Warning signs: Unreported.
Suspect(s)' country of citizenship: Unreported.

Warning signs: Unreported.
Suspect(s)' country of citizenship: Unreported.
Suspect(s)' religious affiliation: Unreported.
Alleged reason for shooting: Fight. Clash between youths from rival neighborhoods.
Metal detectors present?: Unreported.
Location & time of shooting: Unreported.
For more information, contact: Dallas Police Detective Samuel Schiller.
Citations/sources: (A teenage girl, 1991, p. 2A) (Girl shot in gang fight, 1991, p. 5)

#1186
Location of shooting: Donna High School
Date: 2/6/1991
City, State: Donna, TX
Name of victim(s) killed: Raul Calvo (shooter).
Age of victim(s) killed: 15
Name of victim(s) injured: N/A.
Age of victim(s) injured: N/A.
Name of suspect(s)/shooter(s): Raul Calvo.
Age of suspect(s)/shooter(s): 15
Weapon(s): .38-caliber revolver
High capacity magazine(s)?: Unreported.
Weapon(s) legally acquired by suspect(s)/shooter(s)?: No.
# of people killed: 1
# of people injured: 0
Total # of victims: 1
Time suspect(s)/shooter(s) were apprehended or killed?: Suicide.
Suspect(s)' mental illness: Unreported.
Suspect(s)' medication or drug use: Unreported.
Suspect(s)' criminal history: Unreported.
Warning signs: Unreported.
Suspect(s)' country of citizenship: Unreported.
Suspect(s)' religious affiliation: Unreported.
Alleged reason for shooting: Accident. Student shot himself dead while playing Russian roulette.
Metal detectors present?: Unreported.
Location & time of shooting: Shooting occurred inside a biology classroom about 1:25 p.m.
For more information, contact: Donna Police Department Lt. Gilbert Gonzalez and acting Police Chief Antonio Lopez.
Citations/sources: (Student fatally shoots himself, 1991)

#1185

Location of shooting: Booker T Washington High School

Date: 2/19/1991

City, State: New Orleans, LA

Name of victim(s) killed: Demond Hankton.

Age of victim(s) killed: 15

Name of victim(s) injured: Trenece Darton.

Age of victim(s) injured: 18

Name of suspect(s)/shooter(s): Michael Jarrow (shooter) & Marie Robinson (accomplice).

Age of suspect(s)/shooter(s): 21 & 17

Weapon(s): Unreported.

High capacity magazine(s)?: Unreported.

Weapon(s) legally acquired by suspect(s)/shooter(s)?: Unreported.

# of people killed: 1

# of people injured: 1

Total # of victims: 2

Time suspect(s)/shooter(s) were apprehended or killed?: Suspect arrested approximately one month after shooting.

Suspect(s)' mental illness: Unreported.

Suspect(s)' medication or drug use: Unreported.

Suspect(s)' criminal history: Suspect escaped from a state juvenile detention center more than a year before the shooting.

Warning signs: Unreported.

Suspect(s)' country of citizenship: Unreported.

Suspect(s)' religious affiliation: Unreported.

Alleged reason for shooting: Feud.

Metal detectors present?: N/A.

Location & time of shooting: Shooting occurred in school yard around noon. Suspect passed by armed security guard when he entered the school.

For more information, contact: New Orleans Police Department Officer John Marie and Principal Troy J. Vincent.

Citations/sources: (Booker T. Washington, 1991, p. A-9) (Cops probe N.O. student killing, 1991, p. 2) (N.O. police search for killer, 1991, p. D-10) (Escapee charged in death, 1991, p. 19A)

1184

Location of shooting: Woodmont High School

Date: 3/14/1991

City, State: Greenville, SC

Name of victim(s) killed: N/A.

Age of victim(s) killed: N/A.

Suspect(s)' religious affiliation: Unreported.

Alleged reason for shooting: Gang-related. Authority issues. Shooter attempted to shoot a guard in retaliation for being kicked off the schoolyard the previous week, but killed an 11-year old boy in the line of fire instead.

Metal detectors present?: N/A.

Location & time of shooting: Shooting occurred in school yard, beneath the school flagpole, after classes had ended around 3:30 p.m. Shooter opened fire from across the street.

For more information, contact: Sheriff's Sgt. Mike Maynard; Compton Police Detective John Swanson; Compton School District Police & Deputy Rafael Estrada and school counselor Vera Alexander.

Citations/sources: (Russel & Fuetsh, 1991) (Tobar & Fuetsch, 1991)

1181

Location of shooting: Franklin Alternative Middle School

Date: 5/9/1991

City, State: Columbus, OH

Name of victim(s) killed: Armon Williams.

Age of victim(s) killed: 18

Name of victim(s) injured: N/A.

Age of victim(s) injured: N/A.

Name of suspect(s)/shooter(s): Robert L. Jones.

Age of suspect(s)/shooter(s): 15

Weapon(s): Two pistols

High capacity magazine(s)?: Unreported.

Weapon(s) legally acquired by suspect(s)/shooter(s)?: No. Suspect stole the gun from someone who was allegedly harassing him.

# of people killed: 1

# of people injured: 0

Total # of victims: 1

Time suspect(s)/shooter(s) were apprehended or killed?: Unreported.

Suspect(s)' mental illness: Unreported.

Suspect(s)' medication or drug use: Unreported.

Suspect(s)' criminal history: Unreported.

Warning signs: Unreported.

Suspect(s)' country of citizenship: Unreported.

Suspect(s)' religious affiliation: Unreported.

Alleged reason for shooting: Bullying.

Metal detectors present?: N/A.

Location & time of shooting: Shooting occurred outside of the middle school during a spring concert around 6:45 p.m.

For more information, contact: Columbus Police Officer Steve Scruggs and Detective Sharon Ceckitti.

Citations/sources: (Detroit youth faces charges, 1991, p. 2A) (Bullets bounce into school, 1991, p. 5)

#1180
Location of shooting: Coronado Middle School
Date: 5/16/1991
City, State: Kansas City, KS
Name of victim(s) killed: N/A.
Age of victim(s) killed: N/A.
Name of victim(s) injured: Unnamed girl and boy due to age.
Age of victim(s) injured: 13 & 15
Name of suspect(s)/shooter(s): 2 unnamed youths due to age.
Age of suspect(s)/shooter(s): 13 & 15
Weapon(s): Long-barreled pistol-type weapon.
High capacity magazine(s)?: Unreported.
Weapon(s) legally acquired by suspect(s)/shooter(s)?: No.
# of people killed: 0
# of people injured: 2
Total # of victims: 2
Time suspect(s)/shooter(s) were apprehended or killed?: Two suspects were arrested 5 days after shooting.
Suspect(s)' mental illness: Unreported.
Suspect(s)' medication or drug use: Unreported.
Suspect(s)' criminal history: Unreported.
Warning signs: Unreported.
Suspect(s)' country of citizenship: Unreported.
Suspect(s)' religious affiliation: Unreported.
Alleged reason for shooting: Unreported.
Metal detectors present?: Unreported.
Location & time of shooting: Shooting occurred in junior high cafeteria.
For more information, contact: Kansas City Police Sgt. Bill Edwards and Spokesman Donald Ash.

Citations/sources: (Two hurt in junior high, 1991, p. 6C) (Juveniles held in shooting, 1991, p. A3)

#1179
Location of shooting: School of Choice (Grades 6 - 12)
Date: 5/20/1991
City, State: Pahokee, FL

Name of victim(s) killed: Tameica Thames.
Age of victim(s) killed: 15
Name of victim(s) injured: Curtis Robinson & Denton Schoburgh.
Age of victim(s) injured: 16 & 17
Name of suspect(s)/shooter(s): Benjamin Dotson.
Age of suspect(s)/shooter(s): 18
Weapon(s): .380-caliber semiautomatic.
High capacity magazine(s)?: Unreported.
Weapon(s) legally acquired by suspect(s)/shooter(s)?: No. Suspect stole the gun from Alex Torres, age 19 who allegedly had it in a locked bedroom.
# of people killed: 1
# of people injured: 2
Total # of victims: 3
Time suspect(s)/shooter(s) were apprehended or killed?: Suspect was subdued by teachers and school security guards immediately after shooting until Palm Beach County sheriffs arrived.
Suspect(s)' mental illness: Unreported.
Suspect(s)' medication or drug use: Unreported.
Suspect(s)' criminal history: Suspect was charged with criminal mischief on August 19, 1990 in connection with throwing a rock through a trailer window.
Warning signs: Unreported.
Suspect(s)' country of citizenship: Unreported.
Suspect(s)' religious affiliation: Unreported.
Alleged reason for shooting: Feud with another student. Victim was an innocent bystander.
Metal detectors present?: No. N/A.
Location & time of shooting:
For more information, contact: Victim was shot in the schoolyard at approximately 10:30 a.m.
Citations/sources: (Goldberg, 1991, p. A6) (Swart, 1991, p. 4B) (Harris, 1991, p. 4B)

#1178
Location of shooting: Robert A. Millikan Junior High School (Middle school)
Date: 5/22/1991
City, State: Sherman Oaks, CA
Name of victim(s) killed: Alejandro Penaloza.
Age of victim(s) killed: 14
Name of victim(s) injured: N/A.
Age of victim(s) injured: N/A.
Name of suspect(s)/shooter(s): Salvador Humberto Funes, a.k.a. "Blackie" or "Negro."
Age of suspect(s)/shooter(s): 20
Weapon(s): Small caliber weapons.
High capacity magazine(s)?: Unreported.
Weapon(s) legally acquired by suspect(s)/shooter(s)?: Unreported.

# of people killed: 1
# of people injured: 0
Total # of victims: 1
Time suspect(s)/shooter(s) were apprehended or killed?: Unreported.
Suspect(s)' mental illness: Unreported.
Suspect(s)' medication or drug use: Unreported.
Suspect(s)' criminal history: Unreported.
Warning signs: Unreported.
Suspect(s)' country of citizenship: Unreported.
Suspect(s)' religious affiliation: Unreported.
Alleged reason for shooting: Gang-related.
Metal detectors present?: N/A.
Location & time of shooting: Shooting took place in front of school after classes were dismissed.
For more information, contact: Van Nuys Division Homicide and Detective Jim Vojtecky.
Citations/sources: (Banks & Sengupta, 1993) (Braxton, 1991, p. B12)

1177
Location of shooting: Westchester High School
Date: 7/22/1991
City, State: Los Angeles, CA
Name of victim(s) killed: N/A.
Age of victim(s) killed: N/A.
Name of victim(s) injured: Unnamed male student due to age.
Age of victim(s) injured: 16
Name of suspect(s)/shooter(s): Two unidentified assailants in a brown Cadillac.
Age of suspect(s)/shooter(s): Unreported.
Weapon(s): .22-caliber handgun.
High capacity magazine(s)?: Unreported.
Weapon(s) legally acquired by suspect(s)/shooter(s)?: Unreported.
# of people killed: 0
# of people injured: 1
Total # of victims: 1
Time suspect(s)/shooter(s) were apprehended or killed?: Unreported.
Suspect(s)' mental illness: Unreported.
Suspect(s)' medication or drug use: Unreported.
Suspect(s)' criminal history: Unreported.
Warning signs: Unreported.
Suspect(s)' country of citizenship: Unreported.
Suspect(s)' religious affiliation: Unreported.
Alleged reason for shooting: Gang-related.

Metal detectors present?: N/A.

Location & time of shooting: Drive-by shooting in front of school while student was waiting for school bus shortly after 10:30 a.m. Victim was attending summer school.

For more information, contact: Principal Jim Berk, Administrator Harriette Williams and L.A. School District Administrator Diana Munatones.

Citations/sources: (Banks & Sengupta, 1993) (Helfand, 1991, p. B4) (Student shot in drive-by attack, 1991, p. B2)

#1176
Location of shooting: Enterprise Middle School
Date: 7/30/1991
City, State: Compton, CA
Name of victim(s) killed: N/A.
Age of victim(s) killed: N/A.
Name of victim(s) injured: Thearon Steen.
Age of victim(s) injured: 14
Name of suspect(s)/shooter(s): Two unidentified teen-aged gang members.
Age of suspect(s)/shooter(s): Teenaged
Weapon(s): Unreported.
High capacity magazine(s)?: Unreported.
Weapon(s) legally acquired by suspect(s)/shooter(s)?: Unreported.
# of people killed: 0
# of people injured: 1
Total # of victims: 1
Time suspect(s)/shooter(s) were apprehended or killed?: Unreported.
Suspect(s)' mental illness: Unreported.
Suspect(s)' medication or drug use: Unreported.
Suspect(s)' criminal history: Unreported.
Warning signs: Unreported.
Suspect(s)' country of citizenship: Unreported.
Suspect(s)' religious affiliation: Unreported.
Alleged reason for shooting: Gang-related.
Metal detectors present?: Unreported.

Location & time of shooting: Victim was shot while fleeing from gang members on school campus.

For more information, contact: Los Angeles Police.

Citations/sources: (Banks & Sengupta, 1993) (Boy, 14, shot, 1991, p. B2)

#1175
Location of shooting: Wichita State University
Date: 9/2/1991

<u>City, State</u>: Wichita, KS
<u>Name of victim(s) killed</u>: Anthony Jones.
<u>Age of victim(s) killed</u>: 19
<u>Name of victim(s) injured</u>: N/A.
<u>Age of victim(s) injured</u>: N/A.
<u>Name of suspect(s)/shooter(s)</u>: Unreported.
<u>Age of suspect(s)/shooter(s)</u>: Unreported.
<u>Weapon(s)</u>: Unreported.
<u>High capacity magazine(s)?</u>: Unreported.
<u>Weapon(s) legally acquired by suspect(s)/shooter(s)?</u>: Unreported.
<u># of people killed</u>: 1
<u># of people injured</u>: 0
<u>Total # of victims</u>: 1
<u>Time suspect(s)/shooter(s) were apprehended or killed?</u>: Unreported.
<u>Suspect(s)' mental illness</u>: Unreported.
<u>Suspect(s)' medication or drug use</u>: Unreported.
<u>Suspect(s)' criminal history</u>: Unreported.
<u>Warning signs</u>: Unreported.
<u>Suspect(s)' country of citizenship</u>: Unreported.
<u>Suspect(s)' religious affiliation</u>: Unreported.
<u>Alleged reason for shooting</u>: Unreported.
<u>Metal detectors present?</u>: N/A.
<u>Location & time of shooting</u>: Shooting occurred in a parking lot at the Black Arts Festival held on campus.
<u>For more information, contact</u>: Unreported.
<u>Citations/sources</u>: (Gragg v. Wichita State Univ., 1997) (Street war, 1992) (Laviana, 1994)

#1174
<u>Location of shooting</u>: Madison High School
<u>Date</u>: 9/13/1991
<u>City, State</u>: Houston, TX
<u>Name of victim(s) killed</u>: Mario Pittman.
<u>Age of victim(s) killed</u>: 19
<u>Name of victim(s) injured</u>: N/A.
<u>Age of victim(s) injured</u>: N/A.
<u>Name of suspect(s)/shooter(s)</u>: Multiple unidentified shooters from rival high schools in at least three cars.
<u>Age of suspect(s)/shooter(s)</u>: Unreported.
<u>Weapon(s)</u>: Unreported.
<u>High capacity magazine(s)?</u>: Unreported.
<u>Weapon(s) legally acquired by suspect(s)/shooter(s)?</u>: Unreported.

# of people killed: 1
# of people injured: 0
Total # of victims: 1
Time suspect(s)/shooter(s) were apprehended or killed?: Unreported.
Suspect(s)' mental illness: Unreported.
Suspect(s)' medication or drug use: Unreported.
Suspect(s)' criminal history: Unreported.
Warning signs: No.
Suspect(s)' country of citizenship: Unreported.
Suspect(s)' religious affiliation: Unreported.
Alleged reason for shooting: Feud. Rivalry between two schools. Uninvolved student was shot in crossfire.
Metal detectors present?: N/A.
Location & time of shooting: Drive-by shooting occurred outside, after a high school football game at approximately 11:00 p.m.
For more information, contact: Principal Ada Cooper.
Citations/sources: (High school student dies, 1991, p. 7B) (Student killed in post-game, 1991, p. 18A)

#1173
Location of shooting: Woodson North Elementary School (Woodson North School)
Date: 9/17/1991
City, State: Chicago, IL
Name of victim(s) killed: N/A.
Age of victim(s) killed: N/A.
Name of victim(s) injured: Clarence Notree.
Age of victim(s) injured: 44
Name of suspect(s)/shooter(s): A unidentified male youth.
Age of suspect(s)/shooter(s): Unreported.
Weapon(s): 9mm handgun
High capacity magazine(s)?: Unreported.
Weapon(s) legally acquired by suspect(s)/shooter(s)?: Unreported.
# of people killed: 0
# of people injured: 1
Total # of victims: 1
Time suspect(s)/shooter(s) were apprehended or killed?: Suspect not found yet.
Suspect(s)' mental illness: Unreported.
Suspect(s)' medication or drug use: Unreported.
Suspect(s)' criminal history: Unreported.
Warning signs: Unreported.
Suspect(s)' country of citizenship: Unreported.

Suspect(s)' religious affiliation: Unreported.

Alleged reason for shooting: Unreported. Believed to be gang-related.

Metal detectors present?: Unreported.

Location & time of shooting: Shooting occurred in school gym.

For more information, contact: Wentworth Sgt. Dennis Murphy and Chicago Police Department.

Citations/sources: (Morganthau, 1992) (Wiltz, 1991) (After-school teacher wounded, 1991, p. 8) (Coleman, 1991, p. D7)

#1172

Location of shooting: Crosby High School

Date: 9/18/1991

City, State: Crosby, TX

Name of victim(s) killed: Arthur Jack.

Age of victim(s) killed: 17

Name of victim(s) injured: N/A.

Age of victim(s) injured: N/A.

Name of suspect(s)/shooter(s): Lakeeta Cadoree.

Age of suspect(s)/shooter(s): 15

Weapon(s): .38-caliber revolver

High capacity magazine(s)?: Unreported.

Weapon(s) legally acquired by suspect(s)/shooter(s)?: No.

# of people killed: 1

# of people injured: 0

Total # of victims: 1

Time suspect(s)/shooter(s) were apprehended or killed?: Assistant school principal talked shooter into giving up her weapon moments after shooting.

Suspect(s)' mental illness: Unreported.

Suspect(s)' medication or drug use: Unreported.

Suspect(s)' criminal history: None.

Warning signs: Unreported.

Suspect(s)' country of citizenship: Unreported.

Suspect(s)' religious affiliation: Unreported.

Alleged reason for shooting: Argument. Suspect shot the victim because he called her a "bitch."

Metal detectors present?: Unreported.

Location & time of shooting: Unreported.

For more information, contact: Harris County Sheriff's Sgt. Skip Oliver.

Citations/sources: (Morganthau, 1992) (Kennedy, 1991) (High school football star shot, 1991)

#1171

Location of shooting: Nogales High School (School bus)

Date: 9/26/1991
City, State: La Puente, CA
Name of victim(s) killed: N/A.
Age of victim(s) killed: N/A.
Name of victim(s) injured: Two unnamed girls due to age.
Age of victim(s) injured: 15 & 17
Name of suspect(s)/shooter(s): Unreported.
Age of suspect(s)/shooter(s): Unreported.
Weapon(s): 9mm handgun
High capacity magazine(s)?: Unreported.
Weapon(s) legally acquired by suspect(s)/shooter(s)?: Unreported.
# of people killed: 0
# of people injured: 2
Total # of victims: 2
Time suspect(s)/shooter(s) were apprehended or killed?: Suspect(s) not found yet.
Suspect(s)' mental illness: Unreported.
Suspect(s)' medication or drug use: Unreported.
Suspect(s)' criminal history: Unreported.
Warning signs: Unreported.
Suspect(s)' country of citizenship: Unreported.
Suspect(s)' religious affiliation: Unreported.
Alleged reason for shooting: Possibly gang-related.
Metal detectors present?: N/A.
Location & time of shooting: Shooting occurred on a school bus around 12:30 p.m. A car pulled alongside the bus opened fire.
For more information, contact: Sheriff Sgt. Dan Pohl, Supt. Sharon S. Robinson and Rowland Unified School District spokeswoman Diane Ho.
Citations/sources: (Banks & Sengupta, 1993) (Guards posted at schools, 1991, p. B-4) (Utley, 1991, p. B3)

#1170
Location of shooting: Spring Woods High School
Date: 10/2/1991
City, State: Houston, TX
Name of victim(s) killed: N/A.
Age of victim(s) killed: N/A.
Name of victim(s) injured: Dustin Sulak.
Age of victim(s) injured: 16
Name of suspect(s)/shooter(s): Kim Young.
Age of suspect(s)/shooter(s): 16
Weapon(s): Small caliber gun.

High capacity magazine(s)?: Unreported.
Weapon(s) legally acquired by suspect(s)/shooter(s)?:
# of people killed: 0
# of people injured: 1
Total # of victims: 1
Time suspect(s)/shooter(s) were apprehended or killed?: Houston police took suspect into custody at the scene of the shooting, but after the suspect threw the gun into a sewer.
Suspect(s)' mental illness: Unreported.
Suspect(s)' medication or drug use: Unreported.
Suspect(s)' criminal history: Unreported.
Warning signs: Unreported.
Suspect(s)' country of citizenship: Unreported.
Suspect(s)' religious affiliation: Unreported.
Alleged reason for shooting: Accident. Suspect was showing the gun to a friend when it accidentally discharged.
Metal detectors present?: N/A.
Location & time of shooting: Shooting occurred in a school bus shortly before 8:00 a.m.
For more information, contact: Spring Woods Principal, Perry Pope.
Citations/sources: (Abram, 1991, p. 1) (Student shot in leg, 1991, p. 8A) (Houston student shot aboard school bus, 1991, p. 10-A)

#1169
Location of shooting: Dorsey High School
Date: 10/4/1991
City, State: Los Angeles, CA
Name of victim(s) killed: N/A.
Age of victim(s) killed: N/A.
Name of victim(s) injured: Two unnamed students.
Age of victim(s) injured: Unreported.
Name of suspect(s)/shooter(s): 10-15 gang members.
Age of suspect(s)/shooter(s): Unreported.
Weapon(s): Unreported.
High capacity magazine(s)?: Unreported.
Weapon(s) legally acquired by suspect(s)/shooter(s)?: Unreported.
# of people killed: 0
# of people injured: 2
Total # of victims: 2
Time suspect(s)/shooter(s) were apprehended or killed?: Unreported.
Suspect(s)' mental illness: Unreported.
Suspect(s)' medication or drug use: Unreported.
Suspect(s)' criminal history: Unreported.

Warning signs: Unreported.
Suspect(s)' country of citizenship: Unreported.
Suspect(s)' religious affiliation: Unreported.
Alleged reason for shooting: Gang-related.
Metal detectors present?: N/A.
Location & time of shooting: Shooting occurred at a high school football game at Jackie Robinson Stadium around 5:30 p.m.
For more information, contact: LAPD, Sgt. J.J. Resse and School District Spokeswoman Diana Munatones.
Citations/sources: (Shepard & Himmel, 1991, p. B1 & B14) (Shepard, 1991, p. B1 & B14) (Fear of gang violence, 1991, p. 4-D)

#1168
Location of shooting: James Monroe High School
Date: 10/8/1991
City, State: Bronx, NY
Name of victim(s) killed: Tryon Whittaker.
Age of victim(s) killed: 17
Name of victim(s) injured: N/A.
Age of victim(s) injured: N/A.
Name of suspect(s)/shooter(s): Unreported.
Age of suspect(s)/shooter(s): Unreported.
Weapon(s): Unreported.
High capacity magazine(s)?: Unreported.
Weapon(s) legally acquired by suspect(s)/shooter(s)?: Unreported.
# of people killed: 1
# of people injured: 0
Total # of victims: 1
Time suspect(s)/shooter(s) were apprehended or killed?: Unreported.
Suspect(s)' mental illness: Unreported.
Suspect(s)' medication or drug use: Unreported.
Suspect(s)' criminal history: Unreported.
Warning signs: Unreported.
Suspect(s)' country of citizenship: Unreported.
Suspect(s)' religious affiliation: Unreported.
Alleged reason for shooting: Argument.
Metal detectors present?: N/A.
Location & time of shooting: Shooting occurred in front of the school at approximately 9:15 a.m.
For more information, contact: David Whittaker (victim's older brother).
Citations/sources: (McQuiston, 1991) (Lee, 1993)

#1166

Location of shooting: Genevieve Sparks Elementary School

Date: 10/15/1991

City, State: Pasadena, TX

Name of victim(s) killed: N/A.

Age of victim(s) killed: N/A.

Name of victim(s) injured: John Barnett.

Age of victim(s) injured: 7

Name of suspect(s)/shooter(s): Unnamed due to age.

Age of suspect(s)/shooter(s): 13

Weapon(s): .22-caliber rifle

High capacity magazine(s)?: Unreported.

Weapon(s) legally acquired by suspect(s)/shooter(s)?: No.

# of people killed: 0

# of people injured: 1

Total # of victims: 1

Time suspect(s)/shooter(s) were apprehended or killed?: Suspect was arrested the following day after shooting. A neighbor who heard the suspect firing his rifle led the authorities to the suspect after the shooting.

Suspect(s)' mental illness: Unreported.

Suspect(s)' medication or drug use: Unreported.

Suspect(s)' criminal history: Unreported.

Warning signs: Unreported.

Suspect(s)' country of citizenship: Unreported.

Suspect(s)' religious affiliation: Unreported.

Alleged reason for shooting: Accident. Suspect accidentally shot a 2nd grader while shooting at birds and squirrels near the school.

Metal detectors present?: N/A.

Location & time of shooting: Victim was shot while returning to class from the school playground.

For more information, contact: Unreported.

Citations/sources: (Student reportedly shot accidentally, 1991, p. 2B) (Second-grader in stable condition, 1991, p. 19A) (Second-grader shot accidentally, 1991, p. 12A)

#1167

Location of shooting: Monadnock Regional High School

Date: 10/15/1991

City, State: Swanzey, NH

Name of victim(s) killed: N/A.

Age of victim(s) killed: N/A.

Name of victim(s) injured: Two unidentified students.
Age of victim(s) injured: Unreported.
Name of suspect(s)/shooter(s): Unnamed former student dropout.
Age of suspect(s)/shooter(s): 16
Weapon(s): Rifle
High capacity magazine(s)?: Unreported.
Weapon(s) legally acquired by suspect(s)/shooter(s)?: No.
# of people killed: 0
# of people injured: 2
Total # of victims: 2
Time suspect(s)/shooter(s) were apprehended or killed?: Police were able to sneak up on the 16-year-old from behind and disarm him, approximately within 15 minutes after the shooting.
Suspect(s)' mental illness: Unreported.
Suspect(s)' medication or drug use: Unreported.
Suspect(s)' criminal history: Unreported.
Warning signs: Unreported.
Suspect(s)' country of citizenship: Unreported.
Suspect(s)' religious affiliation: Unreported.
Alleged reason for shooting: Unreported.
Metal detectors present?: Unreported.
Location & time of shooting: Unreported location inside the school.
For more information, contact: Swanzey Police Chief Larss A. Ogren.
Citations/sources: (From the files, 2016) (People news, 1992) (Schinella, 2022)

#1165
Location of shooting: A. Maceo Smith High School
Date: 10/23/1991
City, State: Dallas, TX
Name of victim(s) killed: Andrew Gaston.
Age of victim(s) killed: 15
Name of victim(s) injured: N/A.
Age of victim(s) injured: N/A.
Name of suspect(s)/shooter(s): Drumestic Contreal Brown.
Age of suspect(s)/shooter(s): 18
Weapon(s): Unreported.
High capacity magazine(s)?: Unreported.
Weapon(s) legally acquired by suspect(s)/shooter(s)?: Unreported.
# of people killed: 1
# of people injured: 0
Total # of victims: 1

Time suspect(s)/shooter(s) were apprehended or killed?: Suspect surrendered to police shortly after shooting incident.

Suspect(s)' mental illness: Unreported.

Suspect(s)' medication or drug use: Unreported.

Suspect(s)' criminal history: Unreported.

Warning signs: Unreported.

Suspect(s)' country of citizenship: Unreported.

Suspect(s)' religious affiliation: Unreported.

Alleged reason for shooting: Fight. Victim was an innocent bystander watching the fight.

Metal detectors present?: Yes.

Location & time of shooting: Shooting occurred outside the front entrance of the school building shortly after a fight spilled from the school cafeteria shortly before 9:00 a.m. Metal detectors were not in use that day.

For more information, contact: Sgt. Bill Chandler.

Citations/sources: (Student shot at Dallas high, 1991, p. 3B) (School superintendent asks, 1991, p. 2-A) (Dallas student fatally shot, 1991, p. 10-A)

#1164

Location of shooting: University of Iowa

Date: 11/1/1991

City, State: Iowa City, IA

Name of victim(s) killed: Christoph K. Goertz (Faculty Adviser), Robert Alan Smith (Associate Professor), Dr. Linhua Shan, Dwight R. Nicholson (Chairman of Physics & Astronomy Dept.), T. Anne Cleary (Assoc. V.P. of Academic Affairs) and Gang Lu (shooter).

Age of victim(s) killed: 47, 45, 27, 44, 56 & 28

Name of victim(s) injured: Miya Rodolfo-Sioson (Receptionist).

Age of victim(s) injured: 23

Name of suspect(s)/shooter(s): Gang Lu.

Age of suspect(s)/shooter(s): 28

Weapon(s): Taurus .38-caliber revolver and .22-caliber handgun.

High capacity magazine(s)?: No. The .38-caliber revolver only carried six rounds. The .22 was not used.

Weapon(s) legally acquired by suspect(s)/shooter(s)?: Yes.

# of people killed: 6

# of people injured: 1

Total # of victims: 7

Time suspect(s)/shooter(s) were apprehended or killed?: Suicide.

Suspect(s)' mental illness: Not reported.

Suspect(s)' medication or drug use: Not reported.

Suspect(s)' criminal history: None.

Warning signs: Suspect wrote four letters addressed to the media illustrating that he carefully planned the murders. He also mailed $20,000 his sister in China with a short note that read, "When you get the check, deposit it in the bank. Whatever may happen to me, you may know in the future."

Suspect(s)' country of citizenship: China

Suspect(s)' religious affiliation: None.

Alleged reason for shooting: Protest authority. Shooter was a Ph.D. graduate who was denied a major dissertation prize.

Metal detectors present?: N/A.

Location & time of shooting: Shooting occurred on university campus at 3:42 p.m.

For more information, contact: Sheriff Robert Carpenter of Johnson County.

Citations/sources: (Student goes on killing spree, 1991) (Marriott, 1991) (Mann, 1992) (Shipner, 2008) (Armstrong, 1991a, p. 3A)(Armstrong, 1991b, p. 1A) ($2 million bail, 2021)

#1163

Location of shooting: Holland Woods Middle School

Date: 11/5/1991

City, State: Port Huron, MI

Name of victim(s) killed: N/A.

Age of victim(s) killed: N/A.

Name of victim(s) injured: Unnamed male student due to age.

Age of victim(s) injured: 13

Name of suspect(s)/shooter(s): Unnamed male student due to age.

Age of suspect(s)/shooter(s): 13

Weapon(s): .32-caliber revolver and two boxes of bullets.

High capacity magazine(s)?: Unreported.

Weapon(s) legally acquired by suspect(s)/shooter(s)?: No. Suspect stole gun from home.

# of people killed: 0

# of people injured: 1

Total # of victims: 1

Time suspect(s)/shooter(s) were apprehended or killed?: Suspect apprehended by a St. Clair County Sheriff's Deputy less than one hour after shooting.

Suspect(s)' mental illness: Unreported.

Suspect(s)' medication or drug use: Unreported.

Suspect(s)' criminal history: None.

Warning signs: Unreported.

Suspect(s)' country of citizenship: Unreported.

Suspect(s)' religious affiliation: Unreported.

Alleged reason for shooting: Bullying.

Metal detectors present?: Unreported.

Location & time of shooting: Shooting occurred in a reading classroom, around 10:00 a.m.

For more information, contact: Port Huron Police Chief William Corbett, Port Huron Police Captain James Carmody, St. Clair County Sheriff Deputy James Stanley and Superintendent Larry Moeller.

Citations/sources: (Verdin, 1991, p. 7A) (Chronology of a shooting, 1991, p. 7A) (Schaefer, 1991, 4B) (Teenager pulls gun from pack, 1991, p. 4B)

#1162
Location of shooting: Cohen High School
Date: 11/6/1991
City, State: New Orleans, LA
Name of victim(s) killed: Dumas D. Robertson.
Age of victim(s) killed: 15
Name of victim(s) injured: Marlin Jackson.
Age of victim(s) injured: 15
Name of suspect(s)/shooter(s): Robert L. Monroe.
Age of suspect(s)/shooter(s): 19
Weapon(s): Unreported.
High capacity magazine(s)?: Unreported.
Weapon(s) legally acquired by suspect(s)/shooter(s)?: Unreported.
# of people killed: 1
# of people injured: 1
Total # of victims: 2
Time suspect(s)/shooter(s) were apprehended or killed?: Suspect was arrested in his parent's home during the evening of 11/7/1991, one day after the shooting.
Suspect(s)' mental illness: Unreported.
Suspect(s)' medication or drug use: Unreported.
Suspect(s)' criminal history: Unreported.
Warning signs: Unreported.
Suspect(s)' country of citizenship: Unreported.
Suspect(s)' religious affiliation: Unreported.
Alleged reason for shooting: Fight among at least eight female students.
Metal detectors present?: N/A.
Location & time of shooting: Suspect shot from his truck toward a crowd of students who were fighting outside of the school after classes were dismissed at 3:15 p.m.
For more information, contact: New Orleans Police Department Spokesman Marlon Defillo and Principal Leroy Gray.
Citations/sources: (Shooting outside Cohen High, 1991, p. 1) (Man arrested for shooting, 1991, p. 5) (One suspect arrested for murder, 1991, p. 5)

#1161
Location of shooting: Milby High School

Date: 11/14/1991
City, State: Houston, TX
Name of victim(s) killed: N/A.
Age of victim(s) killed: N/A.
Name of victim(s) injured: Francisco Contreras.
Age of victim(s) injured: 18
Name of suspect(s)/shooter(s): Unnamed 9th grade student.
Age of suspect(s)/shooter(s): 16
Weapon(s): .25-caliber handgun
High capacity magazine(s)?: Unreported.
Weapon(s) legally acquired by suspect(s)/shooter(s)?: No.
# of people killed: 0
# of people injured: 1
Total # of victims: 1
Time suspect(s)/shooter(s) were apprehended or killed?: Suspect apprehended by campus security officers shortly after shooting.
Suspect(s)' mental illness: Unreported.
Suspect(s)' medication or drug use: Unreported.
Suspect(s)' criminal history: Unreported.
Warning signs: Unreported.
Suspect(s)' country of citizenship: Unreported.
Suspect(s)' religious affiliation: Unreported.
Alleged reason for shooting: Fight.
Metal detectors present?: No.
Location & time of shooting: Hand-held metal detectors were offered that year, but the principal turned them down because he considered them inefficient. Victim was shot in school hallway, next to cafeteria shortly after noon.
For more information, contact: Houston school district spokeswoman Lisa Bunse, Houston Police Department Spokesman Rick Hartley, Principal Michael McClellan and Assistant Principal Milton Morgan.
Citations/sources: (Houston student shot during fight, 1991, p. 12-A) (Asin & Markley, 1991, p. A1)

1160
Location of shooting: Thomas Jefferson High School
Date: 11/25/1991
City, State: Fort Worth, TX
Name of victim(s) killed: Darryl Sharpe.
Age of victim(s) killed: 16
Name of victim(s) injured: Robert Anderson (computer instructor).
Age of victim(s) injured: 48

Name of suspect(s)/shooter(s): Jason Bentley.
Age of suspect(s)/shooter(s): 14
Weapon(s): 9-millimeter automatic
High capacity magazine(s)?: Unreported.
Weapon(s) legally acquired by suspect(s)/shooter(s)?: No. Gun was purchased on the street for $50.
# of people killed: 1
# of people injured: 1
Total # of victims: 2
Time suspect(s)/shooter(s) were apprehended or killed?: Suspect apprehended several hours after shooting incident.
Suspect(s)' mental illness: Unreported.
Suspect(s)' medication or drug use: Unreported.
Suspect(s)' criminal history: None.
Warning signs: Unreported.
Suspect(s)' country of citizenship: Unreported.
Suspect(s)' religious affiliation: Unreported.
Alleged reason for shooting: Fight. Self-defense claimed, but shot two innocent bystanders. Shooter had drawn his gun to help his brother, who was in a dispute with another student.
Metal detectors present?: No.
Location & time of shooting: Unreported.
For more information, contact: Capt. John J. Finn and Robert Anderson (teacher & victim).
Citations/sources: (Moore, Petrie, Braga, & McLaughlin, 2013, p.198, 266-283) (McFadden, 1991) (People v. Bentley, 1992) (Crews, 2016, p. 7)

#1159
Location of shooting: Delaware State College
Date: 12/8/1991
City, State: Dover, DE
Name of victim(s) killed: N/A.
Age of victim(s) killed: N/A.
Name of victim(s) injured: Keith P. Jarvis.
Age of victim(s) injured: 18
Name of suspect(s)/shooter(s): Maurice T. Vann.
Age of suspect(s)/shooter(s): 18
Weapon(s): .32-caliber Regent handgun
High capacity magazine(s)?: Unreported.
Weapon(s) legally acquired by suspect(s)/shooter(s)?: Unreported.
# of people killed: 0
# of people injured: 1
Total # of victims: 1

Time suspect(s)/shooter(s) were apprehended or killed?: Suspect was arrested one day after the shooting.
　Suspect(s)' mental illness: Unreported.
　Suspect(s)' medication or drug use: Unreported.
　Suspect(s)' criminal history: Unreported.
　Warning signs: Unreported.
　Suspect(s)' country of citizenship: Unreported.
　Suspect(s)' religious affiliation: Unreported.
　Alleged reason for shooting: Feud between suspect and 3 other men. Victim was an innocent bystander.
　Metal detectors present?: N/A.
　Location & time of shooting: Shooting occurred at the college student center parking lot about 2:30 a.m. after a dance.
　For more information, contact: Police spokesman W. James Beauchamp and Kent General Hospital Nursing Supervisor Ruby Price.
　Citations/sources: (Student is shot walking, 1991, p. A3) (Moore, 1991, p. B1)

#1158
Location of shooting: Whiteville High School
Date: 12/26/1991
City, State: Whiteville, NC
Name of victim(s) killed: N/A.
Age of victim(s) killed: N/A.
Name of victim(s) injured: Henry Norton Jr. & Bobby Wilson (bystander).
Age of victim(s) injured: 18 & 25
Name of suspect(s)/shooter(s): Alfonsa George Jr.
Age of suspect(s)/shooter(s): 18
Weapon(s): Unreported.
High capacity magazine(s)?: Unreported.
Weapon(s) legally acquired by suspect(s)/shooter(s)?: Unreported.
# of people killed: 0
# of people injured: 2
Total # of victims: 2
Time suspect(s)/shooter(s) were apprehended or killed?: Suspect was arrested the following day after shooting in the evening.
　Suspect(s)' mental illness: Unreported.
　Suspect(s)' medication or drug use: Unreported.
　Suspect(s)' criminal history: Unreported.
　Warning signs: Unreported.
　Suspect(s)' country of citizenship: Unreported.
　Suspect(s)' religious affiliation: Unreported.

Alleged reason for shooting: Unreported.

Metal detectors present?: No. N/A.

Location & time of shooting: Shooting occurred outside the school gym during a holiday basketball tournament at the high school, in the midst of about 1,000 people in attendance.

For more information, contact: Whiteville Police Department Detective Glenda George and Officer B.R. Benton.

Citations/sources: (Niven, 1991) (Schools will increase security, 1992)

#1157

Location of shooting: Greenwood High School

Date: 1/17/1992

City, State: Greenwood, SC

Name of victim(s) killed: N/A.

Age of victim(s) killed: N/A.

Name of victim(s) injured: Michael Williams.

Age of victim(s) injured: 18

Name of suspect(s)/shooter(s): Unnamed due to age.

Age of suspect(s)/shooter(s): 16

Weapon(s): .32 caliber pistol

High capacity magazine(s)?: Unreported.

Weapon(s) legally acquired by suspect(s)/shooter(s)?: No.

# of people killed: 0

# of people injured: 1

Total # of victims: 1

Time suspect(s)/shooter(s) were apprehended or killed?: School maintenance man disarmed the suspect moments after shooting. The shooter was taken into custody by Greenwood County Sheriff's deputies afterward.

Suspect(s)' mental illness: Unreported.

Suspect(s)' medication or drug use: Unreported.

Suspect(s)' criminal history: Unreported.

Warning signs: Victim claimed he told a school guidance secretary that the suspect was carrying a gun and planned to shoot him an hour and a half before the shooting incident.

Suspect(s)' country of citizenship: Unreported.

Suspect(s)' religious affiliation: Unreported.

Alleged reason for shooting: Feud.

Metal detectors present?: No.

Location & time of shooting: Shooting occurred inside the school hallway, outside of the cafeteria around 11:30 a.m.

For more information, contact: Greenwood County Sheriff, Sam Riley.

Citations/sources: (GHS student faces adult status, 1992, p. 2) (Siltzer, 1992a, p. 1A & 8A) (Siltzerb, 1992, p. 1A & 8A) (Lott, 1992, p. 1A & 8A)

#1156

Location of shooting: Kent State University

Date: 1/29/1992

City, State: Kent, OH

Name of victim(s) killed: N/A.

Age of victim(s) killed: N/A.

Name of victim(s) injured: Sarah Smith.

Age of victim(s) injured: 26

Name of suspect(s)/shooter(s): Mark Cunningham.

Age of suspect(s)/shooter(s): 35

Weapon(s): .38-caliber revolver

High capacity magazine(s)?: No.

Weapon(s) legally acquired by suspect(s)/shooter(s)?: Unreported.

# of people killed: 0

# of people injured: 1

Total # of victims: 1

Time suspect(s)/shooter(s) were apprehended or killed?: Suspect was shot and killed by a Kent police officer in a shootout, 13 days after shooting at Kent University.

Suspect(s)' mental illness: "Anxiety-related disorder."

Suspect(s)' medication or drug use: Unreported.

Suspect(s)' criminal history: Unreported.

Warning signs: Suspect had told a friend that he was afraid of people and that billboards around him were giving him messages.

Suspect(s)' country of citizenship: Unreported.

Suspect(s)' religious affiliation: Unreported.

Alleged reason for shooting: Unreported.

Metal detectors present?: N/A.

Location & time of shooting: Shooting occurred at university campus, at the base of a staircase of White Hall; the college of education, approximately 7:30 p.m.

For more information, contact: Kent Police Captain Dan Fitzpatrick and Police Chief William Lillich.

Citations/sources: (Student shot, wounded on Kent State, 1992, p. 4) (Davis, 1992, p. A1) (Umrigar, 1992a, p. C1 & C3) (Umrigar, 1992b, p. A1 & A8) (Umrigar, 1992c, p. A8) (Motive in shootings, 1992, p. B1)

#1155

Location of shooting: Francis W. Gregory Junior High School (Middle school)

Date: 1/31/1992

City, State: New Orleans, LA

Name of victim(s) killed: N/A.

Age of victim(s) killed: N/A.
Name of victim(s) injured: Unnamed male student due to age.
Age of victim(s) injured: 13
Name of suspect(s)/shooter(s): Two unidentified boys.
Age of suspect(s)/shooter(s): 14 & 15
Weapon(s): Unreported.
High capacity magazine(s)?: Unreported.
Weapon(s) legally acquired by suspect(s)/shooter(s)?: No.
# of people killed: 0
# of people injured: 1
Total # of victims: 1
Time suspect(s)/shooter(s) were apprehended or killed?: Unreported.
Suspect(s)' mental illness: Unreported.
Suspect(s)' medication or drug use: Unreported.
Suspect(s)' criminal history: Unreported.
Warning signs: Unreported.
Suspect(s)' country of citizenship: Unreported.
Suspect(s)' religious affiliation: Unreported.
Alleged reason for shooting: Fight. Victim was trying to run away from the older boys who were beating him up.
Metal detectors present?: Unreported.
Location & time of shooting: Unreported.
For more information, contact: Sgt. Marlon Defillo.
Citations/sources: (School violence, 1992, p. A-16) (School violence growing concern, 1992, p. 4) (Louisiana schools gripped, 1992, p. 17B)

#1154
Location of shooting: Star-Spencer High School
Date: 1/31/1992
City, State: Oklahoma City, OK
Name of victim(s) killed: N/A.
Age of victim(s) killed: N/A.
Name of victim(s) injured: Unreported.
Age of victim(s) injured: 15
Name of suspect(s)/shooter(s): Unreported.
Age of suspect(s)/shooter(s): Unreported.
Weapon(s): Handgun.
High capacity magazine(s)?: Unreported.
Weapon(s) legally acquired by suspect(s)/shooter(s)?: Unreported.
# of people killed: 0
# of people injured: 1

Total # of victims: 1
Time suspect(s)/shooter(s) were apprehended or killed?: Unreported.
Suspect(s)' mental illness: Unreported.
Suspect(s)' medication or drug use: Unreported.
Suspect(s)' criminal history: Unreported.
Warning signs: Unreported.
Suspect(s)' country of citizenship: Unreported.
Suspect(s)' religious affiliation: Unreported.
Alleged reason for shooting: Fight. Victim was an innocent bystander who was shot while watching a fight between two students.
Metal detectors present?: N/A.
Location & time of shooting: Shooting occurred outside of the school at approximately 2:30 p.m. while students were waiting for the school bus.
For more information, contact: District Spokesman Michael Carrier, Police Sgt. Joe Snodgrass, Police Lt. Mel Thee and County Assistant District Attorney John Foley.
Citations/sources: (Kuhlman & Perry, 1992, p. 9) (Perry, 1992)

#1153
Location of shooting: Douglass High School
Date: 2/6/1992
City, State: Oklahoma City, OK
Name of victim(s) killed: Charles W. "Billy" Graham.
Age of victim(s) killed: 17
Name of victim(s) injured: N/A.
Age of victim(s) injured: N/A.
Name of suspect(s)/shooter(s): Joe W. Wallen.
Age of suspect(s)/shooter(s): 14
Weapon(s): Unreported.
High capacity magazine(s)?: Unreported.
Weapon(s) legally acquired by suspect(s)/shooter(s)?: No.
# of people killed: 1
# of people injured: 0
Total # of victims: 1
Time suspect(s)/shooter(s) were apprehended or killed?: Unreported.
Suspect(s)' mental illness: Unreported.
Suspect(s)' medication or drug use: Unreported.
Suspect(s)' criminal history: None.
Warning signs: Unreported.
Suspect(s)' country of citizenship: Unreported.
Suspect(s)' religious affiliation: Unreported.
Alleged reason for shooting: Argument over a girl.

Metal detectors present?: Yes. May not have been in use on the day of the shooting.

Location & time of shooting: Shooting occurred in the school hallway at approximately 2:20 p.m., just as the final classes of the day were getting out.

For more information, contact: District Superintendent Arthur Steller, Principal Walter Mason and District Spokesman L.D. Barney.

Citations/sources: (Perry, 1992) (Aiken, 1992)

#1152
Location of shooting: Booker T. Washington High School
Date: 2/7/1992
City, State: Norfolk, VA
Name of victim(s) killed: Darryl Taylor.
Age of victim(s) killed: 19
Name of victim(s) injured: Ronald Smith.
Age of victim(s) injured: 18
Name of suspect(s)/shooter(s): Charles T. Cabarraf.
Age of suspect(s)/shooter(s): 19
Weapon(s): Automatic pistol
High capacity magazine(s)?: Unreported.
Weapon(s) legally acquired by suspect(s)/shooter(s)?: Unreported.
# of people killed: 1
# of people injured: 1
Total # of victims: 2
Time suspect(s)/shooter(s) were apprehended or killed?: Suspect arrested about six hours after second victim died.

Suspect(s)' mental illness: Unreported.

Suspect(s)' medication or drug use: Unreported.

Suspect(s)' criminal history: Unreported.

Warning signs: Unreported.

Suspect(s)' country of citizenship: Unreported.

Suspect(s)' religious affiliation: Unreported.

Alleged reason for shooting: Dispute. Aftermath of a burglary incident that occurred at one of the victim's home the day before the shooting.

Metal detectors present?: No. N/A.

Location & time of shooting: Shooting occurred outside the back parking lot of the school at 12:47PM.

For more information, contact: Police Chief Henry Henson and Norfolk Police Department Larry Hill.

Citations/sources: (Blattner, 1992) (Saville, 1992, p. C5)

#1151

Location of shooting: Thomas Jefferson High School

Date: 2/26/1992

City, State: Brooklyn, NY

Name of victim(s) killed: Tyrone Sinkler & Ian Moore.

Age of victim(s) killed: 16 & 17

Name of victim(s) injured: N/A.

Age of victim(s) injured: N/A.

Name of suspect(s)/shooter(s): Kahlil Sumpter.

Age of suspect(s)/shooter(s): 15

Weapon(s): .38-caliber Smith & Wesson revolver

High capacity magazine(s)?: Unreported.

Weapon(s) legally acquired by suspect(s)/shooter(s)?: No. Received gun from a friend in order to defend himself. Police said the gun was originally stolen from an off-duty campus police officer at the University of Medicine and Dentistry of New Jersey in Plainfield, N.J.

# of people killed: 2

# of people injured: 0

Total # of victims: 2

Time suspect(s)/shooter(s) were apprehended or killed?: School security guards caught suspect two blocks away from the school immediately after the shooting.

Suspect(s)' mental illness: No.

Suspect(s)' medication or drug use: Unreported.

Suspect(s)' criminal history: Suspect arrested for a prior robbery and received two years of probation.

Warning signs: Unreported.

Suspect(s)' country of citizenship: Unreported.

Suspect(s)' religious affiliation: Unreported.

Alleged reason for shooting: Feud. Shooter and one of the victims were both arrested for a robbery in 1990. Only one of the youths served time in prison. Shooter claimed he feared the victims were going to attack him.

Metal detectors present?: Yes, but they were not used on the day of the shooting.

Location & time of shooting: Shooting occurred on the second floor of the high school.

For more information, contact: Detective Sgt. Michael Race of the 75th Precinct

Citations/sources: (Moore, Petrie, Braga, & McLaughlin, 2013, p.215, 266-283) (Mitchel, 1992) (Kleinfield & Fisher, 1992) (Fried, 1993) (Crews, 2016, p. 7)

#1150

Location of shooting: Robert Fulton Junior High School (Middle school)

Date: 2/28/1992

City, State: Van Nuys, CA

Name of victim(s) killed: N/A.

Age of victim(s) killed: N/A.

Name of victim(s) injured: Two unidentified students.
Age of victim(s) injured: 15 & 15
Name of suspect(s)/shooter(s): John Noguera.
Age of suspect(s)/shooter(s): 18
Weapon(s): Unreported.
High capacity magazine(s)?: Unreported.
Weapon(s) legally acquired by suspect(s)/shooter(s)?: Unreported.
# of people killed: 0
# of people injured: 2
Total # of victims: 2
Time suspect(s)/shooter(s) were apprehended or killed?: Suspect surrendered to the police two days after the shooting.
Suspect(s)' mental illness: Unreported.
Suspect(s)' medication or drug use: Unreported.
Suspect(s)' criminal history: Unreported.
Warning signs: Unreported.
Suspect(s)' country of citizenship: Unreported.
Suspect(s)' religious affiliation: Unreported.
Alleged reason for shooting: Gang-related.
Metal detectors present?: N/A.
Location & time of shooting: Suspect fired six bullets at a group of students standing outside the school approximately 7:35 a.m.
For more information, contact: Chief of Police for the Los Angeles Unified School District Wesley Mitchell, Detective Greg Demirjian and Sgt. Dan Honey.
Citations/sources: (Fernandes & Chu, 1992, p. B14) (Man, 18, charged, 1992, p. B2)

#1149
Location of shooting: Hamilton Middle School
Date: 3/5/1992
City, State: Obetz, OH
Name of victim(s) killed: N/A.
Age of victim(s) killed: N/A.
Name of victim(s) injured: Gregg Johnson.
Age of victim(s) injured: 14
Name of suspect(s)/shooter(s): Gordon W. Dye, Jr.
Age of suspect(s)/shooter(s): 12
Weapon(s): .22-caliber revolver
High capacity magazine(s)?: Unreported.
Weapon(s) legally acquired by suspect(s)/shooter(s)?: No. Suspect stole gun from home.
# of people killed: 0
# of people injured: 1

Total # of victims: 1

Time suspect(s)/shooter(s) were apprehended or killed?: Suspect was disarmed by a teacher moments after the shooting.

Suspect(s)' mental illness: Unreported.

Suspect(s)' medication or drug use: Unreported.

Suspect(s)' criminal history: None.

Warning signs: No.

Suspect(s)' country of citizenship: Unreported.

Suspect(s)' religious affiliation: Unreported.

Alleged reason for shooting: Bullying. Suspect wanted to teach bullies a lesson.

Metal detectors present?: Unreported.

Location & time of shooting: Shooting occurred in school cafeteria during lunch period.

For more information, contact: Franklin County Sheriff's Department Deputy Rick Minerd and Principal John Cornette.

Citations/sources: (Shooting an 'isolated incident,' 1992, p. 2) (Students pleads guilty, 1992, p. 7C) (Boy gets probation, 1992, p. 2)

#1148
Location of shooting: Brandon High School
Date: 3/23/1992
City, State: Brandon, FL
Name of victim(s) killed: N/A.
Age of victim(s) killed: N/A.
Name of victim(s) injured: Brad Shumaker.
Age of victim(s) injured: 17
Name of suspect(s)/shooter(s): Quintus L. Johnson.
Age of suspect(s)/shooter(s): 18
Weapon(s): .25-caliber pistol
High capacity magazine(s)?: Unreported.
Weapon(s) legally acquired by suspect(s)/shooter(s)?: Unreported.
# of people killed: 0
# of people injured: 1
Total # of victims: 1
Time suspect(s)/shooter(s) were apprehended or killed?: Unreported.
Suspect(s)' mental illness: Unreported.
Suspect(s)' medication or drug use: Unreported.
Suspect(s)' criminal history: Unreported.
Warning signs: Unreported.
Suspect(s)' country of citizenship: Unreported.
Suspect(s)' religious affiliation: Unreported.

<u>Alleged reason for shooting</u>: Accident. Firearm accidentally discharged while in the suspect's pocket. Suspect claimed he was carrying the gun for protection from gangs.

<u>Metal detectors present?</u>:

<u>Location & time of shooting</u>: Shooting occurred in an agricultural production class at 8:25 a.m.

<u>For more information, contact</u>: Superintendent Mike Vinson, Police Chief Walker Tucker and City Court Judge Mike Younger.

<u>Citations/sources:</u> (Incident reminds editor, 1997, p. 12A) (Wagster, 1992a, p. 1A) (Wagster, 1992b, p. 1A) (School violence: metro area, 1997, p. 12A)

#1147
<u>Location of shooting</u>: O. Perry Walker High School
<u>Date</u>: 3/31/1992
<u>City, State</u>: New Orleans, LA
<u>Name of victim(s) killed</u>: Jamo or Jomo-Kenyetta Joseph (first name spelled both ways in reporting).
<u>Age of victim(s) killed</u>: 15
<u>Name of victim(s) injured</u>: N/A.
<u>Age of victim(s) injured</u>: N/A.
<u>Name of suspect(s)/shooter(s)</u>: Herman Tureau (a.k.a. Tureaud).
<u>Age of suspect(s)/shooter(s)</u>: 15
<u>Weapon(s)</u>: .38-caliber revolver
<u>High capacity magazine(s)?</u>: Unreported.
<u>Weapon(s) legally acquired by suspect(s)/shooter(s)?</u>: No.
<u># of people killed</u>: 1
<u># of people injured</u>: 0
<u>Total # of victims</u>: 1
<u>Time suspect(s)/shooter(s) were apprehended or killed?</u>: Suspect was arrested at his home in the afternoon of the same day of the shooting.
<u>Suspect(s)' mental illness</u>: Unreported.
<u>Suspect(s)' medication or drug use</u>: Unreported.
<u>Suspect(s)' criminal history</u>: Unreported.
<u>Warning signs</u>: Witnesses testified that the teen had shown off a .38-caliber revolver he brought to school that morning, and had told others that if anyone messed with him, they would be shot.
<u>Suspect(s)' country of citizenship</u>: Unreported.
<u>Suspect(s)' religious affiliation</u>: Unreported.
<u>Alleged reason for shooting</u>: Fight between two groups of teenagers.
<u>Metal detectors present?</u>: Unreported.
<u>Location & time of shooting</u>: Shooting occurred at school breezeway around 8:30 a.m.
<u>For more information, contact</u>: Hospital spokeswoman Linda Hudson, Sgt. Bob Young and U.S. Education Secretary Lamar Alexander.

Citations/sources: (Student, 15, dies, 1991, p. 13A) (Alexander: school's safety, 1992) (Daley, 2017)

#1146
Location of shooting: Zia Middle School
Date: 4/10/1992
City, State: Mesilla (Las Cruces), NM
Name of victim(s) killed: N/A.
Age of victim(s) killed: N/A.
Name of victim(s) injured: Renee Martinez.
Age of victim(s) injured: 14
Name of suspect(s)/shooter(s): Joe Rodriguez, Brian Johnson, Wendell Crabb & Seth Yarter.
Age of suspect(s)/shooter(s): 14, 14, 13 & 13
Weapon(s): .25-caliber semiautomatic pistol
High capacity magazine(s)?: Unreported.
Weapon(s) legally acquired by suspect(s)/shooter(s)?: No.
# of people killed: 0
# of people injured: 1
Total # of victims: 1
Time suspect(s)/shooter(s) were apprehended or killed?: Arrested by a town marshal's officer minutes after the shooting by an irrigation ditch near the school.
Suspect(s)' mental illness: Unreported.
Suspect(s)' medication or drug use: Unreported.
Suspect(s)' criminal history: Unreported.
Warning signs: A fellow student said he saw the suspect load the handgun and showing it to two other guys.
Suspect(s)' country of citizenship: Unreported.
Suspect(s)' religious affiliation: Unreported.
Alleged reason for shooting: Gang-related.
Metal detectors present?: No.
Location & time of shooting: Shooting occurred in school patio area.
For more information, contact: Investigator Terry Lewis, Mesilla Marshal's Department officer Johnny Singh and Sheriff Ray Storment, District Attorney Doug Driggers.
Citations/sources: (Seventh-grader in custody, 1992, p. A-3) (Shock of Zia school shooting, 1992, p. 1B & 2B) (Lopez, 1992, p. D3)

#1145
Location of shooting: Lincoln High School
Date: 4/17/1992
City, State: Dallas, TX
Name of victim(s) killed: Dameon Steadham.

Age of victim(s) killed: 18
Name of victim(s) injured: N/A.
Age of victim(s) injured: N/A.
Name of suspect(s)/shooter(s): John L. Cofield.
Age of suspect(s)/shooter(s): 16
Weapon(s): .38-caliber weapon
High capacity magazine(s)?: Unreported.
Weapon(s) legally acquired by suspect(s)/shooter(s)?: No.
# of people killed: 1
# of people injured: 0
Total # of victims: 1
Time suspect(s)/shooter(s) were apprehended or killed?: Unreported.
Suspect(s)' mental illness: Unreported.
Suspect(s)' medication or drug use: Unreported.
Suspect(s)' criminal history: Unreported.
Warning signs: Unreported. Frequency of gunfire during & after school functions was so well-known that officials of the Dallas PD had previously asked Lincoln High School officials to refrain from sponsoring school functions until adequate police security could be provided.
Suspect(s)' country of citizenship: Unreported.
Suspect(s)' religious affiliation: Unreported.
Alleged reason for shooting: Accident. Celebratory gunfire.
Metal detectors present?: N/A.
Location & time of shooting: Shooting occurred in school parking lot after a school dance in the evening.
For more information, contact: Dallas Police Sgt. Joe DeCorte, Assistant District Attorney George West and Homicide Detective James Murphy; Principal Napoleon Lewis.
Citations/sources: (Leffall v. Dallas Indep. Sch. Dist., 1994) (Lewis, 1992, p. 33A) (Nagorka, 1992, p. 25A)

#1144
Location of shooting: Lindhurst High School
Date: 5/1/1992
City, State: Olivehurst, CA
Name of victim(s) killed: Beamon A. Hill, Judy Davis, Jason E. White & Robert Brens (Civics teacher).
Age of victim(s) killed: 16, 17, 19 & 28
Name of victim(s) injured: Wayne Boggess, Patricia Collazo, Danita Gipson, Donald Graham, Thomas Hinojosai, John Kaze, Sergio Martinez, Jose Rodriguez, Rachel Scarberry & Mireya Yanez.
Age of victim(s) injured: Unreported.
Name of suspect(s)/shooter(s): Eric Houston.

Age of suspect(s)/shooter(s): 20
Weapon(s): 12-gauge shotgun & .22-caliber sawed-off rifle
High capacity magazine(s)?: No.
Weapon(s) legally acquired by suspect(s)/shooter(s)?: Yes.
# of people killed: 4
# of people injured: 10
Total # of victims: 14

Time suspect(s)/shooter(s) were apprehended or killed?: Suspect surrendered to law enforcement approximately 8 and half hours after shooting began, after receiving a "contract" promising him he would serve no more than five-years in a minimum-security prison.

Suspect(s)' mental illness: Suspect's attorney argued he suffered from an organic brain disorder and that molestation from his civics teacher in 1989 caused a post-traumatic stress disorder.

Suspect(s)' medication or drug use: Unreported.

Suspect(s)' criminal history: Unreported.

Warning signs: In early 1992, the suspect on several occasions told his best friend, David Rewerts, that he would like to go to Lindhurst High School and shoot a couple of people.

Suspect(s)' country of citizenship: Unreported.

Suspect(s)' religious affiliation: Unreported.

Alleged reason for shooting: Protest authority. Retaliation for a failing grade in an economics class. Suspect blamed teacher for failing to graduate and the loss of his job and girlfriend. Suspect also accused this former teacher of having molested him.

Metal detectors present?: Unreported.

Location & time of shooting: Suspect entered the school and began shooting in the hallways; holding approximately 85 students hostage.

For more information, contact: Yube County Sheriff Gary Tindel, Sheriff Captain Dennis Moore and Yuba County District Attorney Charles O'Rourke.

Citations/sources: (Klein, 2012, p. 153) (Crews, 2016, p. 7) (Lebrun, 2009, p. 173) (State supreme court upholds, 2012) (Locke, 2018) (4 slain, 10 wounded, p. A1) (Hunt, 1993, p. A2) (People v. Houston, 2012) (Newman, Fox, Harding, Mehta, & Roth, 2004, p.236 & 263) (Morain & Ingram, 1992)

#1143
Location of shooting: Silverado Middle School
Date: 5/14/1992
City, State: Napa, CA
Name of victim(s) killed: N/A.
Age of victim(s) killed: N/A.
Name of victim(s) injured: Two unnamed male students.
Age of victim(s) injured: 14 & 14
Name of suspect(s)/shooter(s): Unnamed due to age.
Age of suspect(s)/shooter(s): 14
Weapon(s): .357-caliber Magnum revolver

High capacity magazine(s)?: Unreported.

Weapon(s) legally acquired by suspect(s)/shooter(s)?: No. Stolen from suspect's father.

# of people killed: 0

# of people injured: 2

Total # of victims: 2

Time suspect(s)/shooter(s) were apprehended or killed?: Teachers surrounded the suspect and convinced him to surrender his gun moments after the shooting and held him until law enforcement arrived.

Suspect(s)' mental illness: Unreported.

Suspect(s)' medication or drug use: Unreported.

Suspect(s)' criminal history: None.

Warning signs: Students revealed that a few weeks prior to the shooting, the suspect brought a gun to school and threatened to kill someone. The students didn't believe him.

Suspect(s)' country of citizenship: Unreported.

Suspect(s)' religious affiliation: Unreported.

Alleged reason for shooting: Bullying.

Metal detectors present?: Unreported.

Location & time of shooting: Shooting occurred in a science classroom at 8:40 a.m.

For more information, contact: Napa Police Chief Dan Monez and science teacher David Duddles.

Citations/sources: (Rossman, 1992, p. A1 & A12) (Flinn, 1992, p. A-1 & A-12)

#1142

Location of shooting: Huntsville Junior High School (Middle school)

Date: 5/14/1992

City, State: Huntsville, TX

Name of victim(s) killed: N/A.

Age of victim(s) killed: N/A.

Name of victim(s) injured: Quinn Ashworth.

Age of victim(s) injured: 15

Name of suspect(s)/shooter(s): Unnamed boy due to age.

Age of suspect(s)/shooter(s): 14

Weapon(s): .38-caliber semiautomatic pistol

High capacity magazine(s)?: Unreported.

Weapon(s) legally acquired by suspect(s)/shooter(s)?: No.

# of people killed: 0

# of people injured: 1

Total # of victims: 1

Time suspect(s)/shooter(s) were apprehended or killed?: Unreported.

Suspect(s)' mental illness: Unreported.

Suspect(s)' medication or drug use: Unreported.

Suspect(s)' criminal history: Unreported.
Warning signs: Unreported.
Suspect(s)' country of citizenship: Unreported.
Suspect(s)' religious affiliation: Unreported.
Alleged reason for shooting: Self-defense. Feud.
Metal detectors present?: Unreported.
Location & time of shooting: Shooting occurred at an open area between the school's main building and a wing about 7:45 am.
For more information, contact: Memorial Hospital Spokeswoman Jill Baine, Huntsville Independent School District Superintendent Dale Dixon and Lt. Gary Howze.
Citations/sources: (Youth acquitted, 1992, p. 2A) (Student who shot 'bully,' 1992, p. 3D) (Junior high boy critical, 1992, p. 9A)

#1141
Location of shooting: Venice High School
Date: 5/29/1992
City, State: Los Angeles, CA
Name of victim(s) killed: N/A.
Age of victim(s) killed: N/A.
Name of victim(s) injured: Three unnamed students.
Age of victim(s) injured: 15, 17 & 18
Name of suspect(s)/shooter(s): Four males in a stolen maroon Honda Civic.
Age of suspect(s)/shooter(s): Unreported.
Weapon(s): Unreported.
High capacity magazine(s)?: Unreported.
Weapon(s) legally acquired by suspect(s)/shooter(s)?: Unreported.
# of people killed: 0
# of people injured: 3
Total # of victims: 3
Time suspect(s)/shooter(s) were apprehended or killed?: Unreported.
Suspect(s)' mental illness: Unreported.
Suspect(s)' medication or drug use: Unreported.
Suspect(s)' criminal history: Unreported.
Warning signs: Unreported.
Suspect(s)' country of citizenship: Unreported.
Suspect(s)' religious affiliation: Unreported.
Alleged reason for shooting: Gang-related.
Metal detectors present?: N/A.
Location & time of shooting: Drive-by shooting around 8:20 a.m..
For more information, contact: Los Angeles Police Officer Steve Cordova, LAPD Lt. George Ibarra, Fire Department Spokesman Mike Little and Principal Bud Jacobs.

Citations/sources: (Banks & Sengupta, 1993) (Timnick, 1992, p. B9) (3 teens shot, 1992, p. A3)

#1140
Location of shooting: Merced High School
Date: 6/6/1992
City, State: Merced, CA
Name of victim(s) killed: N/A.
Age of victim(s) killed: N/A.
Name of victim(s) injured: Tou Lee.
Age of victim(s) injured: 23
Name of suspect(s)/shooter(s): Unreported.
Age of suspect(s)/shooter(s): 17
Weapon(s): Unreported.
High capacity magazine(s)?: Unreported.
Weapon(s) legally acquired by suspect(s)/shooter(s)?: No.
# of people killed: 0
# of people injured: 1
Total # of victims: 1
Time suspect(s)/shooter(s) were apprehended or killed?: Unreported.
Suspect(s)' mental illness: Unreported.
Suspect(s)' medication or drug use: Unreported.
Suspect(s)' criminal history: Unreported.
Warning signs: Unreported.
Suspect(s)' country of citizenship: Unreported.
Suspect(s)' religious affiliation: Unreported.
Alleged reason for shooting: Fight.
Metal detectors present?: N/A.

Location & time of shooting: Shooting occurred during a graduation party between the school gymnasium and the music building at approximately 11:18 p.m., which was open to the public.

For more information, contact: Police Cmdr. Mark Dossetti and School District Spokeswoman Sylvia Christiansen.

Citations/sources: (Washington, 1992, p. B1)

1139
Location of shooting: Palo Duro High School
Date: 9/11/1992
City, State: Amarillo, TX
Name of victim(s) killed: N/A.
Age of victim(s) killed: N/A.

Name of victim(s) injured: Donyel Austin, Bobby Archie, Matthew Mitchel, Marcus Stiles, Norman Winifred & Delmond Carruthers.

Age of victim(s) injured: 15, 15, 16, ?, 17 & 18
Name of suspect(s)/shooter(s): Randy Earl Matthews & an unnamed 15-year-old.
Age of suspect(s)/shooter(s): 17 & 15
Weapon(s): .22-caliber pistol
High capacity magazine(s)?: Unreported.
Weapon(s) legally acquired by suspect(s)/shooter(s)?: No.
# of people killed: 0
# of people injured: 6
Total # of victims: 6
Time suspect(s)/shooter(s) were apprehended or killed?: Unreported.
Suspect(s)' mental illness: Unreported.
Suspect(s)' medication or drug use: Unreported.
Suspect(s)' criminal history: Unreported.
Warning signs: Unreported.
Suspect(s)' country of citizenship: Unreported.
Suspect(s)' religious affiliation: Unreported.
Alleged reason for shooting: Fight.
Metal detectors present?: No.
Location & time of shooting: Shooting took place in a school hallway.
For more information, contact: Amarillo Independent School District Superintendent John Wilson, Police spokesman Helen Smith and Amarillo Special Crimes Sgt. Kevin Dockery.
Citations/sources: (Parents confess fears, 1992, p. 3A) (After shooting, fear may rule, 1992, p. B6) (Distraught father enters elementary school, 1992, p. 2B) (Mayer, 2012, p. 5B) (Teen-ager shoots 6, 1992, p. A12) (Brown, 1992, p. B12)

#1138
Location of shooting: Piney Point Elementary School
Date: 9/18/1992
City, State: Houston, TX
Name of victim(s) killed: N/A.
Age of victim(s) killed: N/A.
Name of victim(s) injured: Lowell Neinast (Houston Police Officer) & David E. Dungan (Houston Police Officer).
Age of victim(s) injured: 29 & 36
Name of suspect(s)/shooter(s): Calvin Charles Bell.
Age of suspect(s)/shooter(s): 44
Weapon(s): Two semiautomatic guns, four ammunition clips, a combat-style hunting knife and a can of mace.
High capacity magazine(s)?: Unreported.
Weapon(s) legally acquired by suspect(s)/shooter(s)?: Unreported.
# of people killed: 0

<u># of people injured</u>: 2

<u>Total # of victims</u>: 2

<u>Time suspect(s)/shooter(s) were apprehended or killed?</u>: Unreported.

<u>Suspect(s)' mental illness</u>: Suspect found not guilty by reason of insanity and was released from a mental facility in 1994.

<u>Suspect(s)' medication or drug use</u>: Suspect recently quit taking medication for depression before shooting.

<u>Suspect(s)' criminal history</u>: None.

<u>Warning signs</u>: Unreported.

<u>Suspect(s)' country of citizenship</u>: Unreported.

<u>Suspect(s)' religious affiliation</u>: Unreported.

<u>Alleged reason for shooting</u>: Protest authority. Suspect was angry about over his son's grades.

<u>Metal detectors present?</u>: Unreported.

<u>Location & time of shooting</u>: Shooting occurred in the school administration office

<u>For more information, contact</u>: Police spokesman John Leggio, Officer Lowell Neinast, Officer David E. Dungan and Officer Leon Martinez III.

<u>Citations/sources</u>: (Distraught father enters elementary school, 1992, p. 1B & 2B) (Son's grades may be tied, 1992, p. A-3) (Mental facility frees, 1994, p. 5D) (Man who opened fire, 1994, p. 7B)

#1137

Location of shooting: Hiram Johnson High School

<u>Date</u>: 9/28/1992

<u>City, State</u>: Sacramento, CA

<u>Name of victim(s) killed</u>: N/A.

<u>Age of victim(s) killed</u>: N/A.

<u>Name of victim(s) injured</u>: Julio Perez & Bernardo Rojas.

<u>Age of victim(s) injured</u>: 16 & 18

<u>Name of suspect(s)/shooter(s)</u>: Tuan Do, Binh Tran, Duy Nguyen, and an unnamed 16-year old boy.

<u>Age of suspect(s)/shooter(s)</u>: 18, 19, 20 & 16

<u>Weapon(s)</u>: Unreported.

<u>High capacity magazine(s)?</u>: Unreported.

<u>Weapon(s) legally acquired by suspect(s)/shooter(s)?</u>: Unreported.

<u># of people killed</u>: 0

<u># of people injured</u>: 2

<u>Total # of victims</u>: 2

<u>Time suspect(s)/shooter(s) were apprehended or killed?</u>: Unreported.

<u>Suspect(s)' mental illness</u>: Unreported.

<u>Suspect(s)' medication or drug use</u>: Unreported.

<u>Suspect(s)' criminal history</u>: Unreported.

<u>Warning signs</u>: Unreported.

Suspect(s)' country of citizenship: Unreported.
Suspect(s)' religious affiliation: Unreported.
Alleged reason for shooting: Fight. Possibly gang-related.
Metal detectors present?: Unreported.
Location & time of shooting: Unreported.
For more information, contact: Sacramento Police Sgt. Bob Mitchell.
Citations/sources: (Two Hiram Johnson students, 1992, p. A2) (Four arrested in high school, 1992, p. A2)

#1136
Location of shooting: John Marshall High School
Date: 9/30/1992
City, State: Rochester, NY
Name of victim(s) killed: N/A.
Age of victim(s) killed: N/A.
Name of victim(s) injured: James Holt.
Age of victim(s) injured: 18
Name of suspect(s)/shooter(s): David Morris.
Age of suspect(s)/shooter(s): 17
Weapon(s): Small caliber handgun
High capacity magazine(s)?: Unreported.
Weapon(s) legally acquired by suspect(s)/shooter(s)?: No.
# of people killed: 0
# of people injured: 1
Total # of victims: 1
Time suspect(s)/shooter(s) were apprehended or killed?: Suspect surrendered to the police with his lawyer 5 days after shooting.
Suspect(s)' mental illness: Unreported.
Suspect(s)' medication or drug use: Unreported.
Suspect(s)' criminal history: Unreported.
Warning signs: Unreported.
Suspect(s)' country of citizenship: Unreported.
Suspect(s)' religious affiliation: Unreported.
Alleged reason for shooting: Dispute over a cassette tape.
Metal detectors present?: No.
Location & time of shooting: Shooting occurred in a crowded school hallway about 11:15 a.m. between classes. Superintendent Manuel Rivera did not favor metal detectors.
For more information, contact: Rochester Police Department and Rochester Schools Superintendent Manuel Rivera.
Citations/sources: (Teen pleads guilty, 1993, p. 2B) (Wertheimer, 1992, p. 1A) (Mills & Morrell, 1992, p. 1B)

#1135
Location of shooting: Hollibrook Elementary School
Date: 10/5/1992
City, State: Houston, TX
Name of victim(s) killed: Luis Mesa.
Age of victim(s) killed: 16
Name of victim(s) injured: N/A.
Age of victim(s) injured: N/A.
Name of suspect(s)/shooter(s): Juan Diaz.
Age of suspect(s)/shooter(s): 15
Weapon(s): Shotgun
High capacity magazine(s)?: Unreported.
Weapon(s) legally acquired by suspect(s)/shooter(s)?: No.
# of people killed: 1
# of people injured: 0
Total # of victims: 1
Time suspect(s)/shooter(s) were apprehended or killed?: Unreported.
Suspect(s)' mental illness: Unreported.
Suspect(s)' medication or drug use: Unreported.
Suspect(s)' criminal history: Unreported.
Warning signs: Unreported.
Suspect(s)' country of citizenship: Unreported.
Suspect(s)' religious affiliation: Unreported.
Alleged reason for shooting: Gang-related.
Metal detectors present?: N/A.
Location & time of shooting: Shooting occurred at the playground of Hollibrook Elementary School.
For more information, contact: Unreported.
Citations/sources: (National School Safety Center, 2010, p. 2) (Roll Call of the Dead, 1993) (Congress of the U.S., 1999, p. 69)

#1134
Location of shooting: Desert View High School
Date: 10/13/1992
City, State: Tucson, AZ
Name of victim(s) killed: Oscar Daniel Leon.
Age of victim(s) killed: 16
Name of victim(s) injured: N/A.
Age of victim(s) injured: N/A.
Name of suspect(s)/shooter(s): Antonio Redondo.

Age of suspect(s)/shooter(s): 19
Weapon(s): .22 caliber pistol
High capacity magazine(s)?: Unreported.
Weapon(s) legally acquired by suspect(s)/shooter(s)?: Unreported.
# of people killed: 1
# of people injured: 0
Total # of victims: 1
Time suspect(s)/shooter(s) were apprehended or killed?: Unreported.
Suspect(s)' mental illness: Unreported.
Suspect(s)' medication or drug use: Unreported.
Suspect(s)' criminal history: Convicted in Pima County Juvenile Court of attempted murder in 1990, attempted aggravated assault, attempted robbery, and attempted burglary charges. Cited for use of marijuana and trespassing in 1990. Convicted of grand theft auto at 12 years old in 1985.
Warning signs: Yes. Approximately 30 minutes before the shooting, the suspect and his friends drove into the school parking lot taunting students by flashing gang signs and pointed a gun at a 14-year old girl sitting in a bus.
Suspect(s)' country of citizenship: Unreported.
Suspect(s)' religious affiliation: Unreported.
Alleged reason for shooting: Gang-related.
Metal detectors present?: No. N/A.
Location & time of shooting: Shooting occurred in the school parking lot as the gunman drove up in a pickup truck around 2:00 p.m.
For more information, contact: Superior Court Judge John Kelly, Deputy County Attorney Teresa Milliken and Defense attorney Eric Larsen.
Citations/sources: (National School Safety Center, 2010, p. 2) (Corella, 1992, p. 1A & 4A) (O'Connell, 1992, p. 1A & 4A) (Salkowski, 1993a, p. 1B) (Salkowski, 1993b, p. 1A & 2A) (Congress of the U.S., 1999, p. 69)

#1133
Location of shooting: Finney High School
Date: 11/4/1992
City, State: Detroit, MI
Name of victim(s) killed: N/A.
Age of victim(s) killed: N/A.
Name of victim(s) injured: Herman Hays, Jasmine Bridgeman, Terrance Carey, Aisha Turner, Council Bellomy III & Nagongi Cann.
Age of victim(s) injured: 14, 15, 15, 16, 17 & 18
Name of suspect(s)/shooter(s): Renard Merkerson, Montrice Coleman & Robert White.
Age of suspect(s)/shooter(s): 18, 18 & 19
Weapon(s): Rifle, sawed-off shotgun and a .22-caliber pistol.
High capacity magazine(s)?: Unreported.

Weapon(s) legally acquired by suspect(s)/shooter(s)?: Unreported.
# of people killed: 0
# of people injured: 6
Total # of victims: 6
Time suspect(s)/shooter(s) were apprehended or killed?: Three suspects were taken into custody late on the same day of the shooting.
Suspect(s)' mental illness: Unreported.
Suspect(s)' medication or drug use: Unreported.
Suspect(s)' criminal history: Unreported.
Warning signs: Unreported.
Suspect(s)' country of citizenship: Unreported.
Suspect(s)' religious affiliation: Unreported.
Alleged reason for shooting: Dispute that started at a pep rally.
Metal detectors present?: No.
Location & time of shooting: Shooting occurred in crowded school hallway shortly after 10:30 a.m.

For more information, contact: Detroit Police Officer Rhoda Virgil-Madison, Superintendent Deborah McGriff & Wayne County Prosecutor's Office and Asst. Prosecutor Andrea Solak.

Citations/sources: (Security tightens after 11 Detroit, 1992, p. 1) (Johnson, 1992, p. 1A & 11A) (Kresnak, 1992, p. 1B) (Alexander, 1992) (Charges dropped in school shooting, 1992, p. 3B) ('I saw everybody running,' 1993, p. 5F & 6F)

#1132
Location of shooting: Mumford High School
Date: 11/4/1992
City, State: Detroit, MI
Name of victim(s) killed: N/A.
Age of victim(s) killed: N/A.
Name of victim(s) injured: DeWayne Boyd.
Age of victim(s) injured: 16
Name of suspect(s)/shooter(s): Allegedly, two reputed gang members from the Six Mile Road Boys gang, later released for lack of evidence.
Age of suspect(s)/shooter(s): 15 & 16
Weapon(s): Unreported.
High capacity magazine(s)?: Unreported.
Weapon(s) legally acquired by suspect(s)/shooter(s)?: Unreported.
# of people killed: 0
# of people injured: 1
Total # of victims: 1
Time suspect(s)/shooter(s) were apprehended or killed?: Two suspects were taken into custody a week after the shooting.

Suspect(s)' mental illness: Unreported.
Suspect(s)' medication or drug use: Unreported.
Suspect(s)' criminal history: Unreported.
Warning signs: Unreported.
Suspect(s)' country of citizenship: Unreported.
Suspect(s)' religious affiliation: Unreported.
Alleged reason for shooting: Gang-related. Feud between rival gangs.
Metal detectors present?: Yes. N/A.
Location & time of shooting: Shooting occurred approximately 3:00 p.m. in front of the school.
For more information, contact: Detroit Police Officer Rhoda Virgil-Madison, Superintendent Deborah McGriff and Mumford Principal Robin Oden.
Citations/sources: (Security tightens after 11 Detroit, 1992, p. 1) (Johnson, 1992, p. 1A & 11A) (Alexander, 1992) ('I saw everybody running,' 1993, p. 5F & 6F)

#1131
Location of shooting: Sherman Elementary School
Date: 11/10/1992
City, State: Sherman, IL
Name of victim(s) killed: Willie Clayborn (shooter).
Age of victim(s) killed: 13
Name of victim(s) injured: N/A.
Age of victim(s) injured: N/A.
Name of suspect(s)/shooter(s): Willie Clayborn.
Age of suspect(s)/shooter(s): 13
Weapon(s): .22-caliber handgun
High capacity magazine(s)?: Unreported.
Weapon(s) legally acquired by suspect(s)/shooter(s)?: No. Classmates claim shooter obtained gun from a 12-year old friend. Police were unable to trace the weapon.
# of people killed: 1
# of people injured: 0
Total # of victims: 1
Time suspect(s)/shooter(s) were apprehended or killed?: Accidental suicide.
Suspect(s)' mental illness: Unreported.
Suspect(s)' medication or drug use: Unreported.
Suspect(s)' criminal history: Unreported.
Warning signs: Shooter was playing with the gun in front of classmates while the teacher's back was turned, but they did not report the incident before the teen accidentally shot himself.
Suspect(s)' country of citizenship: Unreported.
Suspect(s)' religious affiliation: Unreported.
Alleged reason for shooting: Accident. Self-inflicted gunshot while playing with gun in a classroom in front of classmates.

Metal detectors present?: No.

Location & time of shooting: Shooting occurred inside a classroom, in front of classmates while teacher's back was turned.

For more information, contact: Chicago Police Sgt. Stan Zaborac.

Citations/sources: (National School Safety Center, 2010, p. 2) (Hawes & Gottesman, 1992, p. 1 & 10) (Classmates watch boy's fatal shot, 1992, p. A6) (Congress of the U.S., 1999, p. 70)

#1130
Location of shooting: Langham Creek High School
Date: 11/13/1992

City, State: Houston, TX

Name of victim(s) killed: Rita Bertsch Wenzel (Chair of Special Ed. Department) & Stephen (Steve) P. Wenzel (estranged husband of victim).

Age of victim(s) killed: 39 & 39

Name of victim(s) injured: N/A.

Age of victim(s) injured: N/A.

Name of suspect(s)/shooter(s): Stephen (Steve) P. Wenzel.

Age of suspect(s)/shooter(s): 39

Weapon(s): Unreported.

High capacity magazine(s)?: Unreported.

Weapon(s) legally acquired by suspect(s)/shooter(s)?: Unreported.

# of people killed: 2

# of people injured: 0

Total # of victims: 2

Time suspect(s)/shooter(s) were apprehended or killed?: Suicide.

Suspect(s)' mental illness: Unreported.

Suspect(s)' medication or drug use: Unreported.

Suspect(s)' criminal history: Unreported.

Warning signs: Unreported.

Suspect(s)' country of citizenship: Unreported.

Suspect(s)' religious affiliation: Unreported.

Alleged reason for shooting: Dispute. Suspect shot his estranged wife. The two were undergoing a separation, the radio station reported.

Metal detectors present?: N/A.

Location & time of shooting: Shooting occurred in the parking lot, outside the front door of the school about 2:00PM.

For more information, contact: Cypress-Fairbanks Independent School District spokeswoman Donna Shrake.

Citations/sources: (National School Safety Center, 2010, p. 2) (Obituaries, 1992, p. 4-A) (Roll Call of the Dead, 1993) (Fernandez & Roth, 2018) (Congress of the U.S., 1999, p. 70) (Man fatally shoots estranged wife, 1992, p. A9)

#1129

Location of shooting: Fairfield High School

Date: 11/16/1992

City, State: Birmingham, AL

Name of victim(s) killed: Michael Jackson, Jr.

Age of victim(s) killed: 16

Name of victim(s) injured: N/A.

Age of victim(s) injured: N/A.

Name of suspect(s)/shooter(s): Eric Harris, Charles D. Cash, Andre Lama & unnamed boy due to his age.

Age of suspect(s)/shooter(s): 18, 18, 21 & 17

Weapon(s): .38-caliber pistol

High capacity magazine(s)?: Unreported.

Weapon(s) legally acquired by suspect(s)/shooter(s)?: Unreported.

# of people killed: 1

# of people injured: 0

Total # of victims: 1

Time suspect(s)/shooter(s) were apprehended or killed?: The four suspects were charged with murder one month after school shooting.

Suspect(s)' mental illness: Unreported.

Suspect(s)' medication or drug use: Unreported.

Suspect(s)' criminal history: Unreported.

Warning signs: Unreported.

Suspect(s)' country of citizenship: Unreported.

Suspect(s)' religious affiliation: Unreported.

Alleged reason for shooting: Robbery. Victim shot in back of head after a chase by four youths trying to steal victim's athletic Starter jacket.

Metal detectors present?: N/A.

Location & time of shooting: Victim was shot at the doorway of a building that houses the offices of the Fairfield school board around 5:35 p.m. He was there to videotape a school basketball practice.

For more information, contact: Fairfield Mayor Larry Langford was at the scene, Detective Reubin Wilkinson & school Principal Charles McGhee.

Citations/sources: (National School Safety Center, 2010, p. 2) (A murder in Alabama, 1992, p. A3) (Student killed near, 1992, p. 6A) (Suspects indicted, 1993, p. 8A) (Congress of the U.S., 1999, p. 70)

#1128

Location of shooting: Edward Tilden High School

Date: 11/20/1992

City, State: Chicago, IL

Name of victim(s) killed: DeLondyn Lawson.

Age of victim(s) killed: 15

Name of victim(s) injured: Two unnamed students.

Age of victim(s) injured: Unreported.

Name of suspect(s)/shooter(s): Joseph White.

Age of suspect(s)/shooter(s): 15

Weapon(s): Handgun

High capacity magazine(s)?: Unreported.

Weapon(s) legally acquired by suspect(s)/shooter(s)?: No.

# of people killed: 1

# of people injured: 2

Total # of victims: 3

Time suspect(s)/shooter(s) were apprehended or killed?: Unreported.

Suspect(s)' mental illness: Unreported.

Suspect(s)' medication or drug use: Unreported.

Suspect(s)' criminal history: Arrested previous year before the shooting for throwing brick, stones, and bottles at people with 50 other gang-associated youth. Pleaded guilty for stealing stereos from a railroad boxcar.

Warning signs: Unreported.

Suspect(s)' country of citizenship: Unreported.

Suspect(s)' religious affiliation: Unreported.

Alleged reason for shooting: Fight. Gang related. Over a gambling debt. Shooter claimed self-defense.

Metal detectors present?: Yes. Metal detector was not in operation the day of the shooting.

Location & time of shooting: Victims shot in school hallway around 10:00 a.m.

For more information, contact: Circuit Judge Richard Neville and Tilden Principal Hazel Steward.

Citations/sources: (Moore, Petrie, Braga, & McLaughlin, 2013, p.163-164, 177-178, 188, 266-283) (Wilson, 1994) (National School Safety Center, 2010, p. 2) (Thompson, 1992a, p. 1-5) (Prison term, 1994, p. 2-3) (Congress of the U.S., 1999, p. 70)

#1127

Location of shooting: South Park High School

Date: 11/23/1992

City, State: Buffalo, NY

Name of victim(s) killed: N/A.

Age of victim(s) killed: N/A.

Name of victim(s) injured: George Steele (Security Guard).

Age of victim(s) injured: 27

Name of suspect(s)/shooter(s): David Moore (a.k.a. "Dawoo").

Age of suspect(s)/shooter(s): 18

Weapon(s): .380 mm automatic pistol

High capacity magazine(s)?: Unreported.

Weapon(s) legally acquired by suspect(s)/shooter(s)?: No. Moore's attorney said he bought the gun illegally.

# of people killed: 0

# of people injured: 1

Total # of victims: 1

Time suspect(s)/shooter(s) were apprehended or killed?: Suspect was arrested the same day of the shooting.

Suspect(s)' mental illness: Unreported.

Suspect(s)' medication or drug use: Unreported.

Suspect(s)' criminal history: None. The judge ordered Moore to "fully cooperate" with a city program designed to help first-time offenders.

Warning signs: Unreported.

Suspect(s)' country of citizenship: Unreported.

Suspect(s)' religious affiliation: Unreported.

Alleged reason for shooting: Fight stemmed from a neighborhood disagreement. Security guard who was shot was trying to break up a fight between the suspect and another student.

Metal detectors present?: Unreported.

Location & time of shooting: Shooting occurred about 1:15 p.m.

For more information, contact: School Principal Paul Lafornara, Buffalo Police Officer Phillip Tisdale, Erie County Judge John V. Rogowski and District Attorney Kevin M. Dillon.

Citations/sources: (Bookbags banned in Buffalo, 1992, p. B8) (Gryta, 1993, p. C1) (Hammersley & Gryta, 1992, p. B1) (Hammersley, 1992, p. A1 & A7)

#1126

Location of shooting: Robert E. Lee High School

Date: 11/24/1992

City, State: Montgomery, AL

Name of victim(s) killed: N/A.

Age of victim(s) killed: N/A.

Name of victim(s) injured: Candy Cogman (shooter).

Age of victim(s) injured: 18

Name of suspect(s)/shooter(s): Candy Cogman.

Age of suspect(s)/shooter(s): 18

Weapon(s): .22-caliber revolver

High capacity magazine(s)?: Unreported.

Weapon(s) legally acquired by suspect(s)/shooter(s)?: Unreported.

# of people killed: 0

# of people injured: 1

<u>Total # of victims</u>: 1

<u>Time suspect(s)/shooter(s) were apprehended or killed?</u>: The school principal, a teacher, and a fellow student caught the suspect and disarmed her after the shooting.

<u>Suspect(s)' mental illness</u>: Unreported.

<u>Suspect(s)' medication or drug use</u>: Unreported.

<u>Suspect(s)' criminal history</u>: Unreported.

<u>Warning signs</u>: Unreported.

<u>Suspect(s)' country of citizenship</u>: Unreported.

<u>Suspect(s)' religious affiliation</u>: Unreported.

<u>Alleged reason for shooting</u>: Fight over an ex-boyfriend.

<u>Metal detectors present?</u>: Unreported.

<u>Location & time of shooting</u>: Shooting occurred in a school bathroom and hallway, around 7:30 a.m. Suspect shot herself in the finger while firing at another teenager.

<u>For more information, contact</u>: Montgomery Police Capt. Wyatt Gantt, Circuit Judge Joseph Phelps and Deputy District Attorney David Glazner.

<u>Citations/sources</u>: (Smith, 1992, p. 1B & 2B) (Student shot at school, 1992, p. 2A) (Student charged, 1992, p. 1B) (Teen gets 20 years, 1993, p. 2C)

#1125

Location of shooting: Carter G. Woodson School (PreK - 8)

<u>Date</u>: 12/3/1992

<u>City, State</u>: Chicago, IL

<u>Name of victim(s) killed</u>: Frederick (Fritz) Cortez Williams.

<u>Age of victim(s) killed</u>: 19

<u>Name of victim(s) injured</u>: Erica Carter.

<u>Age of victim(s) injured</u>: 25

<u>Name of suspect(s)/shooter(s)</u>: Ray George & another unidentified suspect.

<u>Age of suspect(s)/shooter(s)</u>: 23 & ?

<u>Weapon(s)</u>: .357 Magnum

<u>High capacity magazine(s)?</u>: Unreported.

<u>Weapon(s) legally acquired by suspect(s)/shooter(s)?</u>: Unreported.

<u># of people killed</u>: 1

<u># of people injured</u>: 1

<u>Total # of victims</u>: 2

<u>Time suspect(s)/shooter(s) were apprehended or killed?</u>: Suspect was arrested and charged 11 days after the shooting..

<u>Suspect(s)' mental illness</u>: Unreported.

<u>Suspect(s)' medication or drug use</u>: Unreported.

<u>Suspect(s)' criminal history</u>: Unreported.

<u>Warning signs</u>: Unreported.

<u>Suspect(s)' country of citizenship</u>: Unreported.

Suspect(s)' religious affiliation: Unreported.

Alleged reason for shooting: Unreported.

Metal detectors present?: Unreported.

Location & time of shooting: Victim was shot while playing basketball in school gymnasium in an after-school community program, shortly after 4:00 p.m.

For more information, contact: Lt. Thomas Byrne, Sgt. Edward Griffin and Deputy Jerry Earnest.

Citations/sources: (National School Safety Center, 2010, p. 3) (Roll Call of the Dead, 1993) (Thompson, 1992b, p. 1-1 & 1-14) (Thompson & Kiernan, 1992, p. 1-1 & 1-14) (Suspect denied bond, 1992, p. 2-3) (Congress of the U.S., 1999, p. 70)

#1124

Location of shooting: Bard College of Simon's Rock

Date: 12/14/1992

City, State: Great Barrington, MA

Name of victim(s) killed: Galen C. Gibson (college student) & Nacunan Saez (language professor).

Age of victim(s) killed: 18 & 37

Name of victim(s) injured: Joshua A Faber, Matthew L. David, Thomas McElderry & Teresa Beavers (security guard).

Age of victim(s) injured: 15, 18, 18 & 42

Name of suspect(s)/shooter(s): Wayne Lo

Age of suspect(s)/shooter(s): 18

Weapon(s): Chinese-made SKS 7.62 semiautomatic rifle

High capacity magazine(s)?: Yes. After shooting 6 victims, the suspect still had 30 rounds of ammunition left.

Weapon(s) legally acquired by suspect(s)/shooter(s)?: Yes. Suspect purchased his weapon for $150 at Dave's Sporting Goods store in Pittsfield, Montana, days before the shooting. Ammunition was delivered to the school in the mail from a catalog.

# of people killed: 2

# of people injured: 4

Total # of victims: 6

Time suspect(s)/shooter(s) were apprehended or killed?: Suspect called the police on himself and surrendered to law enforcement 20 minutes after shooting began.

Suspect(s)' mental illness: Defense witnesses testified that the suspect suffered from schizophrenia.

Suspect(s)' medication or drug use: Unreported.

Suspect(s)' criminal history: Unreported.

Warning signs: A basketball teammate recalls suspect asking about where he could get a gun for him in November 1992, but didn't think anything of it. Suspect's hatred for blacks, Jews, homosexuals, and interracial couples was allegedly well-known on campus.

Suspect(s)' country of citizenship: Taiwan.

Suspect(s)' religious affiliation: Christian: Catholic.

Alleged reason for shooting: Mental illness. Defense witnesses testified that the suspect suffered from schizophrenia and believed God had told him to cleanse the campus of homosexuality, drug abuse, and lying.

Metal detectors present?: N/A.

Location & time of shooting: Shooting rampage took place at the entrance of the college campus, in the school library, and at a student dormitory, beginning at 10:20 a.m. and ending at 10:40 a.m.

For more information, contact: Officer Mark Stannard and Prosecutor Gerard Downing.

Citations/sources: (National School Safety Center, 2010) (Bernstein, Renner, & Venema, 1992, p. A1, A12, & A13) (Wayne Lo convicted, 1994, p. 2A) (Pratt, 1992, p. A1 & A4) (Newman, Fox, Harding, Mehta, & Roth, 2004, p.237)

#1123

Location of shooting: Walton's O'Neil High School

Date: 12/14/1992

City, State: Walton, NY

Name of victim(s) killed: N/A.

Age of victim(s) killed: N/A.

Name of victim(s) injured: Virginia Wilcox (Teacher).

Age of victim(s) injured: 49

Name of suspect(s)/shooter(s): Jason A. Hodge.

Age of suspect(s)/shooter(s): 15

Weapon(s): .22-caliber rifle

High capacity magazine(s)?: Unreported.

Weapon(s) legally acquired by suspect(s)/shooter(s)?: No.

# of people killed: 0

# of people injured: 1

Total # of victims: 1

Time suspect(s)/shooter(s) were apprehended or killed?: Students wrestled with suspect for control of the weapon after shooting.

Suspect(s)' mental illness: Unreported.

Suspect(s)' medication or drug use: Unreported.

Suspect(s)' criminal history: None. However, suspect had been sent to the principle multiple times and suspended from other classes in the past.

Warning signs: Suspect had written poems about suicide and killing teachers and parents in the past. The teacher reported it and tried to get the suspect help.

Suspect(s)' country of citizenship: Unreported.

Suspect(s)' religious affiliation: Unreported.

Alleged reason for shooting: Protest authority. Suspect shot his English teacher because he wasn't allowed to read a poem he wrote.

Metal detectors present?: Unreported.

Location & time of shooting: Shooting took place in school English class in front of other students.

For more information, contact: Walton Police Chief Melvin R. Woodin and Delaware County District Attorney Paul F. Eaton Jr.

Citations/sources: (Fullerton & Jump, 1992, p. 1B & 3B) (Student shoots teacher, 1992, p. B12) (Jump, 1993, p. 1A & 6A)

#1122
Location of shooting: Brentwood High School
Date: 1/5/1993
City, State: Brentwood, NY
Name of victim(s) killed: N/A.
Age of victim(s) killed: N/A.
Name of victim(s) injured: Matthew Hunter.
Age of victim(s) injured: 19
Name of suspect(s)/shooter(s): Michael Pearson.
Age of suspect(s)/shooter(s): 20
Weapon(s): Unreported.
High capacity magazine(s)?: Unreported.
Weapon(s) legally acquired by suspect(s)/shooter(s)?: Unreported.
# of people killed: 0
# of people injured: 1
Total # of victims: 1
Time suspect(s)/shooter(s) were apprehended or killed?: Suspect surrendered to Suffolk County Police one day after the shooting at 10:55 p.m.

Suspect(s)' mental illness: Unreported.

Suspect(s)' medication or drug use: Unreported.

Suspect(s)' criminal history: Unreported.

Warning signs: Unreported.

Suspect(s)' country of citizenship: Unreported.

Suspect(s)' religious affiliation: Unreported.

Alleged reason for shooting: Dispute over the theft of a gold chain.

Metal detectors present?: No. Anthony Felicio, president of the Brentwood School Board and other school officials ruled out the use of metal detectors at the high school.

Location & time of shooting: Shooting occurred in the high school gymnasium, during a basketball game at 5:27 p.m.

For more information, contact: Suffolk County Police, Sgt. Paul Fuhrmann, Officer Robert Tooker and Police spokesman Officer Randy Jarett.

Citations/sources: (McQuiston, 1993a, p. B8) (Held in shooting, 1993, p. 15)

#1121
Location of shooting: Norland Senior High School
Date: 1/12/1993
City, State: Miami, FL
Name of victim(s) killed: Conroy Robinson.
Age of victim(s) killed: 18
Name of victim(s) injured: N/A.
Age of victim(s) injured: N/A.
Name of suspect(s)/shooter(s): Unreported shooter & Conroy Robinson (victim).
Age of suspect(s)/shooter(s): ? & 18
Weapon(s): Two guns. One was a semiautomatic pistol.
High capacity magazine(s)?: Unreported.
Weapon(s) legally acquired by suspect(s)/shooter(s)?: Unreported.
# of people killed: 1
# of people injured: 0
Total # of victims: 1
Time suspect(s)/shooter(s) were apprehended or killed?: Unreported.
Suspect(s)' mental illness: Unreported.
Suspect(s)' medication or drug use: Unreported.
Suspect(s)' criminal history: Unreported.
Warning signs: Unreported.
Suspect(s)' country of citizenship: Unreported.
Suspect(s)' religious affiliation: Unreported.
Alleged reason for shooting: Argument over a girl.
Metal detectors present?: No.
Location & time of shooting: Shooting occurred outside of the high school gym about 3:15 p.m., while victim was waiting to be picked up from school by his mother.
For more information, contact: Dade County spokesman Henry Fraind, Police spokesman Israel Reyes and Metro-Dade Police.
Citations/sources: (National School Safety Center, 2010, p. 3) (Yanez & Smith, 1993, p. 4B) (Yanez, 1993, p. 1B & 5B) (Congress of the U.S., 1999, p. 71)

#1120
Location of shooting: East Carter High School
Date: 1/18/1993
City, State: Grayson, KY
Name of victim(s) killed: Deanna McDavid (English teacher) & Marvin Hicks (Head Custodian).
Age of victim(s) killed: 48 & 51

Name of victim(s) injured: N/A.
Age of victim(s) injured: N/A.
Name of suspect(s)/shooter(s): Gary Scott Pennington.
Age of suspect(s)/shooter(s): 17
Weapon(s): .38-caliber revolver
High capacity magazine(s)?: Unreported.
Weapon(s) legally acquired by suspect(s)/shooter(s)?: No. Stolen from suspect's father.
# of people killed: 2
# of people injured: 0
Total # of victims: 2
Time suspect(s)/shooter(s) were apprehended or killed?: Suspect held his classmates hostage for 40 minutes before surrendering to the police.
Suspect(s)' mental illness: Depression.
Suspect(s)' medication or drug use: Unreported.
Suspect(s)' criminal history: Unreported.
Warning signs: One of the suspect's writings concerned one of the teachers (McDavid) who was killed: a book report on a Stephen King novel, "Rage," in which the protagonist, Charlie Decker, shoots his teacher and then tries to convince his classmates he is a hero for doing so.
Suspect(s)' country of citizenship: U.S.A.. Suspect is a native of Elliot County, Kentucky.
Suspect(s)' religious affiliation: Unreported.
Alleged reason for shooting: Protest authority and bullying for suspect's stammering and thick glasses.
Metal detectors present?: No.
Location & time of shooting: Shooting took place in suspect's high school English class, approximately 2:45 p.m.
For more information, contact: Grayson Police Officers Keith Hill and Larry Green, Lincoln County Sheriff Earl Dean McWhorter, Deputies J.D. Smoth & Tim Gambrel and Principal Larry Kiser.
Citations/sources: (National School Safety Center, 2010, p. 3) (Crews, 2016, p. 7) (Lebrun, 2009, p. 173) (Mother says boy, 1993, p. 7C) (Voskuhl, 1993, p. B-2) (Teenage boy indicted, 1993, p. A3) (Congress of the U.S., 1999, p. 71) (Newman, Fox, Harding, Mehta, & Roth, 2004, p.237) (Hart, 2013)

#1119
Location of shooting: Fairfax High School
Date: 1/21/1993
City, State: Los Angeles, CA
Name of victim(s) killed: Demetrius Rice.
Age of victim(s) killed: 16
Name of victim(s) injured: Eliaho (Eli) Kogman.
Age of victim(s) injured: 17

Name of suspect(s)/shooter(s): Unnamed due to age.
Age of suspect(s)/shooter(s): 15
Weapon(s): Ruger Blackhawk .357-magnum pistol
High capacity magazine(s)?: Unreported.
Weapon(s) legally acquired by suspect(s)/shooter(s)?: No. Stolen from suspect's grandfather's closet.
# of people killed: 1
# of people injured: 1
Total # of victims: 2
Time suspect(s)/shooter(s) were apprehended or killed?: Suspect did not attempt to flee and was arrested immediately by school police.
Suspect(s)' mental illness: Unreported.
Suspect(s)' medication or drug use: Unreported.
Suspect(s)' criminal history: Unreported.
Warning signs: Several students said the youth had previously bragged about having a weapon. Another classmate testified that the youth had shown him the gun at school a week before the shooting.
Suspect(s)' country of citizenship: Unreported.
Suspect(s)' religious affiliation: Unreported.
Alleged reason for shooting: Accident. Shooter carried the firearm in his backpack which accidently fired a single bullet that killed one child and injured another.
Metal detectors present?: No.
Location & time of shooting: Shooting occurred in a classroom.
For more information, contact: Los Angeles Police Officer Angela McGill.
Citations/sources: (Banks & Sengupta, 1993) (Lara, 2011) (One student killed, one wounded, 1993) (National School Safety Center, 2010, p. 3) (Moran, 1993) (Mejia & Vives, 2018) (Congress of the U.S., 1999, p. 71)

#1118
Location of shooting: Patricia Roberts Harris Educational Center (PreK - 10)
Date: 1/28/1993
City, State: Washington, DC
Name of victim(s) killed: N/A.
Age of victim(s) killed: N/A.
Name of victim(s) injured: Patrick Layne (Security Guard).
Age of victim(s) injured: 29
Name of suspect(s)/shooter(s): Unnamed gang member.
Age of suspect(s)/shooter(s): 14
Weapon(s): .22-caliber Intratec semiautomatic pistol (Tec-22)
High capacity magazine(s)?: Unreported.
Weapon(s) legally acquired by suspect(s)/shooter(s)?: No.

# of people killed: 0
# of people injured: 1
Total # of victims: 1
Time suspect(s)/shooter(s) were apprehended or killed?: Unreported.
Suspect(s)' mental illness: Unreported.
Suspect(s)' medication or drug use: Unreported.
Suspect(s)' criminal history: Unreported.
Warning signs: Unreported.
Suspect(s)' country of citizenship: Unreported.
Suspect(s)' religious affiliation: Unreported.
Alleged reason for shooting: Gang-related.
Metal detectors present?: Unreported.
Location & time of shooting: Unreported.
For more information, contact: ATF Special Agent Patrick D. Hynes.
Citations/sources: (Greene, 1993) (Gun in Washington, 1993, p. B3) (Agents seek purchasers, 1993, p. A3)

#1117
Location of shooting: Amityville High School
Date: 2/1/1993
City, State: Amityville, NY
Name of victim(s) killed: Randel Artis.
Age of victim(s) killed: 17
Name of victim(s) injured: John Billinger.
Age of victim(s) injured: 17
Name of suspect(s)/shooter(s): Shem S. McCoy.
Age of suspect(s)/shooter(s): 17
Weapon(s): Nine-shot .22-caliber revolver
High capacity magazine(s)?: No.
Weapon(s) legally acquired by suspect(s)/shooter(s)?: No.
# of people killed: 1
# of people injured: 1
Total # of victims: 2
Time suspect(s)/shooter(s) were apprehended or killed?: Unreported.
Suspect(s)' mental illness: Unreported.
Suspect(s)' medication or drug use: Unreported.
Suspect(s)' criminal history: Unreported.
Warning signs: Unreported.
Suspect(s)' country of citizenship: Unreported.
Suspect(s)' religious affiliation: Unreported.
Alleged reason for shooting: Dispute. Fight.

Metal detectors present?: N/A.

Location & time of shooting: Victims shot in the back of the school at approximately 2:20 p.m.

For more information, contact: Suffolk County Police spokesman Lt. John Gierasch.

Citations/sources: (National School Safety Center, 2010, p. 4) (Held in 2 shootings, 1993, p. 1) (Teen shot to death, 1993, p. 5A) (Congress of the U.S., 1999, p. 71) (McQuiston, 1993b)

#1116

Location of shooting: Redmond Junior High School (Middle school)

Date: 2/1/1993

City, State: Redmond, WA

Name of victim(s) killed: Jason Paul Domenico (shooter).

Age of victim(s) killed: 14

Name of victim(s) injured: N/A.

Age of victim(s) injured: N/A.

Name of suspect(s)/shooter(s): Jason Paul Domenico.

Age of suspect(s)/shooter(s): 14

Weapon(s): Antique-reproduction .44-caliber black-powder revolver

High capacity magazine(s)?: Unreported.

Weapon(s) legally acquired by suspect(s)/shooter(s)?: No. Stolen from his father.

# of people killed: 1

# of people injured: 0

Total # of victims: 1

Time suspect(s)/shooter(s) were apprehended or killed?: Suicide.

Suspect(s)' mental illness: None.

Suspect(s)' medication or drug use: Unreported.

Suspect(s)' criminal history: None.

Warning signs: None.

Suspect(s)' country of citizenship: Unreported.

Suspect(s)' religious affiliation: Unreported.

Alleged reason for shooting: Unreported.

Metal detectors present?: N/A.

Location & time of shooting: Student shot himself on school grounds approximately 6:30 a.m. in front of two female students and a parent.

For more information, contact: Investigator Joe Frisino of the medical examiner's office.

Citations/sources: (National School Safety Center, 2010, p. 4) (Lobos, 1993) (Scattarella, 1993) (Congress of the U.S., 1999, p. 72)

#1115

Location of shooting: North Clayton High School

Date: 2/4/1993

City, State: College Park (Atlanta), GA

Name of victim(s) killed: James Holiday.
Age of victim(s) killed: 18
Name of victim(s) injured: N/A.
Age of victim(s) injured: N/A.
Name of suspect(s)/shooter(s): Damon Bernard Sinkfield.
Age of suspect(s)/shooter(s): 17
Weapon(s): .32-caliber pistol
High capacity magazine(s)?: Unreported.
Weapon(s) legally acquired by suspect(s)/shooter(s)?: No.
# of people killed: 1
# of people injured: 0
Total # of victims: 1
Time suspect(s)/shooter(s) were apprehended or killed?: Suspect was disarmed moments after the shooting and held by school officials until police arrived.
Suspect(s)' mental illness: Unreported.
Suspect(s)' medication or drug use: Unreported.
Suspect(s)' criminal history: None.
Warning signs: Unreported. The two students were arguing in the parking lot while 40 students watched.
Suspect(s)' country of citizenship: Unreported.
Suspect(s)' religious affiliation: Unreported.
Alleged reason for shooting: Feud.
Metal detectors present?: N/A.
Location & time of shooting: Victim shot in school parking lot at 3:30 p.m.
For more information, contact: Police Lt. Doug Jewett and Superior Court Judge Matthew O. Simmons.
Citations/sources: (National School Safety Center, 2010, p. 4) (Roll Call of the Dead, 1993) (Minter, 1993, p. G2) (Mistrial is declared, 1994, p. JI-13) (Montgomery, 1995, p. C11) (Congress of the U.S., 1999, p. 72)

#1114
Location of shooting: Washington-Dix Street Academy (High school)
Date: 2/8/1993
City, State: Washington, DC
Name of victim(s) killed: Kenneth W. Jackson.
Age of victim(s) killed: 21
Name of victim(s) injured: N/A.
Age of victim(s) injured: N/A.
Name of suspect(s)/shooter(s): Unreported.
Age of suspect(s)/shooter(s): Unreported.
Weapon(s): Unreported.

High capacity magazine(s)?: Unreported.
Weapon(s) legally acquired by suspect(s)/shooter(s)?: Unreported.
# of people killed: 1
# of people injured: 0
Total # of victims: 1
Time suspect(s)/shooter(s) were apprehended or killed?: Unreported.
Suspect(s)' mental illness: Unreported.
Suspect(s)' medication or drug use: Unreported.
Suspect(s)' criminal history: Unreported.
Warning signs: Unreported.
Suspect(s)' country of citizenship: Unreported.
Suspect(s)' religious affiliation: Unreported.
Alleged reason for shooting: Robbery.
Metal detectors present?: Yes, but used rarely.
Location & time of shooting: Victim shot about 11:00 a.m., just outside an isolated entrance way of the school.
For more information, contact: Washington-Dix Principal Jerome Shelton, School Board President R. David Hall and D.C. Police.
Citations/sources: (National School Safety Center, 2010, p. 4) (Greene, 1993) (Congress of the U.S., 1999, p. 72)

#1113
Location of shooting: Middle River Elementary School (Grades K - 8)
Date: 2/8/1993
City, State: Middle River, MN
Name of victim(s) killed: Eric Melby (shooter).
Age of victim(s) killed: 13
Name of victim(s) injured: N/A.
Age of victim(s) injured: N/A.
Name of suspect(s)/shooter(s): Eric Melby.
Age of suspect(s)/shooter(s): 13
Weapon(s): .30-30 rifle
High capacity magazine(s)?: Unreported.
Weapon(s) legally acquired by suspect(s)/shooter(s)?: No.
# of people killed: 1
# of people injured: 0
Total # of victims: 1
Time suspect(s)/shooter(s) were apprehended or killed?: Suicide.
Suspect(s)' mental illness: Unreported.
Suspect(s)' medication or drug use: Unreported.
Suspect(s)' criminal history: Unreported.

Warning signs: Unreported.

Suspect(s)' country of citizenship: Unreported.

Suspect(s)' religious affiliation: Unreported.

Alleged reason for shooting: Unreported.

Metal detectors present?: Unreported.

Location & time of shooting: Student shot himself in a storeroom by the school music room about 8:00 a.m.

For more information, contact: Superintendent Phil Dyrud.

Citations/sources: (National School Safety Center, 2010, p. 4) (Roll Call of the Dead, 1993) (Boy kills himself, 1993, p. 9B) (Congress of the U.S., 1999, p. 72) (Eighth-grader kills himself, 1993, p. 4B)

#1112
Location of shooting: Kimball High School

Date: 2/18/1993

City, State: Dallas, TX

Name of victim(s) killed: Andrew Castillo.

Age of victim(s) killed: 17

Name of victim(s) injured: N/A.

Age of victim(s) injured: N/A.

Name of suspect(s)/shooter(s): Jesse Estrello.

Age of suspect(s)/shooter(s): 21

Weapon(s): 9mm semi automatic handgun

High capacity magazine(s)?: No. Victim was shot as many as 15 times.

Weapon(s) legally acquired by suspect(s)/shooter(s)?: Unreported.

# of people killed: 1

# of people injured: 0

Total # of victims: 1

Time suspect(s)/shooter(s) were apprehended or killed?: Unreported.

Suspect(s)' mental illness: Unreported.

Suspect(s)' medication or drug use: Unreported.

Suspect(s)' criminal history: Unreported. Suspect was arrested in January 1992 for attempting to shoot his ex-girlfriend and her father. Last Christmas Eve, the suspect threatened to kill his ex-girlfriend at his home after she told him she wanted to leave, according to her affidavit.

Warning signs: In January of the previous year, the suspect tried to kill his ex-girlfriend and her father, according to affidavits filed by the ex-girlfriend and her mother, Carmen Alvarez.

Suspect(s)' country of citizenship: Unreported.

Suspect(s)' religious affiliation: Unreported.

Alleged reason for shooting: Rejection. Suspect was the former boyfriend of the girl who was dating the victim and the father of her 9-month old son.

Metal detectors present?: N/A.

Location & time of shooting: Student was shot while waiting in a car in the school parking lot for his 17-year old girlfriend, Elizabeth Alvarez around 1:00 p.m.

For more information, contact: Police Sgt. Bill Chandler, Police Spokesman Jim Chandler and Judge Charles Rose.

Citations/sources: (National School Safety Center, 2010, p. 4) (Dallas, 1993, p. 8A) (Congress of the U.S., 1999, p. 72) (Brumley, 1993, p. 1A)

#1111
Location of shooting: Reseda High School
Date: 2/22/1993
City, State: Reseda, CA
Name of victim(s) killed: Micheal Shean Easley.
Age of victim(s) killed: 17
Name of victim(s) injured: N/A.
Age of victim(s) injured: N/A.
Name of suspect(s)/shooter(s): Robert Heard.
Age of suspect(s)/shooter(s): 15
Weapon(s): .22-caliber Derringer handgun
High capacity magazine(s)?: Unreported.
Weapon(s) legally acquired by suspect(s)/shooter(s)?: No.
# of people killed: 1
# of people injured: 0
Total # of victims: 1
Time suspect(s)/shooter(s) were apprehended or killed?: Unreported.
Suspect(s)' mental illness: Unreported.
Suspect(s)' medication or drug use: Unreported.
Suspect(s)' criminal history: Shooter has an unspecified previous criminal record and had been transferred between schools at least once because of minor run-ins with school officials.
Warning signs: Shooter bragged the previous week that he was carrying a gun.
Suspect(s)' country of citizenship: Unreported.
Suspect(s)' religious affiliation: Unreported.
Alleged reason for shooting: Gang-related. Stemmed from an argument between members of "rival 'tagging crews,' youths who spray graffiti on walls."
Metal detectors present?: No.
Location & time of shooting: Unreported.
For more information, contact: Detective Phil Quartararo and Deputy Dist. Atty. Bill Ryder.
Citations/sources: (Student shot in school corridor, 1993) (Meyer & Watson, 1993) (Colker & Enriquez, 1993) (National School Safety Center, 2010, p. 4) (Roll Call of the Dead, 1993) (Congress of the U.S., 1999, p. 72)

#1110

Location of shooting: Gloucester High School
Date: 2/26/1993
City, State: Gloucester, MA
Name of victim(s) killed: William "Wilie" Gross (shooter).
Age of victim(s) killed: 15
Name of victim(s) injured: N/A.
Age of victim(s) injured: N/A.
Name of suspect(s)/shooter(s): William "Wilie" Gross.
Age of suspect(s)/shooter(s): 15
Weapon(s): .22 handgun
High capacity magazine(s)?: Unreported.
Weapon(s) legally acquired by suspect(s)/shooter(s)?: No. Student stole gun from his neighbor.
# of people killed: 1
# of people injured: 0
Total # of victims: 1
Time suspect(s)/shooter(s) were apprehended or killed?: Suicide.
Suspect(s)' mental illness: Unreported.
Suspect(s)' medication or drug use: Unreported.
Suspect(s)' criminal history: Unreported.
Warning signs: Unreported.
Suspect(s)' country of citizenship: Unreported.
Suspect(s)' religious affiliation: Unreported.
Alleged reason for shooting: Unreported.
Metal detectors present?: Unreported.
Location & time of shooting: Shooting occurred in school cafeteria in view of several hundred students.
For more information, contact: Biology Teacher/School Crisis Intervention Team Member, Bill Brundage and Guidance Councelor Jack O'Maley.
Citations/sources: (National School Safety Center, 2010, p. 5) (McGeary, 1993, p. 1 & 22) (Congress of the U.S., 1999, p. 72)

#1109
Location of shooting: Harlem High School
Date: 3/18/1993
City, State: Harlem, GA
Name of victim(s) killed: Rodricas Gibson.
Age of victim(s) killed: 15
Name of victim(s) injured: Ricoh Lee.
Age of victim(s) injured: 17
Name of suspect(s)/shooter(s): Edward Byrant Gillom.
Age of suspect(s)/shooter(s): 15

Weapon(s): .38 caliber revolver

High capacity magazine(s)?: Unreported.

Weapon(s) legally acquired by suspect(s)/shooter(s)?: No.

# of people killed: 1

# of people injured: 1

Total # of victims: 2

Time suspect(s)/shooter(s) were apprehended or killed?: Suspect was arrested 100 yards from the school after the shooting.

Suspect(s)' mental illness: Unreported.

Suspect(s)' medication or drug use: Unreported.

Suspect(s)' criminal history: Unreported.

Warning signs: Unreported.

Suspect(s)' country of citizenship: Unreported.

Suspect(s)' religious affiliation: Unreported.

Alleged reason for shooting: Feud over a girl.

Metal detectors present?: Yes. Suspect was not scanned on that day.

Location & time of shooting: Shooting occurred in a crowded school hallway at approximately 8:15 a.m.

For more information, contact: Columbia County Sheriff Gilbert Lopez and John Cook, Eisenhower Medical Center Spokesman Aby Kirkland, Sheriff Otis Hensley and District Attorney Daniel Craig.

Citations/sources: (National School Safety Center, 2010, p. 5) (Roll Call of the Dead, 1993) (One student killed in Harlem, 1993, p. 2A) (One killed, one injured, 1993, p. 4A) (Harlem: shooting suspect, 1993, p. B10) (Congress of the U.S., 1999, p. 73) (School violence: metro area, 1997, p. 12A)

#1108

Location of shooting: Rider College (Now called "Rider University")

Date: 3/21/1993

City, State: Lawrenceville, NJ

Name of victim(s) killed: Kenneth Bernard McBride.

Age of victim(s) killed: 21

Name of victim(s) injured: N/A.

Age of victim(s) injured: N/A.

Name of suspect(s)/shooter(s): Kai Johnson.

Age of suspect(s)/shooter(s): 17

Weapon(s): Handgun

High capacity magazine(s)?: Unreported.

Weapon(s) legally acquired by suspect(s)/shooter(s)?: No.

# of people killed: 1

# of people injured: 0

Total # of victims: 1

Time suspect(s)/shooter(s) were apprehended or killed?: Suspect was arrested on the same day of the shooting.

Suspect(s)' mental illness: Unreported.

Suspect(s)' medication or drug use: Unreported.

Suspect(s)' criminal history: Unreported.

Warning signs: Unreported.

Suspect(s)' country of citizenship: Unreported.

Suspect(s)' religious affiliation: Unreported.

Alleged reason for shooting: Fight.

Metal detectors present?: N/A.

Location & time of shooting: Shooting occurred in the university Student Center parking lot after a Phi Beta Sigma-sponsored dance party about 2:30 a.m.

For more information, contact: Assistant Prosecutor Lewis Korngut, Rider College Spokesman Earle Romme and Rider College President J. Barton Luedeke.

Citations/sources: (Kelley, 1995) (Man acquitted, 1995, p. 15A) (South Jersey news in brief, 1995) (Teen-ager charged in slaying, 1993, p. B4) ((Pearce, 2003)

#1107
Location of shooting: Sumner High School
Date: 3/25/1993

City, State: St. Louis, MO

Name of victim(s) killed: Tony Hall.

Age of victim(s) killed: 17

Name of victim(s) injured: N/A.

Age of victim(s) injured: N/A.

Name of suspect(s)/shooter(s): Lawanda Jackson.

Age of suspect(s)/shooter(s): 17

Weapon(s): .25-caliber pistol

High capacity magazine(s)?: Unreported.

Weapon(s) legally acquired by suspect(s)/shooter(s)?: No.

# of people killed: 1

# of people injured: 0

Total # of victims: 1

Time suspect(s)/shooter(s) were apprehended or killed?: A security guard stopped the suspect before she could leave the building after the shooting.

Suspect(s)' mental illness: Unreported.

Suspect(s)' medication or drug use: Unreported.

Suspect(s)' criminal history: None.

Warning signs: Suspect had told several friends she was either going to kill herself or the victim.

Suspect(s)' country of citizenship: Unreported.

Suspect(s)' religious affiliation: Unreported.

Alleged reason for shooting: Feud. Suspect shot her allegedly physically abusive ex-boyfriend after he got a new girlfriend.

Metal detectors present?: Yes. Hand-held metal detectors used on a "spot basis."

Location & time of shooting: Shooting occurred in a second floor school hallway, just before the first class bell rang.

For more information, contact: Assistant Circuit Attorney Diana Wagner, Defense lawyer Scott N. Rosenblum, Circuit Judge James R. Dowd and City school spokesman Charles E. Burgess.

Citations/sources: (National School Safety Center, 2010, p. 5) (Little, 1993, p. 10 a) (Librach & Little, 1993, p. 3A) (Bryant, 1994, p. 1C) (Congress of the U.S., 1999, p. 73)

#1106

Location of shooting: Albert Ford Middle School

Date: 4/14/1993

City, State: Acushnet, MA

Name of victim(s) killed: Carole Day (school nurse).

Age of victim(s) killed: 52

Name of victim(s) injured: N/A.

Age of victim(s) injured: N/A.

Name of suspect(s)/shooter(s): David Taber.

Age of suspect(s)/shooter(s): 42

Weapon(s): 12-gauge shotgun

High capacity magazine(s)?: Unreported.

Weapon(s) legally acquired by suspect(s)/shooter(s)?: Unreported.

# of people killed: 1

# of people injured: 0

Total # of victims: 1

Time suspect(s)/shooter(s) were apprehended or killed?: School principal immediately grabbed suspect's shotgun and wrestled it from his hands after the shooting.

Suspect(s)' mental illness: History of mental illness. Suspect found not guilty by reason of insanity.

Suspect(s)' medication or drug use: Unreported.

Suspect(s)' criminal history: Suspect set fire to his home before going to the school.

Warning signs: Unreported.

Suspect(s)' country of citizenship: Unreported.

Suspect(s)' religious affiliation: Unreported.

Alleged reason for shooting: Mental illness

Metal detectors present?: No.

Location & time of shooting: Shooting occurred in principal's office around 10:20 a.m.

For more information, contact: Acushnet Police Chief Michael Poitras and Detective Sgt. Donald Medeiros.

Citations/sources: (National School Safety Center, 2010) (Crews, 2016, p. 7) (Gunman kills school nurse, 1993, p. A-2) (Coakley, 1993, p. 17)

#1105

Location of shooting: Grant High School

Date: 4/16/1993

City, State: Sacramento, CA

Name of victim(s) killed: Fred Lawson (Little League Coach).

Age of victim(s) killed: 43

Name of victim(s) injured: N/A.

Age of victim(s) injured: N/A.

Name of suspect(s)/shooter(s): Arthur Tyes.

Age of suspect(s)/shooter(s): 20

Weapon(s): Handgun

High capacity magazine(s)?: Unreported.

Weapon(s) legally acquired by suspect(s)/shooter(s)?: Unreported.

# of people killed: 1

# of people injured: 0

Total # of victims: 1

Time suspect(s)/shooter(s) were apprehended or killed?: Unreported.

Suspect(s)' mental illness: Unreported.

Suspect(s)' medication or drug use: Unreported.

Suspect(s)' criminal history: Suspect was on probation and suspected for committing a robbery on the day of the shooting.

Warning signs: Unreported.

Suspect(s)' country of citizenship: Unreported.

Suspect(s)' religious affiliation: Unreported.

Alleged reason for shooting: Feud. Stray bullet hit little league coach, Fred Lawson in the head.

Metal detectors present?: N/A.

Location & time of shooting: Shooting occurred next to school baseball field during a game.

For more information, contact: Sgt. Bob Mitchell.

Citations/sources: (National School Safety Center, 2010, p. 5) (Blenke, 1993, p. 11) (Fire damages unpopular, 1993, p. A2) (Suspect charged in murder, 1993, p. A2) (Congress of the U.S., 1999, p. 73)

#1104

Location of shooting: Nimitz High School

Date: 5/14/1993

City, State: Irving, TX

Name of victim(s) killed: Jose Balderas, Jr.
Age of victim(s) killed: 17
Name of victim(s) injured: N/A.
Age of victim(s) injured: N/A.
Name of suspect(s)/shooter(s): Max Alexander Martinez.
Age of suspect(s)/shooter(s): 17
Weapon(s): .38-caliber revolver
High capacity magazine(s)?: Unreported.
Weapon(s) legally acquired by suspect(s)/shooter(s)?: No.
# of people killed: 1
# of people injured: 0
Total # of victims: 1
Time suspect(s)/shooter(s) were apprehended or killed?: Shooter was taken into custody a few minutes after the shooting about one block from the school, officials said.
Suspect(s)' mental illness: Unreported.
Suspect(s)' medication or drug use: Unreported.
Suspect(s)' criminal history: Unreported.
Warning signs: Unreported.
Suspect(s)' country of citizenship: Unreported.
Suspect(s)' religious affiliation: Unreported.
Alleged reason for shooting: Dispute over girls.
Metal detectors present?: Unreported.
Location & time of shooting: Shooting occurred in school hallway, minutes before school was let out.
For more information, contact: Police Capt. Travis Hall.
Citations/sources: (Texas teen killed in school, 1993) (Student Killed in Texas School, 1993) (Student dies in shooting, 1993, p. A-5) (Congress of the U.S., 1999, p. 73)

#1103
Location of shooting: Upper Perkiomen High School
Date: 5/24/1993
City, State: Pennsburg, PA
Name of victim(s) killed: Michael Swann.
Age of victim(s) killed: 16
Name of victim(s) injured: N/A.
Age of victim(s) injured: N/A.
Name of suspect(s)/shooter(s): Jason Michael Smith.
Age of suspect(s)/shooter(s): 15
Weapon(s): 9mm Ruger automatic
High capacity magazine(s)?: Unreported.

Weapon(s) legally acquired by suspect(s)/shooter(s)?: No. Suspect stole gun from his mother's boyfriend's locked gun cabinet.

# of people killed: 1

# of people injured: 0

Total # of victims: 1

Time suspect(s)/shooter(s) were apprehended or killed?: Unreported.

Suspect(s)' mental illness: Unreported.

Suspect(s)' medication or drug use: Unreported.

Suspect(s)' criminal history: None.

Warning signs: None. Suspect did not complain to his friends about his problems with his bigger classmate.

Suspect(s)' country of citizenship: Unreported.

Suspect(s)' religious affiliation: Christian.

Alleged reason for shooting: Bullying. Suspect claimed the victim regularly punched, kicked, and pushed him into his locker.

Metal detectors present?: Unreported.

Location & time of shooting: Shooting occurred in front of 20 students in a biology class.

For more information, contact: Montgomery County District Attorney Michael D. Marino, Justice Catherine M. Hummel, Police Officer Andrew Curtis, Police Chief Thomas Liott and School Superintendent Nelson Weber.

Citations/sources: (National School Safety Center, 2010, p. 6) (Roll Call of the Dead, 1993) (Crews, 2016, p. 7) (Landry, 1993, p. A1 & A8) (Funk, 1994, p. B4) (Congress of the U.S., 1999, p. 74)

#1102

Location of shooting: Francis T. Nicholls High School (Renamed KIPP Renaissance High School)

Date: 5/27/1993

City, State: New Orleans, LA

Name of victim(s) killed: Gerald Dordain.

Age of victim(s) killed: 15

Name of victim(s) injured: N/A.

Age of victim(s) injured: N/A.

Name of suspect(s)/shooter(s): Shon Williams.

Age of suspect(s)/shooter(s): 17

Weapon(s): 9mm pistol

High capacity magazine(s)?: Unreported.

Weapon(s) legally acquired by suspect(s)/shooter(s)?: No.

# of people killed: 1

# of people injured: 0

Total # of victims: 1

Time suspect(s)/shooter(s) were apprehended or killed?: Suspect was arrested on a nearby street corner by three officers in route to investigate the school shooting.

Suspect(s)' mental illness: Unreported.

Suspect(s)' medication or drug use: Unreported.

Suspect(s)' criminal history: Unreported.

Warning signs: Unreported.

Suspect(s)' country of citizenship: Unreported.

Suspect(s)' religious affiliation: Unreported.

Alleged reason for shooting: Fight.

Metal detectors present?: N/A. Yes. The school had handheld metal detectors.

Location & time of shooting: Shooting occurred between a sidewalk and a fence on the edge of the school grounds as students were changing classes for final exams.

For more information, contact: New Orleans Police Sgt. Gilbert Johnson and School Board President Cheryl Q. Cramer.

Citations/sources: (National School Safety Center, 2010, p. 6) (Roll Call of the Dead, 1993) (Dropout killed, 1993, p. 2A) (Ex-high school student shot, 1993, p. D-4) (High school quarrel ends, 1993, p. 5) (Congress of the U.S., 1999, p. 74)

#1101

Location of shooting: Wichita State University (Cessna Stadium)

Date: 7/4/1993

City, State: Wichita, KS

Name of victim(s) killed: Barbara Gragg & Anthony Robinson.

Age of victim(s) killed: 54 & 14

Name of victim(s) injured: N/A.

Age of victim(s) injured: N/A.

Name of suspect(s)/shooter(s): Anthony L. Scott.

Age of suspect(s)/shooter(s): 19

Weapon(s): Unreported.

High capacity magazine(s)?: Unreported.

Weapon(s) legally acquired by suspect(s)/shooter(s)?: Unreported.

# of people killed: 2

# of people injured: 0

Total # of victims: 2

Time suspect(s)/shooter(s) were apprehended or killed?: Suspect was apprehended near the scene the same day of the shooting.

Suspect(s)' mental illness: Unreported.

Suspect(s)' medication or drug use: Unreported.

Suspect(s)' criminal history: Suspect had been convicted for aggravated battery and disorderly conduct charges in 1991. He was also convicted for possession of marijuana and cocaine.

Warning signs: Unreported.

Suspect(s)' country of citizenship: Unreported.

Suspect(s)' religious affiliation: Unreported.

Alleged reason for shooting: Gang-related. Female victim (Gragg) was a bystander.

Metal detectors present?: N/A.

Location & time of shooting: Shooting occurred at the Celebrate '93 fireworks show at the university's Cessna track and field stadium.

For more information, contact: Wichita Deputy Police Chief Paul Goward, Wichita State University Police Chief Chuck Rummery, WSU President Gene Hughes and District Attorney Nola Foulston.

Citations/sources: (Finger, 2015) (Roy & Dorsey, 1993) (Thomas, 1993) (Gragg v. Wichita State Univ., 1997) (Laviana, 1994)

#1100

Location of shooting: Weber State University

Date: 7/8/1993

City, State: Ogden, UT

Name of victim(s) killed: Mark Duong (shooter).

Age of victim(s) killed: 28

Name of victim(s) injured: Tuan Nguyen, Sgt. Kent Kiernan (Campus Police Officer) & Richard Hill (University lawyer).

Age of victim(s) injured: Unreported.

Name of suspect(s)/shooter(s): Mark Duong.

Age of suspect(s)/shooter(s): 28

Weapon(s): Semiautomatic handgun

High capacity magazine(s)?: Unreported.

Weapon(s) legally acquired by suspect(s)/shooter(s)?: Unreported.

# of people killed: 1

# of people injured: 3

Total # of victims: 4

Time suspect(s)/shooter(s) were apprehended or killed?: Suspect was killed by police officer after the officer was shot in the face by the suspect and wounded two others.

Suspect(s)' mental illness: Unreported.

Suspect(s)' medication or drug use: Unreported.

Suspect(s)' criminal history: Suspect was at a college grievance hearing for allegedly sexually and physically harassing and threatening a fellow student and his wife.

Warning signs: Unreported.

Suspect(s)' country of citizenship: Vietnam

Suspect(s)' religious affiliation: Unreported.

Alleged reason for shooting: Protest authority. Suspect was at a college grievance hearing for allegedly sexually and physically harassing and threatening a fellow student and his wife.

Metal detectors present?: N/A.

Location & time of shooting: Shooting occurred on college campus around 9:00 a.m., during the suspect's grievance hearing.

For more information, contact: Weber County Sheriff Craig Dearden, Police Sgt Kent Kiernan (victim), University spokesman Ron Cantera and University Police Lt. David Heston.

Citations/sources: (Carter, 1993, p. 6A) (Student shoots 3 at hearing, 1993, p. 9A) (Student opens fire, 1993, p. A7) (WSU releases partial transcript, 1993, p. A2)

#1099
Location of shooting: Theodore Roosevelt High School
Date: 8/3/1993
City, State: Bronx, NY
Name of victim(s) killed: N/A.
Age of victim(s) killed: N/A.
Name of victim(s) injured: Unnamed male student.
Age of victim(s) injured: 18
Name of suspect(s)/shooter(s): Unreported black teen-ager about 6 feet tall and weighing about 180 pounds.
Age of suspect(s)/shooter(s): Unreported.
Weapon(s): Unreported.
High capacity magazine(s)?: Unreported.
Weapon(s) legally acquired by suspect(s)/shooter(s)?: Unreported.
# of people killed: 0
# of people injured: 1
Total # of victims: 1
Time suspect(s)/shooter(s) were apprehended or killed?: Unreported.
Suspect(s)' mental illness: Unreported.
Suspect(s)' medication or drug use: Unreported.
Suspect(s)' criminal history: Unreported.
Warning signs: Unreported.
Suspect(s)' country of citizenship: Unreported.
Suspect(s)' religious affiliation: Unreported.
Alleged reason for shooting: Unreported.
Metal detectors present?: Yes, but were not in use during the summer school.
Location & time of shooting: Shooting occurred in classroom, just before noon.
For more information, contact: Sgt. Edelle James and Board of Education spokesman Frank Sobrino.
Citations/sources: (Bronx student is shot, 1993, p. 22) (Hernandez, 1993)

#1098
Location of shooting: Harper High School
Date: 8/31/1993

City, State: Atlanta, GA
Name of victim(s) killed: Marcus Taylor.
Age of victim(s) killed: 15
Name of victim(s) injured: Reginald Driskol.
Age of victim(s) injured: Unreported.
Name of suspect(s)/shooter(s): Unnamed due to age.
Age of suspect(s)/shooter(s): 15
Weapon(s): .22 caliber handgun
High capacity magazine(s)?: Unreported.
Weapon(s) legally acquired by suspect(s)/shooter(s)?: No.
# of people killed: 1
# of people injured: 1
Total # of victims: 2
Time suspect(s)/shooter(s) were apprehended or killed?: Suspect was chased and caught by school employees after shooting.
Suspect(s)' mental illness: Unreported.
Suspect(s)' medication or drug use: Unreported.
Suspect(s)' criminal history: Unreported.
Warning signs: Unreported.
Suspect(s)' country of citizenship: Unreported.
Suspect(s)' religious affiliation: Unreported.
Alleged reason for shooting: Feud.
Metal detectors present?: No.
Location & time of shooting: Shooting occurred in school cafeteria.
For more information, contact: Police Chief Eldrin Bell and Superintendent Lester Butts.
Citations/sources: (National School Safety Center, 2010, p. 6) (Kelly, 1993, p. C1) (Harper High slaying, 1994, p. G2) (Congress of the U.S., 1999, p. 74)

#1097
Location of shooting: Junction City High School
Date: 9/1/1993
City, State: Junction City, KS
Name of victim(s) killed: N/A.
Age of victim(s) killed: N/A.
Name of victim(s) injured: Shannon Ingle.
Age of victim(s) injured: 14
Name of suspect(s)/shooter(s): Russell A. Williams.
Age of suspect(s)/shooter(s): 15
Weapon(s): .25-caliber handgun
High capacity magazine(s)?: Unreported.
Weapon(s) legally acquired by suspect(s)/shooter(s)?: No.

# of people killed: 0

# of people injured: 1

Total # of victims: 1

Time suspect(s)/shooter(s) were apprehended or killed?: Unreported.

Suspect(s)' mental illness: Unreported.

Suspect(s)' medication or drug use: Unreported.

Suspect(s)' criminal history: Unreported.

Warning signs: Unreported.

Suspect(s)' country of citizenship: Unreported.

Suspect(s)' religious affiliation: Unreported.

Alleged reason for shooting: Argument. Believed to be gang related. Victim was an innocent bystander.

Metal detectors present?: No.

Location & time of shooting: Shooting occurred in school cafeteria.

For more information, contact: Principal Greg Springston and Geary County Attorney Chris Biggs.

Citations/sources: (Fort Riley teen charged, 1993, p. 3) (Teen will be held, 1994, p. B8) (Authorities name youth, 1993, p. A3)

1096

Location of shooting: Roosevelt High School

Date: 9/2/1993

City, State: Dallas, TX

Name of victim(s) killed: DeMarkous McLemore.

Age of victim(s) killed: 15

Name of victim(s) injured: N/A.

Age of victim(s) injured: N/A.

Name of suspect(s)/shooter(s): Unnamed male student due to age.

Age of suspect(s)/shooter(s): 16

Weapon(s): 2 handguns

High capacity magazine(s)?: Unreported.

Weapon(s) legally acquired by suspect(s)/shooter(s)?: No.

# of people killed: 1

# of people injured: 0

Total # of victims: 1

Time suspect(s)/shooter(s) were apprehended or killed?: Suspect turned himself in the evening of the day of the shooting.

Suspect(s)' mental illness: Unreported.

Suspect(s)' medication or drug use: Unreported.

Suspect(s)' criminal history: Unreported.

Warning signs: Unreported.

Suspect(s)' country of citizenship: Unreported.
Suspect(s)' religious affiliation: Unreported.
Alleged reason for shooting: Fight.
Metal detectors present?: Yes. Two metal detectors used for random checks were not in operation on the day of the shooting.
Location & time of shooting: Shooting occurred in school hallway.
For more information, contact: Unreported.
Citations/sources: (National School Safety Center, 2010, p. 6) (Teen-ager dies after shooting, 1993, p. B3) (Student dies after shooting, 1993, p. 2A) (Teen-ager dies in shooting at school, 1993, p. 3B) (Congress of the U.S., 1999, p. 74)

#1095
Location of shooting: Dorsey High School
Date: 9/7/1993
City, State: Los Angeles, CA
Name of victim(s) killed: N/A.
Age of victim(s) killed: N/A.
Name of victim(s) injured: Glenn Browne Jr.
Age of victim(s) injured: 15
Name of suspect(s)/shooter(s): Byrant Boyd.
Age of suspect(s)/shooter(s): 18
Weapon(s): Handgun
High capacity magazine(s)?: Unreported.
Weapon(s) legally acquired by suspect(s)/shooter(s)?: Unreported.
# of people killed: 0
# of people injured: 1
Total # of victims: 1
Time suspect(s)/shooter(s) were apprehended or killed?: Unreported.
Suspect(s)' mental illness: Unreported.
Suspect(s)' medication or drug use: Unreported.
Suspect(s)' criminal history: Unreported.
Warning signs: Unreported.
Suspect(s)' country of citizenship: Unreported.
Suspect(s)' religious affiliation: Unreported.
Alleged reason for shooting: Gang-related. Victim was an innocent bystander.
Metal detectors present?: Yes. Hand-held metal detectors used for random weapon checks.
Location & time of shooting: Shooting occurred inside a crowded school auditorium where more than 150 students were gathered for enrollment at 2:20 p.m.
For more information, contact: LAPD Lt. Sergio Robleto, School superintendent Sid Thompson and L.A. Superior Court Judge James Bascue.

Citations/sources: (Teenage boy shot on first, 1993, p. A1) (L.A. shooting mars 1st day, 1993, p. B3) (Man gets 14 years, 1995, p. 8)

1094
Location of shooting: Central Middle School
Date: 9/17/1993
City, State: Sheridan, WY
Name of victim(s) killed: Kevin Newman (shooter).
Age of victim(s) killed: 29
Name of victim(s) injured: Lindsey Belliveau, Justin Sprague, Danny Schultz & Cory Butler.
Age of victim(s) injured: 11, 11, 12 & 12
Name of suspect(s)/shooter(s): Kevin Newman.
Age of suspect(s)/shooter(s): 29
Weapon(s): Semiautomatic 9mm Ruger pistol & rifle
High capacity magazine(s)?: No. Two 15-round magazines.
Weapon(s) legally acquired by suspect(s)/shooter(s)?: Unreported.
\# of people killed: 1
\# of people injured: 4
Total \# of victims: 5
Time suspect(s)/shooter(s) were apprehended or killed?: Suicide.
Suspect(s)' mental illness: Unreported.
Suspect(s)' medication or drug use: In the suspect's hotel room, there was an open whiskey bottle, beer cans, and prescription medication. There was also an unopened bottle of whiskey in the suspect's backpack.
Suspect(s)' criminal history: Suspect had numerous misdemeanors, no felonies, and had recently received a less-than-honorable discharge from the Navy.
Warning signs: Suspect left suicide note in a Sheridan motel room but did not indicate plans to harm anyone at the middle school.
Suspect(s)' country of citizenship: U.S.A.
Suspect(s)' religious affiliation: Unreported.
Alleged reason for shooting: Unreported. Random act.
Metal detectors present?: N/A.
Location & time of shooting: Suspect opened fire just before 10:00 a.m. toward 31 students in a school football field and then shot himself.
For more information, contact: Teacher Vicky Hanft, Sheridan Police Chief Charley Hendren, Principal Kelly Caroll and Superintendent Russell Carlson.
Citations/sources: (National School Safety Center, 2010, p. 6) (4 students shot, 1993) (Ehli & Blair, 1993, p. 1A & 14A) (Congress of the U.S., 1999, p. 74) (Forster, 1993, p. 1A)

#1093
Location of shooting: Downers Grove South High School

Date: 9/17/1993
City, State: Downers Grove, IL
Name of victim(s) killed: Barrett Modisette.
Age of victim(s) killed: 17
Name of victim(s) injured: N/A.
Age of victim(s) injured: N/A.
Name of suspect(s)/shooter(s): Philip Powell.
Age of suspect(s)/shooter(s): 15
Weapon(s): .25-caliber pistol with six bullets
High capacity magazine(s)?: No.
Weapon(s) legally acquired by suspect(s)/shooter(s)?: No. Suspect bought the weapon from a man on 71st and Rockwell Streets in Chicago.
# of people killed: 1
# of people injured: 0
Total # of victims: 1
Time suspect(s)/shooter(s) were apprehended or killed?: Suspect was arrested shortly after the shooting.
Suspect(s)' mental illness: Unreported.
Suspect(s)' medication or drug use: Unreported.
Suspect(s)' criminal history: Unreported.
Warning signs: Suspect approached a 16-year old classmate and gang-member a few weeks before the shooting and requested his help in buying a gun.
Suspect(s)' country of citizenship: Unreported.
Suspect(s)' religious affiliation: Unreported.
Alleged reason for shooting: Dispute from a week prior to the shooting.
Metal detectors present?: N/A.
Location & time of shooting: Shooting occurred in school parking lot after a football game, dressed as his school's mascot.
For more information, contact: Assistant DuPage State's Atty. John Kinsella and Downers Grove Police Lt. Dave Rechenmacher.
Citations/sources: (Babwin, 1993) (Sjostrom, 1994)

#1092
Location of shooting: Weatherless Elementary School
Date: 9/25/1993
City, State: Washington, DC
Name of victim(s) killed: Jaunice (Launice) Smith & Kervin Brown.
Age of victim(s) killed: 4 & 23
Name of victim(s) injured: N/A.
Age of victim(s) injured: N/A.
Name of suspect(s)/shooter(s): Steven Chadwick, Anthony D. Dawkins & two other gunmen.

Age of suspect(s)/shooter(s): 19, 22, ? & ?
Weapon(s): Pistols
High capacity magazine(s)?: Unreported.
Weapon(s) legally acquired by suspect(s)/shooter(s)?: Unreported.
# of people killed: 2
# of people injured: 0
Total # of victims: 2
Time suspect(s)/shooter(s) were apprehended or killed?: Unreported.
Suspect(s)' mental illness: Unreported.
Suspect(s)' medication or drug use: Unreported.
Suspect(s)' criminal history: Unreported.
Warning signs: Unreported.
Suspect(s)' country of citizenship: Unreported.
Suspect(s)' religious affiliation: Unreported.
Alleged reason for shooting: Gang-related.
Metal detectors present?: N/A.
Location & time of shooting: Shooting occurred at a football game at the elementary school.
For more information, contact: D.C. Superior Court Judge Henry F. Greene.
Citations/sources: (National School Safety Center, 2010, p. 6) (Cockburn, 1993, p. A3) (Two wounded at football game, 1993, p. A2) (2nd murder suspect arrested, 1993, p. 5A) (Lewis, 1995b) (Congress of the U.S., 1999, p. 75)

#1091
Location of shooting: Dover High School
Date: 10/12/1993
City, State: New Castle, DE
Name of victim(s) killed: Laura Beth Moyer (shooter).
Age of victim(s) killed: 16
Name of victim(s) injured: N/A.
Age of victim(s) injured: N/A.
Name of suspect(s)/shooter(s): Laura Beth Moyer.
Age of suspect(s)/shooter(s): 16
Weapon(s): .32-caliber handgun
High capacity magazine(s)?: Unreported.
Weapon(s) legally acquired by suspect(s)/shooter(s)?: No.
# of people killed: 1
# of people injured: 0
Total # of victims: 1
Time suspect(s)/shooter(s) were apprehended or killed?: Suicide.
Suspect(s)' mental illness: Unreported.
Suspect(s)' medication or drug use: Unreported.

Suspect(s)' criminal history: Unreported.
Warning signs: None.
Suspect(s)' country of citizenship: Unreported.
Suspect(s)' religious affiliation: Christian.
Alleged reason for shooting: Unreported.
Metal detectors present?: Unreported.
Location & time of shooting: Student shot herself in a school clinic bathroom about 1:00 p.m.
For more information, contact: Dover Police Captain W. James Beauchamp, Health Teacher Robert F. Neylan and Principal William P. McGlumphy.
Citations/sources: (National School Safety Center, 2010, p. 6) (Obituaries, 1993, p. B4) (Svetvilas, 1993a, p. A1) (Svetvilas, 1993b, p. A1) (Congress of the U.S., 1999, p. 75)

#1090
Location of shooting: J.H. Johnson Junior High School (Middle school)
Date: 10/18/1993
City, State: Washington, DC
Name of victim(s) killed: N/A.
Age of victim(s) killed: N/A.
Name of victim(s) injured: Robert Williams.
Age of victim(s) injured: 13
Name of suspect(s)/shooter(s): Unnamed due to age.
Age of suspect(s)/shooter(s): 15
Weapon(s): Unreported.
High capacity magazine(s)?: Unreported.
Weapon(s) legally acquired by suspect(s)/shooter(s)?: No.
# of people killed: 0
# of people injured: 1
Total # of victims: 1
Time suspect(s)/shooter(s) were apprehended or killed?: Unreported.
Suspect(s)' mental illness: Unreported.
Suspect(s)' medication or drug use: Unreported.
Suspect(s)' criminal history: Unreported.
Warning signs: Unreported.
Suspect(s)' country of citizenship: Unreported.
Suspect(s)' religious affiliation: Unreported.
Alleged reason for shooting: Unreported.
Metal detectors present?: Yes.
Location & time of shooting: Shooting occurred in a school locker room just before 11:30 a.m.
For more information, contact: School Spokeswoman Karen Hinton and Ward 8 D.C. School Board member Linda Moody.
Citations/sources: (Horwitz, 1994) (Castaneda, 1993)

#1089

Location of shooting: Neshoba Central High School

Date: 10/19/1993

City, State: Philadelphia, PA

Name of victim(s) killed: N/A.

Age of victim(s) killed: N/A.

Name of victim(s) injured: Rodney Davis.

Age of victim(s) injured: 15

Name of suspect(s)/shooter(s): Trevone Stribling.

Age of suspect(s)/shooter(s): 15

Weapon(s): .25-caliber pistol

High capacity magazine(s)?: Unreported.

Weapon(s) legally acquired by suspect(s)/shooter(s)?: No.

# of people killed: 0

# of people injured: 1

Total # of victims: 1

Time suspect(s)/shooter(s) were apprehended or killed?: Suspect was arrested about 30 minutes after school officials called the Neshoba County Sheriff's Department.

Suspect(s)' mental illness: Unreported.

Suspect(s)' medication or drug use: Unreported.

Suspect(s)' criminal history: Unreported.

Warning signs: Unreported.

Suspect(s)' country of citizenship: Unreported.

Suspect(s)' religious affiliation: Unreported.

Alleged reason for shooting: Dispute that allegedly stemmed from the Monday sentencing in Neshoba County Justice Court of two men believed to be Stribling's relatives. The suspect accused the victim of (telling) on them.

Metal detectors present?: N/A.

Location & time of shooting: Shooting occurred outside of the school building at approximately 7:55 a.m. after the two students were told to stop arguing and go to class.

For more information, contact: Neshoba County Sheriff Glen Waddell, Principal Jerry Brantley, Superintendent V. C. Manning, Dee Dee Culberson and student who witnessed shooting.

Citations/sources: (Incident reminds editor, 1997, p. 12A) (Philadelphia student shot, 1993, p. 5) (1 Neshoba student shot, 1993, p. 10 a) (School violence: metro area, 1997, p. 12A)

#1088

Location of shooting: Bay Springs High School

Date: 11/4/1993

City, State: Bay Springs, MS

Name of victim(s) killed: Jason Ratcliff.

Age of victim(s) killed: 16

Name of victim(s) injured: N/A.

Age of victim(s) injured: N/A.

Name of suspect(s)/shooter(s): Unreported.

Age of suspect(s)/shooter(s): Unreported.

Weapon(s): .38-caliber handgun

High capacity magazine(s)?: Unreported.

Weapon(s) legally acquired by suspect(s)/shooter(s)?: Unreported.

# of people killed: 1

# of people injured: 0

Total # of victims: 1

Time suspect(s)/shooter(s) were apprehended or killed?: Unreported.

Suspect(s)' mental illness: Unreported.

Suspect(s)' medication or drug use: Unreported.

Suspect(s)' criminal history: Unreported.

Warning signs: Unreported.

Suspect(s)' country of citizenship: Unreported.

Suspect(s)' religious affiliation: Unreported.

Alleged reason for shooting: Unreported.

Metal detectors present?: No.

Location & time of shooting: Victim was shot in the high school band hall after school, preparing to go home with his father, who was a teacher at the school.

For more information, contact: Police Chief Charles Rogers, West Jasper School District Superintendent Charles Lyles and District Attorney Rusty Thornberry.

Citations/sources: (National School Safety Center, 2010) (James, 1993a, p. 1A & 12A) (James, 1993b, p. 1A) (James, 1993c, p. 1A)

#1087

Location of shooting: Terry Parker High School

Date: 11/4/1993

City, State: Jacksonville, FL

Name of victim(s) killed: Richard Jefferson Mitchell.

Age of victim(s) killed: 14

Name of victim(s) injured: N/A.

Age of victim(s) injured: N/A.

Name of suspect(s)/shooter(s): Omar Shareef Jones (shooter), Edward Jerome Goodmand, Marlon Hawkins & Ellis Curry.

Age of suspect(s)/shooter(s): 19, 19, 19 & 16

Weapon(s): Unreported.

High capacity magazine(s)?: Unreported.

Weapon(s) legally acquired by suspect(s)/shooter(s)?: Unreported.

# of people killed: 1
# of people injured: 0
Total # of victims: 1

Time suspect(s)/shooter(s) were apprehended or killed?: Jones confessed to the police the day after the shooting.

Suspect(s)' mental illness: Diagnosed as organically brain damaged at two months old and was classified as borderline "retarded" at school with an IQ of 76 and has the mental age of a child.

Suspect(s)' medication or drug use: Jones was drinking beer and smoking marijuana on the day of the shooting. Justices determined "lack of judgement in a stressful situation would be exacerbated by drugs and alcohol."

Suspect(s)' criminal history: Unreported.

Warning signs: Unreported.

Suspect(s)' country of citizenship: Unreported.

Suspect(s)' religious affiliation: Unreported.

Alleged reason for shooting: Attempted robbery.

Metal detectors present?: N/A.

Location & time of shooting: Victim shot outside of the school building while waiting for his father to pick him up after school.

For more information, contact: State Attorney Harry Shorstein.

Citations/sources: (National School Safety Center, 2010, p. 7) (Grand jury indicts nine, 1993, p. 1B & 5B) (9 Duval teens indicted, 1993, p. 8A) (Duval County grand jury, 1993, p. Metro-3) (Slaying settlement reached, 1997, p. 1B) (Court reverses death sentence, 1998, p. 5B) (Congress of the U.S., 1999, p. 75)

#1086
Location of shooting: New Britain High School
Date: 11/4/1993
City, State: New Britain, CT
Name of victim(s) killed: Miguel DeJesus, Jr.
Age of victim(s) killed: 18
Name of victim(s) injured: N/A.
Age of victim(s) injured: N/A.
Name of suspect(s)/shooter(s): Fernando "Mandy" Rivera, Maurice "Mo" Flanagan & Thomas "Fray" Mejia.
Age of suspect(s)/shooter(s): 19, 25 & 23
Weapon(s): Unreported.
High capacity magazine(s)?: Unreported.
Weapon(s) legally acquired by suspect(s)/shooter(s)?: Unreported.
# of people killed: 1
# of people injured: 0
Total # of victims: 1

Time suspect(s)/shooter(s) were apprehended or killed?: Rivera surrendered to police nearly a year and a half after the murder.

Suspect(s)' mental illness: Unreported.

Suspect(s)' medication or drug use: Unreported.

Suspect(s)' criminal history: Unreported.

Warning signs: Unreported.

Suspect(s)' country of citizenship: Unreported.

Suspect(s)' religious affiliation: Unreported.

Alleged reason for shooting: Gang-related. Shooter was a member of the Los Solidos street gang and victim was member of the Latin Kings gang.

Metal detectors present?: No. N/A.

Location & time of shooting: Victim was shot as he was entering the school building.

For more information, contact: Acting Deputy Police Chief William Sencio, New Britain police spokesman Sgt. Henry Orzel, Superintendent Paul V. Sequeira and Principal Evan Pitkoff.

Citations/sources: (Student shot at a school, 1993) (Springer, 1995) (National School Safety Center, 2010, p. 7) (Carlson, 1993, p. C3) (Kauffman, 1994, p. A7) (Man charged in killing, 1995, p. B1) (Williams, 1994, p. B11) (Congress of the U.S., 1999, p. 75)

#1085

Location of shooting: Center High School

Date: 11/29/1993

City, State: Kansas City, MO

Name of victim(s) killed: DeWayne Bingham.

Age of victim(s) killed: 23

Name of victim(s) injured: N/A.

Age of victim(s) injured: N/A.

Name of suspect(s)/shooter(s): Unnamed boy due to age.

Age of suspect(s)/shooter(s): 15

Weapon(s): Unreported.

High capacity magazine(s)?: Unreported.

Weapon(s) legally acquired by suspect(s)/shooter(s)?: No.

# of people killed: 1

# of people injured: 0

Total # of victims: 1

Time suspect(s)/shooter(s) were apprehended or killed?: Suspect was arrested one day after the shooting.

Suspect(s)' mental illness: Unreported.

Suspect(s)' medication or drug use: Unreported.

Suspect(s)' criminal history: Unreported.

Warning signs: Unreported.

Suspect(s)' country of citizenship: Unreported.

Suspect(s)' religious affiliation: Unreported.

Alleged reason for shooting: Unreported.

Metal detectors present?: N/A.

Location & time of shooting: Drive-by shooting occurred in school parking lot while the victim was waiting in a car to pick up cousin after a basketball game around 9:00 p.m.

For more information, contact: Ad Hoc Group Against Crime Founder Alvin Brooks, Principal Darlene Jones, Kansas City Police Capt. Vince McInerney and Superintendent Ray Feltner.

Citations/sources: (National School Safety Center, 2010, p. 7) (Congress of the U.S., 1999, p. 76) (Montgomeryleslie & Dillon, 1993, , p. A1) (Lozano, 1993, p. C1)

#1084
Location of shooting: Wauwatosa West High School
Date: 12/1/1993

City, State: Wauwatosa, WI

Name of victim(s) killed: Dale Breitlow (Assistant Principal).

Age of victim(s) killed: 46

Name of victim(s) injured: N/A.

Age of victim(s) injured: N/A.

Name of suspect(s)/shooter(s): Leonard D. McDowell.

Age of suspect(s)/shooter(s): 21

Weapon(s): Revolver

High capacity magazine(s)?: Unreported.

Weapon(s) legally acquired by suspect(s)/shooter(s)?: Unreported.

# of people killed: 1

# of people injured: 0

Total # of victims: 1

Time suspect(s)/shooter(s) were apprehended or killed?: Suspect was arrested near his home approximately 25 minutes after the shooting.

Suspect(s)' mental illness: Unreported.

Suspect(s)' medication or drug use: Unreported.

Suspect(s)' criminal history: Arrested in January 1993 for loitering on school property. Arrested for trespassing at Wauwatosa East High School in November 1992. Arrested for battery of a female teacher on November 29, 1990.

Warning signs: Police found hand-written notes in suspect's home indicating he wanted to kill the school principal for having him tossed out of the high school in 1991.

Suspect(s)' country of citizenship: Unreported.

Suspect(s)' religious affiliation: Unreported.

Alleged reason for shooting: Protest authority.

Metal detectors present?: No.

Location & time of shooting: School principal was shot and killed in a second-floor school hallway.

For more information, contact: Wauwatosa Police Chief Barry Weber and Detective William Gehrking.

Citations/sources: (National School Safety Center, 2010, p. 7) (Crews, 2016, p. 7) (Suspect arrested in high school, 1993, p. A-1) (Finkel, 1993, p. B-1) (School killing spurs calls, 1993, p. B-1) (Jury must decide, 1994, p. B-2) (Congress of the U.S., 1999, p. 76)

#1083
Location of shooting: Alfred E. Beach High School
Date: 12/8/1993
City, State: Savannah, GA
Name of victim(s) killed: Jason Kelly.
Age of victim(s) killed: 15
Name of victim(s) injured: N/A.
Age of victim(s) injured: N/A.
Name of suspect(s)/shooter(s): Aron Gilliam.
Age of suspect(s)/shooter(s): 16
Weapon(s): .32-caliber revolver
High capacity magazine(s)?: Unreported.
Weapon(s) legally acquired by suspect(s)/shooter(s)?: No.
# of people killed: 1
# of people injured: 0
Total # of victims: 1
Time suspect(s)/shooter(s) were apprehended or killed?: Unreported.
Suspect(s)' mental illness: Unreported.
Suspect(s)' medication or drug use: Unreported.
Suspect(s)' criminal history: Unreported.
Warning signs: Unreported.
Suspect(s)' country of citizenship: Unreported.
Suspect(s)' religious affiliation: Unreported.
Alleged reason for shooting: Possibly gang-related.
Metal detectors present?: N/A.
Location & time of shooting: Shooting took place a few yards from the school's front entrance, just after classes began at 8:00 a.m.
For more information, contact: Unreported.
Citations/sources: (National School Safety Center, 2010, p. 7) (Savannah: teen to serve 18 months, 1993, p. C4) (Portner, 1998) (Congress of the U.S., 1999, p. 76)

#1082
Location of shooting: Chatsworth High School
Date: 12/15/1993
City, State: Chatsworth, CA

Name of victim(s) killed: N/A.
Age of victim(s) killed: N/A.
Name of victim(s) injured: Gabriel Gettleson.
Age of victim(s) injured: 17
Name of suspect(s)/shooter(s): Unnamed 15-year old (shooter) & 17-year old (accomplice).
Age of suspect(s)/shooter(s): 15 & 17
Weapon(s): .22-caliber pistol
High capacity magazine(s)?: Unreported.
Weapon(s) legally acquired by suspect(s)/shooter(s)?: No.
# of people killed: 0
# of people injured: 1
Total # of victims: 1
Time suspect(s)/shooter(s) were apprehended or killed?: Suspects arrested approximately one week after shooting.
Suspect(s)' mental illness: Unreported.
Suspect(s)' medication or drug use: Unreported.
Suspect(s)' criminal history: 15-year old suspect robbed another teenager in front of Polytechnic High School in Sun Valley earlier that same day.
Warning signs: Unreported.
Suspect(s)' country of citizenship: Unreported.
Suspect(s)' religious affiliation: Unreported.
Alleged reason for shooting: Robbery. Suspects tried to steal victim's backpack.
Metal detectors present?: N/A.
Location & time of shooting: Shooting occurred outside of school while victim was waiting for his mother to pick him up and take him to his job.
For more information, contact: Los Angeles Police Detective Kenneth Crocker.
Citations/sources: (Police arrested two youths, 1993, p. A2) (Moran, 1994, p. A1 & A18) (Shuster, 1994, p. B13)

#1081
Location of shooting: Chelsea High School
Date: 12/16/1993
City, State: Chelsea, MI
Name of victim(s) killed: Joseph Piasecki (Superintendent).
Age of victim(s) killed: 47
Name of victim(s) injured: Ronald Mead (Principal) & Philip Jones (Teacher).
Age of victim(s) injured: 43 & 44
Name of suspect(s)/shooter(s): Stephen Saunders Leith (Science teacher).
Age of suspect(s)/shooter(s): 39
Weapon(s): 9mm Browning semiautomatic pistol
High capacity magazine(s)?: Unreported.

Weapon(s) legally acquired by suspect(s)/shooter(s)?: Unreported.
# of people killed: 1
# of people injured: 2
Total # of victims: 3
Time suspect(s)/shooter(s) were apprehended or killed?: Suspect was apprehended minutes after the shooting. Police found the suspect in his classroom grading papers.
Suspect(s)' mental illness: Suspect was under the care of a psychiatrist for "uncontrollable anger, deep depression, and homicidal fantasies."
Suspect(s)' medication or drug use: Prozac.
Suspect(s)' criminal history: Unreported.
Warning signs: Mark Jenkins, a Michigan Education Association representative for Chelsea teachers called the school minutes before the shooting in order to warn the victim, but he did not take the warning seriously.
Suspect(s)' country of citizenship: Unreported.
Suspect(s)' religious affiliation: Christian.
Alleged reason for shooting: Protest authority and mental illness. Suspect stormed out of a grievance meeting based on a female student's complaints about him.
Metal detectors present?: Unreported.
Location & time of shooting: Science teacher shot superintendent during school staff meeting, inside of the school's administration building.
For more information, contact: Chelsea Police Chief Lenard McDougall.
Citations/sources: (National School Safety Center, 2010, p. 7) (George, Trimer-Hartley, & Adams, 1993, p. 1A & 10 a) (Kageyama, 1993, p. 14A) (Lawyer blames Prozac, 1994, p. 5B) (George, 1994, p. 3B) (Congress of the U.S., 1999, p. 76) (1993 Chelsea school shooter, 2013)

#1080
Location of shooting: Los Altos High School
Date: 1/20/1994
City, State: Hacienda Heights, CA
Name of victim(s) killed: Benjamin Barranza.
Age of victim(s) killed: 17
Name of victim(s) injured: N/A.
Age of victim(s) injured: N/A.
Name of suspect(s)/shooter(s): A carload of teen-agers.
Age of suspect(s)/shooter(s): Unreported.
Weapon(s): Unreported.
High capacity magazine(s)?: Unreported.
Weapon(s) legally acquired by suspect(s)/shooter(s)?: Unreported.
# of people killed: 1
# of people injured: 0
Total # of victims: 1

Time suspect(s)/shooter(s) were apprehended or killed?: Unreported.

Suspect(s)' mental illness: Unreported.

Suspect(s)' medication or drug use: Unreported.

Suspect(s)' criminal history: Unreported.

Warning signs: Unreported.

Suspect(s)' country of citizenship: Unreported.

Suspect(s)' religious affiliation: Unreported.

Alleged reason for shooting: Gang-related.

Metal detectors present?: N/A.

Location & time of shooting: Shooting occurred in school parking lot around 3:15 p.m.

For more information, contact: Sheriff Lt. Leonard Tyko and Principal Donald White.

Citations/sources: (National School Safety Center, 2010, p. 8) (Carlson, 1994, p. 8) (Torres, 1994, p. B4) (Congress of the U.S., 1999, p. 76)

#1079

Location of shooting: Kennard High School

Date: 1/21/1994

City, State: Kennard, TX

Name of victim(s) killed: Joseph Leon Olivo (shooter).

Age of victim(s) killed: 17

Name of victim(s) injured: N/A.

Age of victim(s) injured: N/A.

Name of suspect(s)/shooter(s): Joseph Leon Olivo.

Age of suspect(s)/shooter(s): 17

Weapon(s): .30-30 rifle

High capacity magazine(s)?: Unreported.

Weapon(s) legally acquired by suspect(s)/shooter(s)?: No. Shooter borrowed rifle from a friend during hunting season.

# of people killed: 1

# of people injured: 0

Total # of victims: 1

Time suspect(s)/shooter(s) were apprehended or killed?: Suicide.

Suspect(s)' mental illness: Unreported.

Suspect(s)' medication or drug use: Unreported.

Suspect(s)' criminal history: Unreported.

Warning signs: Unreported.

Suspect(s)' country of citizenship: Unreported.

Suspect(s)' religious affiliation: Unreported.

Alleged reason for shooting: Unreported. Shooter left a note in the classroom describing personal problems.

Metal detectors present?: Unreported.

Location & time of shooting: Suicide occurred in classroom around 8:02 a.m., after the shooter ordered his teacher and fellow classmates to leave the room.

For more information, contact: Houston County Sheriff Jimbo Rains.

Citations/sources: (National School Safety Center, 2010, p. 8) (Student commits suicide, 1994, p. 14-A) (Items of interest, 1994, p. B4) (District news roundup, 1994) (Congress of the U.S., 1999, p. 76)

#1078
Location of shooting: Voorhees College
Date: 1/25/1994
City, State: Denmark, SC
Name of victim(s) killed: N/A.
Age of victim(s) killed: N/A.
Name of victim(s) injured: Gregory Singleton & Anthony Allen.
Age of victim(s) injured: 19 & 23
Name of suspect(s)/shooter(s): Marcus Blakely & Chad A. Gadsden.
Age of suspect(s)/shooter(s): 22 & 22
Weapon(s): Unreported.
High capacity magazine(s)?: Unreported.
Weapon(s) legally acquired by suspect(s)/shooter(s)?: Unreported.
# of people killed: 0
# of people injured: 2
Total # of victims: 2
Time suspect(s)/shooter(s) were apprehended or killed?: Blakely was arrested two days after the shooting at his home. Gadsen was arrested one week after shooting at the college.

Suspect(s)' mental illness: Unreported.

Suspect(s)' medication or drug use: Unreported.

Suspect(s)' criminal history: Unreported.

Warning signs: Unreported.

Suspect(s)' country of citizenship: Unreported.

Suspect(s)' religious affiliation: Unreported.

Alleged reason for shooting: Argument over a girl.

Metal detectors present?: N/A.

Location & time of shooting: Shooting occurred on college campus shortly before 10:00 p.m.

For more information, contact: Voorhees President Leonard E. Dawson, Bamberg County Sheriff Ed Darnell and State Law Enforcement Spokesman Hugh Munn.

Citations/sources: (More info: school shootings, 2010) (Milkie, 1994, p. 1A & 4A) (Hendren, 1994a, p. 1B) (Second man under arrest, 1994, p. 1B) (Suspect jailed in shooting, 1994, p. 2C)

#1077
Location of shooting: Eau Claire High School

Date: 1/25/1994
City, State: Columbia, SC
Name of victim(s) killed: Earnest Dunlap.
Age of victim(s) killed: 16
Name of victim(s) injured: N/A.
Age of victim(s) injured: N/A.
Name of suspect(s)/shooter(s): Floyd Eugene Brown.
Age of suspect(s)/shooter(s): 18
Weapon(s): Unreported.
High capacity magazine(s)?: Unreported.
Weapon(s) legally acquired by suspect(s)/shooter(s)?: Unreported.
# of people killed: 1
# of people injured: 0
Total # of victims: 1
Time suspect(s)/shooter(s) were apprehended or killed?: Suspect was arrested at his Columbia home shortly after the shooting.
Suspect(s)' mental illness: Unreported.
Suspect(s)' medication or drug use: Unreported.
Suspect(s)' criminal history: Unreported.
Warning signs: Unreported.
Suspect(s)' country of citizenship: Unreported.
Suspect(s)' religious affiliation: Unreported.
Alleged reason for shooting: Argument. Self-defense.
Metal detectors present?: No.
Location & time of shooting: Shooting took place in school third-floor hallway at the beginning of a break in classes.
For more information, contact: Police Chief Charles Austin, Richland School District Spokesman Buddy Price and Superintendent John Stevenson.
Citations/sources: (Jones, 1994, p. 1A & 4A) (Jury: Brown innocent, 1995, p. 8B)

#1076
Location of shooting: Washington Elementary School
Date: 1/27/1994
City, State: San Jose, CA
Name of victim(s) killed: Osvaldo Mojarro Rios.
Age of victim(s) killed: 22
Name of victim(s) injured: N/A.
Age of victim(s) injured: N/A.
Name of suspect(s)/shooter(s): Francisco Anthony Valdez (shooter), Joseph Aguilera Jr., Joseph Mamone Jr., Steve Gonzales & Mario Abrego.
Age of suspect(s)/shooter(s): 18, 18, 19, 19 & 20

Weapon(s): Semiautomatic pistol

High capacity magazine(s)?: Unreported.

Weapon(s) legally acquired by suspect(s)/shooter(s)?: Unreported.

# of people killed: 1

# of people injured: 0

Total # of victims: 1

Time suspect(s)/shooter(s) were apprehended or killed?: Valdez was arrested the day after the shooting. Abrego, Gonzalaes, Aguilera, & Mamone were arrested 1 and 2 days after the shooting in raids by San Jose police along with nine juveniles.

Suspect(s)' mental illness: Unreported.

Suspect(s)' medication or drug use: Unreported.

Suspect(s)' criminal history: Unreported.

Warning signs: Unreported.

Suspect(s)' country of citizenship: Unreported.

Suspect(s)' religious affiliation: Unreported.

Alleged reason for shooting: Gang-related. Suspects mistakenly thought victim was a rival gang member.

Metal detectors present?: N/A.

Location & time of shooting: Victim was shot in the school parking lot in a car with his wife while waiting for their son to be released from school.

For more information, contact: San Jose Police Officer Michael Piscitello, Principal Al Moreno, Deputy District Attorneys Kurt Kumli & Mike Fitzsimmons.

Citations/sources: (National School Safety Center, 2010, p. 8) (Court of Appeal, Sixth District, 1997) (Congress of the U.S., 1999, p. 76) (Fischer & Guido, 1994, p. 1B) (Boubion, 1994, p. 1B) (South Bay - arrest in killing, 1994, p. A21) (Barnacle, 1994, p. 1B)

#1075

Location of shooting: Marcus Whitman Middle School

Date: 1/31/1994

City, State: Seattle, WA

Name of victim(s) killed: Neal Summers (U.S. history teacher).

Age of victim(s) killed: 45

Name of victim(s) injured: N/A.

Age of victim(s) injured: N/A.

Name of suspect(s)/shooter(s): Darrell Allen Cloud.

Age of suspect(s)/shooter(s): 24

Weapon(s): AR-15 semiautomatic rifle

High capacity magazine(s)?: Unreported.

Weapon(s) legally acquired by suspect(s)/shooter(s)?: Unreported.

# of people killed: 1

# of people injured: 0

Total # of victims: 1

Time suspect(s)/shooter(s) were apprehended or killed?: Shooter was taken into custody about 29 hours after shooting with assistance from public.

Suspect(s)' mental illness: Unreported.

Suspect(s)' medication or drug use: Unreported.

Suspect(s)' criminal history: Went to trial for "displaying a weapon to intimidate" on a highway a year before the shooting.

Warning signs: Unreported.

Suspect(s)' country of citizenship: Unreported.

Suspect(s)' religious affiliation: Unreported.

Alleged reason for shooting: Sexual abuse. Shooter claimed he was driven to kill teacher due to years of alleged sexual abuse that began when shooter was 14.

Metal detectors present?: Unreported.

Location & time of shooting: Teacher shot in school hallway at 6:20 a.m.

For more information, contact: Seattle Police, Police Spokesman Sean O'Donnell and Teachers Larry and Anne Temple.

Citations/sources: (Angelos, et al., 1994) (Jury convicts man of killing, 1995) (National School Safety Center, 2010, p. 8) (Police arrest man, 1994, p. 5B) (Man is convicted, 1995, p. 7B) (Seattle man who killed, 1994) (Teacher in Seattle, 1994, p. 3B) (Congress of the U.S., 1999, p. 77) (School shootings in Washington, 2012)

#1074

Location of shooting: South Carolina State University

Date: 2/4/1994

City, State: Orangeburg, SC

Name of victim(s) killed: N/A.

Age of victim(s) killed: N/A.

Name of victim(s) injured: Stanley Montgomery III, William Little & Frederick Ellis.

Age of victim(s) injured: 20, 20 & 20

Name of suspect(s)/shooter(s): Marcus White & Steven White.

Age of suspect(s)/shooter(s): 20 & 21

Weapon(s): .25-caliber semiautomatic gun & a revolver.

High capacity magazine(s)?: Unreported.

Weapon(s) legally acquired by suspect(s)/shooter(s)?: Unreported.

# of people killed: 0

# of people injured: 3

Total # of victims: 3

Time suspect(s)/shooter(s) were apprehended or killed?: Suspects turned themselves in to police one day after the shooting.

Suspect(s)' mental illness: Unreported.

Suspect(s)' medication or drug use: Alcohol. Suspects were "drinking heavily."

Suspect(s)' criminal history: Steven White had four prior convictions, including 5 years of imprisonment for a 1989 charge of disturbing a school, second-degree burglary, possession of marijuana and petty larceny. Marcus White had no prior convictions.

Warning signs: Unreported.

Suspect(s)' country of citizenship: Unreported.

Suspect(s)' religious affiliation: Christian: Baptist.

Alleged reason for shooting: Fight. Wrestling.

Metal detectors present?: N/A

Location & time of shooting: Shooting occurred in college dormitory room around 10:00 p.m.

For more information, contact: SCSU President Dr. Barbara R. Hatton and VP of Development and Institutional Advancement Dr. Thomas Stewart.

Citations/sources: (More info: school shootings, 2010) (In wake of shooting, 1994, p. 10B) (York, 1994, p. 1A & 7A) (Hendren, 1994a, February 8, p. 1A & 7A) (S.C. State shooting, 1994, p. 2A)

#1073
Location of shooting: Lee County School Services Building

Date: 2/7/1994

City, State: Fort Myers, FL

Name of victim(s) killed: James A. Adams (School Superintendent) & Larry Ray Shelton (shooter).

Age of victim(s) killed: 57 & 48

Name of victim(s) injured: N/A.

Age of victim(s) injured: N/A.

Name of suspect(s)/shooter(s): Larry Ray Shelton (Former special education teacher).

Age of suspect(s)/shooter(s): 48

Weapon(s): .38 caliber revolver

High capacity magazine(s)?: Unreported.

Weapon(s) legally acquired by suspect(s)/shooter(s)?: Unreported.

# of people killed: 2

# of people injured: 0

Total # of victims: 2

Time suspect(s)/shooter(s) were apprehended or killed?: Suicide.

Suspect(s)' mental illness: Unreported.

Suspect(s)' medication or drug use: Unreported.

Suspect(s)' criminal history: None.

Warning signs: Suspect pinned a farewell note to a lamp in his bedroom of his friend's home, requesting to be cremated and to check the news that night. His friend discovered the note approximately 30 minutes after the shooting.

Suspect(s)' country of citizenship: Unreported.

Suspect(s)' religious affiliation: Unreported.

Alleged reason for shooting: Possibly due to financial troubles and unemployment.

Metal detectors present?: Unreported.

Location & time of shooting: Shooting occurred outside victim's third-floor school office at 2:50 p.m.

For more information, contact: Unreported.

Citations/sources: (National School Safety Center, 2010, p. 8) (Francheschina & Melsek, 1994, p. 1A & 4A) (Congress of the U.S., 1999, p. 77)

1072

Location of shooting: Osborn High School

Date: 2/8/1994

City, State: Detroit, MI

Name of victim(s) killed: Steven Watkins.

Age of victim(s) killed: 19

Name of victim(s) injured: N/A.

Age of victim(s) injured: N/A.

Name of suspect(s)/shooter(s): Gunman in a white Eagle Premier vehicle.

Age of suspect(s)/shooter(s): Unreported.

Weapon(s): Unreported.

High capacity magazine(s)?: Unreported.

Weapon(s) legally acquired by suspect(s)/shooter(s)?: Unreported.

# of people killed: 1

# of people injured: 0

Total # of victims: 1

Time suspect(s)/shooter(s) were apprehended or killed?: Unreported.

Suspect(s)' mental illness: Unreported.

Suspect(s)' medication or drug use: Unreported.

Suspect(s)' criminal history: Unreported.

Warning signs: Unreported.

Suspect(s)' country of citizenship: Unreported.

Suspect(s)' religious affiliation: Unreported.

Alleged reason for shooting: Unreported.

Metal detectors present?: N/A.

Location & time of shooting: Victim shot in school parking lot while in his car.

For more information, contact: District Security Head Charles Mitchell.

Citations/sources: (National School Safety Center, 2010, p. 8) (2nd slaying from gunfire, 1994, p. 8B) (Collier, 1994, p. 4E)

#1071

Location of shooting: Kemper Military School and College (Private military high school and college)

Date: 3/1/1994

City, State: Boonville, MO
Name of victim(s) killed: Robin Michelle Coleman & Richard Vancena.
Age of victim(s) killed: 33 & 58
Name of victim(s) injured: N/A.
Age of victim(s) injured: N/A.
Name of suspect(s)/shooter(s): Dante D. Hayes.
Age of suspect(s)/shooter(s): 33
Weapon(s): 12-gauge shotgun
High capacity magazine(s)?: Unreported.
Weapon(s) legally acquired by suspect(s)/shooter(s)?: Unreported.
# of people killed: 2
# of people injured: 0
Total # of victims: 2
Time suspect(s)/shooter(s) were apprehended or killed?: Suspect surrendered approximately 10 hours after shooting and after holding two other people hostage for 5 hours.
Suspect(s)' mental illness: Unreported.
Suspect(s)' medication or drug use: Alcohol.
Suspect(s)' criminal history: Unreported.
Warning signs: Unreported.
Suspect(s)' country of citizenship: Unreported.
Suspect(s)' religious affiliation: Unreported.
Alleged reason for shooting: Argument. Intoxicated by alcohol. Suspect intended to kill his wife following an argument. When asked why he did it, the suspect said, "Those people was in my business."
Metal detectors present?: Unreported.
Location & time of shooting: Shooting occurred in the military school mess hall cafeteria approximately 8:45 a.m.
For more information, contact: Sheriff Paul Milne, KMIZ TV Reporter Travis Ford, Circuit Judge Donald Barnes, Patrol Cpl. Tim Hull, Mess hall worker Anna Hayes, Missouri State Highway Patrol and Prosecutor Doug Abele.
Citations/sources: (Defendant unrestrained, 1994, p. 5B) (Man surrendered after two killed, 1994, p. 1B) (Life sentences, 1994, p. 4)

#1070
Location of shooting: Eastern High School
Date: 3/9/1994
City, State: Washington, DC
Name of victim(s) killed: N/A.
Age of victim(s) killed: N/A.
Name of victim(s) injured: Jerome Cook.
Age of victim(s) injured: 17

Name of suspect(s)/shooter(s): Cornell Andrew Cheeks Jr.
Age of suspect(s)/shooter(s): 17
Weapon(s): Unreported.
High capacity magazine(s)?: Unreported.
Weapon(s) legally acquired by suspect(s)/shooter(s)?: No.
# of people killed: 0
# of people injured: 1
Total # of victims: 1
Time suspect(s)/shooter(s) were apprehended or killed?: Unreported.
Suspect(s)' mental illness: Unreported.
Suspect(s)' medication or drug use: Marijuana. Suspect acknowledged having a substance abuse problem.
Suspect(s)' criminal history: Unreported.
Warning signs: Unreported.
Suspect(s)' country of citizenship: Unreported.
Suspect(s)' religious affiliation: Unreported.
Alleged reason for shooting: Argument because one had bumped into the other.
Metal detectors present?: Yes. Two metal detectors and an X-ray machine.
Location & time of shooting: Shooting occurred outside the school cafeteria, where 500 students were eating lunch, around 11:00 a.m.
For more information, contact: Principal Ralph H. Neal, Mayor Sharon Pratt Kelly, Police Chief Fred Thomas, School Superintendent Franklin L. Smith and Inspector William O. Ritchie.
Citations/sources: (Frazier, 1996) (Horwitz, 1994) (Castaneda & Lewis, 1994)

#1069
Location of shooting: Goose Creek High School
Date: 3/15/1994
City, State: Charleston, SC
Name of victim(s) killed: Michael Ryan Spann.
Age of victim(s) killed: 18
Name of victim(s) injured: Mario Jones & Stan Dawson.
Age of victim(s) injured: 16 & 21
Name of suspect(s)/shooter(s): Randolph T. Johnson (shooter), Lang Wolfe, Jerice Oiver & John Doughty.
Age of suspect(s)/shooter(s): 20, 18, 17 & 17
Weapon(s): Revolver
High capacity magazine(s)?: Unreported.
Weapon(s) legally acquired by suspect(s)/shooter(s)?: Unreported.
# of people killed: 1
# of people injured: 2
Total # of victims: 3

Time suspect(s)/shooter(s) were apprehended or killed?: Three of the suspects were caught within the hour.

Suspect(s)' mental illness: Unreported.

Suspect(s)' medication or drug use: Unreported.

Suspect(s)' criminal history: Wolfe had a previous assault charge.

Warning signs: Unreported.

Suspect(s)' country of citizenship: Unreported.

Suspect(s)' religious affiliation: Unreported.

Alleged reason for shooting: Fight.

Metal detectors present?: N/A.

Location & time of shooting: Shooting occurred in school parking lot approximately 3:15 p.m.

For more information, contact: Berkeley County Sheriff Ray Isett, Berkeley County Maj. E. G. Erickson, Assistant Principal Charlie Davis and Principal John Fulmer.

Citations/sources: (National School Safety Center, 2010, p. 8) (More info: school shootings, 2010) (School shooting in Goose Creek, 1994, p. 2B) (Patrols requested, 1994, p. 12) (Goose Creek school shooting, 1994, p. 1A & 7A) (Bond set for four, 1994, p. 2B) (Man sentenced to life, 1994, p. 2B) (Congress of the U.S., 1999, p. 77)

#1068

Location of shooting: Ballard High School

Date: 3/23/1994

City, State: Seattle, WA

Name of victim(s) killed: Melissa "Missie" Fernandez.

Age of victim(s) killed: 16

Name of victim(s) injured: Unnamed student.

Age of victim(s) injured: Unreported.

Name of suspect(s)/shooter(s): Brian Keith Ronquillo (shooter), Jerome Reyes, & Caesar Sarausad.

Age of suspect(s)/shooter(s): 16, 18 & 20

Weapon(s): Handgun

High capacity magazine(s)?: Unreported.

Weapon(s) legally acquired by suspect(s)/shooter(s)?: No.

# of people killed: 1

# of people injured: 1

Total # of victims: 2

Time suspect(s)/shooter(s) were apprehended or killed?: Ronquillo turned himself into police 3 days after the shooting.

Suspect(s)' mental illness: Unreported.

Suspect(s)' medication or drug use: Unreported.

Suspect(s)' criminal history: Unreported.

Warning signs: Unreported.

<u>Suspect(s)' country of citizenship</u>: Unreported.

<u>Suspect(s)' religious affiliation</u>: Unreported.

<u>Alleged reason for shooting</u>: Gang-related. Victim was an innocent bystander.

<u>Metal detectors present?</u>: N/A.

<u>Location & time of shooting</u>: Drive-by shooting on the north side of the school shortly after 1:30 p.m.

<u>For more information, contact</u>: Seattle Police Dep. Spokesman Sean O'Donnell and Seattle police spokeswoman Vinette Tichi.

<u>Citations/sources</u>: (National School Safety Center, 2010, p. 9) (Seattle teen turns himself in, 1994, p. 3B) (Girl wounded in drive-by, p. A4) (Congress of the U.S., 1999, p. 77) (School shootings in Washington, 2012)

#1067

<u>Location of shooting</u>: Etowah High School

<u>Date</u>: 3/25/1994

<u>City, State</u>: Woodstock, GA

<u>Name of victim(s) killed</u>: Brian Head (shooter).

<u>Age of victim(s) killed</u>: 15

<u>Name of victim(s) injured</u>: N/A.

<u>Age of victim(s) injured</u>: N/A.

<u>Name of suspect(s)/shooter(s)</u>: Brian Head.

<u>Age of suspect(s)/shooter(s)</u>: 15

<u>Weapon(s)</u>: 9mm pistol

<u>High capacity magazine(s)?</u>: Unreported.

<u>Weapon(s) legally acquired by suspect(s)/shooter(s)?</u>: No. Student stole gun from his family.

<u># of people killed</u>: 1

<u># of people injured</u>: 0

<u>Total # of victims</u>: 1

<u>Time suspect(s)/shooter(s) were apprehended or killed?</u>: Suicide.

<u>Suspect(s)' mental illness</u>: Unreported.

<u>Suspect(s)' medication or drug use</u>: Unreported.

<u>Suspect(s)' criminal history</u>: Unreported.

<u>Warning signs</u>: Unreported.

<u>Suspect(s)' country of citizenship</u>: Unreported.

<u>Suspect(s)' religious affiliation</u>: Unreported.

<u>Alleged reason for shooting</u>: Bullying. Teasing about victim's weight.

<u>Metal detectors present?</u>: Yes. Handheld metal detectors are used only when someone is suspected of carry a weapon.

<u>Location & time of shooting</u>: Shooting occurred in school classroom.

<u>For more information, contact</u>: Etowah economics teacher Bill Watkins and Cherokee County Sheriff Roger Garrison.

Citations/sources: (National School Safety Center, 2010, p. 9) (Hendrick, 1994, p. B1) (Jacobson, 1994, p. C6) (Teen kills himself, 1994, p. 2A)

#1066
Location of shooting: McNeil High School
Date: 4/5/1994
City, State: Austin, TX
Name of victim(s) killed: N/A.
Age of victim(s) killed: N/A.
Name of victim(s) injured: Alison Mentzer & Reshonda Sparkman.
Age of victim(s) injured: 17 & 18
Name of suspect(s)/shooter(s): 3 students.
Age of suspect(s)/shooter(s): 16, 16 & 16
Weapon(s): TZ75 Parabellum handgun (9mm).
High capacity magazine(s)?: No. Gun was loaded with 12 bullets.
Weapon(s) legally acquired by suspect(s)/shooter(s)?: No. Stolen from a school mate.
# of people killed: 0
# of people injured: 2
Total # of victims: 2
Time suspect(s)/shooter(s) were apprehended or killed?: Unreported.
Suspect(s)' mental illness: Unreported.
Suspect(s)' medication or drug use: Unreported.
Suspect(s)' criminal history: One of the suspects were on probation for burglary.
Warning signs: Unreported.
Suspect(s)' country of citizenship: Unreported.
Suspect(s)' religious affiliation: Unreported.
Alleged reason for shooting: Accident. Gun Accidently discharged in student's backpack, injuring two students.
Metal detectors present?: Yes. Handheld metal detectors.
Location & time of shooting: Shooting occurred in an anatomy classroom, at approximately 10:00 a.m.
For more information, contact: Chief Deputy Floyd Hacker, Travis County Sheriff Lt. Scott Burroughs, Travis County Sheriff Spokesman Deputy Andy Saenz, McNeil High School Principal Alan Veach and teacher Pat Crutsinger.
Citations/sources: (Welch, 1994, p. 1) (Burgees, 1994, p. A1 & A17) (Burgess & Vargas, 1994, p. A1 & A7)

#1065
Location of shooting: Largo High School
Date: 4/8/1994
City, State: Largo, MD

Name of victim(s) killed: N/A.
Age of victim(s) killed: N/A.
Name of victim(s) injured: Barrington Miles, Jr. (Teacher).
Age of victim(s) injured: 46
Name of suspect(s)/shooter(s): Warren Emmanuel Graham Jr.
Age of suspect(s)/shooter(s): 17
Weapon(s): 9mm pistol (police service weapon) and two magazines of ammunition.
High capacity magazine(s)?: No.
Weapon(s) legally acquired by suspect(s)/shooter(s)?: No. Stolen from suspect's father, who is a police officer.
# of people killed: 0
# of people injured: 1
Total # of victims: 1
Time suspect(s)/shooter(s) were apprehended or killed?: Unreported.
Suspect(s)' mental illness: Unreported.
Suspect(s)' medication or drug use: Unreported.
Suspect(s)' criminal history: Unreported.
Warning signs: Unreported.
Suspect(s)' country of citizenship: Unreported.
Suspect(s)' religious affiliation: Unreported.
Alleged reason for shooting: Protest authority. Teacher interrupted the sale of the suspect's stolen gun.
Metal detectors present?: Unreported.
Location & time of shooting: Shooting occurred while teacher was entering a second floor boys' restroom while on hall duty about 8:50 a.m.
For more information, contact: County District Judge Sheila Tillerson, Computer Science Teacher (victim) Barrington Miles Jr. and Schools Spokesman Bonnie Jenkins.
Citations/sources: (Teacher shot with cop's gun, 1994, p. 6A) (Bail set for officer's son, 1994, p. 2B) (Official urges plan, 1994, p. B-5)

#1064
Location of shooting: Margaret Leary Elementary School
Date: 4/12/1994
City, State: Butte, MT
Name of victim(s) killed: Jeremy Bullock.
Age of victim(s) killed: 11
Name of victim(s) injured: N/A.
Age of victim(s) injured: N/A.
Name of suspect(s)/shooter(s): James Osmanson.
Age of suspect(s)/shooter(s): 10
Weapon(s): .22-calliber semiautomatic handgun.

High capacity magazine(s)?: Unreported.
Weapon(s) legally acquired by suspect(s)/shooter(s)?: No.
# of people killed: 1
# of people injured: 0
Total # of victims: 1
Time suspect(s)/shooter(s) were apprehended or killed?: Suspect surrendered his gun to a teacher after the shooting.
Suspect(s)' mental illness: Unreported.
Suspect(s)' medication or drug use: Unreported.
Suspect(s)' criminal history: Unreported.
Warning signs: Unreported.
Suspect(s)' country of citizenship: Unreported.
Suspect(s)' religious affiliation: Unreported.
Alleged reason for shooting: Bullying. Missed intended target. Suspect was teased because his parents have AIDS.
Metal detectors present?: N/A.
Location & time of shooting: Victim shot in school playground, just before classes began in the morning.
For more information, contact: Butte Sheriff John McPherson, Detective Capt. John Walsh, Butte School Superintendent Bill Nachatilo and Butte Youth Court Judge Mark Sullivan.
Citations/sources: (National School Safety Center, 2010, p. 9) (Crews, 2016, p. 7) (Anez, 1994, p. 1A) (DelBonis, 1994b, p. A1 & A6) (DelBonis, 1994a, p. 1A & 8A) (Fenner, 1994, p. 1C)

#1063
Location of shooting: 49th Street Elementary School
Date: 4/13/1994
City, State: Los Angeles, CA
Name of victim(s) killed: Jorge David Licea (shooter).
Age of victim(s) killed: 10
Name of victim(s) injured: N/A.
Age of victim(s) injured: N/A.
Name of suspect(s)/shooter(s): Jorge David Licea.
Age of suspect(s)/shooter(s): 10
Weapon(s): .380-caliber semiautomatic handgun,
High capacity magazine(s)?: Unreported.
Weapon(s) legally acquired by suspect(s)/shooter(s)?: No. Stolen from shooter's father who kept it stashed under his mattress.
# of people killed: 1
# of people injured: 0
Total # of victims: 1
Time suspect(s)/shooter(s) were apprehended or killed?: Suicide.

Suspect(s)' mental illness: Unreported.

Suspect(s)' medication or drug use: Unreported.

Suspect(s)' criminal history: None.

Warning signs: None.

Suspect(s)' country of citizenship: U.S.A.: Los Angeles, CA

Suspect(s)' religious affiliation: Christian: Catholic.

Alleged reason for shooting: Unreported. Possibly due to receiving a one-day, informal suspension for cursing the day before the shooting.

Metal detectors present?: N/A.

Location & time of shooting: Shooting occurred in front of the school building as classmates filed into school.

For more information, contact: Los Angeles Police Detective John Garcia, Principal Lemuel Chavis and Psychologist Richard Lieberman.

Citations/sources: (National School Safety Center, 2010, p. 9) (Kata, 1994, p. B12 & B17) (Klein, 1994, p. A1 & A31) (Congress of the U.S., 1999, p. 78)

#1062

Location of shooting: William Smith Special School, a National Christian Academy affiliate (Private Christian high school)

Date: 4/18/1994

City, State: Fort Washington, MD

Name of victim(s) killed: N/A.

Age of victim(s) killed: N/A.

Name of victim(s) injured: Rodriguez Durden.

Age of victim(s) injured: 17

Name of suspect(s)/shooter(s): Quintin G. Carson.

Age of suspect(s)/shooter(s): 16

Weapon(s): .22-caliber revolver.

High capacity magazine(s)?: Unreported.

Weapon(s) legally acquired by suspect(s)/shooter(s)?: No. Suspect told detectives he purchased the gun from a "crackhead" or drug addict.

# of people killed: 0

# of people injured: 1

Total # of victims: 1

Time suspect(s)/shooter(s) were apprehended or killed?: Arrested moments after the shooting by patrol officers who found him hiding in a toolshed in the back yard of a home several blocks from the school.

Suspect(s)' mental illness: Unreported.

Suspect(s)' medication or drug use: Unreported.

Suspect(s)' criminal history: Suspect was expelled from a public school six months prior to the shooting after he allegedly threatened a classmate with a replica of a handgun. The present school officials claim they were unaware of the suspects expulsion.

Warning signs: Unreported.

Suspect(s)' country of citizenship: Unreported.

Suspect(s)' religious affiliation: Christian.

Alleged reason for shooting: Argument over a girl.

Metal detectors present?: No.

Location & time of shooting: Unreported.

For more information, contact: Prince George's County police, Academy Administrator Rev. Fred Snowden, District Court Judge Sherrie Krauser and Police Investigator Alan Gibson.

Citations/sources: (Jeter, 1994a) (Teen held without bond, 1994, p. 26B) (Jeter, 1994b)

#1061

Location of shooting: East Norriton Middle School

Date: 4/19/1994

City, State: Norristown, PA

Name of victim(s) killed: N/A.

Age of victim(s) killed: N/A.

Name of victim(s) injured: Chanel Perkins.

Age of victim(s) injured: 12

Name of suspect(s)/shooter(s): Michael Anthony Stenson.

Age of suspect(s)/shooter(s): 13

Weapon(s): .25-caliber semiautomatic pistol.

High capacity magazine(s)?: Unreported.

Weapon(s) legally acquired by suspect(s)/shooter(s)?: No. Stolen from a tenant living at the suspect's house.

# of people killed: 0

# of people injured: 1

Total # of victims: 1

Time suspect(s)/shooter(s) were apprehended or killed?: Unreported.

Suspect(s)' mental illness: Unreported.

Suspect(s)' medication or drug use: Unreported.

Suspect(s)' criminal history: Unreported.

Warning signs: Unreported.

Suspect(s)' country of citizenship: Unreported.

Suspect(s)' religious affiliation: Unreported.

Alleged reason for shooting: Bullying. Suspect was frequently physically and verbally bullied by the victim and other students.

Metal detectors present?: N/A.

Location & time of shooting: Suspect shot the gun from inside a school bus window as the victim was stepping out.

For more information, contact: Norristown Police Chief Thomas Stone, Norristown Area School District Superintendent Michael Woodall and Montgomery County Juvenile Court Judge Maurino J. Rossanese.

Citations/sources: (Boy shoots girl, 1994, p. 4) (King & Downs, 1994, p. B1 & B10) (King, 1994, p. B1 & B3)

#1060
Location of shooting: John Trotwood Moore Middle School
Date: 4/21/1994
City, State: Nashville, TN
Name of victim(s) killed: Terrance Murray.
Age of victim(s) killed: 13
Name of victim(s) injured: N/A.
Age of victim(s) injured: N/A.
Name of suspect(s)/shooter(s): Jeremy Byrant.
Age of suspect(s)/shooter(s): 14
Weapon(s): .25-caliber pistol
High capacity magazine(s)?: Unreported.
Weapon(s) legally acquired by suspect(s)/shooter(s)?: No.
# of people killed: 1
# of people injured: 0
Total # of victims: 1
Time suspect(s)/shooter(s) were apprehended or killed?: Unreported.
Suspect(s)' mental illness: Unreported.
Suspect(s)' medication or drug use: Unreported.
Suspect(s)' criminal history: Unreported.
Warning signs: Unreported.
Suspect(s)' country of citizenship: Unreported.
Suspect(s)' religious affiliation: Unreported.
Alleged reason for shooting: Accident. Shooter didn't know gun passed to him in class was loaded.
Metal detectors present?: Unreported.
Location & time of shooting: Shooting occurred in a classroom while watching a video of "Beauty and the Beast" with classmates.
For more information, contact: Metro Nashville Police Chief Robert Kirchner & Metro Nashville school superintendent Richard Benjamin.
Citations/sources: (Seventh grader shot, 1994) (7th-grade boy shot to death, 1994) (National School Safety Center, 2010, p. 9) (Congress of the U.S., 1999, p. 78)

#1059

Location of shooting: North Miami High School

Date: 5/2/1994

City, State: North Miami, FL

Name of victim(s) killed: Edvard Almonor.

Age of victim(s) killed: 18

Name of victim(s) injured: N/A.

Age of victim(s) injured: N/A.

Name of suspect(s)/shooter(s): Tyhno Rock.

Age of suspect(s)/shooter(s): 18

Weapon(s): .380-caliber semiautomatic pistol

High capacity magazine(s)?: Unreported.

Weapon(s) legally acquired by suspect(s)/shooter(s)?: Unreported.

# of people killed: 1

# of people injured: 0

Total # of victims: 1

Time suspect(s)/shooter(s) were apprehended or killed?: Arrested approximately 45 minutes after shooting.

Suspect(s)' mental illness: Unreported.

Suspect(s)' medication or drug use: Unreported.

Suspect(s)' criminal history: Unreported.

Warning signs: Unreported.

Suspect(s)' country of citizenship: Unreported.

Suspect(s)' religious affiliation: Unreported.

Alleged reason for shooting: Accident. Shooter was showing gun to friends in school parking lot during lunch period.

Metal detectors present?: N/A.

Location & time of shooting: Shooting occurred in school parking lot during lunch period.

For more information, contact: North Miami Police Detective Kathleen Ruggiero.

Citations/sources: (National School Safety Center, 2010, p. 9) (Student in shooting dies, 1994, p. 3B) (Charges elevated, 1994, p. 8) (Congress of the U.S., 1999, p. 78)

#1058

Location of shooting: Ottumwa High School

Date: 7/25/1994

City, State: Ottumwa, IA

Name of victim(s) killed: Jeramy Wayne Allen.

Age of victim(s) killed: 15

Name of victim(s) injured: N/A.

Age of victim(s) injured: N/A.

Name of suspect(s)/shooter(s): Michael P. Coffman.

Age of suspect(s)/shooter(s): 16

Weapon(s): .22-caliber revolver

High capacity magazine(s)?: Unreported.

Weapon(s) legally acquired by suspect(s)/shooter(s)?: No. Stolen from suspect's father's locked gun case.

# of people killed: 1

# of people injured: 0

Total # of victims: 1

Time suspect(s)/shooter(s) were apprehended or killed?: Apprehended several hours after shooting.

Suspect(s)' mental illness: Unreported.

Suspect(s)' medication or drug use: Unreported.

Suspect(s)' criminal history: Unreported.

Warning signs: Several students claimed the suspect boasted about his intent to "put a cap" into the victim.

Suspect(s)' country of citizenship: Unreported.

Suspect(s)' religious affiliation: Unreported.

Alleged reason for shooting: Argument.

Metal detectors present?: N/A.

Location & time of shooting: Shooting occurred outside of the school after a driver education class.

For more information, contact: Iowa State Patrol Trooper Robert Coffman and District Judge Phillip Collet.

Citations/sources: (National School Safety Center, 2010, p. 10) (Siebert, 1994, p. 1M) (Santiago, 1995, p. 2A) (Congress of the U.S., 1999, p. 78)

#1057

Location of shooting: Hollywood High School

Date: 9/7/1994

City, State: Los Angeles, CA

Name of victim(s) killed: Rolando Ruiz.

Age of victim(s) killed: 17

Name of victim(s) injured: N/A.

Age of victim(s) injured: N/A.

Name of suspect(s)/shooter(s): Three gang members.

Age of suspect(s)/shooter(s): Unreported.

Weapon(s): Unreported.

High capacity magazine(s)?: Unreported.

Weapon(s) legally acquired by suspect(s)/shooter(s)?: Unreported.

# of people killed: 1

# of people injured: 0

Total # of victims: 1
Time suspect(s)/shooter(s) were apprehended or killed?: Unreported.
Suspect(s)' mental illness: Unreported.
Suspect(s)' medication or drug use: Unreported.
Suspect(s)' criminal history: Unreported.
Warning signs: Unreported.
Suspect(s)' country of citizenship: Unreported.
Suspect(s)' religious affiliation: Unreported.
Alleged reason for shooting: Gang-related.
Metal detectors present?: N/A.
Location & time of shooting: Shooting occurred on outside school lawn by rival gang members about 3:45 p.m. shortly after school ended.
For more information, contact: Hollywood High Principal Jeanne Hon and Los Angeles Police Department Detective Mike Pasquale.
Citations/sources: (National School Safety Center, 2010, p. 10) (Teen fatally shot, 1994, p. A1) (Riccardi & Chavez, 1994, p. B12) (Congress of the U.S., 1999, p. 79)

#1056
Location of shooting: South Florence High School
Date: 9/13/1994
City, State: Florence, SC
Name of victim(s) killed: N/A.
Age of victim(s) killed: N/A.
Name of victim(s) injured: Anastasia Purvis & Jerome Greene.
Age of victim(s) injured: 15 & 19
Name of suspect(s)/shooter(s): Taheen Kirven.
Age of suspect(s)/shooter(s): 18
Weapon(s): 9mm handgun
High capacity magazine(s)?: Unreported.
Weapon(s) legally acquired by suspect(s)/shooter(s)?: Unreported.
# of people killed: 0
# of people injured: 2
Total # of victims: 2
Time suspect(s)/shooter(s) were apprehended or killed?: Suspect was arrested two hours after shooting in a relative's house.
Suspect(s)' mental illness: Unreported.
Suspect(s)' medication or drug use: Unreported.
Suspect(s)' criminal history: Unreported.
Warning signs: Unreported.
Suspect(s)' country of citizenship: Unreported.
Suspect(s)' religious affiliation: Unreported.

Alleged reason for shooting: Unreported.

Metal detectors present?: Unreported.

Location & time of shooting: Shooting occurred in school hallway.

For more information, contact: Florence County Sheriff Lt. Johnny Abraham, Principal Curtis Boswell, Sheriff Jimmy Gregg and U.S. Magiztrate E.S. Swearingen.

Citations/sources: (Two teens shot at South Florence, 1994, p. 3B) (Two teens shot at high school, 1994, p. 11 & 12) (Suspect in school shootings, 1994, p. 3C)

#1055

Location of shooting: Sheepshead Bay High School

Date: 9/14/1994

City, State: Brooklyn, NY

Name of victim(s) killed: N/A.

Age of victim(s) killed: N/A.

Name of victim(s) injured: Maurice Ferguson.

Age of victim(s) injured: 15

Name of suspect(s)/shooter(s): David Estrada.

Age of suspect(s)/shooter(s): 16 or 17

Weapon(s): .32-caliber semi-automatic

High capacity magazine(s)?: Unreported.

Weapon(s) legally acquired by suspect(s)/shooter(s)?: No. Gun was unregistered.

# of people killed: 0

# of people injured: 1

Total # of victims: 1

Time suspect(s)/shooter(s) were apprehended or killed?: Suspect arrested minutes after the shooting.

Suspect(s)' mental illness: Unreported.

Suspect(s)' medication or drug use: Unreported.

Suspect(s)' criminal history: Both the suspect and victim have "petty" juvenile records.

Warning signs: Unreported.

Suspect(s)' country of citizenship: Unreported.

Suspect(s)' religious affiliation: Unreported.

Alleged reason for shooting: Feud. Victim's older brother claimed there was a feud between the suspect and victim. Suspect claimed the shooting was an accident.

Metal detectors present?: Yes.

Location & time of shooting: Shooting occurred at 1:40 p.m. in school hallway–ten minutes after the handheld metal detectors were turned off. Only the 14th or 15th student was scanned.

For more information, contact: Brooklyn Detective Capt. Richard Ward, Assistant Chief Commanding Officer Michael Markman, Police Chief William Bratton and Police Spokesman Sgt. Edward Caro.

Citations/sources: (Mangan, 1994, p. C8) (Student shot, wounded, 1994, p. 5C) (Student critically injured, 1994, p. B4) (Chiang, Mangan, Marzuli, & Speyer, 1994, p. 20)

#1054
Location of shooting: Grimsley High School
Date: 10/12/1994
City, State: Greensboro, NC
Name of victim(s) killed: Nicholas Alexander Atkinson (shooter).
Age of victim(s) killed: 16
Name of victim(s) injured: Bill Whites (Assistant Principal).
Age of victim(s) injured: 59
Name of suspect(s)/shooter(s): Nicholas Alexander Atkinson.
Age of suspect(s)/shooter(s): 16
Weapon(s): 9mm handgun
High capacity magazine(s)?: Unreported.
Weapon(s) legally acquired by suspect(s)/shooter(s)?: No.
# of people killed: 1
# of people injured: 1
Total # of victims: 2
Time suspect(s)/shooter(s) were apprehended or killed?: Suicide.
Suspect(s)' mental illness: Unreported.
Suspect(s)' medication or drug use: Unreported.
Suspect(s)' criminal history: In July of the same year, the suspect led sheriff deputies on a high-speed car chase in his grandmother's Cadillac.
Warning signs: Unreported.
Suspect(s)' country of citizenship: Unreported.
Suspect(s)' religious affiliation: Unreported.
Alleged reason for shooting: Protest authority. Suspect had been suspended for smoking the day before the shooting.
Metal detectors present?: N/A.
Location & time of shooting: Shooting occurred outside of school, near the school busses at approximately 3:35 p.m.
For more information, contact: Principal Bill Whites (victim), Principal Tom Penland, Police Sgt. D.B. Wood and School Bus Driver Joel Hairston.
Citations/sources: (National School Safety Center, 2010, p. 10) (Hunt visits school, 1994, p. 2A) (Student kills self, 1994, p. 2B) (Swofford, 1994) (Congress of the U.S., 1999, p. 79)

#1053
Location of shooting: Wickliffe Middle School
Date: 11/7/1994
City, State: Wickliffe, OH

Name of victim(s) killed: Peter Christopher (School Custodian).
Age of victim(s) killed: 41
Name of victim(s) injured: James J. Anderson (Assistant Principal), Thomas Schmidt (Patrolman), Lowell Grimm (Industrial Arts Teacher) & Keith A. Ledeger (shooter).
Age of victim(s) injured: 51, 47, 50 & 37
Name of suspect(s)/shooter(s): Keith A. Ledeger
Age of suspect(s)/shooter(s): 37
Weapon(s): 12-gauge shotgun
High capacity magazine(s)?: Unreported.
Weapon(s) legally acquired by suspect(s)/shooter(s)?: Unreported.
# of people killed: 1
# of people injured: 4
Total # of victims: 5
Time suspect(s)/shooter(s) were apprehended or killed?: Suspect was nonfatally shot and apprehended by a police officer during shooting.
Suspect(s)' mental illness: Diagnosed chronic paranoid schizophrenia.
Suspect(s)' medication or drug use: Unreported.
Suspect(s)' criminal history: Unreported.
Warning signs: Unreported.
Suspect(s)' country of citizenship: Unreported.
Suspect(s)' religious affiliation: Unreported.
Alleged reason for shooting: Unreported.
Metal detectors present?: Unreported.
Location & time of shooting: Shooting occurred in the school office about 2:00 p.m.
For more information, contact: Police Chief Jim Fox, Officer Thomas Schmidt (victim), Assistant Principal James J. Anderson (victim) and Teacher Lowell Grimm.
Citations/sources: (National School Safety Center, 2010, p. 10) (Crews, 2016, p. 7) (Motive sought for shooting, p. A1) (Community waits for justice, 1994, p. 5) (Gunman kills one, wounds three, 1994, p. 6) (Congress of the U.S., 1999, p. 79) (Reed, 2012)

#1052
Location of shooting: West Delaware High School
Date: 11/8/1994
City, State: Manchester, IA
Name of victim(s) killed: N/A.
Age of victim(s) killed: N/A.
Name of victim(s) injured: Julie Shaw (High School Secretary) & Linda Mickens (High School Secretary).
Age of victim(s) injured: Unreported.
Name of suspect(s)/shooter(s): Chad Welcher.
Age of suspect(s)/shooter(s): 16

Weapon(s): 12-gauge shotgun
High capacity magazine(s)?: Unreported.
Weapon(s) legally acquired by suspect(s)/shooter(s)?: No.
\# of people killed: 0
\# of people injured: 2
Total \# of victims: 2
Time suspect(s)/shooter(s) were apprehended or killed?: Suspect was apprehended at his home shortly after the shooting.
Suspect(s)' mental illness: Unreported.
Suspect(s)' medication or drug use: Unreported.
Suspect(s)' criminal history: Suspect was recently suspended for three days after setting off a smoke bomb in the school.
Warning signs: Suspect told another youth that he intended to shoot the school administrator.
Suspect(s)' country of citizenship: Unreported.
Suspect(s)' religious affiliation: Unreported.
Alleged reason for shooting: Protest authority. Suspect attempted to kill a school administrator after getting into trouble at school.
Metal detectors present?: No.
Location & time of shooting: Suspect shot through the school office window from the hallway about 2:00 p.m.
For more information, contact: Julie Shaw (victim), Manchester Police Chief Bruce Trapp, Superintendent Joseph Kirchoff and Delaware County Attorney Lou Walker.
Citations/sources: (Teen charged after firing, 1994, p. 1M) (Hovelson, 1994, p. 1M) (Swinton, 1994, p. 1)

\#1051
Location of shooting: Stadium High School
Date: 11/15/1994
City, State: Tacoma, WA
Name of victim(s) killed: Thorin Baldwin (shooter).
Age of victim(s) killed: 17
Name of victim(s) injured: N/A.
Age of victim(s) injured: N/A.
Name of suspect(s)/shooter(s): Thorin Baldwin
Age of suspect(s)/shooter(s): 17
Weapon(s): Handgun
High capacity magazine(s)?: Unreported.
Weapon(s) legally acquired by suspect(s)/shooter(s)?: No. Stolen from parents.
\# of people killed: 1
\# of people injured: 0
Total \# of victims: 1

Time suspect(s)/shooter(s) were apprehended or killed?: Suicide.

Suspect(s)' mental illness: Unreported.

Suspect(s)' medication or drug use: Unreported.

Suspect(s)' criminal history: Unreported.

Warning signs: Shooter's friend, Alex Auty, said he patted his pocket and said he was carrying a gun during the afternoon he committed suicide. Auty thought the shooter was kidding.

Suspect(s)' country of citizenship: Unreported.

Suspect(s)' religious affiliation: Unreported.

Alleged reason for shooting: Unreported.

Metal detectors present?: Unreported.

Location & time of shooting: Shooting occurred on the third floor of the school in the afternoon.

For more information, contact: School Board President Pat McCarthy.

Citations/sources: (National School Safety Center, 2010) (Porterfield, Gordon, & Marchionni, 1994, p. A1)

#1050
Location of shooting: University of Albany
Date: 12/14/1994

City, State: Albany, NY

Name of victim(s) killed: N/A.

Age of victim(s) killed: N/A.

Name of victim(s) injured: Jason McEnaney

Age of victim(s) injured: 19

Name of suspect(s)/shooter(s): Ralph J. Tortorici.

Age of suspect(s)/shooter(s): 26

Weapon(s): Remington .270-caliber rifle

High capacity magazine(s)?: Unreported.

Weapon(s) legally acquired by suspect(s)/shooter(s)?: Unreported.

# of people killed: 0

# of people injured: 1

Total # of victims: 1

Time suspect(s)/shooter(s) were apprehended or killed?: Suspect was disarmed by the hostages two hours after entering the classroom.

Suspect(s)' mental illness: Defense attorney claimed suspect suffered from schizophrenia. Suspect was found sane by jury.

Suspect(s)' medication or drug use: Unreported.

Suspect(s)' criminal history: Faced cocaine possession charges from a November 29, 1994 arrest. History of motor-vehicle violations and had his license revoked three years prior to shooting.

Warning signs: Unreported.

Suspect(s)' country of citizenship: Unreported.

Suspect(s)' religious affiliation: Unreported.

Alleged reason for shooting: Protest authority. Suspect had a grievance over financial aid and wanted to speak with President Clinton, Governor Mario Cuomo, and the SUNY at Albany bursar.

Metal detectors present?: N/A.

Location & time of shooting: Shooting occurred on a university campus within a school classroom after 11:00 a.m. as the suspect held 35 students hostage for 2 hours.

For more information, contact: Albany Deputy Police Chief Robert Grebert and Jason McEnaney (victim who disarmed suspect).

Citations/sources: (Bauder, 1994, p. A-2) (Hughes, 1994, p. 4A) (Gunman found to be incompetent, 1995, p. A6)

#1049
Location of shooting: Cardozo Senior High School (Cardozo Education Campus)
Date: 1/5/1995
City, State: Washington, DC
Name of victim(s) killed: Antar A. Hall.
Age of victim(s) killed: 16
Name of victim(s) injured: N/A.
Age of victim(s) injured: N/A.
Name of suspect(s)/shooter(s): Unnamed youth (shooter) & Phillip Baines (accomplice).
Age of suspect(s)/shooter(s): 14 & 19
Weapon(s): .380-caliber pistol
High capacity magazine(s)?: Unreported.
Weapon(s) legally acquired by suspect(s)/shooter(s)?: No. Suspect received weapon from Baines, who was also charged with first-degree murder in victim's death.
# of people killed: 1
# of people injured: 0
Total # of victims: 1
Time suspect(s)/shooter(s) were apprehended or killed?: Unreported.
Suspect(s)' mental illness: Unreported.
Suspect(s)' medication or drug use: Unreported.
Suspect(s)' criminal history: Baines was arrested Jan. 31st in Rialto, California, on a robbery charge.
Warning signs: Unreported.
Suspect(s)' country of citizenship: Unreported.
Suspect(s)' religious affiliation: Unreported.
Alleged reason for shooting: Argument.
Metal detectors present?: Yes.
Location & time of shooting: Shooting occurred at the entrance to the school.
For more information, contact: Inspector Charles E. Collins.

Citations/sources: (National School Safety Center, 2010, p. 11) (Murder suspect, 1995, p. A7) (Duggan & Melillo, 1995) (Lewis, 1995a) (Congress of the U.S., 1999, p. 79) (Cardozo High School III, 2006)

#1048
Location of shooting: Palm Beach Gardens High School
Date: 1/10/1995
City, State: Palm Beach Gardens, FL
Name of victim(s) killed: Robert Warthen (shooter).
Age of victim(s) killed: 15
Name of victim(s) injured: N/A.
Age of victim(s) injured: N/A.
Name of suspect(s)/shooter(s): Robert Warthen.
Age of suspect(s)/shooter(s): 15
Weapon(s): Silver-plated .25-caliber Raven semiautomatic pistol
High capacity magazine(s)?: Unreported.
Weapon(s) legally acquired by suspect(s)/shooter(s)?: No.
# of people killed: 1
# of people injured: 0
Total # of victims: 1
Time suspect(s)/shooter(s) were apprehended or killed?: Suicide.
Suspect(s)' mental illness: Unreported.
Suspect(s)' medication or drug use: Unreported.
Suspect(s)' criminal history: Unreported.
Warning signs: 45 minutes before the student shot himself, he left a message on his sister's answering machine, telling her she was his favorite sister and that he will miss her and loved her, then said goodbye and hung up.
Suspect(s)' country of citizenship: Unreported.
Suspect(s)' religious affiliation: Unreported.
Alleged reason for shooting: Unreported.
Metal detectors present?: No.
Location & time of shooting: Student shot himself in an open hallway near the school cafeteria.
For more information, contact: Palm Beach Gardens Chief James O. Fitzgerald, Coach Barry Hill, Chief of School Board Police Jim Kelly and School Board Spokeswoman Sue Walters.
Citations/sources: (National School Safety Center, 2010, p. 11) (Nealy, 1995, p. 2B) (Athans, 1995, p. 3B) (Congress of the U.S., 1999, p. 79)

#1047
Location of shooting: Garfield High School
Date: 1/12/1995

City, State: Seattle, WA
Name of victim(s) killed: N/A.
Age of victim(s) killed: N/A.
Name of victim(s) injured: Rachel Thompson & Hassan Coaxum Jr.
Age of victim(s) injured: 15 & 18
Name of suspect(s)/shooter(s): Unnamed student due to age.
Age of suspect(s)/shooter(s): 15
Weapon(s): 9mm gun
High capacity magazine(s)?: Unreported.
Weapon(s) legally acquired by suspect(s)/shooter(s)?: No. Suspect stole gun from his grandfather's glove compartment.
# of people killed: 0
# of people injured: 2
Total # of victims: 2
Time suspect(s)/shooter(s) were apprehended or killed?: Suspect was arrested after the shooting in a field outside the school by two on-duty officers assigned to the school.
Suspect(s)' mental illness: Unreported.
Suspect(s)' medication or drug use: Unreported.
Suspect(s)' criminal history: Unreported.
Warning signs: Unreported.
Suspect(s)' country of citizenship: Unreported.
Suspect(s)' religious affiliation: Unreported.
Alleged reason for shooting: Argument and fight.
Metal detectors present?: No.
Location & time of shooting: Shooting occurred in a school stairwell, near the cafeteria filled with over 100 students.
For more information, contact: Rachel Gruenwald (victim), Seattle Public Schools Assistant Superintendent Arlene Ackerman, Police Spokesman Sean O'Donnell, School Board President Linda Harris and Garfield Principal Ammon McWashington.
Citations/sources: (Henderson & Lilly, 1995) (Gruenwald & Smith, 2018) (2 wounded in school, 1995, p. 4B) (Haines, Birkland, Lilly, & Simon, 1995)

#1046
Location of shooting: Sacred Heart School (Private Catholic Christian PreK - 8 school)
Date: 1/23/1995
City, State: Redlands, CA
Name of victim(s) killed: John Sirola Jr. (shooter)
Age of victim(s) killed: 13
Name of victim(s) injured: Richard Facciolo (Principal).
Age of victim(s) injured: 43
Name of suspect(s)/shooter(s): John Sirola Jr.

Age of suspect(s)/shooter(s): 13

Weapon(s): 12-guage sawed-off shotgun

High capacity magazine(s)?: Unreported.

Weapon(s) legally acquired by suspect(s)/shooter(s)?: No.

# of people killed: 1

# of people injured: 1

Total # of victims: 2

Time suspect(s)/shooter(s) were apprehended or killed?: Suicide.

Suspect(s)' mental illness: Unreported.

Suspect(s)' medication or drug use: Unreported.

Suspect(s)' criminal history: Unreported.

Warning signs: Unreported.

Suspect(s)' country of citizenship: Unreported.

Suspect(s)' religious affiliation: Christian: Catholic.

Alleged reason for shooting: Protest authority. Suspect had problems with dress code and authority. Suspect shot principal 90 minutes after being told he needed to improve his attitude.

Metal detectors present?: Unreported.

Location & time of shooting: Suspect shot the principal in his office and then shot himself outside of the school.

For more information, contact: Principal Richard Facciolo (victim), Police Spokesman Sgt. Marc Tilson, Redlands Police Chief Lewis Nelson, Footnall Coach Takishi Kinji and Suspect's sixth-grade teacher Judy Monroe.

Citations/sources: (National School Safety Center, 2010, p. 11) (Montano, 1995, p. B1) (Hanna, 1995, p. B1) (Gorman, 1995, p. A3 & A18) (Congress of the U.S., 1999, p. 80) (Church & Valenzuela, 1995, p. A1 & A6)

#1045

Location of shooting: University of North Carolina

Date: 1/26/1995

City, State: Chapel Hill, NC

Name of victim(s) killed: Kevin Reichardt & Ralph W. Walker, Jr.

Age of victim(s) killed: 20 & 42

Name of victim(s) injured: Bill Leone, Demetrise Stephenson (Chapel Hill Police Officer) & Wendell Williamson (shooter).

Age of victim(s) injured: 26, 24 & 26

Name of suspect(s)/shooter(s): Wendell Williamson.

Age of suspect(s)/shooter(s): 26

Weapon(s): .30-caliber semiautomatic M-1 Garland rifle and 75 8-round magazine clips.

High capacity magazine(s)?: No.

Weapon(s) legally acquired by suspect(s)/shooter(s)?: No. Suspect stole the weapon from his father's home.

# of people killed: 2

# of people injured: 3

Total # of victims: 5

Time suspect(s)/shooter(s) were apprehended or killed?: Suspect was shot in the legs during the shooting and tackled by a bystander.

Suspect(s)' mental illness: Schizophrenic. Declared insane by the courts and placed in a mental institution.

Suspect(s)' medication or drug use: Suspect prescribed medication for "delusional order grandiose" by his psychiatrist a year before the shooting.

Suspect(s)' criminal history: Unreported.

Warning signs: Unreported.

Suspect(s)' country of citizenship: Unreported.

Suspect(s)' religious affiliation: Unreported.

Alleged reason for shooting: Unreported.

Metal detectors present?: N/A.

Location & time of shooting: Shooting occurred outside on a university campus around 2:00 p.m.

For more information, contact: Anne Arundel County Police, Orange County District Attorney Carl Fox, Chapel Hill Police Officer Demetrise Stephenson (victim) and Police spokesman Jane Cousins.

Citations/sources: (Shooting victim was exemplary, 1995, p. 2B) (North Carolina gunman, 195, p. A3) (Victim of shooting rampage, 1995, p. C5) (M-1 Garland cuts, 1997, p. 1-9) (Terzian, 1998, p. 13A) ('I just did it,' 1995, p. 2B)

#1044

Location of shooting: Chadron Middle School

Date: 2/8/1995

City, State: Chadron, NE

Name of victim(s) killed: N/A.

Age of victim(s) killed: N/A.

Name of victim(s) injured: Andy Pope (Teacher).

Age of victim(s) injured: 35

Name of suspect(s)/shooter(s): Unreported.

Age of suspect(s)/shooter(s): 13

Weapon(s): Unreported.

High capacity magazine(s)?: Unreported.

Weapon(s) legally acquired by suspect(s)/shooter(s)?: No.

# of people killed: 0

# of people injured: 1

Total # of victims: 1

Time suspect(s)/shooter(s) were apprehended or killed?: Unreported.

Suspect(s)' mental illness: Unreported.
Suspect(s)' medication or drug use: Unreported.
Suspect(s)' criminal history: Unreported.
Warning signs: Unreported.
Suspect(s)' country of citizenship: Unreported.
Suspect(s)' religious affiliation: Unreported.
Alleged reason for shooting: Unreported.
Metal detectors present?: Unreported.
Location & time of shooting: Teacher shot while teaching in his social studies classroom.
For more information, contact: Unreported.
Citations/sources: (Coach shot at Nebraska, 1995) (Among worst U.S. school, 2011)

#1043
Location of shooting: Lake Worth High School
Date: 6/14/1995
City, State: Lake Worth, FL
Name of victim(s) killed: N/A.
Age of victim(s) killed: N/A.
Name of victim(s) injured: Erica Mosely & Dieuly Aristilde.
Age of victim(s) injured: 14 & 18
Name of suspect(s)/shooter(s): Alexander F. Kucer.
Age of suspect(s)/shooter(s): 19
Weapon(s): .45-caliber pistol
High capacity magazine(s)?: Unreported.
Weapon(s) legally acquired by suspect(s)/shooter(s)?: No. Suspect paid $100 for a gun stolen from a suburban West Palm Beach home, 8 months prior to the shooting.
# of people killed: 0
# of people injured: 2
Total # of victims: 2
Time suspect(s)/shooter(s) were apprehended or killed?: Suspect turned himself in to the Lake Worth Police Department about 10:15 p.m., approximately ten hours after the shooting.
Suspect(s)' mental illness: Unreported.
Suspect(s)' medication or drug use: Unreported.
Suspect(s)' criminal history: Convicted in 1993 of aggravated assault with a weapon after throwing two ninja-style knives at another student.
Warning signs: Unreported.
Suspect(s)' country of citizenship: U.S.A.
Suspect(s)' religious affiliation: Unreported.
Alleged reason for shooting: Fight. Feud between suspect and one of the victims since middle school.
Metal detectors present?: N/A.

Location & time of shooting: Shooting occurred in school parking lot just after final exams, at approximately 12:20 p.m.

For more information, contact: Lake Worth Police Crime Scene Supervisor Harold Ruslander.

Citations/sources: (Paola, 1995, p. 1A & 19A) (Staletovich, 1995a, p. 1A) (Staletovich, 1995b, June 16, p. 4B)

#1042
Location of shooting: Memorial Middle School
Date: 8/29/1995
City, State: Laredo, TX
Name of victim(s) killed: Elizabeth "Lizzy" Rivera.
Age of victim(s) killed: 12
Name of victim(s) injured: N/A.
Age of victim(s) injured: N/A.
Name of suspect(s)/shooter(s): Jonah Iverson.
Age of suspect(s)/shooter(s): 12
Weapon(s): .25 caliber automatic pistol
High capacity magazine(s)?: Unreported.
Weapon(s) legally acquired by suspect(s)/shooter(s)?: No.
# of people killed: 1
# of people injured: 0
Total # of victims: 1
Time suspect(s)/shooter(s) were apprehended or killed?: Unreported.
Suspect(s)' mental illness: Unreported.
Suspect(s)' medication or drug use: Unreported.
Suspect(s)' criminal history: Unreported.
Warning signs: Unreported.
Suspect(s)' country of citizenship: Unreported.
Suspect(s)' religious affiliation: Unreported.
Alleged reason for shooting: Accident.
Metal detectors present?: No.
Location & time of shooting: Victim was shot in the girl's bathroom at the middle school.

For more information, contact: Principal Sammy Moreno, Webb County Court-at-law Judge Jesus Garza and LISD public information officer Veronica Castillon.

Citations/sources: (National School Safety Center, 2010, p. 12) (Congress of the U.S., 1999, p. 80) (Reddick, 2005)

#1041
Location of shooting: Cypress Junior High School (Middle School)
Date: 9/12/1995
City, State: Memphis, TN

Name of victim(s) killed: Torenzo Maurice Bell.
Age of victim(s) killed: 15
Name of victim(s) injured: N/A.
Age of victim(s) injured: N/A.
Name of suspect(s)/shooter(s): Columbus Coffer.
Age of suspect(s)/shooter(s): 15
Weapon(s): .38 caliber handgun.
High capacity magazine(s)?: Unreported.
Weapon(s) legally acquired by suspect(s)/shooter(s)?: No.
# of people killed: 1
# of people injured: 0
Total # of victims: 1
Time suspect(s)/shooter(s) were apprehended or killed?: Unreported.
Suspect(s)' mental illness: Unreported.
Suspect(s)' medication or drug use: Unreported.
Suspect(s)' criminal history: Unreported.
Warning signs: Unreported.
Suspect(s)' country of citizenship: Unreported.
Suspect(s)' religious affiliation: Unreported.
Alleged reason for shooting: Fight. Argument.
Metal detectors present?: Unreported.
Location & time of shooting: Victim shot in school hallway approximately 8:45 a.m.
For more information, contact: Police Homicide Investigator Major A.L. Gray.
Citations/sources: (National School Safety Center, 2010, p. 12) (Teen killed in junior high, p. 2B) (Congress of the U.S., 1999, p. 81)

#1040
Location of shooting: Olathe North High School
Date: 9/14/1995
City, State: Olathe, KS
Name of victim(s) killed: Wilson Montenegro & Jerrell Frazier.
Age of victim(s) killed: 15 & 19
Name of victim(s) injured: Ryan Spornitz, Johnny Bruce and two other unnamed male students.
Age of victim(s) injured: 18, 23, ? & ?
Name of suspect(s)/shooter(s): Alfred Jerome Williams Jr.
Age of suspect(s)/shooter(s): 17
Weapon(s): .22-caliber Jennings semiautomatic handgun
High capacity magazine(s)?: Unreported.
Weapon(s) legally acquired by suspect(s)/shooter(s)?: No.
# of people killed: 2

# of people injured: 4

Total # of victims: 6

Time suspect(s)/shooter(s) were apprehended or killed?: Unreported.

Suspect(s)' mental illness: Unreported.

Suspect(s)' medication or drug use: Unreported.

Suspect(s)' criminal history: Unreported.

Warning signs: Unreported.

Suspect(s)' country of citizenship: Unreported.

Suspect(s)' religious affiliation: Unreported.

Alleged reason for shooting: Feud over a local high school football game.

Metal detectors present?: N/A.

Location & time of shooting: Drive-by shooting into a crowd gathered in the school parking lot during a Sunday evening pickup football game.

For more information, contact: District Judge Robery Jones, School Spokeswoman Michelle Dubay, Principal Charles Nichols, Assistant Johnson County Prosecutor Roger Nordeen and Olathe Police Lt. Joe Pruett.

Citations/sources: (National School Safety Center, 2010, p. 12) (Congress of the U.S., 1999, p. 81) (Bad blood between schools, 1995, p. 12B) (Teen charged in killings, 1995, p. A3) (Teen-ager charged, 1995, p. 13A) (Hay, 2002, p. 3A)

#1039

Location of shooting: Tavares Middle School

Date: 9/29/1995

City, State: Tavares, FL

Name of victim(s) killed: Joey Summerall

Age of victim(s) killed: 13

Name of victim(s) injured: N/A.

Age of victim(s) injured: N/A.

Name of suspect(s)/shooter(s): Keith Eugene Johnson.

Age of suspect(s)/shooter(s): 14

Weapon(s): 9mm semiautomatic handgun

High capacity magazine(s)?: No. Victim was shot with 13 bullets. One bullet was left in the chamber.

Weapon(s) legally acquired by suspect(s)/shooter(s)?: No. Shooter stole the unsecured gun from a 26-year old family friend/neighbor, who left the loaded 9mm next to the pillow on his bed.

# of people killed: 1

# of people injured: 0

Total # of victims: 1

Time suspect(s)/shooter(s) were apprehended or killed?: Deputy Sheriffs caught the shooter about 15 minutes after shooting.

Suspect(s)' mental illness: Unreported.

Suspect(s)' medication or drug use: Unreported.

Suspect(s)' criminal history: Shooter was suspended from Tavares Middle School four or five times the previous year.

Warning signs: Several students acknowledged that shooter talked about the shooting on the bus ride to school and even showed them the gun. However, no one told an adult.

Suspect(s)' country of citizenship: Unreported.

Suspect(s)' religious affiliation: Unreported.

Alleged reason for shooting: Feud. A friend of the victim told him the shooter had a gun and was planning to settle a score.

Metal detectors present?: Unreported.

Location & time of shooting: Victim shot in school courtyard.

For more information, contact: Tavares Police Chief Norb Thomas, Captain David Myers (retired) and the victim's aunt Detective Elaine Howard (Davis) (also retired).

Citations/sources: (Hayes, 2015) (Murphy & Weber, 1995) (Shaw, 1995) (National School Safety Center, 2010, p. 12) (Congress of the U.S., 1999, p. 81)

#1038
Location of shooting: Blackville-Hilda High School

Date: 10/12/1995

City, State: Blackville, SC

Name of victim(s) killed: Phyllis Senn (Math Teacher) & Toby R. Sincino (shooter).

Age of victim(s) killed: 56 & 16

Name of victim(s) injured: John Thompson.

Age of victim(s) injured: 38

Name of suspect(s)/shooter(s): Toby R. Sincino.

Age of suspect(s)/shooter(s): 16

Weapon(s): .32-caliber revolver

High capacity magazine(s)?: Unreported.

Weapon(s) legally acquired by suspect(s)/shooter(s)?: No. Gun was stolen from a car the year before.

# of people killed: 2

# of people injured: 1

Total # of victims: 3

Time suspect(s)/shooter(s) were apprehended or killed?: Suicide.

Suspect(s)' mental illness: Unreported.

Suspect(s)' medication or drug use: Unreported.

Suspect(s)' criminal history: None. Suspect was suspended from school the previous year, but was on probationary status.

Warning signs: Unreported.

Suspect(s)' country of citizenship: Unreported.

Suspect(s)' religious affiliation: Unreported.

Alleged reason for shooting: Possibly to protest authority. Suspect was suspended for making a rude gesture on the school bus & was already on probation after being expelled the previous year and was facing an expulsion hearing soon because of the suspension.

Metal detectors present?: Unreported.

Location & time of shooting: Unreported.

For more information, contact: SLED Chief Robert Stewart and Superintendent Richard Huggans.

Citations/sources: (More info: school shootings, 2010, p. 12) (National School Safety Center, 2010, p. 12) (Crews, 2016, p. 7) (Congress of the U.S., 1999, p. 81) (Smith, 1995, p. 1A & 7A) (Burgdorf, 1995, p. 1A) (Newman, Fox, Harding, Mehta, & Roth, 2004, p.237)

#1037
Location of shooting: Lindbergh High School
Date: 10/13/1995
City, State: St. Louis, MO
Name of victim(s) killed: N/A.
Age of victim(s) killed: N/A.
Name of victim(s) injured: Unnamed due to age.
Age of victim(s) injured: Unreported.
Name of suspect(s)/shooter(s): Unnamed due to age.
Age of suspect(s)/shooter(s): Unreported.
Weapon(s): Unreported.
High capacity magazine(s)?: Unreported.
Weapon(s) legally acquired by suspect(s)/shooter(s)?: Unreported.
# of people killed: 0
# of people injured: 1
Total # of victims: 1
Time suspect(s)/shooter(s) were apprehended or killed?: Suspect was taken into custody by police in the afternoon of the same day at school.

Suspect(s)' mental illness: Unreported.

Suspect(s)' medication or drug use: Unreported.

Suspect(s)' criminal history: Unreported.

Warning signs: Unreported.

Suspect(s)' country of citizenship: Unreported.

Suspect(s)' religious affiliation: Unreported.

Alleged reason for shooting: Gang-related.

Metal detectors present?: N/A.

Location & time of shooting: Shooting occurred on a school bus at approximately 6:30 a.m.

For more information, contact: Voluntary Interdistrict Student Transportation Office operations supervisor Tim Kirkman.

Citations/sources: (Student held after school bus, 1995, p. 4A) (Yaqub, 1995, p. 1A & 4A)

#1036

Location of shooting: Lake Howell High School

Date: 10/23/1995

City, State: Winter Park, FL

Name of victim(s) killed: N/A.

Age of victim(s) killed: N/A.

Name of victim(s) injured: Expeditas "Odette" Reyes (shooter).

Age of victim(s) injured: 16

Name of suspect(s)/shooter(s): Expeditas "Odette" Reyes.

Age of suspect(s)/shooter(s): 16

Weapon(s): .25-caliber blue steel Beretta

High capacity magazine(s)?: Unreported.

Weapon(s) legally acquired by suspect(s)/shooter(s)?: No. Suspect stole the gun from her mother.

# of people killed: 0

# of people injured: 1

Total # of victims: 1

Time suspect(s)/shooter(s) were apprehended or killed?: Suspect turned herself in 3 weeks after the shooting, after lying to investigators that two hooded men attacked her.

Suspect(s)' mental illness: Unreported.

Suspect(s)' medication or drug use: Unreported.

Suspect(s)' criminal history: Unreported.

Warning signs: Unreported.

Suspect(s)' country of citizenship: Unreported.

Suspect(s)' religious affiliation: Unreported.

Alleged reason for shooting: Accident. Self-inflicted wound. Suspect brought a gun to school because she dreamed she would be threatened with a knife.

Metal detectors present?: Unreported.

Location & time of shooting: Shooting occurred between two school buildings as suspect was on her way to a guidance counselor's office at 7:55 a.m.

For more information, contact: Assistant state attorney Joe d'Achille; Principal Don Smith and Sheriff Don Eslinger.

Citations/sources: (Taylor, 1995, p. D-3) (McBreen, 1995, p. A-1)

#1035

Location of shooting: Richland High School

Date: 11/15/1995

City, State: Lynnville, TN

Name of victim(s) killed: Diane Collins & Carolyn Foster (Business teacher).

Age of victim(s) killed: 14 & 58

Name of victim(s) injured: Carol Yancey (Math Teacher).
Age of victim(s) injured: 50
Name of suspect(s)/shooter(s): James Ellison "Jamie" Rouse.
Age of suspect(s)/shooter(s): 17
Weapon(s): .22 caliber Remington Viper semiautomatic rifle
High capacity magazine(s)?: Unreported.
Weapon(s) legally acquired by suspect(s)/shooter(s)?: No.
# of people killed: 2
# of people injured: 1
Total # of victims: 3
Time suspect(s)/shooter(s) were apprehended or killed?: Suspect was wrestled to the ground after shooting.
Suspect(s)' mental illness: Unreported.
Suspect(s)' medication or drug use: Suspect began drinking and doing drugs in high school.
Suspect(s)' criminal history: Unreported.
Warning signs: The suspect told five friends. One friend drove shooter to school on the morning of the attack. "He saw that I had the gun," recalls Rouse. "I remember him making some, a comment like, 'So, you're really going to do it, aren't you?' The suspect said, 'I guess I wanted someone to stop me.'"
Suspect(s)' country of citizenship: Unreported.
Suspect(s)' religious affiliation: Unreported.
Alleged reason for shooting: Bullying, physical abuse from father, and to Protest authority. Shooter claims he was bullied by classmates for being small and too quiet. In high school, he was "ostracized by kids who thought he worshiped the devil." Blamed school and teachers.
Metal detectors present?: Unreported.
Location & time of shooting: Shooting occurred in school hallway.
For more information, contact: Unreported.
Citations/sources: (Leung, 2018) (National School Safety Center, 2010, p. 13) (Crews, 2016, p. 7) (Congress of the U.S., 1999, p. 82) (Newman, Fox, Harding, Mehta, & Roth, 2004, p.237 & 245) (School violence: metro area, 1997, p. 12A) (U.S. Supreme Court rules, 2016)

#1034
Location of shooting: Oxon Hill High School
Date: 12/14/1995
City, State: Oxon Hill, MD
Name of victim(s) killed: Charles "Chuckie" Marsh.
Age of victim(s) killed: 17
Name of victim(s) injured: N/A.
Age of victim(s) injured: N/A.
Name of suspect(s)/shooter(s): Masked youths.
Age of suspect(s)/shooter(s): Unreported.

<u>Weapon(s)</u>: Unreported.
<u>High capacity magazine(s)?</u>: Unreported.
<u>Weapon(s) legally acquired by suspect(s)/shooter(s)?</u>: No.
<u># of people killed</u>: 1
<u># of people injured</u>: 0
<u>Total # of victims</u>: 1
<u>Time suspect(s)/shooter(s) were apprehended or killed?</u>: Unreported.
<u>Suspect(s)' mental illness</u>: Unreported.
<u>Suspect(s)' medication or drug use</u>: Unreported.
<u>Suspect(s)' criminal history</u>: Unreported.
<u>Warning signs</u>: Unreported.
<u>Suspect(s)' country of citizenship</u>: Unreported.
<u>Suspect(s)' religious affiliation</u>: Unreported.
<u>Alleged reason for shooting</u>: Robbery. Suspects stole victim's coat.
<u>Metal detectors present?</u>: N/A.
<u>Location & time of shooting</u>: Shot in front of school bus stop.
<u>For more information, contact</u>: Unreported.
<u>Citations/sources</u>: (National School Safety Center, 2010, p. 13) (Frazier, 1996) (Congress of the U.S., 1999, p. 82)

#1033
Location of shooting: Girard High School
<u>Date</u>: 1/2/1996
<u>City, State</u>: Girald, PA
<u>Name of victim(s) killed</u>: John Pegg (shooter).
<u>Age of victim(s) killed</u>: 16
<u>Name of victim(s) injured</u>: N/A.
<u>Age of victim(s) injured</u>: N/A.
<u>Name of suspect(s)/shooter(s)</u>: John Pegg.
<u>Age of suspect(s)/shooter(s)</u>: 16
<u>Weapon(s)</u>: Unreported.
<u>High capacity magazine(s)?</u>: Unreported.
<u>Weapon(s) legally acquired by suspect(s)/shooter(s)?</u>: No.
<u># of people killed</u>: 1
<u># of people injured</u>: 0
<u>Total # of victims</u>: 1
<u>Time suspect(s)/shooter(s) were apprehended or killed?</u>: Suicide.
<u>Suspect(s)' mental illness</u>: Unreported.
<u>Suspect(s)' medication or drug use</u>: Unreported.
<u>Suspect(s)' criminal history</u>: Unreported.
<u>Warning signs</u>: Unreported.

Suspect(s)' country of citizenship: Unreported.
Suspect(s)' religious affiliation: Unreported.
Alleged reason for shooting: Unreported.
Metal detectors present?: Unreported.
Location & time of shooting: Student shot himself in the head in a school stairway just after 8:00 a.m.
For more information, contact: Superintendent Wally Blucas
Citations/sources: (National School Safety Center, 2010, p. 13) (Congress of the U.S., 1999, p. 82) (Teen shoots himself, 1996, p. 2) (Suicide at Erie school, 1996, p. B-3)

#1032
Location of shooting: Winston Education Center (Martha H. Winston Community School, Grades PreK - 8)
Date: 1/19/1996
City, State: Washington, D.C.
Name of victim(s) killed: Damion Blocker.
Age of victim(s) killed: 14
Name of victim(s) injured: N/A.
Age of victim(s) injured: N/A.
Name of suspect(s)/shooter(s): Darrick Evans (shooter) & William Arnell Batchelor Jr. (accomplice).
Age of suspect(s)/shooter(s): 16 & 18
Weapon(s): Revolver
High capacity magazine(s)?: Unreported.
Weapon(s) legally acquired by suspect(s)/shooter(s)?: No.
# of people killed: 1
# of people injured: 0
Total # of victims: 1
Time suspect(s)/shooter(s) were apprehended or killed?: Unreported.
Suspect(s)' mental illness: Unreported.
Suspect(s)' medication or drug use: Unreported.
Suspect(s)' criminal history: Unreported.
Warning signs: Unreported.
Suspect(s)' country of citizenship: Unreported.
Suspect(s)' religious affiliation: Unreported.
Alleged reason for shooting: Feud.
Metal detectors present?: Unreported.
Location & time of shooting: Victim was shot in school stairwell.
For more information, contact: Unreported.
Citations/sources: (Miller, 1997) (National School Safety Center, 2010, p. 13) (Crews, 2016, p. 7) (Congress of the U.S., 1999, p. 82) (Death in the schools, 1997, p. 2E) (Brown & Kyriakos, 1996)

#1031

Location of shooting: East High School

Date: 1/26/1996

City, State: Memphis, TN

Name of victim(s) killed: Glenn Taylor, Jr.

Age of victim(s) killed: 15

Name of victim(s) injured: N/A.

Age of victim(s) injured: N/A.

Name of suspect(s)/shooter(s): Maria Maclin.

Age of suspect(s)/shooter(s): Unreported.

Weapon(s): Unreported.

High capacity magazine(s)?: Unreported.

Weapon(s) legally acquired by suspect(s)/shooter(s)?: No.

# of people killed: 1

# of people injured: 0

Total # of victims: 1

Time suspect(s)/shooter(s) were apprehended or killed?: Unreported.

Suspect(s)' mental illness: Unreported.

Suspect(s)' medication or drug use: Unreported.

Suspect(s)' criminal history: Unreported.

Warning signs: Unreported.

Suspect(s)' country of citizenship: Unreported.

Suspect(s)' religious affiliation: Unreported.

Alleged reason for shooting: Fight stemming from $100 allegedly stolen from the victim's sister and the slashing of suspect's sister's tires.

Metal detectors present?: N/A.

Location & time of shooting: Shooting occurred in school parking lot after a high school basketball game.

For more information, contact: Unreported.

Citations/sources: (National School Safety Center, 2010, p. 13) (Congress of the U.S., 1999, p. 83) (State v. Maria Maclin, 1998)

#1030

Location of shooting: Frontier Junior High School (Middle School)

Date: 2/2/1996

City, State: Moses Lake, WA

Name of victim(s) killed: Manuel Vela, Arnold F. Fritz & Leona D. Caires (Teacher).

Age of victim(s) killed: 14, 14 & 49

Name of victim(s) injured: Natalie Hintz.

Age of victim(s) injured: 13.

Name of suspect(s)/shooter(s): Barry Dale Loukaitis.
Age of suspect(s)/shooter(s): 14
Weapon(s): Hunting rifle, two handguns and a cartridge belt with 70 rounds of ammunition.
High capacity magazine(s)?: Unreported.
Weapon(s) legally acquired by suspect(s)/shooter(s)?: No.
# of people killed: 3
# of people injured: 1
Total # of victims: 4
Time suspect(s)/shooter(s) were apprehended or killed?: Suspect was disarmed and apprehended by physical education teacher, John M. Lane, shortly after shooting began.
Suspect(s)' mental illness: Depressed and possibly mentally ill. Suspect's mother planned to commit suicide.
Suspect(s)' medication or drug use: Unreported.
Suspect(s)' criminal history: Unreported.
Warning signs: Told friends, it would be "cool" to go on a killing spree like the characters in the movie "Natural Born Killers." Students reported hearing two days before incident that Loukitas "was going to kill someone before he died."
Suspect(s)' country of citizenship: Unreported.
Suspect(s)' religious affiliation: Unreported.
Alleged reason for shooting: Bullying.
Metal detectors present?: Unreported.
Location & time of shooting: Victims shot in school classroom at approximately 2:00 p.m.
For more information, contact: Police Chief Dean Mitchell; Sgt. Dennis Duke and Physical Education Teacher John M. Lane.
Citations/sources: (National School Safety Center, 2010, p. 13 & 14) (Crews, 2016, p. 6) (Lebrun, 2009, p. 173 & 174) (Congress of the U.S., 1999, p. 83) (Young student kills teacher, 1996, p. A3) (Honors student arrested, 1996, p. A-6) (Geranios, 2017a) (Newman, Fox, Harding, Mehta, & Roth, 2004, p.237, 248, & 252) (School shootings in Washington, 2012) (School violence: metro area, 1997, p. 12A)

#1029
Location of shooting: Mid-Peninsula High School
Date: 2/8/1996
City, State: Menlo Park, CA
Name of victim(s) killed: Douglas Bradley (shooter).
Age of victim(s) killed: 16
Name of victim(s) injured: Unnamed male due to age.
Age of victim(s) injured: 14
Name of suspect(s)/shooter(s): Douglas Bradley.
Age of suspect(s)/shooter(s): 16
Weapon(s): .38-caliber revolver

High capacity magazine(s)?: Unreported.
Weapon(s) legally acquired by suspect(s)/shooter(s)?: No.
# of people killed: 1
# of people injured: 1
Total # of victims: 2
Time suspect(s)/shooter(s) were apprehended or killed?: Suicide.
Suspect(s)' mental illness: Clinically depressed.
Suspect(s)' medication or drug use: Unreported.
Suspect(s)' criminal history: Unreported.
Warning signs: Suspect had voiced suicidal thoughts. He also asked two friends to help him get a gun, but they did not comply.
Suspect(s)' country of citizenship: Unreported.
Suspect(s)' religious affiliation: Unreported.
Alleged reason for shooting: Depression. Upset over problems with girlfriend.
Metal detectors present?: N/A.
Location & time of shooting: Shooting took place on the school basketball courts, just before 11:00 a.m.
For more information, contact: Palo Alto Police Agent Jean Krahulec, School Headmaster Philip Bliss and Police Officer Tami Gage.
Citations/sources: (National School Safety Center, 2010, p. 14) (Congress of the U.S., 1999, p. 83) (Mitchell, 1996, p. A-3) (Boy in high school shooting spree, 1996, p. C-8)

#1028
Location of shooting: West Philadelphia High School
Date: 2/16/1996
City, State: Philadelphia, PA
Name of victim(s) killed: N/A.
Age of victim(s) killed: N/A.
Name of victim(s) injured: Rojah Morris.
Age of victim(s) injured: 16
Name of suspect(s)/shooter(s): Lamar Congleton.
Age of suspect(s)/shooter(s): 18
Weapon(s): Silver handgun
High capacity magazine(s)?: Unreported.
Weapon(s) legally acquired by suspect(s)/shooter(s)?: Unreported.
# of people killed: 0
# of people injured: 1
Total # of victims: 1
Time suspect(s)/shooter(s) were apprehended or killed?: Suspect turned himself in three days after the shooting.
Suspect(s)' mental illness: Unreported.

Suspect(s)' medication or drug use: Unreported.

Suspect(s)' criminal history: Unreported.

Warning signs: Unreported.

Suspect(s)' country of citizenship: Unreported.

Suspect(s)' religious affiliation: Unreported.

Alleged reason for shooting: Robbery. Victim tried to break a $20 bill, but was robbed by drug dealers. The suspect shot him when he tried to get his money back.

Metal detectors present?: Unreported.

Location & time of shooting: Shooting occurred in the school basement.

For more information, contact: Common Please Judge Tama Myers and Assistant District Attorney Elizabeth Greenfield.

Citations/sources: (Bello, 1996, p. 23) (Woodall, 1996, p. B2)

#1027

Location of shooting: Jenkins High School

Date: 2/22/1996

City, State: Savannah, GA

Name of victim(s) killed: Dwayne Cedric Martin.

Age of victim(s) killed: 17

Name of victim(s) injured: N/A.

Age of victim(s) injured: N/A.

Name of suspect(s)/shooter(s): Keith Antoine Green.

Age of suspect(s)/shooter(s): 15

Weapon(s): .380 semi-automatic pistol

High capacity magazine(s)?: Unreported.

Weapon(s) legally acquired by suspect(s)/shooter(s)?: No.

# of people killed: 1

# of people injured: 0

Total # of victims: 1

Time suspect(s)/shooter(s) were apprehended or killed?: Unreported.

Suspect(s)' mental illness: Unreported.

Suspect(s)' medication or drug use: Unreported.

Suspect(s)' criminal history: In 1994, suspect was convicted for obstructing a police officer and disorderly conduct at Wilder Middle School, armed robbery, robbery and battery.

Warning signs: Unreported.

Suspect(s)' country of citizenship: Unreported.

Suspect(s)' religious affiliation: Unreported.

Alleged reason for shooting: Feud that lasted several days.

Metal detectors present?: N/A.

Location & time of shooting: Shooting occurred outside the science technology school building.

For more information, contact: Acting Chatham County Police Manager Billy Freeman.

Citations/sources: (National School Safety Center, 2010, p. 14) (Congress of the U.S., 1999, p. 83) (2 deaths stun students, 1996, p. B5) (Death suit, 1996, p. C9)

#1026

Location of shooting: Beaumont High School

Date: 2/29/1996

City, State: St. Louis, MO

Name of victim(s) killed: Diamond Taylor (unborn child) & Kyunia Taylor.

Age of victim(s) killed: 6 months in mother's womb & 15

Name of victim(s) injured: Richard Lanemann (Bus Driver).

Age of victim(s) injured: 60

Name of suspect(s)/shooter(s): Malik J. Nettles (shooter) and Mark Boyd (Contracted shooter).

Age of suspect(s)/shooter(s): 21 & 29

Weapon(s): 9mm pistol

High capacity magazine(s)?: Unreported.

Weapon(s) legally acquired by suspect(s)/shooter(s)?: Unreported.

# of people killed: 2

# of people injured: 1

Total # of victims: 3

Time suspect(s)/shooter(s) were apprehended or killed?: Suspect arrested 2 months after shooting. Nettles surrendered to police on April 30, 1996 after the 9mm pistol taken from him by police was found connected to Taylor's death. Boyd was indicted on May 31, 1996.

Suspect(s)' mental illness: Unreported.

Suspect(s)' medication or drug use: Unreported.

Suspect(s)' criminal history: Unreported.

Warning signs: Unreported.

Suspect(s)' country of citizenship: Unreported.

Suspect(s)' religious affiliation: Unreported.

Alleged reason for shooting: Contract killing. Boyd paid Nettles $4,000 to kill Taylor because she was fathering his baby whom he allegedly believed would be born retarded.

Metal detectors present?: N/A.

Location & time of shooting: Shooting occurred on a school bus.

For more information, contact: St. Louis Homicide Commander Capt. David Heath.

Citations/sources: (National School Safety Center, 2010, p. 14) (Congress of the U.S., 1999, p. 83) (Bryan, 1996a, p. 10 a) (Bryant, 1998, p. 15) (Bower, 1996, p. 1D & 12D) (Grand jury indicts man, 1996, p. 5B) (Chronology in killing, 1996, p. 7A)

1025

Location of shooting: North Stanly High School

Date: 3/11/1996

City, State: New London, NC
Name of victim(s) killed: Jamie Hurley (shooter).
Age of victim(s) killed: 15
Name of victim(s) injured: N/A.
Age of victim(s) injured: N/A.
Name of suspect(s)/shooter(s): Jamie Hurley.
Age of suspect(s)/shooter(s): 15
Weapon(s): 9mm pistol
High capacity magazine(s)?: No. The weapon only had 9 bullets.
Weapon(s) legally acquired by suspect(s)/shooter(s)?: No.
# of people killed: 1
# of people injured: 0
Total # of victims: 1
Time suspect(s)/shooter(s) were apprehended or killed?: Suicide.
Suspect(s)' mental illness: Unreported.
Suspect(s)' medication or drug use: Unreported.
Suspect(s)' criminal history: Unreported.
Warning signs: No.
Suspect(s)' country of citizenship: Unreported.
Suspect(s)' religious affiliation: Unreported.
Alleged reason for shooting: Unreported.
Metal detectors present?: Unreported.
Location & time of shooting: Student shot himself inside of his 4-period algebra class, just before taking a quiz.
For more information, contact: Sheriff Joe Lowder.
Citations/sources: (National School Safety Center, 2010, p. 14) (Congress of the U.S., 1999, p. 83) (Troubled teen's in-school suicide, 1996, p. 2A)

#1024
Location of shooting: Talladega High School
Date: 4/11/1996
City, State: Talladega, AL
Name of victim(s) killed: Bobby Roberson, Jr.
Age of victim(s) killed: 18
Name of victim(s) injured: N/A.
Age of victim(s) injured: N/A.
Name of suspect(s)/shooter(s): Steven Curry.
Age of suspect(s)/shooter(s): 16
Weapon(s): 12-gauge shotgun
High capacity magazine(s)?: Unreported.
Weapon(s) legally acquired by suspect(s)/shooter(s)?: No.

# of people killed: 1

# of people injured: 0

Total # of victims: 1

Time suspect(s)/shooter(s) were apprehended or killed?: Suspect ran into the principal's office after the shooting and was taken into custody by Talladega Police.

Suspect(s)' mental illness: Unreported.

Suspect(s)' medication or drug use: Unreported.

Suspect(s)' criminal history: Unreported.

Warning signs: Unreported.

Suspect(s)' country of citizenship: Unreported.

Suspect(s)' religious affiliation: Unreported.

Alleged reason for shooting: Argument.

Metal detectors present?: N/A.

Location & time of shooting: Shooting occurred in school parking lot about 3:00 p.m.

For more information, contact: Unreported.

Citations/sources: (National School Safety Center, 2010, p. 14) (Congress of the U.S., 1999, p. 84) (Teen charged in classmate's death, 1996, p. 12A)

#1023

Location of shooting: Alexander Junior High School (Middle School)

Date: 4/15/1996

City, State: Brookhaven, MS

Name of victim(s) killed: N/A.

Age of victim(s) killed: N/A.

Name of victim(s) injured: Travis Pendelton.

Age of victim(s) injured: 16

Name of suspect(s)/shooter(s): Don Harvey Bolds.

Age of suspect(s)/shooter(s): 15

Weapon(s): Shotgun

High capacity magazine(s)?: Unreported.

Weapon(s) legally acquired by suspect(s)/shooter(s)?: No.

# of people killed: 0

# of people injured: 1

Total # of victims: 1

Time suspect(s)/shooter(s) were apprehended or killed?: Unreported.

Suspect(s)' mental illness: Unreported.

Suspect(s)' medication or drug use: Unreported.

Suspect(s)' criminal history: Unreported.

Warning signs: Suspect hid the shotgun in his pants' leg, concealed it under his coat and boarded his school bus. Some witnesses said they noticed the suspect walking "stiff-legged" after getting off the bus.

Suspect(s)' country of citizenship: Unreported.
Suspect(s)' religious affiliation: Unreported.
Alleged reason for shooting: Feud.
Metal detectors present?: Unreported.
Location & time of shooting: Shooting occurred just before 8:00 a.m. on the school's campus.
For more information, contact: Brookhaven Police Chief Fred McKee and District Attorney Dunn Lampton.
Citations/sources: (School violence: metro area, 1997, p. 12A) (Student feud ends with Lincoln, 1996, p. 1) (Brookhaven teen facing, 1996, p. 4B)

#1022
Location of shooting: Bingham Middle School
Date: 5/14/1996
City, State: Taylorsville, UT
Name of victim(s) killed: Justin Allgood (shooter).
Age of victim(s) killed: 15
Name of victim(s) injured: Sula Bearden (Bus driver).
Age of victim(s) injured: 37
Name of suspect(s)/shooter(s): Justin Allgood.
Age of suspect(s)/shooter(s): 15
Weapon(s): .357-caliber Magnum
High capacity magazine(s)?: Unreported.
Weapon(s) legally acquired by suspect(s)/shooter(s)?: No. Suspect stole weapon from parent's gun cabinet.
# of people killed: 1
# of people injured: 1
Total # of victims: 2
Time suspect(s)/shooter(s) were apprehended or killed?: Suicide.
Suspect(s)' mental illness: Unreported.
Suspect(s)' medication or drug use: Unreported.
Suspect(s)' criminal history: None.
Warning signs: Unreported.
Suspect(s)' country of citizenship: Unreported.
Suspect(s)' religious affiliation: Unreported.
Alleged reason for shooting: Unreported. Possibly due to grief over death of friend, Jason Collier, in a car accident. Shooter boarded a school bus, shot the driver, then commandeering the bus crashing it then committed suicide. Two obituaries of his dead friends were with his body.
Metal detectors present?: N/A
Location & time of shooting: Shooting occurred on school bus.
For more information, contact: Bus Driver Sula Bearden (victim), Salt Lake City Sheriff Aaron Kennard, Sgt. Jim Potter and Retired Sheriff Deputy Dick Johnson.

Citations/sources: (National School Safety Center, 2010, p. 14) (Congress of the U.S., 1999, p. 84) (High schooler crashes hijacked bus, 1996, p. A2)

#1021
Location of shooting: West Valley High School
Date: 6/4/1996
City, State: Hemet, CA
Name of victim(s) killed: Stasiu Neil Kowalski (shooter).
Age of victim(s) killed: 16
Name of victim(s) injured: N/A.
Age of victim(s) injured: N/A.
Name of suspect(s)/shooter(s): Stasiu Neil Kowalski
Age of suspect(s)/shooter(s): 16
Weapon(s): Unreported.
High capacity magazine(s)?: Unreported.
Weapon(s) legally acquired by suspect(s)/shooter(s)?: No.
# of people killed: 1
# of people injured: 0
Total # of victims: 1
Time suspect(s)/shooter(s) were apprehended or killed?: Suicide.
Suspect(s)' mental illness: Unreported.
Suspect(s)' medication or drug use: Unreported.
Suspect(s)' criminal history: Unreported.
Warning signs: Unreported.
Suspect(s)' country of citizenship: Unreported.
Suspect(s)' religious affiliation: Unreported.
Alleged reason for shooting: Unreported.
Metal detectors present?: N/A.
Location & time of shooting: Shooting occurred near the football field in the northeast corner of the school campus about the same time his classmates were arriving for school.
For more information, contact: Principal Jim Smith, Hemet Sgt. Joe Nevarez, Riverside County Sheriff's Department Spokesman Sgt. Mark Lohman, Football Coach Jim Wiesen and School District Psychologist Glenn Schumacher.
Citations/sources: (National School Safety Center, 2010) (Arballo & Moore, 1996, p. B01) (Moore & Arballo, 1996, p. B01)

#1020
Location of shooting: John Marshall High School
Date: 7/26/1996
City, State: Los Angeles, CA
Name of victim(s) killed: N/A.

Age of victim(s) killed: N/A.
Name of victim(s) injured: Alex Merida & Angela Hernandez.
Age of victim(s) injured: Unreported.
Name of suspect(s)/shooter(s): Yohao Albert Rivas.
Age of suspect(s)/shooter(s): 18
Weapon(s): 9mm handgun
High capacity magazine(s)?: Unreported.
Weapon(s) legally acquired by suspect(s)/shooter(s)?: Unreported.
# of people killed: 0
# of people injured: 2
Total # of victims: 2
Time suspect(s)/shooter(s) were apprehended or killed?: Suspect fled to his English class after the shooting where he was apprehended by law enforcement.
Suspect(s)' mental illness: Unreported.
Suspect(s)' medication or drug use: Unreported.
Suspect(s)' criminal history: Unreported.
Warning signs: Unreported.
Suspect(s)' country of citizenship: Unreported.
Suspect(s)' religious affiliation: Unreported.
Alleged reason for shooting: Gang-related.
Metal detectors present?: Unreported.
Location & time of shooting: Shooting occurred in a school stairway.
For more information, contact: Deputy Dist. Attorney James Jacobs, Principal Steve Quon, Assistant Superintendent Dan Isaacs and United Teachers-Los Angeles President Day Higuchi.
Citations/sources: (Pyle, 1996a, p. B3) (Pyle, 1996b, p. B3) (Violent death in our schools, 1998, p. 8A)

#1019
Location of shooting: San Diego State University
Date: 8/15/1996
City, State: San Diego, CA
Name of victim(s) killed: Constantinos S. Lyrintzis (Professor), Chen Liang (Professor) & D. Preston Lowrey III (Professor).
Age of victim(s) killed: 36, 32 & 44
Name of victim(s) injured: N/A.
Age of victim(s) injured: N/A.
Name of suspect(s)/shooter(s): Frederick Martin Davidson.
Age of suspect(s)/shooter(s): 36
Weapon(s): 9mm handgun & five spare 15-round magazines
High capacity magazine(s)?: No. 15-round magazines.
Weapon(s) legally acquired by suspect(s)/shooter(s)?: Unreported.

# of people killed: 3

# of people injured: 0

Total # of victims: 3

Time suspect(s)/shooter(s) were apprehended or killed?: Suspect was arrested a few minutes after the shooting by campus police.

Suspect(s)' mental illness: Unreported.

Suspect(s)' medication or drug use: Unreported.

Suspect(s)' criminal history: Unreported.

Warning signs: No. Suspect's roommate said he did not appear upset prior to the shooting.

Suspect(s)' country of citizenship: Unreported.

Suspect(s)' religious affiliation: Unreported.

Alleged reason for shooting: Protest authority. Suspect believed the three professors had conspired to keep him from getting a job.

Metal detectors present?: N/A.

Location & time of shooting: Shooting occurred in a laboratory classroom on the college campus at about 2:05 p.m.

For more information, contact: Police Lt. Jim Collins, Sgt. Rod Vandiver, Professor Joseph Katz, Graduate Dean James Cobble and Superior Court Judge William Mudd.

Citations/sources: (Slain professors called tough, p. A6) (Police: grad student hid gun, p. A6) (San Diego professors' slayer, p. A6) (Student charged in fatal shootings, 1996, p. A1 & A8) (Graduate gunman, 1996, p. A3)

#1018

Location of shooting: University of Texas

Date: 8/26/1996

City, State: San Antonio, TX

Name of victim(s) killed: Stephen Sorenson (Library employee) & Gregory Heath Tidwell (shooter).

Age of victim(s) killed: 54 & 25

Name of victim(s) injured: N/A.

Age of victim(s) injured: N/A.

Name of suspect(s)/shooter(s): Gregory Heath Tidwell.

Age of suspect(s)/shooter(s): 25

Weapon(s): .357 snub nose revolver

High capacity magazine(s)?: Unreported.

Weapon(s) legally acquired by suspect(s)/shooter(s)?: Unreported.

# of people killed: 2

# of people injured: 0

Total # of victims: 2

Time suspect(s)/shooter(s) were apprehended or killed?: Suicide.

Suspect(s)' mental illness: Unreported.

Suspect(s)' medication or drug use: Unreported.
Suspect(s)' criminal history: Unreported.
Warning signs: Unreported.
Suspect(s)' country of citizenship: Unreported.
Suspect(s)' religious affiliation: Unreported.
Alleged reason for shooting: Unreported.
Metal detectors present?: N/A.
Location & time of shooting: Shooting occurred in a university administration office on the second floor of the John Peace Library Building at approximately 4:45 p.m.
For more information, contact: UTSA Police Lt. Dan Pena, University spokeswoman Roxanne Llewellyn and USTA Police Chief Ron Seacrist.
Citations/sources: (Murder-suicide likely, 1996, p. A10) (Police say shootings, 1996, p. 3A)

#1017
Location of shooting: Penn State University
Date: 9/17/1996
City, State: University Park, PA
Name of victim(s) killed: Melanie Spalla.
Age of victim(s) killed: 21
Name of victim(s) injured: Nicholas Mensah
Age of victim(s) injured: 19
Name of suspect(s)/shooter(s): Jillian Pekkanen Robbins.
Age of suspect(s)/shooter(s): 19
Weapon(s): 7mm Mauser rifle & 7-inch stiletto-type knife
High capacity magazine(s)?: Unreported.
Weapon(s) legally acquired by suspect(s)/shooter(s)?: Unreported.
# of people killed: 1
# of people injured: 1
Total # of victims: 2
Time suspect(s)/shooter(s) were apprehended or killed?: A student disarmed the suspect during the shooting.
Suspect(s)' mental illness: Suspect had a history of manic-depression.
Suspect(s)' medication or drug use: Unreported.
Suspect(s)' criminal history: None.
Warning signs: Weeks before the shooting, the suspect had attempted suicide by swallowing a bunch of pills after being served divorce papers and sought treatment at a mental hospital.
Suspect(s)' country of citizenship: Unreported.
Suspect(s)' religious affiliation: Unreported.
Alleged reason for shooting: Unreported.
Metal detectors present?: N/A

<u>Location & time of shooting</u>: Shooting occurred on the Penn State lawn in front of the student union building.

<u>For more information, contact</u>: Penn State Director of Police Services Thomas R. Harmon, Uni-Mart co-worker Carol Witmer, Brendon Malovrh and student who disarmed the suspect.

<u>Citations/sources</u>: (Ivey, 1996a, p. A3) (Ivey, 1996b, p. 3A) (Ivey, 1996c, p. A1 & A10) (Friends, family remember victim, 1996, p. A2)

#1016

<u>Location of shooting</u>: DeKalb Alternative School (Grades 6-12)

<u>Date</u>: 9/25/1996

<u>City, State</u>: Stone Mountain, GA

<u>Name of victim(s) killed</u>: Dr. Horace P. Morgan (English teacher).

<u>Age of victim(s) killed</u>: 49

<u>Name of victim(s) injured</u>: N/A.

<u>Age of victim(s) injured</u>: N/A.

<u>Name of suspect(s)/shooter(s)</u>: David Dubose Jr.

<u>Age of suspect(s)/shooter(s)</u>: 16

<u>Weapon(s)</u>: .38-caliber revolver

<u>High capacity magazine(s)?</u>: Unreported.

<u>Weapon(s) legally acquired by suspect(s)/shooter(s)?</u>: No.

<u># of people killed</u>: 1

<u># of people injured</u>: 0

<u>Total # of victims</u>: 1

<u>Time suspect(s)/shooter(s) were apprehended or killed?</u>: Suspect was arrested moments after the shooting.

<u>Suspect(s)' mental illness</u>: Suspect found not guilty by reason of insanity.

<u>Suspect(s)' medication or drug use</u>: Unreported.

<u>Suspect(s)' criminal history</u>: Unreported.

<u>Warning signs</u>: Unreported.

<u>Suspect(s)' country of citizenship</u>: Unreported.

<u>Suspect(s)' religious affiliation</u>: Unreported.

<u>Alleged reason for shooting</u>: Unreported.

<u>Metal detectors present?</u>: Unreported.

<u>Location & time of shooting</u>: Teacher shot repeatedly in school hallway moments after the first period class bell at 8:30 a.m.

<u>For more information, contact</u>: Chief District Attorney John Petrey and Student witness Emanjula Brown.

<u>Citations/sources</u>: (National School Safety Center, 2010, p. 15) (Crews, 2016, p. 6) (Congress of the U.S., 1999, p. 84) (Oglesby, 1996, p. C8)

#1015

Location of shooting: Crestview Middle School
Date: 9/26/1996
City, State: St. Louis, MO
Name of victim(s) killed: N/A.
Age of victim(s) killed: N/A.
Name of victim(s) injured: Jodi Henry & Ghazi Khalil.
Age of victim(s) injured: 13 & 28
Name of suspect(s)/shooter(s): Two men.
Age of suspect(s)/shooter(s): Unreported.
Weapon(s): Unreported.
High capacity magazine(s)?: Unreported.
Weapon(s) legally acquired by suspect(s)/shooter(s)?: Unreported.
# of people killed: 0
# of people injured: 2
Total # of victims: 2
Time suspect(s)/shooter(s) were apprehended or killed?: Unreported.
Suspect(s)' mental illness: Unreported.
Suspect(s)' medication or drug use: Unreported.
Suspect(s)' criminal history: Unreported.
Warning signs: Unreported.
Suspect(s)' country of citizenship: Unreported.
Suspect(s)' religious affiliation: Unreported.
Alleged reason for shooting: Accident. Stray bullet from gun fight.
Metal detectors present?: N/A
Location & time of shooting: Shooting involved a stray bullet that his the victim in a school bus around 3:15 p.m.
For more information, contact: Officer Mark Sorocko.
Citations/sources: (Bryan, 1996b, p. 1A & 10 a) (Girl riding bus caught, 1996, p. 2B) (O'Neil, 1996, p. 4C)

#1014
Location of shooting: Smedley Elementary School
Date: 10/2/1996
City, State: Philadelphia, PA
Name of victim(s) killed: Lealoa "Jenny" Coles & Stacey Buxton-Boyd (Parent).
Age of victim(s) killed: 19 & 26
Name of victim(s) injured: N/A.
Age of victim(s) injured: N/A.
Name of suspect(s)/shooter(s): Steven Boyd.
Age of suspect(s)/shooter(s): 25
Weapon(s): Semiautomatic pistol

High capacity magazine(s)?: Unreported.
Weapon(s) legally acquired by suspect(s)/shooter(s)?: Unreported.
# of people killed: 2
# of people injured: 0
Total # of victims: 2
Time suspect(s)/shooter(s) were apprehended or killed?: Unreported.
Suspect(s)' mental illness: Unreported.
Suspect(s)' medication or drug use: Unreported.
Suspect(s)' criminal history: Police records show the suspect was charged April 15 and May 26 with violating a restraining order filed by Stacey Buxton-Boyd. Suspect also had a criminal record dating back to 1982 for robbery, drug violations and assault.
Warning signs: Unreported.
Suspect(s)' country of citizenship: Unreported.
Suspect(s)' religious affiliation: Unreported.
Alleged reason for shooting: Rejection. Suspect shot and killed his estranged wife and her cousin while waiting for the cousin's children to be dismissed from school.
Metal detectors present?: N/A.
Location & time of shooting: Shooting occurred in school parking lot at approximately 2:40 p.m.
For more information, contact: Unreported.
Citations/sources: (National School Safety Center, 2010, p. 15) (Congress of the U.S., 1999, p. 84) (Angeles, 1996, p. 5) (Gibbons, 1996, p. B2) (School violence: metro area, 1997, p. 12A)

#1013
Location of shooting: St. Bernard High School (Private Catholic Christian school)
Date: 10/4/1996
City, State: Playa Del Rey, CA
Name of victim(s) killed: Earoll Michael Thomas.
Age of victim(s) killed: 18
Name of victim(s) injured: Costromas Abercrombie.
Age of victim(s) injured: 18
Name of suspect(s)/shooter(s): Derald Givens.
Age of suspect(s)/shooter(s): 17
Weapon(s): .22-caliber handgun
High capacity magazine(s)?: Unreported.
Weapon(s) legally acquired by suspect(s)/shooter(s)?: No.
# of people killed: 1
# of people injured: 1
Total # of victims: 2
Time suspect(s)/shooter(s) were apprehended or killed?: Unreported.
Suspect(s)' mental illness: Unreported.

Suspect(s)' medication or drug use: Unreported.
Suspect(s)' criminal history: Unreported.
Warning signs: Unreported.
Suspect(s)' country of citizenship: Unreported.
Suspect(s)' religious affiliation: Unreported.
Alleged reason for shooting: Argument.
Metal detectors present?: N/A
Location & time of shooting: Victim shot and killed on an athletic track shortly after 10:00 p.m. following a football game between Jordan and St. Bernard High Schools.
For more information, contact: Homicide Detective Joe Lumbreras and Cal State Northridge head coach Ron Ponciano.
Citations/sources: (National School Safety Center, 2010, p. 15) (Congress of the U.S., 1999, p. 84) (High school player charged, 1996, p. B4) (Yarborough, 1996, p. B1) (Beck, 1998, p. SS6)

#1012
Location of shooting: Jacksonville Senior High School
Date: 10/9/1996
City, State: Sherwood, AR
Name of victim(s) killed: James Earl Routt.
Age of victim(s) killed: 20
Name of victim(s) injured: N/A.
Age of victim(s) injured: N/A.
Name of suspect(s)/shooter(s): Willis Ward Johnson.
Age of suspect(s)/shooter(s): 14
Weapon(s): .22-caliber revolver.
High capacity magazine(s)?: Unreported.
Weapon(s) legally acquired by suspect(s)/shooter(s)?: No.
# of people killed: 1
# of people injured: 0
Total # of victims: 1
Time suspect(s)/shooter(s) were apprehended or killed?: Unreported.
Suspect(s)' mental illness: Unreported.
Suspect(s)' medication or drug use: Unreported.
Suspect(s)' criminal history: Unreported.
Warning signs: Unreported.
Suspect(s)' country of citizenship: Unreported.
Suspect(s)' religious affiliation: Unreported.
Alleged reason for shooting: Feud.
Metal detectors present?: Unreported.
Location & time of shooting: Shooting occurred in school bus around 4:30 p.m.
For more information, contact: Police Chief James Crockett

Citations/sources: (National School Safety Center, 2010, p. 15) (Congress of the U.S., 1999, p. 85) (Student killed on school bus, 1996, p. 7A)

#1011
Location of shooting: Purdue University
Date: 10/16/1996
City, State: West Lafayette, IN
Name of victim(s) killed: Jay T. Severson (Residence Hall counselor) & Jarrod Allen Eskew (shooter).
Age of victim(s) killed: 27 & 18
Name of victim(s) injured: N/A.
Age of victim(s) injured: N/A.
Name of suspect(s)/shooter(s): Jarrod Allen Eskew.
Age of suspect(s)/shooter(s): 18
Weapon(s): 12-gauge sawed-off shotgun
High capacity magazine(s)?: Unreported.
Weapon(s) legally acquired by suspect(s)/shooter(s)?: Unreported.
# of people killed: 2
# of people injured: 0
Total # of victims: 2
Time suspect(s)/shooter(s) were apprehended or killed?: Suicide.
Suspect(s)' mental illness: Unreported.
Suspect(s)' medication or drug use: Police found cocaine in suspect's dormitory room.
Suspect(s)' criminal history: Unreported.
Warning signs: Unreported.
Suspect(s)' country of citizenship: Unreported.
Suspect(s)' religious affiliation: Christian.
Alleged reason for shooting: Unreported.
Metal detectors present?: N/A
Location & time of shooting: Shooting took place on a university third-floor dorm room around 2:50 p.m.
For more information, contact: Unreported.
Citations/sources: (Gerrety & Rahner, 1996, p. B1) (Fleming, 1996, p. A6) (Calm back but not normalcy, 1996, p. G-1)

#1010
Location of shooting: Sumner High School
Date: 10/31/1996
City, State: St. Louis, MO
Name of victim(s) killed: Lamon Jones.
Age of victim(s) killed: 17

Name of victim(s) injured: N/A.
Age of victim(s) injured: N/A.
Name of suspect(s)/shooter(s): Kembert Thomas.
Age of suspect(s)/shooter(s): 15
Weapon(s): Small caliber pistol
High capacity magazine(s)?: Unreported.
Weapon(s) legally acquired by suspect(s)/shooter(s)?: No.
# of people killed: 1
# of people injured: 0
Total # of victims: 1
Time suspect(s)/shooter(s) were apprehended or killed?: Arrested four days after shooting.
Suspect(s)' mental illness: Unreported.
Suspect(s)' medication or drug use: Unreported.
Suspect(s)' criminal history: Unreported.
Warning signs: Unreported.
Suspect(s)' country of citizenship: Unreported.
Suspect(s)' religious affiliation: Unreported.
Alleged reason for shooting: Fight involving several students.
Metal detectors present?: Yes.
Location & time of shooting: Shooting took place on a second-floor hallway. Suspect brought a pistol into the school through a side door that had been opened from the inside so he could avoid the walk-through metal detector at the school's main entrance about 8:20 a.m.

For more information, contact: St. Louis Police Chief Ronald Henderson, St. Louis Public School Superintendent Cleveland Hammonds Jr. and Mayor Freeman Bosley Jr..

Citations/sources: (National School Safety Center, 2010, p. 15) (Holleman, 1996) (Congress of the U.S., 1999, p. 85) (Bryan & Autman, 1996, p. 1A &12A)

#1009
Location of shooting: George W. Wingate High School
Date: 1/8/1997
City, State: Brooklyn, NY
Name of victim(s) killed: Dwight (Jamel) Archer.
Age of victim(s) killed: 18
Name of victim(s) injured: Booker (Teddy) Dixon, William Garcia & an unnamed student.
Age of victim(s) injured: 15, 16 & 15
Name of suspect(s)/shooter(s): Ricardo Lara, Alonza Soto & Aguilino Soto.
Age of suspect(s)/shooter(s): 20, 18 & 18
Weapon(s): Unreported.
High capacity magazine(s)?: Unreported.
Weapon(s) legally acquired by suspect(s)/shooter(s)?: Unreported.
# of people killed: 1

# of people injured: 3

Total # of victims: 4

Time suspect(s)/shooter(s) were apprehended or killed?: Unreported.

Suspect(s)' mental illness: Unreported.

Suspect(s)' medication or drug use: Unreported.

Suspect(s)' criminal history: Unreported.

Warning signs: Unreported.

Suspect(s)' country of citizenship: Unreported.

Suspect(s)' religious affiliation: Unreported.

Alleged reason for shooting: Argument.

Metal detectors present?: N/A.

Location & time of shooting: Shooting occurred at a basketball court outside the school during class at 1:15 p.m.

For more information, contact: Police Spokesman Sgt. Sean Crowley, Board of Education Spokesman David Golub, Schools Chancellor Rudy Crew and Board of Education President William Thompson.

Citations/sources: (National School Safety Center, 2010, p. 15) (Congress of the U.S., 1999, p. 85) (Farrell & Jamieson, 1997, p. 3C) (Fenner & Claffey, 1997, p. 19) (South Shore student dies, 1997, p. 5)

#1008

Location of shooting: Conniston Middle School

Date: 1/27/1997

City, State: West Palm Beach, FL

Name of victim(s) killed: John Pierre Kamel.

Age of victim(s) killed: 14

Name of victim(s) injured: N/A.

Age of victim(s) injured: N/A.

Name of suspect(s)/shooter(s): Tronneal Mangum.

Age of suspect(s)/shooter(s): 13

Weapon(s): .38-caliber pistol

High capacity magazine(s)?: Unreported.

Weapon(s) legally acquired by suspect(s)/shooter(s)?: No. Gun was stolen from a the previous owner's car, years before the shooting.

# of people killed: 1

# of people injured: 0

Total # of victims: 1

Time suspect(s)/shooter(s) were apprehended or killed?: Police caught up with the suspect in a classroom, presumably less than 30 minutes after the shooting.

Suspect(s)' mental illness: Suspect's attorney, Peter Grable, claimed the suspect had suffered brain damage from a car accident. However, no psychiatric exams were performed.

Suspect(s)' medication or drug use: Unreported.

Suspect(s)' criminal history: Unreported.

Warning signs: Classmates said the shooter had carried a gun to school before. A student on the school bus testified he witnessed the suspect tell another boy he was going to use the gun.

Suspect(s)' country of citizenship: Unreported.

Suspect(s)' religious affiliation: Unreported.

Alleged reason for shooting: Feud. Shooting occurred over a fight over an alleged stolen watch, a CD, and a beeper (pager).

Metal detectors present?: N/A.

Location & time of shooting: Shooting occurred outside of school on a sidewalk, approximately 8:40 a.m.

For more information, contact: West Palm Beach Police Officer John Claypool, Circuit Judge Roger Colton, State Attorney Barry Krischer, Schools Police Chief Jim Kelly and Schools Superintendent Joan Kowal.

Citations/sources: (Ragland, Patrick, & Barszewski, 1997) (Sweeney, 2017) (National School Safety Center, 2010, p. 15) (Congress of the U.S., 1999, p. 85) (Sterghos, 1998, p. 1A & 18A)

#1007

Location of shooting: Bunche Early Childhood Development Center (PreK - Kindergarten)

Date: 1/31/1997

City, State: Tulsa, OK

Name of victim(s) killed: Cecil Herndon.

Age of victim(s) killed: 73

Name of victim(s) injured: N/A.

Age of victim(s) injured: N/A.

Name of suspect(s)/shooter(s): Harold Douglas Glover.

Age of suspect(s)/shooter(s): 68

Weapon(s): .357 Magnum

High capacity magazine(s)?: Unreported.

Weapon(s) legally acquired by suspect(s)/shooter(s)?: Unreported.

# of people killed: 1

# of people injured: 0

Total # of victims: 1

Time suspect(s)/shooter(s) were apprehended or killed?: Unreported.

Suspect(s)' mental illness: Unreported.

Suspect(s)' medication or drug use: Unreported.

Suspect(s)' criminal history: Unreported.

Warning signs: Unreported.

Suspect(s)' country of citizenship: Unreported.

Suspect(s)' religious affiliation: Unreported.

Alleged reason for shooting: Self-defense. Argument over who would take their 4-year old grandson home.

    Metal detectors present?: Unreported.

    Location & time of shooting: Unreported.

    For more information, contact: Assistant District Attorney Tim Harris.

    Citations/sources: (Gun carrier faces, 1997, p. 5) (Jury acquits Tulsa man, 1999, p. 5)

#1006

Location of shooting: Wingfield High School

Date: 2/6/1997
City, State: Jackson, MS
Name of victim(s) killed: N/A.
Age of victim(s) killed: N/A.
Name of victim(s) injured: Johnny Lindsey.
Age of victim(s) injured: 17
Name of suspect(s)/shooter(s): Elliot Crosby.
Age of suspect(s)/shooter(s): 16
Weapon(s): Unreported.
High capacity magazine(s)?: Unreported.
Weapon(s) legally acquired by suspect(s)/shooter(s)?: No.
# of people killed: 0
# of people injured: 1
Total # of victims: 1
Time suspect(s)/shooter(s) were apprehended or killed?: Suspect was arrested 5 days after drive-by shooting.

    Suspect(s)' mental illness: Unreported.

    Suspect(s)' medication or drug use: Unreported.

    Suspect(s)' criminal history: Unreported.

    Warning signs: Unreported.

    Suspect(s)' country of citizenship: Unreported.

    Suspect(s)' religious affiliation: Unreported.

    Alleged reason for shooting: Dispute. Shooting may have been linked to a fight over a car radio that was stolen from the victim's car and possible mistaken identity.

    Metal detectors present?: N/A

    Location & time of shooting: Drive-by shooting.

    For more information, contact: Judge David Rozier, Jackson Public Schools interim Superintendent Dan Merit, Assistant Superintendent Ron Sellers and Methodist Medical Center Spokeswoman Jana Fuss.

    Citations/sources: (Wingfield teen moved, 1997, p. 3B) (Bland, 1997, p. 3B) (Oeth, 1997, p. 1A & 13A) (School violence: metro area, 1997, p. 12A)

#1005
Location of shooting: Ohio State University-Wexner Center for the Arts
Date: 2/10/1997
City, State: Columbus, OH
Name of victim(s) killed: Michael Blankenship (Ohio State Police Officer) & Mark Edgerton (shooter).
Age of victim(s) killed: 43 & 40
Name of victim(s) injured: N/A.
Age of victim(s) injured: N/A.
Name of suspect(s)/shooter(s): Mark Edgerton.
Age of suspect(s)/shooter(s): 40
Weapon(s): Two guns.
High capacity magazine(s)?: Unreported.
Weapon(s) legally acquired by suspect(s)/shooter(s)?: Unreported.
# of people killed: 2
# of people injured: 0
Total # of victims: 2
Time suspect(s)/shooter(s) were apprehended or killed?: Suicide.
Suspect(s)' mental illness: Unreported.
Suspect(s)' medication or drug use: Unreported.
Suspect(s)' criminal history: Unreported.
Warning signs: Unreported.
Suspect(s)' country of citizenship: Unreported.
Suspect(s)' religious affiliation: Unreported.
Alleged reason for shooting: Robbery. Victim was shot while responding to a reported theft.
Metal detectors present?: N/A.
Location & time of shooting: Shooting occurred on a university campus in a gallery in the largely unoccupied Wexner Center for the Arts shortly after it opened.
For more information, contact: OSU Police Chief Ron Michalec, Upper Arlington Police Sgt. Paul Schaumburg, Lt. Michael Brining, Officer Sandra J. Niciu (victim's partner) and University President Gordon Gee.
Citations/sources: (Police ID former Ohio State employee, 2015) (Suspect in killing found dead, 1997, p. 3) (Seewer, 1997, p. C8)

#1004
Location of shooting: Bethel Regional High School
Date: 2/19/1997
City, State: Bethel, AK
Name of victim(s) killed: Joshua Palacios & Ronald Dale Edwards (School Principal).
Age of victim(s) killed: 16 & 50
Name of victim(s) injured: Shane McIntyre & Russell Lamont.

Age of victim(s) injured: Unreported.

Name of suspect(s)/shooter(s): Evan Ramsey (shooter), Matthew Charles (Accomplice) & James Randall.

Age of suspect(s)/shooter(s): 16, 14 & 14

Weapon(s): 12-gauge shotgun

High capacity magazine(s)?: No.

Weapon(s) legally acquired by suspect(s)/shooter(s)?: No. Shooter stole it from his legal guardian's home.

# of people killed: 2

# of people injured: 2

Total # of victims: 4

Time suspect(s)/shooter(s) were apprehended or killed?: Suspect was apprehended moments after shooting the school principal, but just before he was able to kill himself.

Suspect(s)' mental illness: Depression.

Suspect(s)' medication or drug use: Unreported.

Suspect(s)' criminal history: Unreported.

Warning signs: Suspect planned the shooting and drew up a hit list with two friends two weeks before the shooting; warned younger brother he was planning to shut down the school for an entire year; and told a female student not to come to school on the day he was going to bring a shotgun to school.

Suspect(s)' country of citizenship: Unreported.

Suspect(s)' religious affiliation: Unreported.

Alleged reason for shooting: Bullying, rejection, protest authority, troubled family life, and abuse in foster homes.

Metal detectors present?: Unreported.

Location & time of shooting: Shooting occurred in the school common area just before classes started.

For more information, contact: Foster parent Sue Hare and Bethel Police Officer Chris Walker.

Citations/sources: (Demer, 2017) (McBride, 2017) (National School Safety Center, 2010, p. 16) (Crews, 2016, p. 6) (Lebrun, 2009, p. 174) (Congress of the U.S., 1999, p. 85) (Newman, Fox, Harding, Mehta, & Roth, 2004, p.155, 237, & 253) (Fainaru, 1998, p. A1, A10 & A11)

#1003

Location of shooting: First Coast High School

Date: 2/20/1997

City, State: Jacksonville, FL

Name of victim(s) killed: Melissa Chambliss (shooter).

Age of victim(s) killed: 17

Name of victim(s) injured: N/A.

Age of victim(s) injured: N/A.

Name of suspect(s)/shooter(s): Melissa Chambliss.
Age of suspect(s)/shooter(s): 17
Weapon(s): Pistol
High capacity magazine(s)?: Unreported.
Weapon(s) legally acquired by suspect(s)/shooter(s)?: No.
# of people killed: 1
# of people injured: 0
Total # of victims: 1
Time suspect(s)/shooter(s) were apprehended or killed?: Suicide.
Suspect(s)' mental illness: Unreported.
Suspect(s)' medication or drug use: Unreported.
Suspect(s)' criminal history: Unreported.
Warning signs: Unreported.
Suspect(s)' country of citizenship: Unreported.
Suspect(s)' religious affiliation: Unreported.
Alleged reason for shooting: Dispute. Student shot herself during a dispute with her coach. She was disheartened after performing poorly at a softball tryout for a scholarship to Santa Fe Community College in Gainesville.
Metal detectors present?: N/A.
Location & time of shooting: Student shot herself on the school baseball field.
For more information, contact: First Coast Principal Hardy Fletcher.
Citations/sources: (National School Safety Center, 2010, p. 16) (Congress of the U.S., 1999, p. 85) (Softball player dies, 1997, p. 3B) (Teen shoots herself, 1997, p. 10 a)

#1002
Location of shooting: Rancho High School
Date: 2/20/1997
City, State: Las Vegas, NV
Name of victim(s) killed: N/A.
Age of victim(s) killed: N/A.
Name of victim(s) injured: Unnamed male student due to age.
Age of victim(s) injured: 16
Name of suspect(s)/shooter(s): Martin Hernandez, a.k.a. "Flaco."
Age of suspect(s)/shooter(s): 14
Weapon(s): 9mm handgun
High capacity magazine(s)?: Unreported.
Weapon(s) legally acquired by suspect(s)/shooter(s)?: No.
# of people killed: 0
# of people injured: 1
Total # of victims: 1

Time suspect(s)/shooter(s) were apprehended or killed?: Suspect was arrested on April 9, 2019, approximately a month and a half after the drive-by shooting. A school police officer recognized him from a wanted poster.

Suspect(s)' mental illness: Unreported.
Suspect(s)' medication or drug use: Unreported.
Suspect(s)' criminal history: Unreported.
Warning signs: Unreported.
Suspect(s)' country of citizenship: Unreported.
Suspect(s)' religious affiliation: Unreported.
Alleged reason for shooting: Gang-related.
Metal detectors present?: N/A
Location & time of shooting: Drive-by shooting.
For more information, contact: School district police spokesman Ken Young.
Citations/sources: (Vegas schools, 1997, p. 1) (Rancho High shootings, p. 2B) (Scott, 1997)

#1001
Location of shooting: Pershing High School
Date: 3/17/1997
City, State: Detroit, MI
Name of victim(s) killed: Kenneth Baumgart.
Age of victim(s) killed: 16
Name of victim(s) injured: N/A.
Age of victim(s) injured: N/A.
Name of suspect(s)/shooter(s): Darrell Hagerman (shooter), Michael McCune & Larry Walker.
Age of suspect(s)/shooter(s): 16, 15 & 15
Weapon(s): Unreported.
High capacity magazine(s)?: Unreported.
Weapon(s) legally acquired by suspect(s)/shooter(s)?: No.
# of people killed: 1
# of people injured: 0
Total # of victims: 1

Time suspect(s)/shooter(s) were apprehended or killed?: McCune was arrested at about 6:00 p.m., approximately 4 hours and 15 minutes after the shooting. Hagerman and Walker were arrested at 12:45 a.m. Tuesday, approximately 10 hours after the shooting.

Suspect(s)' mental illness: Unreported.
Suspect(s)' medication or drug use: Unreported.
Suspect(s)' criminal history: Unreported.
Warning signs: Unreported.
Suspect(s)' country of citizenship: Unreported.
Suspect(s)' religious affiliation: Unreported.
Alleged reason for shooting: Fight. Feud.

Metal detectors present?: N/A

Location & time of shooting: Shooting occurred in school parking lot.

For more information, contact: Detroit Mayor Dennis Archer, Detroit Police Chief Isaiah McKinnon and Head of the Gang Squad Lt. Gerard Simon.

Citations/sources: (National School Safety Center, 2010, p. 16) (Congress of the U.S., 1999, p. 86) (Kresnak, 1997, p. 1A & 2A) (Kresnak & Siegel, 1997, 1A & 7A)

#1000
Location of shooting: McKinley Technical High School
Date: 4/15/1997
City, State: Washington, DC
Name of victim(s) killed: N/A.
Age of victim(s) killed: N/A.
Name of victim(s) injured: Joseph Bailey.
Age of victim(s) injured: 23
Name of suspect(s)/shooter(s): Dujuan Hopkins.
Age of suspect(s)/shooter(s): 18
Weapon(s): .22-caliber semiautomatic pistol
High capacity magazine(s)?: Unreported.
Weapon(s) legally acquired by suspect(s)/shooter(s)?: Unreported.
# of people killed: 0
# of people injured: 1
Total # of victims: 1
Time suspect(s)/shooter(s) were apprehended or killed?: Unreported.
Suspect(s)' mental illness: Unreported.
Suspect(s)' medication or drug use: Unreported.
Suspect(s)' criminal history: Unreported.
Warning signs: Unreported.
Suspect(s)' country of citizenship: Unreported.
Suspect(s)' religious affiliation: Unreported.

Alleged reason for shooting: Feud. Victim had been in an argument the night before the shooting during a neighborhood basketball game with someone who had vowed "to get him."

Metal detectors present?: Yes.

Location & time of shooting: Suspect bypassed the unmanned metal detector at the front entrance of the school. Victim was shot while playing basketball in the school gymnasium shortly after 1:00 p.m.

For more information, contact: 5th District Police Cmdr. Reginald Smith, McKinley Principal James Campbell and Assistant Superintendent Ralph Neal.

Citations/sources: (Thompson & Beamon, 1997) (Student pleads not guilty, 1997)

#999

Location of shooting: City-as-School (High school)
Date: 4/30/1997
City, State: New York City, NY
Name of victim(s) killed: N/A.
Age of victim(s) killed: N/A.
Name of victim(s) injured: Cornelius Ray.
Age of victim(s) injured: 19
Name of suspect(s)/shooter(s): Unreported.
Age of suspect(s)/shooter(s): Unreported.
Weapon(s): .380-caliber semi-automatic weapon
High capacity magazine(s)?: Unreported.
Weapon(s) legally acquired by suspect(s)/shooter(s)?: Unreported.
# of people killed: 0
# of people injured: 1
Total # of victims: 1
Time suspect(s)/shooter(s) were apprehended or killed?: Unreported.
Suspect(s)' mental illness: Unreported.
Suspect(s)' medication or drug use: Unreported.
Suspect(s)' criminal history: Unreported.
Warning signs: Unreported.
Suspect(s)' country of citizenship: Unreported.
Suspect(s)' religious affiliation: Unreported.
Alleged reason for shooting: Argument over a girl.
Metal detectors present?: N/A.
Location & time of shooting: Shooting occurred outside of the school.
For more information, contact: Unreported.
Citations/sources: (Marzulli, 1997, p. 24) (School steps shooting, 1997, p. 7C)

#998
Location of shooting: Pearl High School
Date: 10/1/1997
City, State: Pearl, MS
Name of victim(s) killed: Mary Woodham (Suspect's mother), Christina Menefee, & Lydia Kay Dew.
Age of victim(s) killed: 50, 16 & 17
Name of victim(s) injured: Alan Westbrook, Jerry Safely, Joni Palmer & the last four victims were unreported.
Age of victim(s) injured: Unreported.
Name of suspect(s)/shooter(s): Luke Woodham (shooter), Justin Sledge (accessory) & Grant Boyette (accessory).
Age of suspect(s)/shooter(s): 16, 16 & 18

Weapon(s): .30-30 hunting rifle, butcher knife & aluminum baseball bat.
High capacity magazine(s)?: Unreported.
Weapon(s) legally acquired by suspect(s)/shooter(s)?: No.
# of people killed: 3
# of people injured: 7
Total # of victims: 10
Time suspect(s)/shooter(s) were apprehended or killed?: Unreported.
Suspect(s)' mental illness: Unreported.
Suspect(s)' medication or drug use: Unreported.
Suspect(s)' criminal history: Suspect wrote about how he and an accomplice beat his dog, Sparkle, then set it on fire and threw it in a pond. "I'll never forget the sound of her breaking under my might. I hit her so hard I knocked the fur off her neck . . . it was true beauty," he wrote.
Warning signs: Suspect gave his manifesto and a will to a friend, minutes before the shooting. The suspect claimed friends saved him from suicide twice. Boyette was the head of a demonic cult known as "Kroth" that plotted violence.
Suspect(s)' country of citizenship: Unreported.
Suspect(s)' religious affiliation: Boyette was a Christian: Baptist. The suspect and six other arrested teenagers had formed a demonic cult known as "Kroth."
Alleged reason for shooting: Bullying, rejection, and abuse ("Always beaten, always hated" written in suspect's manifesto).
Metal detectors present?: N/A
Location & time of shooting: Suspect killed his mother before going to school to shoot other students outside of the school as students waited for school to begin.
For more information, contact: District Attorney John Kitchens, Assistant District Attorney Rick Mitchell, Rankin County Circuit Judge Samac Richardson, Police investigator Greg Eklund, Police Chief Billy Slade, Pearl School Superintendent Bill Dodson and Psychologist Mick Jepson.
Citations/sources: (Kimmel & Mahler, 2003, p. 1447 & 1454) (National School Safety Center, 2010, p. 17) (Crews, 2016, p. 6) (Lebrun, 2009, p. 174) (Congress of the U.S., 1999, p. 87) (Newman, Fox, Harding, Mehta, & Roth, 2004, p. 47, 237, & 249) (Boyette charged in death, 1998, p. 7A) (Pressley, 1997) (Rossilli, 1998, 1A & 8A) (Butch, 1998, p. 1A & 8A) (Woodham v. State, 2001)

#997
Location of shooting: Lew Wallace High School
Date: 10/10/1997
City, State: Gary, IN
Name of victim(s) killed: Kellie Franklin.
Age of victim(s) killed: 18
Name of victim(s) injured: Mahogany Mead & Andre Johnson.
Age of victim(s) injured: 15 & 19
Name of suspect(s)/shooter(s): Gustavo McQuay.
Age of suspect(s)/shooter(s): 20

Weapon(s): .38-caliber weapon

High capacity magazine(s)?: Unreported.

Weapon(s) legally acquired by suspect(s)/shooter(s)?: Unreported.

# of people killed: 1

# of people injured: 2

Total # of victims: 3

Time suspect(s)/shooter(s) were apprehended or killed?: Suspect turned himself in to the police at approximately 5:30 a.m., 8 hours after the shooting.

Suspect(s)' mental illness: Unreported.

Suspect(s)' medication or drug use: Unreported.

Suspect(s)' criminal history: Unreported.

Warning signs: Unreported.

Suspect(s)' country of citizenship: Unreported.

Suspect(s)' religious affiliation: Unreported.

Alleged reason for shooting: Gang-related.

Metal detectors present?: N/A.

Location & time of shooting: Shooting occurred at a Homecoming high school football game against Horace Mann High at approximately 9:30 p.m.

For more information, contact: Mayor Scott King, Police Detective Anthony Titus and Horace Mann High School coach James Piggee.

Citations/sources: (Kiesling, 1997, p. B-2) (Gary mayor bans nighttime, 1997, p. B8)

#996
Location of shooting: Lakeview Centennial High School

Date: 10/14/1997

City, State: Garland, TX

Name of victim(s) killed: Armando Montiel.

Age of victim(s) killed: 19

Name of victim(s) injured: N/A.

Age of victim(s) injured: N/A.

Name of suspect(s)/shooter(s): Armando Montiel.

Age of suspect(s)/shooter(s): 19

Weapon(s): .22-caliber revolver

High capacity magazine(s)?: Unreported.

Weapon(s) legally acquired by suspect(s)/shooter(s)?: Unreported.

# of people killed: 1

# of people injured: 0

Total # of victims: 1

Time suspect(s)/shooter(s) were apprehended or killed?: Suicide.

Suspect(s)' mental illness: Unreported.

Suspect(s)' medication or drug use: Unreported.

Suspect(s)' criminal history: Unreported.

Warning signs: Unreported.

Suspect(s)' country of citizenship: Unreported.

Suspect(s)' religious affiliation: Unreported.

Alleged reason for shooting: Unreported. Possibly depression. Distraught over his friend's (Leslie Enfield, age 16) suicide.

Metal detectors present?: Unreported.

Location & time of shooting: Student committed suicide in school bathroom.

For more information, contact: Police Spokesman Joel Bettes.

Citations/sources: (National School Safety Center, 2010, p. 17) (News Clip: H.S. Suicide, 1997) (Congress of the U.S., 1999, p. 88) (Student shoots self, 1997, p. 2A)

#995
Location of shooting: Lincoln Memorial Middle School
Date: 10/15/1997

City, State: Palmetto, FL

Name of victim(s) killed: N/A.

Age of victim(s) killed: N/A.

Name of victim(s) injured: Trent Bernard Murray.

Age of victim(s) injured: 13

Name of suspect(s)/shooter(s): Brandon Lee Hartsoe.

Age of suspect(s)/shooter(s): 13

Weapon(s): .38-caliber handgun

High capacity magazine(s)?: Unreported.

Weapon(s) legally acquired by suspect(s)/shooter(s)?: No. Suspect stole weapon from his mother's live-in boyfriend.

# of people killed: 0

# of people injured: 1

Total # of victims: 1

Time suspect(s)/shooter(s) were apprehended or killed?: Unreported.

Suspect(s)' mental illness: Unreported.

Suspect(s)' medication or drug use: Unreported.

Suspect(s)' criminal history: Unreported.

Warning signs: Unreported.

Suspect(s)' country of citizenship: Unreported.

Suspect(s)' religious affiliation: Unreported.

Alleged reason for shooting: Argument from previous day.

Metal detectors present?: Unreported.

Location & time of shooting: Shooting occurred near the school gym during a class change at approximately 12:30 p.m.

<u>For more information, contact</u>: Sheriff Spokesman Dave Bristow and Circuit Court Judge Peter Dubensky.

<u>Citations/sources</u>: Shooting occurred near the school gym during a class change at approximately 12:30 p.m.

#994
<u>Location of shooting</u>: John Glenn High School
<u>Date</u>: 10/22/1997
<u>City, State</u>: Norwalk, CA
<u>Name of victim(s) killed</u>: Catherine Theresa Tran & Khoa Truc "Robert" Dang (shooter)
<u>Age of victim(s) killed</u>: 16 & 21
<u>Name of victim(s) injured</u>: N/A.
<u>Age of victim(s) injured</u>: N/A.
<u>Name of suspect(s)/shooter(s)</u>: Khoa Truc "Robert" Dang.
<u>Age of suspect(s)/shooter(s)</u>: 21
<u>Weapon(s)</u>: 9mm semiautomatic handgun
<u>High capacity magazine(s)?</u>: Unreported.
<u>Weapon(s) legally acquired by suspect(s)/shooter(s)?</u>: Unreported.
<u># of people killed</u>: 2
<u># of people injured</u>: 0
<u>Total # of victims</u>: 2
<u>Time suspect(s)/shooter(s) were apprehended or killed?</u>: Suicide.
<u>Suspect(s)' mental illness</u>: Unreported.
<u>Suspect(s)' medication or drug use</u>: Unreported.
<u>Suspect(s)' criminal history</u>: Unreported.
<u>Warning signs</u>: The victim's brother alleged the victim told her family that "he (the suspect) was crazy and he wanted to kill himself."
<u>Suspect(s)' country of citizenship</u>: Unreported.
<u>Suspect(s)' religious affiliation</u>: Unreported.
<u>Alleged reason for shooting</u>: Rejection. Suspect committed suicide after killing his girlfriend who had recently broke up with him and went to the school football game with another boy the same night they broke up.
<u>Metal detectors present?</u>: No. N/A.
<u>Location & time of shooting</u>: Shooting occurred on a tree-shaded corner of the school at around 7:45 a.m.
<u>For more information, contact</u>: Superintendent Ginger Shattuck and Government Teacher Irwin Karasik.
<u>Citations/sources</u>: (National School Safety Center, 2010, p. 18) (Congress of the U.S., 1999, p. 88) (Counselors helping Norwalk, 1997, p. A4) (Leeds & Riccardo, 1997, p. A1 & A18)

#993
Location of shooting: Ribault High School
Date: 11/7/1997
City, State: Jacksonville, FL
Name of victim(s) killed: Gary L. White, Jr.
Age of victim(s) killed: 14
Name of victim(s) injured: El Omar Downs.
Age of victim(s) injured: 17
Name of suspect(s)/shooter(s): James David Campbell.
Age of suspect(s)/shooter(s): 18
Weapon(s): Unreported.
High capacity magazine(s)?: Unreported.
Weapon(s) legally acquired by suspect(s)/shooter(s)?: Unreported.
# of people killed: 1
# of people injured: 1
Total # of victims: 2
Time suspect(s)/shooter(s) were apprehended or killed?: Suspect surrendered two days after the shooting.
Suspect(s)' mental illness: Unreported.
Suspect(s)' medication or drug use: Unreported.
Suspect(s)' criminal history: Unreported.
Warning signs: Unreported.
Suspect(s)' country of citizenship: Unreported.
Suspect(s)' religious affiliation: Unreported.
Alleged reason for shooting: Unreported.
Metal detectors present?: N/A
Location & time of shooting: Shooting occurred outside of the high school.
For more information, contact: Unreported.
Citations/sources: (Teen-age suspect surrenders, 1997, p. 6B) (Teen charged in student's killing, 1997, p. 5B) (Teenager pleads guilty, 1998, p. D-6)

#992
Location of shooting: Creekside Elementary School
Date: 11/13/1997
City, State: Sacramento, CA
Name of victim(s) killed: Mike Logsdon (Father of 6-year old daughter at the school).
Age of victim(s) killed: 49
Name of victim(s) injured: N/A.
Age of victim(s) injured: N/A.
Name of suspect(s)/shooter(s): Jess Perry West.
Age of suspect(s)/shooter(s): 39

Weapon(s): Unreported.
High capacity magazine(s)?: Unreported.
Weapon(s) legally acquired by suspect(s)/shooter(s)?: Unreported.
# of people killed: 1
# of people injured: 0
Total # of victims: 1
Time suspect(s)/shooter(s) were apprehended or killed?: Suspect was arrested hours after the shooting after holding three people hostage in their home.
Suspect(s)' mental illness: Unreported.
Suspect(s)' medication or drug use: Unreported.
Suspect(s)' criminal history: Suspect was on parole after serving 6 years on a 12-year term for false imprisonment.
Warning signs: Unreported.
Suspect(s)' country of citizenship: Unreported.
Suspect(s)' religious affiliation: Unreported.
Alleged reason for shooting: Custody dispute with the victim.
Metal detectors present?: N/A.
Location & time of shooting: Victim was shot in his van in the school parking lot, while waiting for his children to come out of school.
For more information, contact: Unreported.
Citations/sources: (National School Safety Center, 2010, p. 18) (Congress of the U.S., 1999, p. 88) (Father shot to death, 1997, p. A-12) (Dad killed at school, 1997, p. C-2)

#991
Location of shooting: Heath High School
Date: 12/1/1997
City, State: West Paducah, KY
Name of victim(s) killed: Nichole Hadley, Kayce Steger, & Jessica James.
Age of victim(s) killed: 14, 15 & 17
Name of victim(s) injured: Shelley Schaberg, Melissa "Missy" Jenkins, Kelly Hard, Hollan Holm, & Craig Keene.
Age of victim(s) injured: 17, 15, 16, 14 & 15
Name of suspect(s)/shooter(s): Michael Carneal.
Age of suspect(s)/shooter(s): 14
Weapon(s): 2 shotguns, 2 semiautomatic rifles, a pistol, and 700 rounds of ammunition.
High capacity magazine(s)?: Unreported.
Weapon(s) legally acquired by suspect(s)/shooter(s)?: No. Shooter stole firearms from his father's closet and from a friend's father's garage.
# of people killed: 3
# of people injured: 5
Total # of victims: 8

Time suspect(s)/shooter(s) were apprehended or killed?: Shooter surrendered to school principle after firing 10 bullets from a 11-round magazine within approximately 12 seconds.

Suspect(s)' mental illness: Diagnosed with "dysthymia, and schizotypal personality disorder with borderline and paranoid features" by defense psychiatrist.

Suspect(s)' medication or drug use: No.

Suspect(s)' criminal history: Minor theft.

Warning signs: Told two 9th grade boys & a 9th grade girl on Nov 26 that "Monday is going to be a day of reckoning." Had weapons wrapped in a blanket, claiming they were props for a science project. Showed a 10th grade boy his gun & said it would be "cool to walk down the hall and kill people."

Suspect(s)' country of citizenship: Unreported.

Suspect(s)' religious affiliation: Christian: Lutheran.

Alleged reason for shooting: Rejection. One victim was a girl he had unreturned crush on. Trying to impress friends and seek acceptance. Bullying - Acquaintances said the shooter had been teased by older high school students, incl. teenagers in the prayer group and on the school's football team.

Metal detectors present?: No.

Location & time of shooting: Shooting occurred next to the principal's office at about 7:45 a.m.

For more information, contact: Psychiatrist Dewey Cornell, Deputy Mark Hayden, Psychologist Dr. Kathleen O'Connor and McCracken District Judge Donna Dixon.

Citations/sources: (Adams, 2014) (UPI Focus, 1997) (Braun & Pasternak, 1997) (Third student dies, 1997) (Moore, Petrie, Braga, & McLaughlin, 2013, p.132, 140, 146, 151, 266-283) (Landman, 2013, p. 3) (Newman, Fox, Harding, Mehta, & Roth, 2004, p. 22-32, 119, 157, & 238) (Kimmel & Mahler, 2003, p. 9) (National School Safety Center, 2010, p. 18) (Crews, 2016, p. 6) (Lebrun, 2009, p. 174) (Congress of the U.S., 1999, p. 88) (Harding, Fox & Mehta, 2002, p. 185, 187 & 198) (Fleshler, Chokey, Huriash & Trischitta, 2018, p. 1A & 9A) (Student indicted, 1997, p. A-4) (Kinsey, 1997, p. 9A)

#990
Location of shooting: Stamps High School
Date: 12/15/1997
City, State: Stamps, AR
Name of victim(s) killed: N/A.
Age of victim(s) killed: N/A.
Name of victim(s) injured: LeTisia Finley & Grover Henderson.
Age of victim(s) injured: 15 &17
Name of suspect(s)/shooter(s): Joseph "Colt" Todd.
Age of suspect(s)/shooter(s): 14
Weapon(s): .22-caliber rifle
High capacity magazine(s)?: Unreported.
Weapon(s) legally acquired by suspect(s)/shooter(s)?: No.

# of people killed: 0
# of people injured: 2
Total # of victims: 2

Time suspect(s)/shooter(s) were apprehended or killed?: Suspect was arrested four days after the shooting.

Suspect(s)' mental illness: Unreported.

Suspect(s)' medication or drug use: Unreported.

Suspect(s)' criminal history: None.

Warning signs: Unreported.

Suspect(s)' country of citizenship: Unreported.

Suspect(s)' religious affiliation: Unreported.

Alleged reason for shooting: Bullying. Suspect claimed he was being pushed and shoved. He claimed students were telling him to give them money in order to keep from being beat up.

Metal detectors present?: N/A.

Location & time of shooting: Suspect shot his victims in the school parking lot while hiding in in a nearby woods.

For more information, contact: Lafayette County Sheriff Sherry Kennedy and Sheriff John Kilgore.

Citations/sources: (Newman, Fox, Harding, Mehta, & Roth, 2004, p. 238) (Two students wounded, 1997) (Stamps teen accused, 1997) (Attorney files appeal, 1998) (Teen arrested for shooting, 1997)

#989
Location of shooting: South Texas Community College
Date: 1/13/1998
City, State: McAllen, TX
Name of victim(s) killed: Carlos Hernandez (College security guard)
Age of victim(s) killed: 32
Name of victim(s) injured: Melinda Singleterry, Julio Rivera & Mary Hernandez.
Age of victim(s) injured: 19, 20 & 27
Name of suspect(s)/shooter(s): Roberto Ivanovich Ojeda Hernandez & another masked gunman.

Age of suspect(s)/shooter(s): 19 & ?

Weapon(s): Either one or two AK-47 assault rifles.

High capacity magazine(s)?: Unreported.

Weapon(s) legally acquired by suspect(s)/shooter(s)?: Unreported.

# of people killed: 1
# of people injured: 3
Total # of victims: 4

Time suspect(s)/shooter(s) were apprehended or killed?: Roberto Ivanovich Ojeda Hernandez was arrested by Mexico's Federal Ministerial Police in July 2018, twenty years after the school shooting.

Suspect(s)' mental illness: Unreported.

Suspect(s)' medication or drug use: Unreported.

Suspect(s)' criminal history: Unreported.

Warning signs: Unreported.

Suspect(s)' country of citizenship: Mexico.

Suspect(s)' religious affiliation: Unreported.

Alleged reason for shooting: Robbery.

Metal detectors present?: N/A.

Location & time of shooting: Shooting occurred in a college office where students were registering for classes at approximately 6:45 p.m.

For more information, contact: Police Spokesman Mitch Reinitz McAllen, STCC President Shirley Reed and McAllen Police Chief Victor Rodriguez.

Citations/sources: (Sandoval, 1998, p. 1A & 4A) (DeLeon, 1998, p. 4A) (Smith, 2019) (Reegan, 2022)

#988
Location of shooting: Joel Elias Spingarn High School
Date: 1/13/1998
City, State: Washington, DC
Name of victim(s) killed: Adilah Gaither.
Age of victim(s) killed: 16
Name of victim(s) injured: N/A.
Age of victim(s) injured: N/A.
Name of suspect(s)/shooter(s): Octavious M. Clarke.
Age of suspect(s)/shooter(s): 17
Weapon(s): Unreported.
High capacity magazine(s)?: Unreported.
Weapon(s) legally acquired by suspect(s)/shooter(s)?: No.
# of people killed: 1
# of people injured: 0
Total # of victims: 1
Time suspect(s)/shooter(s) were apprehended or killed?: Suspect was arrested in his home the following day after the shooting occurred, after midnight.

Suspect(s)' mental illness: Unreported.

Suspect(s)' medication or drug use: Unreported.

Suspect(s)' criminal history: Unreported.

Warning signs: Unreported.

Suspect(s)' country of citizenship: Unreported.

Suspect(s)' religious affiliation: Unreported.

Alleged reason for shooting: Accident. Suspect's lawyer claimed shooting was an accident. Witnesses told police that seconds before the shooting, Clarke asked Adilah for her telephone number and she refused to give it to him.

Metal detectors present?: N/A.

Location & time of shooting: Shooting occurred at a bus stop outside at the high school by an Exxon gas station.

For more information, contact: D.C. Superior Court Judge Frederick H. Weisberg.

Citations/sources: (National School Safety Center, 2010) (Fern & Mooar, 1998) (Slevin, 1998)

#987
Location of shooting: Hoboken High School
Date: 2/12/1998
City, State: Hoboken, NJ
Name of victim(s) killed: John A. Sacci Jr. (Social studies teacher) & Geraisimov V. Metaxas (shooter).
Age of victim(s) killed: 48 & 61
Name of victim(s) injured: N/A.
Age of victim(s) injured: N/A.
Name of suspect(s)/shooter(s): Geraisimov V. Metaxas
Age of suspect(s)/shooter(s): 61
Weapon(s): .380-caliber semiautomatic handgun
High capacity magazine(s)?: Unreported.
Weapon(s) legally acquired by suspect(s)/shooter(s)?: No.
# of people killed: 2
# of people injured: 0
Total # of victims: 2
Time suspect(s)/shooter(s) were apprehended or killed?: Suicide.
Suspect(s)' mental illness: None.
Suspect(s)' medication or drug use: Unreported.
Suspect(s)' criminal history: None.
Warning signs: Unreported.
Suspect(s)' country of citizenship: Unreported.
Suspect(s)' religious affiliation: Unreported.

Alleged reason for shooting: Rejection. Suspect believed his wife was having an affair with the victim, who a teacher at the school.

Metal detectors present?: N/A.

Location & time of shooting: Shooting occurred outside of the school in view of other students.

For more information, contact: Hoboken Police Chief Carmen LaBruno, Hudson County Prosecutor Assistant Terry Hull and Principal Frank Stano.

Citations/sources: (National School Safety Center, 2010, p. 18) (Congress of the U.S., 1999, p. 89) (Herszenhorn, 1998)

#986
Location of shooting: Reed City Middle School
Date: 2/25/1998
City, State: Reed City, MI
Name of victim(s) killed: Vincent D. Garofalo (shooter).
Age of victim(s) killed: 13
Name of victim(s) injured: N/A.
Age of victim(s) injured: N/A.
Name of suspect(s)/shooter(s): Vincent D. Garofalo.
Age of suspect(s)/shooter(s): 13
Weapon(s): .22-caliber rifle smuggled into school in a base guitar case.
High capacity magazine(s)?: Unreported.
Weapon(s) legally acquired by suspect(s)/shooter(s)?: No. Shooter's father bought his son the rifle for hunting and target shooting.
# of people killed: 1
# of people injured: 0
Total # of victims: 1
Time suspect(s)/shooter(s) were apprehended or killed?: Suicide.
Suspect(s)' mental illness: Unreported.
Suspect(s)' medication or drug use: Unreported.
Suspect(s)' criminal history: Unreported.
Warning signs: Two days before the shooting, the shooter told several friends, "something big is going to happen on Wednesday (the day before his 14th birthday), but it would be over before school started." He also said he wouldn't be around to see his birthday. In September, the shooter dictated his will to a friend, telling him how his belongings should be divided if he should die.
Suspect(s)' country of citizenship: Unreported.
Suspect(s)' religious affiliation: Unreported.
Alleged reason for shooting: Unreported.
Metal detectors present?: Unreported.
Location & time of shooting: Shooter shot himself in the school hallway in front of his locker at approximately 8:00 a.m.
For more information, contact: Reed City Police Chief William (Bill) Riemersma and Superintendent David Killips.
Citations/sources: (National School Safety Center, 2010) (Christoff, 1998, p. 1B & 6B)(Eighth-grader kills himself, 1998, p.2) (Leith, 1998, p. 2B)

#985
Location of shooting: George C. Marshall High School

Date: 2/27/1998

City, State: Fairfax, VA

Name of victim(s) killed: David Clinton Albrecht

Age of victim(s) killed: 17

Name of victim(s) injured: N/A.

Age of victim(s) injured: N/A.

Name of suspect(s)/shooter(s): Michael Chuop (shooter), Saeed Sheikh, Peter Hanvichid & unnamed accomplice due to age.

Age of suspect(s)/shooter(s): 18, 19, 16 & 17

Weapon(s): .22-caliber rifle

High capacity magazine(s)?: Unreported.

Weapon(s) legally acquired by suspect(s)/shooter(s)?: Unreported.

# of people killed: 1

# of people injured: 0

Total # of victims: 1

Time suspect(s)/shooter(s) were apprehended or killed?: Unreported.

Suspect(s)' mental illness: Unreported.

Suspect(s)' medication or drug use: Unreported.

Suspect(s)' criminal history: Unreported.

Warning signs: Unreported.

Suspect(s)' country of citizenship: Unreported.

Suspect(s)' religious affiliation: Unreported.

Alleged reason for shooting: Gang-related. Shooting was intended for the friend of the suspect who had been in a fight with a gang member the day before.

Metal detectors present?: N/A.

Location & time of shooting: Suspect was shot while sitting in his car in the school parking lot.

For more information, contact: Circuit Judge Michael McWeeny.

Citations/sources: (National School Safety Center, 2010, p. 19) (Congress of the U.S., 1999, p. 89) (Teen sentenced to 17 years, 1998, p. B3) (Teen pleads guilty to assault, 1998, p. C6)

#984

Location of shooting: Westside Middle School

Date: 3/24/1998

City, State: Jonesboro, AR

Name of victim(s) killed: Brittany R. Varner, Natalie Brooks, Paige Ann Herring, Stephanie Johnson, & Shannon Wright (Teacher).

Age of victim(s) killed: 11, 11, 12, 12 & 32

Name of victim(s) injured: Lynette Thetford (Teacher), Candice Porter, Jennifer Jacobs, and the rest were unreported.

Age of victim(s) injured: 42, 11, 12, ?, ?, ?, ?, ?, ? & ?

Name of suspect(s)/shooter(s): Mitchell Scott Johnson & Andrew Douglas Golden.

Age of suspect(s)/shooter(s): 13 & 11

Weapon(s): .60-06 Remington rifle, Ruger .44 Magnum rifle, Universal .30 carbine rifle, Davis industry .38 special two-shot, FIE .380 handgun, Ruger .357 revolver, Remington model 742 .30-06 rifle, Smith & Wesson .38 pistol, Buddie Arms Double Deuce two-shot Derringer, Charter Arms .38 special pistol, Star .380 semiautomatic pistol, six knives, & two speed loader pistols.

High capacity magazine(s)?: Unreported.

Weapon(s) legally acquired by suspect(s)/shooter(s)?: No. Seven firearms stolen from Andrew Golden's grandfather's house, hanging on a wall for display. 3 firearms were stolen from Golden's father. Golden was unable to access his own firearms because they were locked in a steel safe.

# of people killed: 5

# of people injured: 10

Total # of victims: 15

Time suspect(s)/shooter(s) were apprehended or killed?: Police apprehended suspects approximately 10 minutes after the shooting.

Suspect(s)' mental illness: No & no.

Suspect(s)' medication or drug use: No & no.

Suspect(s)' criminal history: Mitchel was brought before a juvenile court for molestation of a two-year old girl.

Warning signs: Students heard Johnson say, "Tomorrow you will find out if you live or die," and he "had a lot of killing to do." Another student overheard Golden say he planned to bring guns to school and kill people. The student told his father who notified the school counselor.

Suspect(s)' country of citizenship: U.S.A.

Suspect(s)' religious affiliation: Christian.

Alleged reason for shooting: Bullying. Revenge. Rejection by at least two of the female victims. Johnson claims he only intended to scare people, with anger as his motive. Golden was "mad at teacher." Both felt "put upon" by fellow students. Golden claimed being led to the crime by Johnson.

Metal detectors present?: N/A.

Location & time of shooting: Shooting occurred outside of the school after the suspects pulled the fire alarm and forced staff and students to evacuated the building.

For more information, contact: School Administrator Denise Simpson and Principal Karen Curtner.

Citations/sources: (A school shooting in Jonesboro, 2018) (Kifner, Bragg, Johnson, & Verhovek, 1998) (Schwartz, 1998) (Moore, Petrie, Braga, & McLaughlin, 2013, p. 101, 103-105, 107, 109-116, & 266-283)

(Bragg, 1998) (Roberts, 2005) (Brantley, 2017) (Landman, 2013, p. 3) (National School Safety Center, 2010, p. 19) (Kellerman, 1999, p. 2) (Crews, 2016, p. 6) (Lebrun, 2009, p. 174) (Congress of the U.S., 1999, p. 89) (Newman, Fox, Harding, Mehta, & Roth, 2004, p. 39-40, 158-159, & 238) (Ford, 2019) (Children, parents work, 1998, p. 14A)

#983

Location of shooting: Coldwater High School

Date: 3/25/1998

City, State: Coldwater, MI

Name of victim(s) killed: Harley Davidson Carlisle (shooter).

Age of victim(s) killed: 18

Name of victim(s) injured: N/A.

Age of victim(s) injured: N/A.

Name of suspect(s)/shooter(s): Harley Davidson Carlisle.

Age of suspect(s)/shooter(s): 18

Weapon(s): 12-gauge shotgun

High capacity magazine(s)?: Unreported.

Weapon(s) legally acquired by suspect(s)/shooter(s)?: No. Shooter stole weapon from his father's house.

# of people killed: 1

# of people injured: 0

Total # of victims: 1

Time suspect(s)/shooter(s) were apprehended or killed?: Suicide.

Suspect(s)' mental illness: Unreported.

Suspect(s)' medication or drug use: Unreported.

Suspect(s)' criminal history: Unreported.

Warning signs: Unreported.

Suspect(s)' country of citizenship: Unreported.

Suspect(s)' religious affiliation: Unreported.

Alleged reason for shooting: Unreported.

Metal detectors present?: N/A.

Location & time of shooting: Student shot himself in his own car while parked in the school parking lot on the west end, around 7:50 a.m.

For more information, contact: Police Chief Gary Chester, Principal Fred Hobart, and Band Director David Carman.

Citations/sources: (National School Safety Center, 2010) (Motley, 1998, p. 1A & 2A)

#982

Location of shooting: Grey Culbreth Middle School

Date: 3/30/1998

City, State: Chapel Hill, NC

Name of victim(s) killed: Unnamed female student due to age (shooter).

Age of victim(s) killed: 13

Name of victim(s) injured: N/A.

Age of victim(s) injured: N/A.

Name of suspect(s)/shooter(s): Unnamed female student due to age.

Age of suspect(s)/shooter(s): 13
Weapon(s): Unreported.
High capacity magazine(s)?: Unreported.
Weapon(s) legally acquired by suspect(s)/shooter(s)?: No.
# of people killed: 1
# of people injured: 0
Total # of victims: 1
Time suspect(s)/shooter(s) were apprehended or killed?: Suicide.
Suspect(s)' mental illness: Unreported.
Suspect(s)' medication or drug use: Unreported.
Suspect(s)' criminal history: Unreported.
Warning signs: Unreported. Shooter talked about problems at home.
Suspect(s)' country of citizenship: Unreported.
Suspect(s)' religious affiliation: Unreported.
Alleged reason for shooting: Unreported.
Metal detectors present?: Unreported.
Location & time of shooting: Shooting occurred in school bathroom at around 10:55 a.m.
For more information, contact: Superintendent Neal Pedersen.
Citations/sources: (National School Safety Center, 2010, p. 20) (Congress of the U.S., 1999, p. 89) (Parsons, 1998, p. A2) (Student kills self, 1998, p. 6B)

#981
Location of shooting: Pardeeville Elementary School
Date: 4/13/1998
City, State: Pardeeville, WI
Name of victim(s) killed: N/A.
Age of victim(s) killed: N/A.
Name of victim(s) injured: Ralph Pulver (Janitor).
Age of victim(s) injured: 40
Name of suspect(s)/shooter(s): Michael T. LaReau & an unnamed boy.
Age of suspect(s)/shooter(s): 15 & 14
Weapon(s): .22-caliber revolver.
High capacity magazine(s)?: Unreported.
Weapon(s) legally acquired by suspect(s)/shooter(s)?: No. Gun was stolen from a local pizzeria where the suspect worked.
# of people killed: 0
# of people injured: 1
Total # of victims: 1
Time suspect(s)/shooter(s) were apprehended or killed?: LaReau was arrested just after midnight, approximately 3 hours after the shooting.
Suspect(s)' mental illness: Unreported.

Suspect(s)' medication or drug use: Unreported.

Suspect(s)' criminal history: Unreported.

Warning signs: Unreported.

Suspect(s)' country of citizenship: Unreported.

Suspect(s)' religious affiliation: Unreported.

Alleged reason for shooting: Attempted robbery. Suspects attempted to steal the victim's car.

Metal detectors present?: Unreported.

Location & time of shooting: Shooting occurred around 9:00 p.m. Victim was shot through a school door window when he refused to give his car keys to the suspects.

For more information, contact: Court Judge Daniel George, Assistant District Attorney Barbara Reinhold, Sheriff Steven R. Rowe, and Pardeeville Police Chief Robert Briedenbach.

Citations/sources: (Piper, 1998, p. 1A) (15-year old will be tried, 1998, p. 5B) (Teen sentenced to 40 years, 1999, p. A12)

#980
Location of shooting: Culver City High School

Date: 4/22/1998

City, State: Culver City, CA

Name of victim(s) killed: N/A.

Age of victim(s) killed: N/A.

Name of victim(s) injured: Two unnamed boys.

Age of victim(s) injured: 15 & 16

Name of suspect(s)/shooter(s): Two unnamed teenagers.

Age of suspect(s)/shooter(s): 15 & 16

Weapon(s): Small-caliber handgun.

High capacity magazine(s)?: Unreported.

Weapon(s) legally acquired by suspect(s)/shooter(s)?: No.

# of people killed: 0

# of people injured: 2

Total # of victims: 2

Time suspect(s)/shooter(s) were apprehended or killed?: Suspects were arrested 5 days after the shooting.

Suspect(s)' mental illness: Unreported.

Suspect(s)' medication or drug use: Unreported.

Suspect(s)' criminal history: Unreported.

Warning signs: Unreported.

Suspect(s)' country of citizenship: Unreported.

Suspect(s)' religious affiliation: Unreported.

Alleged reason for shooting: Gang-related.

Metal detectors present?: N/A.

Location & time of shooting: Drive-by shooting occurred in front of the school.

For more information, contact: Culver City Police Lt. Ray Scheu, Culver City Spokeswoman Randi Joseph, and Principal Marvin Brown.

Citations/sources: (2 teenagers arrested, 1998, p. B4) (Goldman, 1998, p. B12 & B13)

#979
Location of shooting: James W. Parker Middle School
Date: 4/24/1998
City, State: Edinboro, PA
Name of victim(s) killed: John Gillette (Science Teacher).
Age of victim(s) killed: 48
Name of victim(s) injured: Unreported.
Age of victim(s) injured: 14, 14, & ?
Name of suspect(s)/shooter(s): Andrew Jerome Wurst.
Age of suspect(s)/shooter(s): 14
Weapon(s): .25-caliber semiautomatic handgun.
High capacity magazine(s)?: No. 10-round magazine.
Weapon(s) legally acquired by suspect(s)/shooter(s)?: No. Stolen from father.
# of people killed: 1
# of people injured: 3
Total # of victims: 4
Time suspect(s)/shooter(s) were apprehended or killed?: Shooter apprehended by next door business owner, 10 minutes after shooting.
Suspect(s)' mental illness: Preschizophrenic ideation diagnosed by defense psychiatrist. Suspect claimed he suffered from depression for 4 years.
Suspect(s)' medication or drug use: Shooter carried a small amount of marijuana. Drank alcohol and used marijuana in the 8th grade.
Suspect(s)' criminal history: Unreported.
Warning signs: Left suicide note at home on his pillow. Gave hints to friends no one took seriously. Had another friend feel the gun under his shirt before the shooting.
Suspect(s)' country of citizenship: Unreported.
Suspect(s)' religious affiliation: Christian: Catholic.
Alleged reason for shooting: Unreported. Possible revenge. Shooter made general statements that he wanted to "kill nine people" he hated and then kill himself.
Metal detectors present?: Yes. Use of metal detector wands failed.
Location & time of shooting: Shooting occurred on the patio of a restaurant where a graduation dance was being held for 240 students.
For more information, contact: Edinboro Mayor Clifford Allen, Pennsylvania State Police Spokesman Mark Zaleski, and State Police Cpl. Kirby Ames.
Citations/sources: (Moore, Petrie, Braga, & McLaughlin, 2013, p.70, 72-76, 266-283) (National School Safety Center, 2010, p. 20) (Crews, 2016, p. 6) (Congress of the U.S., 1999, p. 89) (Newman, Fox, Harding, Mehta, & Roth, 2004, p. 238 & 247) (Pennsylvania students cope, 1998)

#978

Location of shooting: Philadelphia Elementary School

Date: 4/28/1998

City, State: Pomona, CA

Name of victim(s) killed: Hector Manuel Lopez & Andres Azocar.

Age of victim(s) killed: 14 & 17

Name of victim(s) injured: Unnamed boy due to age.

Age of victim(s) injured: 15

Name of suspect(s)/shooter(s): Unnamed boy due to age.

Age of suspect(s)/shooter(s): 14

Weapon(s): Unreported.

High capacity magazine(s)?: Unreported.

Weapon(s) legally acquired by suspect(s)/shooter(s)?: No.

# of people killed: 2

# of people injured: 1

Total # of victims: 3

Time suspect(s)/shooter(s) were apprehended or killed?: Suspect was arrested two days after shooting.

Suspect(s)' mental illness: Unreported.

Suspect(s)' medication or drug use: Unreported.

Suspect(s)' criminal history: Unreported.

Warning signs: Unreported.

Suspect(s)' country of citizenship: Unreported.

Suspect(s)' religious affiliation: Unreported.

Alleged reason for shooting: Argument. Rival between two party crews.

Metal detectors present?: N/A.

Location & time of shooting: Shooting took place behind the elementary school at a basketball court.

For more information, contact: Cpl. Robert Bocanegra.

Citations/sources: (National School Safety Center, 2010, p. 20) (Lebrun, 2009, p. 174) (14-year-old held in slayings, 1998, p. B2) (Shooting arrest, 1998, A10)

#977

Location of shooting: Dr. Antonia Pantoja Community School (Public School 18) (Grades PreK - 8)

Date: 5/1/1998

City, State: Buffalo, NY

Name of victim(s) killed: Norma Roman (parent).

Age of victim(s) killed: 30

Name of victim(s) injured: Margaret Beals (teacher's aide).

Age of victim(s) injured: Unreported.
Name of suspect(s)/shooter(s): Juan A. Roman.
Age of suspect(s)/shooter(s): 37
Weapon(s): .357 Magnum.
High capacity magazine(s)?: Unreported.
Weapon(s) legally acquired by suspect(s)/shooter(s)?: No. Stolen from another sheriff deputy who shared a gun locker with the suspect.
# of people killed: 1
# of people injured: 1
Total # of victims: 2
Time suspect(s)/shooter(s) were apprehended or killed?: Suspect was arrested 9 minutes after the shooting, several blocks away from the school.
Suspect(s)' mental illness: Defense lawyer claimed suspect was seeing a psychiatrist.
Suspect(s)' medication or drug use: Antidepressants.
Suspect(s)' criminal history: Suspect was ordered to surrender his own three guns, and his gun locker key, after being served an order of protection sought by his wife on April 21, 1998.
Warning signs: Unreported. Suspect revealed to his pastor that he was having marriage problems and asked him to pray for him.
Suspect(s)' country of citizenship: Unreported.
Suspect(s)' religious affiliation: Christian (Church of God, Buffalo, NY).
Alleged reason for shooting: Custody dispute. Suspect was a sheriff's deputy who was arguing with and shot his estranged wife as she went into the school.
Metal detectors present?: Unreported.
Location & time of shooting: Shooting occurred inside the school office.
For more information, contact: Deputy Police Commissioner John Battle and Erie County Sheriff Patrick Gallivan.
Citations/sources: (National School Safety Center, 2010, p. 20) (Police: man shoots, 1998, p. 5A) (Ex-jail guard admits, 1998, p. 2B) (Slay suspect was psychiatric, 1998, p. A7)

#976
Location of shooting: Lincoln County High School
Date: 5/19/1998
City, State: Fayetteville, TN
Name of victim(s) killed: Robert "Nick" Creson.
Age of victim(s) killed: 18
Name of victim(s) injured: N/A.
Age of victim(s) injured: N/A.
Name of suspect(s)/shooter(s): Jacob Lee Davis.
Age of suspect(s)/shooter(s): 18
Weapon(s): Marlin .22 caliber Magnum rifle.
High capacity magazine(s)?: Unreported.

Weapon(s) legally acquired by suspect(s)/shooter(s)?: No. Suspect had taken the rifle from his father who kept 4 guns in the house.

# of people killed: 1

# of people injured: 0

Total # of victims: 1

Time suspect(s)/shooter(s) were apprehended or killed?: Suspect immediately surrendered after the shooting.

Suspect(s)' mental illness: Dr. William D. Kenner, a specialist in child and adolescent psychiatry, testified the suspect was suffering from a severe depressive disorder. The doctor further explained the suspect had a "genetic predisposition" for depression and mental illness.

Suspect(s)' medication or drug use: Unreported.

Suspect(s)' criminal history: None.

Warning signs: On March 1998, the suspect wrote a letter to the victim's girlfriend, stating he wanted to shoot the victim while reciting lyrics to a Smashing Pumpkins song. "I want to put a three inch diameter hole in his chest from a 12 gauge. I want to dip my finger in his blood and write the words to the song Mayonnaise on his truck."

Suspect(s)' country of citizenship: Unreported.

Suspect(s)' religious affiliation: Unreported.

Alleged reason for shooting: Argument over a girl both the suspect and victim had dated.

Metal detectors present?: N/A.

Location & time of shooting: Shooting occurred in the school parking lot after 2:00 p.m.

For more information, contact: Fayetteville Police Chief Tom Barnes, Principal Jim Stewart, and Police Detective Bill Wood.

Citations/sources: (Another Fatal School Shooting, 1998) (Student Dies in School Shooting, 1998) (National School Safety Center, 2010, p. 20) (Lebrun, 2009, p. 174 & 175) (Tennessee highschool student, 1998) (Sharp, 1998, p. 3A) (Tate v. Davis, 2001)

#975

Location of shooting: Thurston High School

Date: 5/21/1998

City, State: Springfield, OR

Name of victim(s) killed: Bill Kinkel (Suspect's father), Faith Kinkel (Suspect's mother), Mikael Nickolauson, and Ben Walker.

Age of victim(s) killed: 59, 57, 17, & 16

Name of victim(s) injured: Jake Ryker, Jennifer Alldredge, unreported,...

Age of victim(s) injured: 17, 17, unreported,...

Name of suspect(s)/shooter(s): Kip Philip Kinkel.

Age of suspect(s)/shooter(s): 15

Weapon(s): .22 caliber semiautomatic Ruger rifle, his father's 9mm Glock pistol, .22 caliber Ruger semiautomatic pistol, 1,127 rounds of ammunition, and a hunting knife.

High capacity magazine(s)?: Yes. At least one 50-round magazine clip.

Weapon(s) legally acquired by suspect(s)/shooter(s)?: Yes and No: .22 rifle was purchased as a gift from shooter's father. 9mm was stolen from shooter's father. The .22 stolen pistol was secretly purchased from a friend.

# of people killed: 4

# of people injured: 24

Total # of victims: 28

Time suspect(s)/shooter(s) were apprehended or killed?: Suspect wrestled to the ground by five classmates (Jake Ryker, Joshua Ryker, Doud Ure, David Ure, and Adam Walberger) a few minutes after the shooting began.

Suspect(s)' mental illness: Diagnosed with a learning disability in 1992-1993. Also diagnosed with Major Depressive Disorder by psychologist, Dr. Jeffrey Hicks.

Suspect(s)' medication or drug use: Shooter had been off of Prozac for at least 9 months.

Suspect(s)' criminal history: Arrested for throwing rocks off a highway overpass on January 4, 1997. Suspended from school twice for violent acts April 23-29, 1997. Arrested for having a gun in his school locker on May 20, 1998. Caught shoplifting CDs.

Warning signs: Some students said Kinkel used to make odd statements about building a bomb or committing violence, but few people took him seriously.

Suspect(s)' country of citizenship: U.S.A.

Suspect(s)' religious affiliation: Unreported.

Alleged reason for shooting: Bullying. Students claim that the shooter was mad about insults from seniors.

Metal detectors present?: No.

Location & time of shooting: Shooting began in a school hallway towards the cafeteria around 7:55 a.m.

For more information, contact: Springfield Police Chief Jerry Smith and pastor/volunteer firefighter Mark Clark.

Citations/sources: (Frontline: the killer at Thurston High, 1998) (8 years later, 2006) (Egan, 1998) (Kimmel & Mahler, 2003, p. 1455) (National School Safety Center, 2010, p. 20) (Crews, 2016, p. 6) (Lebrun, 2009, p. 175) (Newman, Fox, Harding, Mehta, & Roth, 2004, p. 238 & 259) (Brandon & Haynes, 1998, p. 1 & 16) (Thurston High reopens, 1998, p. A3) (Longman, 1998, p. 6A)

#974

Location of shooting: Jersey Village High School

Date: 5/21/1998

City, State: Houston, TX

Name of victim(s) killed: N/A.

Age of victim(s) killed: N/A.

Name of victim(s) injured: Jamie Anderson.

Age of victim(s) injured: 17

Name of suspect(s)/shooter(s): Marko Antonio Guerrero.

Age of suspect(s)/shooter(s): 17

Weapon(s): .38-caliber revolver.

High capacity magazine(s)?: Unreported.

Weapon(s) legally acquired by suspect(s)/shooter(s)?: No.

# of people killed: 0

# of people injured: 1

Total # of victims: 1

Time suspect(s)/shooter(s) were apprehended or killed?: Suspect apprehended more than an hour after the shooting.

Suspect(s)' mental illness: Unreported.

Suspect(s)' medication or drug use: Unreported.

Suspect(s)' criminal history: Unreported.

Warning signs: Unreported.

Suspect(s)' country of citizenship: Unreported.

Suspect(s)' religious affiliation: Unreported.

Alleged reason for shooting: Accident. Weapon in suspect's backpack accidentally discharged. Suspect claimed he had received threats off-campus and been carrying the weapon since May 1st.

Metal detectors present?: Unreported.

Location & time of shooting: Shooting occurred in a science classroom as class was letting out for the day.

For more information, contact: Principal Dan Troxell and Harris County Precinct 4 Chief Deputy Constable Karen Moore.

Citations/sources: (Lebrun, 2009, p. 175) (Houston area teen shot, 1998, p. 7A) (Houston student suffers, 1998, p. 2A)

#973

Location of shooting: Rialto High School

Date: 5/21/1998

City, State: Rialto, CA

Name of victim(s) killed: Ricardo Martin (shooter).

Age of victim(s) killed: 15

Name of victim(s) injured: N/A.

Age of victim(s) injured: N/A.

Name of suspect(s)/shooter(s): Ricardo Martin

Age of suspect(s)/shooter(s): 15

Weapon(s): .38-caliber pistol.

High capacity magazine(s)?: Unreported.

Weapon(s) legally acquired by suspect(s)/shooter(s)?: No. Stolen from the suspect's family's home.

# of people killed: 1

# of people injured: 0

Total # of victims: 1

Time suspect(s)/shooter(s) were apprehended or killed?: Suicide.
Suspect(s)' mental illness: Unreported.
Suspect(s)' medication or drug use: Unreported.
Suspect(s)' criminal history: Unreported.
Warning signs: Unreported.
Suspect(s)' country of citizenship: Unreported.
Suspect(s)' religious affiliation: Unreported.
Alleged reason for shooting: Depression and bullying. Reportedly distraught over not advancing to tenth grade and upset about being teased about the way he dressed.
Metal detectors present?: Not reported.
Location & time of shooting: Shooting occurred in the school quadrangle at approximately 7:00 a.m.
For more information, contact: Los Angeles Police Lt. W. D. Smith and Loma Linda University Medical Center Spokeswoman Anita Rockwell.
Citations/sources: (National School Safety Center, 2010, p. 20) (Teen shoots self, 1998, p. C-8) (Boy, 15 dies, 1998, p. A23)

#972
Location of shooting: Washington Middle School
Date: 5/27/1998
City, State: Pasadena, CA
Name of victim(s) killed: Salvador Gabriel Diaz.
Age of victim(s) killed: 14
Name of victim(s) injured: Cesar Escamilla.
Age of victim(s) injured: 20
Name of suspect(s)/shooter(s): Miguel Angel Estrada.
Age of suspect(s)/shooter(s): 19
Weapon(s): Unreported.
High capacity magazine(s)?: Unreported.
Weapon(s) legally acquired by suspect(s)/shooter(s)?: Unreported.
# of people killed: 1
# of people injured: 1
Total # of victims: 2
Time suspect(s)/shooter(s) were apprehended or killed?: Unreported.
Suspect(s)' mental illness: Unreported.
Suspect(s)' medication or drug use: Unreported.
Suspect(s)' criminal history: Unreported.
Warning signs: Unreported.
Suspect(s)' country of citizenship: Unreported.
Suspect(s)' religious affiliation: Unreported.
Alleged reason for shooting: Gang-related.

Metal detectors present?: Unreported.

Location & time of shooting: Shooting occurred on the campus grounds around 6:15 p.m.

For more information, contact: Pasadena Police Lt. Keith Jones.

Citations/sources: (National School Safety Center, 2010, p. 21) (Boy, 14, killed, 1998, p. B4) (Suspect sought in slaying, 1998, p. B2)

#971

Location of shooting: Stranahan High School

Date: 5/29/1998

City, State: Fort Lauderdale, FL

Name of victim(s) killed: Nichole Weiser (Teacher) & Michael Grammig (shooter).

Age of victim(s) killed: 26 & 29

Name of victim(s) injured: N/A.

Age of victim(s) injured: N/A.

Name of suspect(s)/shooter(s): Michael Grammig.

Age of suspect(s)/shooter(s): 29

Weapon(s): 9mm handgun.

High capacity magazine(s)?: Unreported.

Weapon(s) legally acquired by suspect(s)/shooter(s)?: Unreported.

# of people killed: 2

# of people injured: 0

Total # of victims: 2

Time suspect(s)/shooter(s) were apprehended or killed?: Suicide.

Suspect(s)' mental illness: Unreported.

Suspect(s)' medication or drug use: Unreported.

Suspect(s)' criminal history: Unreported.

Warning signs: A year before the shooting, the suspect told the victim, "If I ever see you with any other guy I'll kill you.

Suspect(s)' country of citizenship: Unreported.

Suspect(s)' religious affiliation: Unreported.

Alleged reason for shooting: Rejection. The victim was the suspect's ex-girlfriend.

Metal detectors present?: N/A.

Location & time of shooting: Victim was shot in school parking lot, minutes before classes began, shortly before 7:30 a.m.

For more information, contact: Detective Sgt. Tim Bronson and Broward County School Spokeswoman Sisty Walsh.

Citations/sources: (National School Safety Center, 2010, p. 21) (Huriash, 1998, p. 6B) (Ex-boyfriend kills teacher, 1998, p. 2A) (King, Borden, & Kelley, 1998)

#970

Location of shooting: Armstrong High School

Date: 6/15/1998
City, State: Richmond, VA
Name of victim(s) killed: N/A.
Age of victim(s) killed: N/A.
Name of victim(s) injured: Gregory Carter (History teacher and basketball coach) & Eloise Wilson (volunteer aide).
Age of victim(s) injured: 45 & 74
Name of suspect(s)/shooter(s): Quinshawn Booker.
Age of suspect(s)/shooter(s): 14
Weapon(s): .32-caliber Llama semiautomatic handgun.
High capacity magazine(s)?: Unreported.
Weapon(s) legally acquired by suspect(s)/shooter(s)?: No.
# of people killed: 0
# of people injured: 2
Total # of victims: 2
Time suspect(s)/shooter(s) were apprehended or killed?: After the shooting, a school police officer chased the suspect and arrested him three blocks away.
Suspect(s)' mental illness: Unreported.
Suspect(s)' medication or drug use: Unreported.
Suspect(s)' criminal history: Unreported.
Warning signs: Unreported.
Suspect(s)' country of citizenship: Unreported.
Suspect(s)' religious affiliation: Unreported.
Alleged reason for shooting: Argument between two groups of juveniles. Law enforcement believed victims were not intended targets.
Metal detectors present?: Unreported.
Location & time of shooting: Shooting occurred in school hallway around 10:00 a.m.
For more information, contact: Mayor Larry Chavis, Sgt. Jerry Baskette, Deputy Police Chief Theresa Gooch, School Police Officer Ron Brown, and Richmond Commonwealth Attorney David Hicks.
Citations/sources: (Lebrun, 2009, p. 175) (News: teacher, employee, 1998) (Baskerville, 1998, p. A1 & A4) (No bail in school shootings, 1998, p. 6A)

#969
Location of shooting: Herbert Hoover High School
Date: 9/10/1998
City, State: Glendale, CA
Name of victim(s) killed: Avetis "Avo" Demirchyan.
Age of victim(s) killed: 15
Name of victim(s) injured: N/A.
Age of victim(s) injured: N/A.

Name of suspect(s)/shooter(s): Artiom Badalyan.

Age of suspect(s)/shooter(s): 17

Weapon(s): Handgun.

High capacity magazine(s)?: Unreported.

Weapon(s) legally acquired by suspect(s)/shooter(s)?: No.

# of people killed: 1

# of people injured: 0

Total # of victims: 1

Time suspect(s)/shooter(s) were apprehended or killed?: Suspect surrendered one month after the shooting.

Suspect(s)' mental illness: Unreported.

Suspect(s)' medication or drug use: Unreported.

Suspect(s)' criminal history: Suspect had been arrested as a juvenile on suspicion of battery and disruption of school.

Warning signs: Unreported.

Suspect(s)' country of citizenship: Unreported.

Suspect(s)' religious affiliation: Unreported.

Alleged reason for shooting: Fight following a lunchtime insult.

Metal detectors present?: Yes. N/A.

Location & time of shooting: Shooting occurred in school faculty parking lot.

For more information, contact: Glendale Police Sgt. Rick Young.

Citations/sources: (National School Safety Center, 2010, p. 21) (Blankstein & Moore, 1998) (Helfand, 1998, p. B3) (Moore, 1998, p. B8) (Mother asks for no jail time, 1999, p. E6)

#968

Location of shooting: North Miami Senior High School

Date: 9/29/1998

City, State: North Miami, FL

Name of victim(s) killed: N/A.

Age of victim(s) killed: N/A.

Name of victim(s) injured: Jackie Valcourt, Reginald Georges, Lesonie Walker (Business Education teacher).

Age of victim(s) injured: 15, 17 & ?

Name of suspect(s)/shooter(s): Felly Petit-Frere (shooter) and Occi Eliezer.

Age of suspect(s)/shooter(s): 17 & 18

Weapon(s): Unreported.

High capacity magazine(s)?: Unreported.

Weapon(s) legally acquired by suspect(s)/shooter(s)?: No.

# of people killed: 0

# of people injured: 3

Total # of victims: 3

Time suspect(s)/shooter(s) were apprehended or killed?: Eliezer was arrested the night of the shooting. Petit-Frere was arrested a day after the shooting.

Suspect(s)' mental illness: Unreported.

Suspect(s)' medication or drug use: Unreported.

Suspect(s)' criminal history: Unreported.

Warning signs: Unreported.

Suspect(s)' country of citizenship: Unreported.

Suspect(s)' religious affiliation: Unreported.

Alleged reason for shooting: Feud based on a fight from the day before the shooting.

Metal detectors present?: Yes. Handheld metal detectors.

Location & time of shooting: Shooting occurred in a school hallway, just outside the cafeteria at 12:32 p.m.

For more information, contact: Detective Kathleen Ruggiero and Principal Charles Hankerson. (Ramirez & Cazares, 1998, p. 8B) (Shootings injure teacher, 1998, p. 7B) (Viega, 1998, p. 5B)

Citations/sources:

#967
Location of shooting: Leesburg High School
Date: 9/30/1998
City, State: Leesburg, FL
Name of victim(s) killed: N/A.
Age of victim(s) killed: N/A.
Name of victim(s) injured: Unnamed male due to age.
Age of victim(s) injured: 17
Name of suspect(s)/shooter(s): Unnamed male due to age.
Age of suspect(s)/shooter(s): 17
Weapon(s): .22-caliber gun.
High capacity magazine(s)?: Unreported.
Weapon(s) legally acquired by suspect(s)/shooter(s)?: No.
# of people killed: 0
# of people injured: 1
Total # of victims: 1
Time suspect(s)/shooter(s) were apprehended or killed?: Unreported.
Suspect(s)' mental illness: Unreported.
Suspect(s)' medication or drug use: Unreported.
Suspect(s)' criminal history: Unreported.
Warning signs: Unreported.
Suspect(s)' country of citizenship: Unreported.
Suspect(s)' religious affiliation: Unreported.

Alleged reason for shooting: Protest authority. Suspect was unhappy about being sent to public school after years of home schooling.

Metal detectors present?: N/A.

Location & time of shooting: Shooting occurred at the school football field at 8:48 a.m.

For more information, contact: Leesburg Police Captain Hal Reeves, School board member Jimmy Conner, Assistant Superintendent Jerry Cox, and Principal Wayne McLeod.

Citations/sources: (Quigley & Fernandez, 1998, p. 1 & 6) (Quigley, 1998, p. 1 & 5)

#966

Location of shooting: Central High School

Date: 1/8/1999

City, State: Carrollton, GA

Name of victim(s) killed: Andrea Garrett and Jeff Miller (shooter).

Age of victim(s) killed: 15 & 17

Name of victim(s) injured: N/A.

Age of victim(s) injured: N/A.

Name of suspect(s)/shooter(s): Jeff Miller.

Age of suspect(s)/shooter(s): 17

Weapon(s): .22-caliber pistol.

High capacity magazine(s)?: Unreported.

Weapon(s) legally acquired by suspect(s)/shooter(s)?: No. Gun was stolen from a locked gun case in Garrett's home.

# of people killed: 2

# of people injured: 0

Total # of victims: 2

Time suspect(s)/shooter(s) were apprehended or killed?: Suicide.

Suspect(s)' mental illness: Unreported.

Suspect(s)' medication or drug use: Unreported.

Suspect(s)' criminal history: Unreported.

Warning signs: Miller made statements to other students that he might not be around much longer. Allegedly, the couple had each given away favorite possessions to friends before the shooting.

Suspect(s)' country of citizenship: Unreported.

Suspect(s)' religious affiliation: Unreported.

Alleged reason for shooting: Suicide pact. The couple allegedly were under parental pressure to break up.

Metal detectors present?: No.

Location & time of shooting: Shooting occurred in a girl's bathroom during the school's first period.

For more information, contact: Carroll County Sheriff Tony Reeves and Principal Scott Cowart.

Citations/sources: (National School Safety Center, 2010, p. 21) (Cowles & Ellis, 1999, p. C1 & C2) (Warner & Scott, 1999, p. F1)

#965

Location of shooting: Harry S. Truman High School

Date: 1/14/1999

City, State: The Bronx, NY

Name of victim(s) killed: N/A.

Age of victim(s) killed: N/A.

Name of victim(s) injured: Kahinnon Clarke and Lamar Williams.

Age of victim(s) injured: 16 & 18

Name of suspect(s)/shooter(s): Camillo Douglas.

Age of suspect(s)/shooter(s): 16

Weapon(s): Semiautomatic pistol.

High capacity magazine(s)?: Unreported.

Weapon(s) legally acquired by suspect(s)/shooter(s)?: No.

# of people killed: 0

# of people injured: 2

Total # of victims: 2

Time suspect(s)/shooter(s) were apprehended or killed?: Suspect was apprehended by police minutes after the shooting, after he crashed his car into a tree and tried to flee on foot.

Suspect(s)' mental illness: Unreported.

Suspect(s)' medication or drug use: Unreported.

Suspect(s)' criminal history: Unreported.

Warning signs: Unreported.

Suspect(s)' country of citizenship: Unreported.

Suspect(s)' religious affiliation: Unreported.

Alleged reason for shooting: Feud. Police believed the shooting may have been in response to a stabbing, in what was apparently a turf war, a day earlier.

Metal detectors present?: N/A.

Location & time of shooting: Shooting took place on the sidewalk in front of the school around 9:00 a.m.

For more information, contact: Assistant Chief James Lawrence and Board of Education Spokeswoman Karen Crowe.

Citations/sources: (Claffey, Olmeda, & Goldiner, 1999, p. 80) (Roane, 1999)

#964

Location of shooting: Richland High School

Date: 1/21/1999

City, State: North Richland Hills, TX

Name of victim(s) killed: Randall James (shooter).

Age of victim(s) killed: 16

Name of victim(s) injured: N/A.

Age of victim(s) injured: N/A.
Name of suspect(s)/shooter(s): Randall James.
Age of suspect(s)/shooter(s): 16
Weapon(s): 9mm handgun
High capacity magazine(s)?: Unreported.
Weapon(s) legally acquired by suspect(s)/shooter(s)?: No.
# of people killed: 1
# of people injured: 0
Total # of victims: 1
Time suspect(s)/shooter(s) were apprehended or killed?: Suicide.
Suspect(s)' mental illness: Unreported.
Suspect(s)' medication or drug use: Unreported.
Suspect(s)' criminal history: Unreported.
Warning signs: Unreported.
Suspect(s)' country of citizenship: Unreported.
Suspect(s)' religious affiliation: Unreported.
Alleged reason for shooting: Unreported.
Metal detectors present?: Unreported.
Location & time of shooting: Shooting occurred in school bathroom stall shortly after the first bell.
For more information, contact: Investigator Larry Irving.
Citations/sources: (National School Safety Center, 2010, p. 22) (Boy shoots himself, 1999, p. A8) (In other news, 1999, p. 5B)

#963
Location of shooting: Ombudsman Education Service Center (High School)
Date: 2/11/1999
City, State: Elgin, IL
Name of victim(s) killed: Hugo Rodriguez.
Age of victim(s) killed: 14
Name of victim(s) injured: N/A.
Age of victim(s) injured: N/A.
Name of suspect(s)/shooter(s): Rickey L. Quezada (shooter) and Pablo O. Morales (accomplice).
Age of suspect(s)/shooter(s): 15 & 19
Weapon(s): .45-caliber handgun.
High capacity magazine(s)?: Unreported.
Weapon(s) legally acquired by suspect(s)/shooter(s)?: No.
# of people killed: 1
# of people injured: 0
Total # of victims: 1

Time suspect(s)/shooter(s) were apprehended or killed?: Quezada was arrested 5 days after the shooting at a Wheeling home. Morales was also arrested 5 days after the shooting at his own home.

Suspect(s)' mental illness: Unreported.

Suspect(s)' medication or drug use: Unreported.

Suspect(s)' criminal history: Unreported.

Warning signs: Unreported. Ombudsman Education Service Center is an alternative school for at-risk teens.

Suspect(s)' country of citizenship: Unreported.

Suspect(s)' religious affiliation: Unreported.

Alleged reason for shooting: Gang-related.

Metal detectors present?: No.

Location & time of shooting: Shooting occurred in a classroom.

For more information, contact: Judge Philip DiMarzio, Elgin Police Detective Jesse Padron, Detective Jim Lullo, Ombudsman co-owner Lori Sweeny, and Ombudsman President James Boyle.

Citations/sources: (National School Safety Center, 2010, p. 22) (Holt & Karuhn, 1999, p. Section 2-5) (Krol, 1999, p. Section 1-4) (Ferkenhoff & Quintanilla, 1999, p. Section 2-1 & 6)

962

Location of shooting: Columbine High School

Date: 4/20/1999

City, State: Littleton, CO

Name of victim(s) killed: Cassie Bernall, Steven Curnow, Corey DePooter, Kelly Fleming, Matthew Kechter, Daniel Mauser, Daniel Rohrbough, William "Dave" Sanders, Rachel Scott, Isaiah Shoels, John Tomlin, Lauren Townsend, Kyle Velasquez, Eric Harris (shooter), and Dylan Klebold (shooter).

Age of victim(s) killed: 17, 14, 17, 16, 16, 15, 15, 47, 17, 18, 16, 18, 16, 18, & 17

Name of victim(s) injured: Evan Todd, Sean Graves, Mark Taylor, Michael (Mike) Johnson, Makai Hall, Lance Kirklin, Nicole Nowlen, Adam Kyler, Richard Castaldo, Mark Kintgen, Patrick Ireland, Kasey Ruegsegger, Jennifer Doyle, Stephanie Munson, Danny (Dan) Steepleton, Brian Anderson, Valeen Schnurr, Lisa Kreutz, Jeanna Park, Nicholas (Nick) Foss, Joyce Jankowski, Patricia (Pat) Nielson, Stephen Austin Eubanks, unreported, unreported, unreported, and unreported.

Age of victim(s) injured: 15, 15, 15, 15, 16, 16, 16, 16, 17, 17, 17, 17, 17, 17, 17, 18, 18, 18, 18, 45, 45, ?, ?, ?, ?, & ?

Name of suspect(s)/shooter(s): Eric Harris and Dylan Klebold.

Age of suspect(s)/shooter(s): 18 & 17

Weapon(s): Intratec TEC-DC9 semi-automatic pistol, Hi-Point 995 Carbine pistol, Savage 67H pump-action shotgun, Stevens 311D double barreled sawed-off shotgun, 100 rounds of ammunition, 99 explosives, and 4 knives.

High capacity magazine(s)?: Yes. No details mentioned.

Weapon(s) legally acquired by suspect(s)/shooter(s)?: No. Illegally purchased by shooters from Mark Manes, who was sentenced to six years in prison.

# of people killed: 16

# of people injured: 27

Total # of victims: 43

Time suspect(s)/shooter(s) were apprehended or killed?: Suicide. Shooters committed suicide approximately 49 minutes after shooting began.

Suspect(s)' mental illness: Eric Haris complained of depression, anger, and suicidal thoughts to psychiatrist.

Suspect(s)' medication or drug use: Eric Harris had been taking Luvox for a year and a half, prior to school attack.

Suspect(s)' criminal history: Both suspects were arrested in January 1998 for theft. Pled guilty and sent to a juvenile diversion program.

Warning signs: Shooter's sister claimed he "joked around in class about shooting people. He acted like he had a gun, but no one took him seriously." Eric Harris' journal entries express his admiration for Nazis and swastikas, his admission of being a racist, his hatred of his own appearance, his lack of self-esteem, and his desire to kill and instill fear in others.

Suspect(s)' country of citizenship: U.S.A.

Suspect(s)' religious affiliation: Unreported.

Alleged reason for shooting: Bullying. Physical and verbal. Psychopathic behavior.

Metal detectors present?: Unreported.

Location & time of shooting: The suspects placed a 20-pound propane bomb in the cafeteria at 11:10 a.m., then began shooting students in the library and hallways around 11:19 a.m. before killing themselves in the school's library at approximately 12:08 p.m.

For more information, contact: Judge Robert Blackburn, Colorado Attorney General Ken Salazar, Psychiatrist Dr. Frank Ochberg, and FBI Supervisory Special Agent Dwayne Fuselier.

Citations/sources: (Columbine Shooting, 2018) (Landman, 2013, p. 5) (National School Safety Center, 2010, p. 22 & 23) (Crews, 2016, p. 6) (Lebrun, 2009, p. 175) (Newman, Fox, Harding, Mehta, & Roth, 2004, p. 139, 238, & 247) (Fleshler, Chokey, Huriash & Trischitta, 2018, p. 1A & 9A) (Columbine High School, 2019) (Cullen, 2004) (Cabell: Columbine killers, 2003) (Levenson, 2025) (Conditions of school shooting victims, 1999) (Conditions of the wounded, 1999) (Obmascik, 2019) (Ontiveroz, 2019) (Langman Ph.D., 2014) (Jefferson County Sheriff's Office, 2017)

#961

Location of shooting: Martin Luther King Jr. Middle School

Date: 4/22/1999

City, State: Atlanta, GA

Name of victim(s) killed: Geno Vaelette Jerome Thomas.

Age of victim(s) killed: 13

Name of victim(s) injured: N/A.

Age of victim(s) injured: N/A.

Name of suspect(s)/shooter(s): Horace "Bubba" Holt Jr.
Age of suspect(s)/shooter(s): 17
Weapon(s): Revolver.
High capacity magazine(s)?: Unreported.
Weapon(s) legally acquired by suspect(s)/shooter(s)?: No.
# of people killed: 1
# of people injured: 0
Total # of victims: 1
Time suspect(s)/shooter(s) were apprehended or killed?: Suspect turned himself in two days after the shooting.
Suspect(s)' mental illness: Unreported.
Suspect(s)' medication or drug use: Unreported.
Suspect(s)' criminal history: Suspect was previously arrested for fighting, but was given a copy of the charges instead of being booked into jail.
Warning signs: Unreported.
Suspect(s)' country of citizenship: Unreported.
Suspect(s)' religious affiliation: Unreported.
Alleged reason for shooting: Unreported.
Metal detectors present?: N/A.
Location & time of shooting: Victim was shot in a parking lot next to the school at 9:45 p.m., after a school jazz and dance recital.
For more information, contact: Homicide Squad Supervisor Sgt. Cecil Mann, Maj. Mickey Lloyd, Mayor Bill Campbell, Atlanta Homicide Sgt. Scott Bennett, Detectives Bret Zimbrick, Dale Kelly, and A.B. Calhoun.
Citations/sources: (Carter, 2000) (National School Safety Center, 2010, p. 23) (Carter & Ffrench-Parker, 1999, p. G1 & G6) (Warner, 1999, p. F1)

#960
Location of shooting: Scotlandville Middle School
Date: 4/22/1999
City, State: Scotlandville, LA
Name of victim(s) killed: N/A.
Age of victim(s) killed: N/A.
Name of victim(s) injured: Unnamed girl due to age.
Age of victim(s) injured: 14
Name of suspect(s)/shooter(s): Murphy Young (shooter) and Jonathan Wells (accomplice).
Age of suspect(s)/shooter(s): 14 & 14
Weapon(s): .22-caliber pistol.
High capacity magazine(s)?: Unreported.
Weapon(s) legally acquired by suspect(s)/shooter(s)?: No.
# of people killed: 0

<u># of people injured</u>: 1

<u>Total # of victims</u>: 1

<u>Time suspect(s)/shooter(s) were apprehended or killed?</u>: Suspect was arrested within hours of the shooting.

<u>Suspect(s)' mental illness</u>: Unreported.

<u>Suspect(s)' medication or drug use</u>: Unreported.

<u>Suspect(s)' criminal history</u>: Young had previously been arrested for having a gun near a school campus.

<u>Warning signs</u>: Unreported.

<u>Suspect(s)' country of citizenship</u>: Unreported.

<u>Suspect(s)' religious affiliation</u>: Unreported.

<u>Alleged reason for shooting</u>: Argument.

<u>Metal detectors present?</u>: N/A.

<u>Location & time of shooting</u>: Victim was shot outside, between two school buildings at about 12:30 p.m. Suspect shot the wrong student from 100 yards away.

<u>For more information, contact</u>: East Baton Rouge Parish Sheriff's Office Lt. Darrell Oneal and Baton Rouge General Medical Center Spokeswoman Jace Dobrowolski.

<u>Citations/sources</u>: (Teen-age girl is wounded, 1999, p. 17A) (School incidents probed, 1999, p. 2)

#959
Location of shooting: Heritage High School

<u>Date</u>: 5/20/1999

<u>City, State</u>: Conyers, GA

<u>Name of victim(s) killed</u>: N/A.

<u>Age of victim(s) killed</u>: N/A.

<u>Name of victim(s) injured</u>: Drake Hoy, Ryan Rosa, Jason Cheek, Brian Barnhardt, Cania Collins, and Stephanie Laster.

<u>Age of victim(s) injured</u>: 18, 18, 17, 16, 15, & 15

<u>Name of suspect(s)/shooter(s)</u>: Anthony B. "T.J." Solomon, Jr.

<u>Age of suspect(s)/shooter(s)</u>: 15

<u>Weapon(s)</u>: .22-caliber rifle and .357 magnum revolver.

<u>High capacity magazine(s)?</u>: No. Standard 12-round rifle.

<u>Weapon(s) legally acquired by suspect(s)/shooter(s)?</u>: No. Stolen from his step-father's locked gun cabinet.

<u># of people killed</u>: 0

<u># of people injured</u>: 6

<u>Total # of victims</u>: 6

<u>Time suspect(s)/shooter(s) were apprehended or killed?</u>: Shooter surrendered firearm to principal within 12 minutes of shooting.

Suspect(s)' mental illness: Yes. Attention deficit disorder. Diagnosed with clinical depression -- possibly dysthymic disorder.

Suspect(s)' medication or drug use: Ritalin.

Suspect(s)' criminal history: None.

Warning signs: Shooter brought a gun to school a month before the shooting and showed it to a friend who then reported him to the school office. Told friends he was going to shoot his classmates. Threatened to blow up his classroom. Suicidal threats.

Suspect(s)' country of citizenship: U.S.A.

Suspect(s)' religious affiliation: Christian

Alleged reason for shooting: Mental illness, rejection and influence from Columbine shooting. Distraught over a breakup with his girlfriend.

Metal detectors present?: Unreported.

Location & time of shooting: Shooting occurred in one of the common areas of the school approximately 7:30 a.m.

For more information, contact: Former Assistant Principal Cecil Brinkley, Rockdale County District Attorney Richard Read, Forensic Psychologist James Edwards, and Juvenile Judge Court Judge William Schneider.

Citations/sources: (Moore, Petrie, Braga, & McLaughlin, 2013, p.25, 38-40, 52, 54, 266-283) (Queen, 2016) (Cloud, 1999) (Lebrun, 2009, p. 175) (Newman, Fox, Harding, Mehta, & Roth, 2004, p. 238) (Stafford, 2000, p. JR5) (Stafford, 1999, p. C1 & C6) (Jones, 1999, p. 1A & 2A) (Quinn, 2015)

#958
Location of shooting: Jasper County Comprehensive High School
Date: 8/25/1999
City, State: Monticello, GA
Name of victim(s) killed: Amanda Gaylynne Tanquary (shooter).
Age of victim(s) killed: 16
Name of victim(s) injured: N/A.
Age of victim(s) injured: N/A.
Name of suspect(s)/shooter(s): Amanda Gaylynne Tanquary.
Age of suspect(s)/shooter(s): 16
Weapon(s): Unreported.
High capacity magazine(s)?: Unreported.
Weapon(s) legally acquired by suspect(s)/shooter(s)?: No.
# of people killed: 1
# of people injured: 0
Total # of victims: 1
Time suspect(s)/shooter(s) were apprehended or killed?: Suicide.
Suspect(s)' mental illness: Unreported.
Suspect(s)' medication or drug use: Unreported.
Suspect(s)' criminal history: Unreported.

Warning signs: Unreported.
Suspect(s)' country of citizenship: Unreported.
Suspect(s)' religious affiliation: Unreported.
Alleged reason for shooting: Unreported.
Metal detectors present?: N/A.
Location & time of shooting: Student shot herself in a pickup truck parked in the school parking lot. Her body was discovered shortly after 9:00 a.m.
For more information, contact: Jasper County Superintendent Julian Cope, Student Services Director Mike Newton, and Jasper County Emergency Management Director Ed Westbrook.
Citations/sources: (National School Safety Center, 2010, p. 23) (Williams, 1999a, p. A-8)

#957
Location of shooting: Vines High School
Date: 9/7/1999
City, State: Plano, TX
Name of victim(s) killed: Brent Austin (shooter)
Age of victim(s) killed: 16
Name of victim(s) injured: N/A.
Age of victim(s) injured: N/A.
Name of suspect(s)/shooter(s): Brent Austin
Age of suspect(s)/shooter(s): 16
Weapon(s): Small caliber handgun.
High capacity magazine(s)?: Unreported.
Weapon(s) legally acquired by suspect(s)/shooter(s)?: No. Gun stolen from parents.
# of people killed: 1
# of people injured: 0
Total # of victims: 1
Time suspect(s)/shooter(s) were apprehended or killed?: Suicide.
Suspect(s)' mental illness: Unreported.
Suspect(s)' medication or drug use: Unreported.
Suspect(s)' criminal history: Unreported.
Warning signs: Unreported.
Suspect(s)' country of citizenship: Unreported.
Suspect(s)' religious affiliation: Unreported.
Alleged reason for shooting: Unreported.
Metal detectors present?: Unreported.
Location & time of shooting: Student shot himself in school boy's bathroom stall about 12:30 p.m.
For more information, contact: Plano Police Spokesman Carl Duke.
Citations/sources: (National School Safety Center, 2010, p. 23) (Muscanere, 1999a, p. 1A) (Muscanere, 1999b, p. 1A)

#956
Location of shooting: Santa Teresa High School
Date: 9/9/1999
City, State: San Jose, CA
Name of victim(s) killed: Marcos Sarabia (shooter).
Age of victim(s) killed: 16
Name of victim(s) injured: N/A.
Age of victim(s) injured: N/A.
Name of suspect(s)/shooter(s): Marcos Sarabia
Age of suspect(s)/shooter(s): 16
Weapon(s): Handgun.
High capacity magazine(s)?: Unreported.
Weapon(s) legally acquired by suspect(s)/shooter(s)?: No.
# of people killed: 1
# of people injured: 0
Total # of victims: 1
Time suspect(s)/shooter(s) were apprehended or killed?: Suicide.
Suspect(s)' mental illness: Unreported.
Suspect(s)' medication or drug use: Unreported.
Suspect(s)' criminal history: None.
Warning signs: No.
Suspect(s)' country of citizenship: Unreported.
Suspect(s)' religious affiliation: Unreported.
Alleged reason for shooting: Unreported.
Metal detectors present?: No.
Location & time of shooting: Student shot himself in school bathroom at approximately 8:20 a.m.
For more information, contact: San Jose Acting Deputy Chief Donald Anders, Superintendent Joe Coto, and Deputy District Superintendent Bill Kugler.
Citations/sources: (National School Safety Center, 2010, p. 24) (Teen kills self in San Jose, 1999, p. A-5) (Squatriglia, Lynem, & Gaura, 1999)

#955
Location of shooting: John Bartram High School
Date: 10/4/1999
City, State: Philadelphia, PA
Name of victim(s) killed: N/A.
Age of victim(s) killed: N/A.
Name of victim(s) injured: William Burke (Assistant Principal).
Age of victim(s) injured: 61

Name of suspect(s)/shooter(s): Eric L. Coxen.
Age of suspect(s)/shooter(s): 15
Weapon(s): .25-caliber handgun.
High capacity magazine(s)?: Unreported.
Weapon(s) legally acquired by suspect(s)/shooter(s)?: No.
# of people killed: 0
# of people injured: 1
Total # of victims: 1
Time suspect(s)/shooter(s) were apprehended or killed?: Unreported.
Suspect(s)' mental illness: Unreported.
Suspect(s)' medication or drug use: Unreported.
Suspect(s)' criminal history: None.
Warning signs: Unreported.
Suspect(s)' country of citizenship: Unreported.
Suspect(s)' religious affiliation: Unreported.
Alleged reason for shooting: Accident. Principal confronted the student who was suspected of carrying a gun. During a struggle with the student, the gun discharged from his pants pocket.
Metal detectors present?: Yes, but metal detectors were not yet operational.
Location & time of shooting: Shooting occurred shortly after 10:00 a.m.
For more information, contact: Philadelphia Police Officer Susan Williams, Police Spokeswoman Carmen Torres, Superintendent David Hornbeck, Assistant District Attorney Steven Collier, and Municipal Judge Robert Merriweather.
Citations/sources: (Rubinkam, 1999, p. C7) (Conroy, 1999, p. 6) (Dean & Kim, 1999, p. 3)

#954
Location of shooting: Ed W. Clark High School
Date: 10/11/1999
City, State: Las Vegas, NV
Name of victim(s) killed: N/A.
Age of victim(s) killed: N/A.
Name of victim(s) injured: Cesar Berber and Antonio Arroyo.
Age of victim(s) injured: 15 & 16
Name of suspect(s)/shooter(s): Maynor David Villanueva and Tony Tejada.
Age of suspect(s)/shooter(s): 18 & 14
Weapon(s): .357 revolver.
High capacity magazine(s)?: Unreported.
Weapon(s) legally acquired by suspect(s)/shooter(s)?: Unreported.
# of people killed: 0
# of people injured: 2
Total # of victims: 2

Time suspect(s)/shooter(s) were apprehended or killed?: Las Vegas Metropolitan Police officers arrested Villanueva shortly after the shooting. Villanueva escaped in a stolen car, crashed the vehicle, then robbed a 10-year-old child of his bicycle at knife point and continued to flee on the bicycle.

Suspect(s)' mental illness: Unreported.
Suspect(s)' medication or drug use: Unreported.
Suspect(s)' criminal history: Unreported.
Warning signs: Unreported.
Suspect(s)' country of citizenship: Unreported.
Suspect(s)' religious affiliation: Unreported.
Alleged reason for shooting: Gang-related.
Metal detectors present?: N/A.
Location & time of shooting: Shooting occurred outside of the school at approximately 2:30 p.m. while twenty to forty other students were in the area.

For more information, contact: School District Spokeswoman Mary Stanley-Larsen, Clark County School District Police Officer Sgt. Ken Young, and Clark County Eighth Judicial District Court Judge Joseph T. Bonaventure.

Citations/sources: (2 Vegas students wounded, 1999, p. 2B) (School shooting, 1999, p. A10) (Man pleads guilty, 2000, p. A3) (Villanueva v. State, 2001)

#953
Location of shooting: San Fernando High School
Date: 10/21/1999
City, State: San Fernando, CA
Name of victim(s) killed: N/A.
Age of victim(s) killed: N/A.
Name of victim(s) injured: Unnamed male student due to age.
Age of victim(s) injured: 17
Name of suspect(s)/shooter(s): Three unnamed males due to age.
Age of suspect(s)/shooter(s): 16, 16, & 16
Weapon(s): Unreported.
High capacity magazine(s)?: Unreported.
Weapon(s) legally acquired by suspect(s)/shooter(s)?: No.
# of people killed: 0
# of people injured: 1
Total # of victims: 1
Time suspect(s)/shooter(s) were apprehended or killed?: Suspects were arrested hours after the shooting.

Suspect(s)' mental illness: Unreported.
Suspect(s)' medication or drug use: Unreported.
Suspect(s)' criminal history: Unreported.

Warning signs: Unreported.
Suspect(s)' country of citizenship: Unreported.
Suspect(s)' religious affiliation: Unreported.
Alleged reason for shooting: Gang-related.
Metal detectors present?: N/A.
Location & time of shooting: Shooting occurred outside of the school about 2:40 p.m. just outside the school's child care center.
For more information, contact: LAPD Lt. Rick Papke, LAPD Sgt. Steve Nassief, State Senator Richard Alarcon, principal Philip Saldivar, and teacher Rodney Cash.
Citations/sources: (Manzano & Fox, 1999, p. B1 & B8) (Sauerwein, 1999, p. B15)

#952
Location of shooting: Martin Luther King Jr. High School
Date: 10/26/1999
City, State: Philadelphia, PA
Name of victim(s) killed: Donald McNeil.
Age of victim(s) killed: 16
Name of victim(s) injured: N/A.
Age of victim(s) injured: N/A.
Name of suspect(s)/shooter(s): Larry Burton and Keyen Hill.
Age of suspect(s)/shooter(s): 19 & 17
Weapon(s): Tec-9 machine pistol & shotgun.
High capacity magazine(s)?: Unreported.
Weapon(s) legally acquired by suspect(s)/shooter(s)?: No.
# of people killed: 1
# of people injured: 0
Total # of victims: 1
Time suspect(s)/shooter(s) were apprehended or killed?: Suspects were arrested shortly after the shooting after a high speed chase with police. The suspects collided their station wagon with a parked car.
Suspect(s)' mental illness: Unreported.
Suspect(s)' medication or drug use: Unreported.
Suspect(s)' criminal history: Burton was previously incarcerated.
Warning signs: Unreported.
Suspect(s)' country of citizenship: Unreported.
Suspect(s)' religious affiliation: Unreported.
Alleged reason for shooting: Dispute over a mistaken argument between the victim and Burton's sister.
Metal detectors present?: Yes. N/A.
Location & time of shooting: Shooting in a parking lot in front of the school at approximately 1:30 p.m.

For more information, contact: District Spokeswoman Pam Weddington, Groban Silverberg, Judge Marsha H. Neifield, and Assistant District Attorney Randolph Williams.

Citations/sources: (National School Safety Center, 2010, p. 25) (Snyder & Moran, 1999, p. B1 & B4) (Racher, 1999, p. 23) (Haney, Brennan & Silary, 1999, p. 11)

#951

Location of shooting: Dorchester High School

Date: 11/3/1999

City, State: Boston, MA

Name of victim(s) killed: N/A.

Age of victim(s) killed: N/A.

Name of victim(s) injured: Willie Furr.

Age of victim(s) injured: 16

Name of suspect(s)/shooter(s): Willie Furr and an unreported suspect.

Age of suspect(s)/shooter(s): 16 & ?

Weapon(s): Unreported.

High capacity magazine(s)?: No. Police found 7 rounds in the magazine.

Weapon(s) legally acquired by suspect(s)/shooter(s)?: No. The firearm's serial number had been obscured by abrasion and drilling.

# of people killed: 0

# of people injured: 1

Total # of victims: 1

Time suspect(s)/shooter(s) were apprehended or killed?: Unreported.

Suspect(s)' mental illness: Unreported.

Suspect(s)' medication or drug use: Unreported.

Suspect(s)' criminal history: Furr was charged with charges of armed carjacking, kidnapping, armed robbery, and assault and battery with a dangerous weapon on May 13, 1998.

Warning signs: Unreported.

Suspect(s)' country of citizenship: Unreported.

Suspect(s)' religious affiliation: Unreported.

Alleged reason for shooting: Unreported.

Metal detectors present?: N/A.

Location & time of shooting: Shooting occurred in school parking lot around 7:45 a.m.

For more information, contact: School Police Officer Lt. Mike Hennessey.

Citations/sources: (Daley, 1999, p. B1 & B6) (Commonwealth v. Furr, 2003)

#950

Location of shooting: Dickinson High School

Date: 11/17/1999

City, State: Dickinson, TX

Name of victim(s) killed: N/A.

Age of victim(s) killed: N/A.
Name of victim(s) injured: Galacio Torres.
Age of victim(s) injured: 15
Name of suspect(s)/shooter(s): Two unnamed males due to age.
Age of suspect(s)/shooter(s): 14 & 16
Weapon(s): .22-caliber pistol.
High capacity magazine(s)?: Unreported.
Weapon(s) legally acquired by suspect(s)/shooter(s)?: No.
# of people killed: 0
# of people injured: 1
Total # of victims: 1
Time suspect(s)/shooter(s) were apprehended or killed?: At least one suspect was arrested within three hours of the shooting, when the suspect led police to where the gun was hidden.
Suspect(s)' mental illness: Unreported.
Suspect(s)' medication or drug use: Unreported.
Suspect(s)' criminal history: Unreported.
Warning signs: Unreported.
Suspect(s)' country of citizenship: Unreported.
Suspect(s)' religious affiliation: Unreported.
Alleged reason for shooting: Accident.
Metal detectors present?: Yes. Handheld metal detectors, but they were not being used.
Location & time of shooting: Shooting occurred in school bathroom minutes before school began.
For more information, contact: Dickinson Police Chief Morales and Principal Michael LaTouche.
Citations/sources: (Williams, 1999b, p. A1 & A7) (Falgoust, 1999, p. A1 & A7) (15-year old wounded, 1999, p. 5B)

#949
Location of shooting: North High School
Date: 11/18/1999
City, State: Denver, CO
Name of victim(s) killed: N/A.
Age of victim(s) killed: N/A.
Name of victim(s) injured: Unnamed boy due to age.
Age of victim(s) injured: 15
Name of suspect(s)/shooter(s): Unnamed boy due to age.
Age of suspect(s)/shooter(s): 15
Weapon(s): Handgun.
High capacity magazine(s)?: Unreported.
Weapon(s) legally acquired by suspect(s)/shooter(s)?: No.

# of people killed: 0

# of people injured: 1

Total # of victims: 1

Time suspect(s)/shooter(s) were apprehended or killed?: Suspect went to his third-floor classroom where he was assigned that period within approximately 30 minutes after the shooting.

Suspect(s)' mental illness: Unreported.

Suspect(s)' medication or drug use: Unreported.

Suspect(s)' criminal history: Unreported.

Warning signs: Unreported.

Suspect(s)' country of citizenship: Unreported.

Suspect(s)' religious affiliation: Unreported.

Alleged reason for shooting: Accident. Self-inflicted shooting.

Metal detectors present?: Unreported.

Location & time of shooting: Shooting occurred near the school's old main entrance just after noon.

For more information, contact: Police Sgt. Tony Lombard, Principal Joe Sandoval, Police Spokeswoman Detective Virginia Lopez, and Superintendent Chip Zullinger.

Citations/sources: (Robinson, 1999, p. B-02) (Weber & Washington, 1999, p. 5A) (Gutierrez, 1999, p. 28A)

#948
Location of shooting: Deming Middle School

Date: 11/19/1999

City, State: Deming, NM

Name of victim(s) killed: Araceli Tena.

Age of victim(s) killed: 13

Name of victim(s) injured: N/A.

Age of victim(s) injured: N/A.

Name of suspect(s)/shooter(s): Victor Cordova Jr.

Age of suspect(s)/shooter(s): 12

Weapon(s): .22-caliber handgun.

High capacity magazine(s)?: Unreported.

Weapon(s) legally acquired by suspect(s)/shooter(s)?: No. Gun was stolen from home.

# of people killed: 1

# of people injured: 0

Total # of victims: 1

Time suspect(s)/shooter(s) were apprehended or killed?: Police apprehended the suspect within five minutes of confronting him in the school lobby.

Suspect(s)' mental illness: Depression, according to suspect's attorneys.

Suspect(s)' medication or drug use: Unreported.

Suspect(s)' criminal history: Unreported.

Warning signs: Suspect made suicidal remarks in the Spring of 1999 after his mother died of cancer.

Suspect(s)' country of citizenship: U.S.A.

Suspect(s)' religious affiliation: Unreported.

Alleged reason for shooting: Unreported. Suicide attempt gone awry, according to suspect's defense lawyers.

Metal detectors present?: Unreported.

Location & time of shooting: Shooting occurred in the lobby of the school as students were returning from lunch at approximately 12:45 p.m.

For more information, contact: Police Chief Michael Carillo, District Judge V. Lee Vesley, Dr. Thomas Thompson, Dr. Abraham Fiszbein, and District Attorney Jim Foy.

Citations/sources: (National School Safety Center, 2010, p. 25) (Crews, 2016, p. 6) (Lebrun, 2009, p. 175) (Boy held in shooting, 1999) (Brenner, 2000, p. 1 & 2) (Boy sent to prison, 2000, p. 17) (Thompson, 2000, p. A1 & A2)

#947
Location of shooting: Fort Gibson Middle School
Date: 12/6/1999

City, State: Fort Gibson, OK

Name of victim(s) killed: N/A.

Age of victim(s) killed: N/A.

Name of victim(s) injured: Bradley Schindel, Savana Knowles, Cody Chronister, William "Bily" Railey, and an unnamed student.

Age of victim(s) injured: 12, 12, 13, 13 & ?

Name of suspect(s)/shooter(s): Seth Trickney

Age of suspect(s)/shooter(s): 13

Weapon(s): 9mm semiautomatic handgun.

High capacity magazine(s)?: No. Standard 15-round magazine.

Weapon(s) legally acquired by suspect(s)/shooter(s)?: No. Suspect stole firearm and magazine clip from his father, who worked for the Bureau of Indian Affairs at the time.

# of people killed: 0

# of people injured: 5

Total # of victims: 5

Time suspect(s)/shooter(s) were apprehended or killed?: Shooter was apprehended "within seconds" after shooting began by Science Teacher Ron Holuby.

Suspect(s)' mental illness: Unreported.

Suspect(s)' medication or drug use: Three weeks before the shooting, the suspect had been injected with an overdose of the prescription poison ivy drug Kenalog.

Suspect(s)' criminal history: None.

Warning signs: Yes. Shooter's sister claimed he "joked around in class about shooting people. He acted like he had a gun, but no one took him seriously."

Suspect(s)' country of citizenship: Unreported.

Suspect(s)' religious affiliation: Christian.

Alleged reason for shooting: Protest authority. Rejection. The former honor student also testified he felt pressure to perform well at school. He also claimed an obsession with the military, fascination with Columbine school massacre in Colorado and a perceived lack of attention from parents.

Metal detectors present?: N/A.

Location & time of shooting: Shooting occurred outside of the school as students were waiting to enter for the start of classes at approximately 7:45 a.m.

For more information, contact: Police Chief Richard Slader, Toxicologist Dr. William Banner, Sheriff's Deputy Terry Chang, Science Teacher Ronnie Holuby, Governor Frank Keating, District Attorney John David Luton.

Citations/sources: (Romano, 1999) (Ruble, 1999, p. A1 & A4) (Gun in school shooting was father's, 1999) (Jackson, 1999) (Lebrun, 2009, p. 175) (Newman, Fox, Harding, Mehta, & Roth, 2004, p. 239) (School shooter may end up, 2003) (Hutchinson, 1999, p. 12-A)

2

About the Author

Luis D. Aponte
Photo by Bob Lasky

Luis D. Aponte is a librarian, U.S. Air Force veteran, and the author of four books and eBooks on school shootings: *A Safe Place: How to Prevent the Next School Shooting* and *The Ultimate U.S. School Shooting Reference Guide, Volumes 1-3*. His work has been published in Virginia's Mt. Vernon Gazette and Fairfax Connection newspapers and the peer-reviewed EDUCATION journal. Luis resides in Virginia, where he enjoys forest bathing in national parks with his wife, making films, and spoiling their adopted orange tabby cat, Ellie.

In 1992-1993, Luis attended Marjory Stoneman Douglas High School in Parkland, Florida, but dropped out during his junior year due to the threat of gun violence on campus. Approximately 25 years later, the same school experienced one of the worst school shootings in U.S. history. Since then, Luis has dedicated his research skills as a librarian to finding patterns in 1,204 U.S. school shooting incidents over 30 years, aiming to help save children's lives.

Originally from Savannah, Georgia, Luis earned his master's degree in Library and Information Science from the University of South Florida, his bachelor's degree in Communications – Film & Video from Florida Atlantic University, and his associate's degree in Computer Science from Broward College in Florida, all with honors. He was also a member and historian for his local chapters of the Golden Key International Honour Society and Phi Theta Kappa International College Honor Society.

Luis hopes his books on school shootings will help bring communities together to save lives. Children and educators deserve to feel safe in schools without the threat of gun violence.

3

Connect With Me

Website: www.ASafePlaceBook.com
Linktree: https://linktr.ee/LuisAponte
Facebook: @ASafePlaceBook
Instagram: @ASafePlaceBook
Bluesky: @ASafePlaceBook.bsky.social
YouTube: @ASafePlaceBook

4

Other Titles by Luis D. Aponte

eBooks distributed by **Draft2Digital.com**.
Physical books distributed by **IngramSpark.com**.
A Safe Place is also available as an eAudiobook on major platforms via **Voices by INaudio**.

A Safe Place: How to Prevent the Next School Shooting

The Ultimate U.S. School Shooting Reference Guide: Volume 1: 1990-1999

The Ultimate U.S. School Shooting Reference Guide: Volume 2: 2000-2009

The Ultimate U.S. School Shooting Reference Guide: Volume 3: 2010-2019

5

Notes

1204 - Compton High School

Shots from car wound youth at high school. (1990, January 10). *Los Angeles Times*. Retrieved from http://articles.latimes.com/1990-01-10/local/me-136_1_compton-high-school

Fuetsch, M. (1990, May 13). Latest ideas for school cuts touch off uproar. *Los Angeles Times*, p. J3. Retrieved from https://www.newspapers.com/image/175391261/?terms=%22Compton%2BHigh%2BSchool%22

1203 - Central High School

Middleton, T. (1990, January 16). Two wounded in school shooting, racial tensions blamed. *United Press International*. Retrieved from https://www.upi.com/Archives/1990/01/16/Two-wounded-in-school-shooting-racial-tensions-blamed/1799632466000/

1202 - Taft High School

Paralyzed for life: stray bullet still didn't sway Cincy teen's faith. (1990, November 19). *Chronicle-Telegram, The*, p. 29.

Noble, G. (2017, April 6). From the vault: in 1990, Derrick Turnbow symbolized best and worst of city wracked by gun violence. *WCPO*. Retrieved from https://www.wcpo.com/news/our-community/from-the-vault/from-the-vault-derrick-turnbow-symbolized-best-and-worst-of-city-wracked-by-gun-violence

1201 - New Utrecht High School

Black youth shot by whites. (1990, March 28). *Freelance Star, The*, p. 6. Retrieved from https://news.google.com/newspapers?id=LeFLAAAAIBAJ&pg=4139,5070023

Hevesi, D. (1990, March 28). A black is shot in a high school in Bensonhurst. *New York Times, The*. Retrieved from https://www.nytimes.com/1990/03/28/nyregion/a-black-is-shot-in-a-high-school-in-bensonshurst.html

1200 - Skyline High School

Student is shot at Dallas campus. (1990, April 4). *Galveston Daily News, The*, p. 11-A

Mittelstadt, M. (1990, April 4). Student shot at Dallas School. *Monitor, The*, p. 4A. Retrieved from https://www.newspapers.com/image/322875319/?terms=Skyline%2BHigh%2BSchool%2Bshooting

1199 - Manuel Arts High School

Adams, D. (1990, May 4). Gang shooting at Manuel Arts High School in 1990 [Video file]. *KCOP-TV News 13*. Retrieved from https://www.dailymotion.com/video/x2vpwx9

Sahagun, L., & Churm, S. (1990, May 2). Racial, gang tensions lead to violence at 3 schools. *Los Angeles Times*, p. A20. Retrieved from https://www.newspapers.com/image/175160387/?terms=Manual%2BArts%2Bhigh%2Bschool%2C

Ethnic tensions start high school mayhem. (1990, May 3). *Ukiah Daily Journal*, p. 7. Retrieved from https://www.newspapers.com/image/1262320/?terms=freddy%2Btapia%2C

1198 - Mount Pleasant High School

2 teens arrested in schoolyard killing. (1990, May 6, 1990). *San Francisco Examiner*, p. B-8. Retrieved from https://www.newspapers.com/image/462261165/?terms=Mount%2BPleasant%2BHigh%2BSchool%2Bshooting

Quintero, F. (1992, June 16). Group wants hate-crime charge against them. *San Jose Mercury News*, pp 8B.

Shooting suspect. (1990, May 15). *San Francisco Examiner, The*, p. A-19. Retrieved from https://www.newspapers.com/image/462164747/?terms=Mount%2BPleasant%2BHigh%2BSchool%2C

Boy, 15, fatally shot on campus. (1990, May 5). *San Francisco Examiner, The*, p. A-2. Retrieved from https://www.newspapers.com/image/462253086/?terms=Mount%2BPleasant%2BHigh%2BSchool%2C

1197 - Waynesburg Elementary School

Joint services planned for Waynesburg couple. (1990, May 11). *Advocate-Messenger, The*, p. A2. Retrieved from https://www.newspapers.com/image/137937156/?terms=Waynesburg%2BElementary%2BSchool%2C

Stevens, V. S. (1990, May 10). Man guns down school secretary. *Advocate-Messenger, The*, p. A1. Retrieved from https://www.newspapers.com/image/137936977/?terms=Waynesburg%2BElementary%2BSchool%2C

Kentucky man kills wife, self. (1990, May 11). *Leaf-Chronicle, The*, p. 9A. Retrieved from https://www.newspapers.com/image/467684696/?terms=Waynesburg%2BElementary%2BSchool%2C

1196 - Hickman County High School

Schoonover, S. (1990, May 23). Called grand jury session possible in Hickman case. *Tennessean, The*, p. 1B. Retrieved from https://www.newspapers.com/image/112431046/?terms=Hickman%2BCounty%2BHigh%2BSchool%2C

Teacher charged in killing. (1990, May 22). *Journal and Courier*, p. A3. Retrieved from https://www.newspapers.com/image/264083316/?terms=Hickman%2BCounty%2BHigh%2BSchool%2C

Teacher charged in slaying. (1990. May 22). *New York Times, The*. Retrieved from https://www.nytimes.com/1990/05/22/us/teacher-charged-in-slaying.html

1195 - Adams Elementary School

Police say father shot toddler, self. (1990, June 1). *Longview News-Journal*, p. 8-A. Retrieved from https://www.newspapers.com/image/213770638/?terms=Police%2Bsay%2Bfather%2Bshot%2Btoddler%2C%2Bself%2C

San Antonian shoots baby, self. (1990, June 1). *Austin American-Statesman*, p. B3. Retrieved from https://www.newspapers.com/image/358507593/?terms=Sunrise%2BElementary%2BSchool%2Band

1194 - Sunrise Elementary School

Two students hit in drive-by shooting. (1990, June 1). *Longview News-Journal*, p. 8-A. Retrieved from https://www.newspapers.com/image/213770638/?terms=Two%2Bstudents%2Bhit%2Bin%2Bdrive-by%2Bshooting%2C

2 Fort Worth students shot from passing car. (1990, June 1). *Austin American-Statesman*, p. B3. Retrieved from https://www.newspapers.com/image/358507593/?terms=Sunrise%2BElementary%2BSchool%2Band

2 schoolchildren hurt in drive-by shooting. (1990, June 1). *El Paso Times*, p. 4B. Retrieved from https://www.newspapers.com/image/431528264/?terms=Sunrise%2BElementary%2BSchool%2Band

1193 - Myers Park High School

Shots kill teenager, injure man at football game. (1990, August 26). *Atlanta Journal and Constitution, The*, p. D-10. Retrieved from https://www.newspapers.com/image/400340582/?terms=Myers%2BPark%2BHigh%2BSchool%2C

One dead, one injured after shooting Friday. (1990, August 26). *Rocky Mount Telegram*, p. 33. Retrieved from https://www.newspapers.com/image/337786762/?terms=%22One%2Bdead%2C%2Bone%2Binjured%22

Charlotte schools move times for high school football games. (1990, August 29). *Gaffney Ledger, The*, p. 13-A. Retrieved from https://www.newspapers.com/image/78539745/?terms=Myers%2BPark%2BHigh%2BSchool%2C

Youth shot, killed during football game. (1990, August 26). *Asheville Citizen-Times*, p14A. Retrieved from https://www.newspapers.com/image/199848611/?terms=Myers%2BPark%2BHigh%2BSchool%2C

Police charge 2 teens in death at football game. (1990, August 26). *Index-Journal, The*, p. 4A. Retrieved from https://www.newspapers.com/image/70156559/?terms=Myers%2BPark%2BHigh%2BSchool%2C

1192 - Eldorado High School

Shoro, M. & Delaney, M. (2018, September 12). 1 dead in shooting at North Las Vegas high school. *Las Vegas Review-Journal*. Retrieved from https://www.reviewjournal.com/crime/homicides/1-dead-in-shooting-at-north-las-vegas-high-school/

Smith, J. (2016, January 10). Convicted killer out but still serving life. *Las Vegas Review-Journal*. Retrieved from https://www.reviewjournal.com/uncategorized/convicted-killer-out-but-still-serving-life/

Grove, B. (1998, June 20). Memories linger for victim's mother. *Las Vegas Sun*. Retrieved from https://lasvegassun.com/news/1998/jun/20/memories-linger-for-victims-mother/

1191 - Sam Houston High School

3 San Antonio teens wounded. (1990, September 12). *Victoria Advocate, The*, p. 3C. Retrieved from https://www.newspapers.com/image/432704435/?terms=3%2BSan%2BAntonio%2Bteens%2Bwounded%2C

School shooting part of a bigger gang problem. (1990, September 13). *New Braunfels Herald-Zeitung*, p. 6. Retrieved from https://www.newspapers.com/image/9761158/?terms=Sam%2BHouston%2BHigh%2BSchool%2C

3 teens hurt in high school shooting. (1990, September 12). *El Paso Times*, p. 3B. Retrieved from https://www.newspapers.com/image/431385574/?terms=Sam%2BHouston%2BHigh%2BSchool%2C

Shannon, K. (1990, September 12). School shooting hurts 3. *Times, The*, p. 13A. Retrieved from https://www.newspapers.com/image/217306522/?terms=%22Kenneth%2BWolford%22

1190 - William Hardin Adamson High School

Nevins, A. (1990, October 3). Adamson high school student wounded in drive-by shooting. *Dallas Morning News*, p. 32A

1189 - Naaman Forest High School

Assistant principal shot. (1990, October 31). *Odessa American, The*, p. 14A. Retrieved from https://www.newspapers.com/image/300370142/?terms=Naaman%2BForest%2BHigh%2BSchool%2C

Mother accused of shooting principal. (1990, October 31). *El Paso Times*, p. 3B. Retrieved from https://www.newspapers.com/image/431542021/?terms=Naaman%2BForest%2BHigh%2BSchool%2C

1188 - Richardson High School

Miller, B., & Nevins, A. (1991, January 8). Richardson teen-ager kills himself in front of classmates. *Dallas Morning News, The*. Retrieved from http://www.fivehorizons.com/songs/aug99/jeremy_article.shtml

H.S. students recovering after shocking suicide. (1991, January 9). *Monitor, The*, p. 4A. Retrieved from https://www.newspapers.com/image/322789445/?terms=Richardson%2BHigh%2BSchool%2C

Student shoots, kills himself. (1991, January 9). *Odessa American, The*, p. 2B. Retrieved from https://www.newspapers.com/image/297920056/?terms=Richardson%2BHigh%2BSchool%2C

1187 - John B. Hood Middle School

A teenage girl. (1991, January 18). *Marshall News Messenger, The*, p. 2A. Retrieved from https://www.newspapers.com/image/331229871/?terms=Hood%2BMiddle%2BSchool%2C

Girl shot in gang fight. (1991, January 19). *Del Rio News Herald*. Retrieved from https://www.newspapers.com/image/9546048/?terms=John%2BB.%2BHood%2BMiddle%2BSchool%2C

1186 - Donna High School

Student fatally shoots himself. (1991, February 7). *Victoria Advocate, The*, p. 4C.

1185 - Booker T Washington High School

Booker T. Washington: always time to cry. (1991, February 24). *Town Talk, The*, p. A-9. Retrieved from https://www.newspapers.com/image/216895876/?terms=Booker%2BT.%2BWashington%2BHigh%2BSchool%2Bshooting

Cops probe N.O. student killing. (1991, February 21). *St. Mary and Franklin Banner-Tribune*, p. 2. Retrieved from https://www.newspapers.com/image/473061678

N.O. police search for killer of student. (1991, February 21). *Town Talk, The*, p. D-10. Retrieved from https://www.newspapers.com/image/216895341/?terms=Booker%2BT%2BWashington%2BHigh%2BSchool%2C%2BMichael%2BJarrow

Escapee charged in death of student. (1991, March 24). *Times, The*, p. 19A. Retrieved from https://www.newspapers.com/image/217968468/?terms=Booker%2BT%2BWashington%2BHigh%2BSchool%2C%2BMichael%2BJarrow

1184 - Woodmont High School

Moore, T. (1991a, March 15). 5 shot outside Woodmont High. *Greenville News, The*, p. 1A & 6A. Retrieved from https://www.newspapers.com/image/192044425/?terms=Woodmont%2BHigh%2BSchool%2C

Moore, T. (1991b, March 22). Police make first arrests in Woodmont High School shootings. *Greenville News, The*, p. 2C. Retrieved from https://www.newspapers.com/image/192033170/?terms=Woodmont%2BHigh%2BSchool%2C

4 injured at high school. (1991, March 15). *Gaffney Ledger, The*, p. 9. Retrieved from https://www.newspapers.com/image/79394443/?terms=Woodmont%2BHigh%2BSchool%2C

Burns, M. (1992, April 9). Man gets 15 years in school shooting. *Greenville News, The*, p. 1C. Retrieved from https://www.newspapers.com/image/192382156/?terms=lincoln%2Bhigh%2Bschool%2Bshooting

1183 - Garinger High School

Extra security at high school after shooting. (1991, March 27). *Asheville Citizen-Times*, p. 2B. Retrieved from https://www.newspapers.com/image/200149579/?terms=Garinger%2BHigh%2BSchool%2C

Previous dispute prompted shooting. (1991, March 26). *Evening Telegram, The*, p. 3. Retrieved from https://www.newspapers.com/image/337904196/?terms=Garinger%2BHigh%2BSchool%2C

1182 - Ralph J. Bunche Middle School

Russel, R. & Fuetsh, M. (1991, April 24). Shot fired at guard kills boy at school: violence: the 11-year-old was struck as he left a Compton campus. Police say youths had targeted a security officer because of an earlier incident. *Los Angeles Times*. Retrieved from http://articles.latimes.com/1991-04-24/local/me-536_1_security-guard

Tobar, H., & Fuetsch, M. (1991, April 25). School assaults bring tragedy to Compton. *Los Angeles Times*. Retrieved from https://www.latimes.com/archives/la-xpm-1991-04-25-mn-828-story.html

1181 - Franklin Alternative Middle School

Detroit youth faces charges in the death of Columbus man. (1991, May 12). *Newark Advocate, The*, p. 2A. Retrieved from https://www.newspapers.com/image/289233212/?terms=Franklin%2BAlternative%2BMiddle%2BSchool%2C

Bullets bounce into school parking lot. (1991, May 10). *Tribune, The*, p. 5. Retrieved from https://www.newspapers.com/image/322673018/?terms=Franklin%2BAlternative%2BMiddle%2BSchool%2C

1180 - Coronado Middle School

Two hurt in junior high shooting. (1991, May 17). *Greenville News, The*, p. 6C. Retrieved from https://www.newspapers.com/image/191945199/?terms=Coronado%2BMiddle%2BSchool%2C

Juveniles held in shooting. (1991, May 22). *Manhattan Mercury, The*, p. A3. Retrieved from https://www.newspapers.com/image/424946125/?terms=Coronado%2BMiddle%2BSchool%2C

1179 - School of Choice (Grades 6 - 12)

Goldberg, K. (1991, May 21). Florida girl fatally shot as bystander in schoolyard. *Republic, The*, p. A6. Retrieved from https://www.newspapers.com/image/147306128/?terms=School%2Bof%2BChoice%2C

Swart, K. (1991, May 22). Students feel sadness, anger after shootings. *South Florida Sun-Sentinel*, p. 4B. Retrieved from https://www.newspapers.com/image/238280330

Harris, C. (1991, May 22). School coping with student's death. *Palm Beach Post, The*, p. 4B. Retrieved from https://www.newspapers.com/image/132202726/?terms=Benjamin%2BDotson%2C

1178 - Robert A. Millikan Junior High School (Middle school)

Banks, S. & Sengupta, S. (1993, January 22). Student Shot to Death in Fairfax High Class: Violence: Classmate was handling a .357 magnum in his backpack, officials say. Another youth is wounded. *Los Angeles Times*. Retrieved from http://articles.latimes.com/1993-01-22/news/mn-1693_1_fairfax-high-school

Braxton, G. (1991, May 26). Police seek gang member in 2 killings. *Los Angeles Times*, p. B12. Retrieved from https://www.newspapers.com/image/176951271/?terms=Robert%2BA.%2BMillikan%2BJunior%2BHigh%2BSchool%2C

1177 - Westchester High School

Banks, S. & Sengupta, S. (1993, January 22). Student Shot to Death in Fairfax High Class: Violence: Classmate was handling a .357 magnum in his backpack, officials say. Another youth is wounded. *Los Angeles Times*. Retrieved from http://articles.latimes.com/1993-01-22/news/mn-1693_1_fairfax-high-school

Helfand, D. (1991, July 25). Westchester High School student injured in gang-related shooting. *Los Angeles Times*, p. B4. Retrieved from https://www.newspapers.com/image/176655612/?terms=Westchester%2BHigh%2BSchool%2C

Student shot in drive-by attack at RTD bus stop. (1991, July 23). *Los Angeles Times*, p. B2. Retrieved from https://www.newspapers.com/image/176589608/?terms=Westchester%2BHigh%2BSchool%2C

1176 - Enterprise Middle School

Banks, S. & Sengupta, S. (1993, January 22). Student Shot to Death in Fairfax High Class: Violence: Classmate was handling a .357 magnum in his backpack, officials say. Another youth is wounded. *Los Angeles Times*. Retrieved from http://articles.latimes.com/1993-01-22/news/mn-1693_1_fairfax-high-school

Boy, 14, shot while visiting school campus. (1991, July 31). *Los Angeles Times*, p. B2. Retrieved from https://www.newspapers.com/image/176991255/?terms=Enterprise%2BMiddle%2BSchool%2C

1175 - Wichita State University

Gragg v. Wichita State Univ., 261 Kan. 1037, 934 P.2d 121, 1997 Kan. LEXIS 80 (Supreme Court of KansasMarch 14, 1997, Opinion filed). https://edb.pbclibrary.org:2293/api/document?collection=cases&id=urn:contentItem:3RX4-2XT0-003F-D08B-00000-00&context=1516831

Street war: police interview shows gang life in Wichita. (1992, April 21). *Salina Journal, The (Salina, Kansas)*, p. 8. Retrieved from https://www.newspapers.com/image/1795645/

Laviana, H. (1994, June 10). Probe wasn't 'sloppy', WSU police chief says. *Wichita Eagle, The (KS)*, p. 1D. Retrieved from NewsBank: Access World News: https://infoweb-newsbank-

com.ezproxy.lib.usf.edu/apps/news/document-view?p=AWNB&docref=news/
0EADB60F7A993602

1174 - Madison High School

High school student dies in post-game shoot-out. (1991, September 15). *Odessa American, The*, p. 7B. Retrieved from https://www.newspapers.com/image/300631069/?terms=Madison%2BHigh%2BSchool%2C

Student killed in post-game fight. (1991, September 15). *Monitor, The*, p. 18A. Retrieved from https://www.newspapers.com/image/322872467/?terms=Madison%2BHigh%2BSchool%2C

1173 - Woodson North Elementary School (Woodson North School)

Morganthau, T. (1992, March 8). It's not just New York... *Newsweek*. Retrieved from https://www.newsweek.com/its-not-just-new-york-195928

Wiltz, T. (1991, September 19). After-school Gym Teacher Wounded As Shots Ring Out In Gym. *Chicago Tribune*. Retrieved from http://articles.chicagotribune.com/1991-09-19/news/9103110236_1_gangs-after-school-gym

After-school teacher wounded. (1991, September 19). *Chicago Tribune*, p. 8. Retrieved from https://www.newspapers.com/image/389507006/?terms=Clarence%2BNotree%2C

Coleman, B. C. (1991, September 25). Gangs, violence are hard to stop in Chicago schools. *Northwest Herald*, p. D7. Retrieved from https://www.newspapers.com/image/192942186/?terms=Clarence%2BNotree%2C

1172 - Crosby High School

Morganthau, T. (1992, March 8). It's not just New York... *Newsweek*. Retrieved from https://www.newsweek.com/its-not-just-new-york-195928

Kennedy, J. M. (1991, October 10). Column one: America's students: armed and dangerous: as many as 90,000 schoolchildren carry guns to class every day. And serious injuries are on the rise as campus violence spirals out of control. *Los Angeles Times*. Retrieved from http://articles.latimes.com/1991-10-10/news/mn-455_1_school-violence

High school football star shot to death in cafeteria line. (1991, September 18). *Associated Press, The*. Retrieved from https://www.apnews.com/8534975e9f93353fc5808864343c26d6

1171 - Nogales High School (School bus)

Banks, S. & Sengupta, S. (1993, January 22). Student Shot to Death in Fairfax High Class: Violence: Classmate was handling a .357 magnum in his backpack, officials say. Another youth is wounded. *Los Angeles Times*. Retrieved from http://articles.latimes.com/1993-01-22/news/mn-1693_1_fairfax-high-school

Guards posted at schools in wake of gun attack on bus. (1991, September 29). *Ukiah Daily Journal*, p. B-4. Retrieved from https://www.newspapers.com/image/8884994/?terms=Nogales%2BHigh%2BSchool%2C

Utley, M. (1991, September 27). Gunman opens fire on school bus; 2 hurt. *Los Angeles Times*, p. B3. Retrieved from https://www.newspapers.com/image/176800644/?terms=Nogales%2BHigh%2BSchool%2C

1170 - Spring Woods High School

Abram, L. (1991, October 2). Spring Branch student shot on school bus. *Houston Chronicle*, p. 1

Student shot in leg during ride to school. (1991, October 3). *El Paso Times*, p. 8A. Retrieved from https://www.newspapers.com/image/436338268/?terms=dustin%2BSulak%2C

Houston student shot aboard school bus. (1991, October 3). *Longview News-Journal*, p. 10-A. Retrieved from https://www.newspapers.com/image/220107719/?terms=dustin%2BSulak%2C

1169 - Dorsey High School

Shepard, E., & Himmel, N. (1991, October 5). Shootings halt high school football games; 2 wounded. *Los Angeles Times*, p. B1 & B14 Retrieved from https://www.newspapers.com/image/175398232/?terms=Roosevelt%2BHigh%2BSchool%2C

Shepard, E. (1991, October 6). Schools study tighter security at games. *Los Angeles Times*, p. B1 & B14. Retrieved from https://www.newspapers.com/image/175452253/?terms=Roosevelt%2BHigh%2BSchool%2C

Fear of gang violence leads to football forfeit. (1991, October 31). *Billings Gazette, The*, p. 4-D. Retrieved from https://www.newspapers.com/image/412560945/?terms=Dorsey%2BHigh%2BSchool%2B%2C

1168 - James Monroe High School

McQuiston, J. T. (1991, October 9). A Bronx youth is shot to death outside a school. *New York Times, The*. Retrieved from https://www.nytimes.com/1991/10/09/nyregion/a-bronx-youth-is-shot-to-death-outside-a-school.html

Lee, F. (1993, November 13). Bas times get worse at Bronx high school as closing looms. *New York Times, The*. Retrieved from https://www.nytimes.com/1993/11/13/nyregion/bad-times-get-worse-at-bronx-high-school-as-closing-looms.html

1167 - Monadnock Regional High School

From the files Oct. 15, 2016. (2016, October 15). *Sentinel Source*. Retrieved from https://www.sentinelsource.com/news/local/from-the-files-oct/article_9e9f4e93-7810-5896-aa30-ce17d05e8a68.html

People news. (1992, October 7). *Education Week*. Retrieved from https://www.edweek.org/education/people-news/1992/10

Schinella, T. (2022, May 25). NH superintendents say schools are safe, plans in place with police. *Patch.com*. Retrieved from https://patch.com/new-hampshire/concord-nh/nh-superintendents-say-schools-are-safe-plans-place-police

1166 - Genevieve Sparks Elementary School

Student reportedly shot accidentally. (1991, October 18). *Odessa American, The* , p. 2B. Retrieved from https://www.newspapers.com/image/300231582/?terms=Genevieve%2BSparks%2BElementary%2BSchool%2C

Second-grader in stable condition. (1991, October 18). *Times, The*, p. 19A. Retrieved from https://www.newspapers.com/image/220447029/?terms=Genevieve%2BSparks%2BElementary%2BSchool%2C

Second-grader shot accidentally by teen. (1991, October 18). *El Paso Times*, p. 12A. Retrieved from https://www.newspapers.com/image/436343260/?terms=Genevieve%2BSparks%2BElementary%2BSchool%2C

1165 - A. Maceo Smith High School

Student shot at Dallas high school. (1991, October 24). *Odessa American, The*, p. 3B. Retrieved from https://www.newspapers.com/image/300241588/?terms=spring%2Bwoods%2Bhigh%2Bschool%2C%2Bshooting

School superintendent asks for tighter security. (1991, October 26). *Galveston Daily News, The*, p. 2-A. Retrieved from https://www.newspapers.com/image/17141188/?terms=A.%2BMaceo%2BSmith%2BHigh%2BSchool%2C

Dallas student fatally shot at high school. (1991, October 24). *Victoria Advocate*, p. 10-A. Retrieved from https://www.newspapers.com/image/432325748/?terms=A.%2BMaceo%2BSmith%2BHigh%2BSchool%2C

1164 - University of Iowa

Student goes on killing spree at Iowa campus. (1991, November 2). *Chicago Tribune*. Retrieved from https://www.chicagotribune.com/news/ct-xpm-1991-11-02-9104080686-story.html

Marriott, M. (1991, November 4). Iowa gunman was torn by academic challenge. *New York Times, The*. Retrieved from https://www.nytimes.com/1991/11/04/us/iowa-gunman-was-torn-by-academic-challenge.html

Mann, J. (1992, June 7). The physics of revenge: when Dr. Lu Gang's American dream died, six people died with it. *Los Angeles Times*. Retrieved from http://articles.latimes.com/1992-06-07/magazine/tm-411_1_lu-gang

Shipner, R. (2008, December 10). Miya Rodolfo-Sioson, 1968-2008. *Berkeley Daily Planet, The*. Retrieved from http://www.berkeleydailyplanet.com/issue/2008-12-11/article/31784

Armstrong, V. (1991a, November 4). Gunman's letters reveal killings planned to redress grievances. *Iowa City Press Citizen*, p. 3A. Retrieved from https://www.newspapers.com/image/205831707/?terms=Gang%2BLu%2C

Armstrong, V. (1991b, November 5). Ceremony honors victims. *Iowa City Press-Citizen*, p. 1A. Retrieved from https://www.newspapers.com/image/205831731/?terms=Robert%2BA.%2BSmith%2C

$2 million bail in shooting. (2021, August 22). *Chicago Tribune*. Retrieved from https://www.chicagotribune.com/2009/01/17/2-million-bail-in-shooting-2/

1163 - Holland Woods Middle School

Verdin, T. (1991, November 6). Looking for a motive. *Herald Times, The*, p. 7A. Retrieved from https://www.newspapers.com/image/212453073/?terms=Holland%2BWoods%2BMiddle%2BSchool%2C

Chronology of a shooting. (1991, November 6). Looking for a motive. *Herald Times, The*, p. 7A. Retrieved from https://www.newspapers.com/image/212453073/?terms=Holland%2BWoods%2BMiddle%2BSchool%2C

Schaefer, J. (1991, November 6). Middle school student shot, injured in Port Huron class. *Detroit Free Press*, p. 4B. Retrieved from https://www.newspapers.com/image/100238831/?terms=Holland%2BWoods%2BMiddle%2BSchool%2C

Teenager pulls gun from pack, shoots classmate. (1991, November 6). *Lansing State Journal*, p. 4B. Retrieved from https://www.newspapers.com/image/205110238/?terms=Holland%2BWoods%2BMiddle%2BSchool%2C

1162 - Cohen High School

Shooting outside Cohen High School kills one, another wounded. (1991, November 7). *Crowley Post-Signal, The*, p. 1. Retrieved from https://www.newspapers.com/image/469885494/?terms=Cohen%2BHigh%2BSchool%2C

Man arrested for shooting N.O. student. (1991, November 11). *Daily Review, The*, p. 5. Retrieved from https://www.newspapers.com/image/470001457/?terms=Cohen%2BHigh%2BSchool%2C

One suspect arrested for murder of student. (1991, November 8). *St. Mary and Franklin Banner-Tribune*, p. 5. Retrieved from https://www.newspapers.com/image/472856271/?terms=Robert%2BL.%2BMonroe%2C

1161 - Milby High School

Houston student shot during fight. (1991, November 15). *Galveston Daily News, The*, p. 12-A. Retrieved from https://www.newspapers.com/image/17145244/?terms=Milby%2BHigh%2BSchool%2C

Asin, S., & Markley, M. (1991, November 15). Shooting at school fuels calls for more security. *Houston Chronicle*, p. A1.

1160 - Thomas Jefferson High School

Moore, M. H., Petrie, C. V., Braga, A. A., & McLaughlin, B. L. (2013). *Deadly lessons: understanding lethal school violence*. Washington, D.C.: The National Academy Press.

McFadden, R. D. (1991, November 26). 16-year-old is shot to death in a high school in Brooklyn. *New York Times, The*. Retrieved from https://www.nytimes.com/1991/11/26/nyregion/16-year-old-is-shot-to-death-in-a-high-school-in-brooklyn.html

People v. Bentley, 155 Misc. 2d 169; 587 N.Y.S.2d 540; 1992 N.Y. Misc. LEXIS 394. Retrieved from www.lexisnexis.com/us/lnlib

Crews, G. A. (2016). *Critical Examinations of School Violence and Disturbance in K-12 Education*, p. 6 & 7. Hershey, PA: Information Science Reference.

1159 - Delaware State College

Student is shot walking on campus. (1991, December 11). *Central New Jersey Home News, The* (New Brunswick, New Jersey), p. A3. Retrieved from https://www.newspapers.com/image/318017564/?terms=%22Delaware%2Bstate%2Bcollege%22%2C

Moore, R. (1991, December 12). DelState shooting incident underscores factional feud. *News Journal, The* (Wilmington, Delaware), p. B1. Retrieved from https://www.newspapers.com/image/158874605/?terms=%22Delaware%2Bstate%2Bcollege%22%2C

1158 - Whiteville High School

Niven, D. (1991, December 1991). Man charged in shooting at school. *Fayetteville Observer, The*. Retrieved from http://nl.newsbank.com

Schools will increase security. (1992, January 20). *Winston-Salem Journal*, p. 38. Retrieved from https://www.newspapers.com/image/940802156/?match=1&terms=Whiteville%20High%20School

1157 - Greenwood High School

GHS student faces adult status hearing. (1992, March 5). *Index-Journal, The*, p. 2. Retrieved from https://www.newspapers.com/image/69815372/

Siltzer, J. (1992a, January 19). Shocked students show fear, disbelief following shooting. *Index-Journal, The*, p. 1A & 8A. Retrieved from https://www.newspapers.com/image/69774275/?terms=Greenwood%2BHigh%2BSchool%2C

Siltzer, J. (1992b, January 19). Williams in good condition. *Index-Journal, The*, p. 1A & 8A. Retrieved from https://www.newspapers.com/image/69774275/?terms=Greenwood%2BHigh%2BSchool%2C

Lott, J. (1992, January 19). Wounded student said he told secretary about gun. *Index-Journal, The*. Retrieved from https://www.newspapers.com/image/69774275/?terms=Greenwood%2BHigh%2BSchool%2C

1156 - Kent State University

Student shot, wounded on Kent State campus. (1992, January 30). *Blade, The*, p. 4. Retrieved from https://news.google.com/newspapers?id=UoxPAAAAIBAJ&pg=5274,6996772

Davis, G. (1992, January 30). Kent State grad student shot in chest, hospitalized. *Akron Beacon Journal, The*, p. A1. Retrieved from https://www.newspapers.com/image/153811100/?terms=Kent%2BState%2BUniversity%2C

Umrigar, T. (1992a, February 1). Shot Kent student leaves hospital. *Akron Beacon Journal, The*, p. C1 & C3. Retrieved from https://www.newspapers.com/image/154578188

Umrigar, T. (1992b, February 12). Kent police chief backs policeman's split-second decision that brought a fatal halt to a shooting suspect's campus attack. *Akron Beacon Journal, The*, p. A1 & A8. Retrieved from https://www.newspapers.com/image/153541048/

Umrigar, T. (1992c, February 12). Suspect's death can't restore sense of safety. *Akron Beacon Journal, The*, p. A8. Retrieved from https://www.newspapers.com/image/153541590/?terms=Kent%2BState%2BUniversity%2C%2Bshooting%2C

Motive in shootings remains a mystery. (1991, February 25). *Akron Beacon Journal, The*, p. B1. Retrieved from https://www.newspapers.com/image/154213998/?terms=Mark%2BCunningham

1155 - Francis W. Gregory Junior High School (Middle school)

School violence. (1992, February 2). *Town Talk, The*, p. A-16. Retrieved from https://www.newspapers.com/image/218234824/?terms=Francis%2BW.%2BGregory%2BJunior%2BHigh%2BSchool%2C

School violence growing concern all over Louisiana. (1992, February 3). *Daily Review, The*, p. 4. Retrieved from https://www.newspapers.com/image/470391931/

Louisiana schools gripped by tension. (1992, February 2). *Times, The*, p. 17B. Retrieved from https://www.newspapers.com/image/219065907/?terms=Francis%2BW.%2BGregory%2BJunior%2BHigh%2BSchool%2C

1154 - Star-Spencer High School

Kuhlman, J., & Perry, J. (1992, February 1). Star Spencer student shot while watching fistfight. *Daily Oklahoman, The*, p. 9. Retrieved from https://www.newspapers.com/image/453580930/?terms=Star-Spencer%2BHigh%2BSchool%2C

Perry, J. (1992, February 8). City campuses close after shooting death security, searches stepped up. *Oklahoman, The*. Retrieved from https://oklahoman.com/article/2384331/city-campuses-close-after-shooting-death-security-searches-stepped-up

1153 - Douglass High School

Perry, J. (1992, February 8). City campuses close after shooting death security, searches stepped up. *Oklahoman, The*. Retrieved from https://oklahoman.com/article/2384331/city-campuses-close-after-shooting-death-security-searches-stepped-up

Aiken, C. (1992, December 30). Teen pleads guilty in Douglass slaying. *Oklahoman, The*. Retrieved from https://www.oklahoman.com/story/news/1992/12/30/teen-pleads-guilty-in-douglass-slaying/62472098007/

1152 - Booker T. Washington High School

Blattner, B. (1992, February, 8). Teens shot outside high school. *Daily Press*. Retrieved from https://www.dailypress.com/news/dp-xpm-19920208-1992-02-08-9202080051-story.html

Saville, K. (1992, February 9). 19-year-old Norfolk man held in shootings. *Daily Press*. Retrieved from https://www.newspapers.com/image/237297303/?terms=Norfolk%2Bhigh%2Bschool%2C

1151 - Thomas Jefferson High School

Moore, M. H., Petrie, C. V., Braga, A. A., & McLaughlin, B. L. (2013). *Deadly lessons: understanding lethal school violence*. Washington, D.C.: The National Academy Press.

Mitchel, A. (1992, February 27). 2 Teen-Agers Shot to Death in a Brooklyn School. *New York Times, The*. Retrieved from https://www.nytimes.com/1992/02/27/nyregion/2-teen-agers-shot-to-death-in-a-brooklyn-school.html

Kleinfield, N. R., & Fisher, I. (1992, March 1). The fatal vortex: collision of 3 lives in east New York. *New York Times, The*. Retrieved from https://www.nytimes.com/1992/03/01/nyregion/the-fatal-vortex-collision-of-3-lives-in-east-new-york.html

Fried, J. P. (1993, September 8). Youth receives maximum prison term in 2 students' killings. *New York Times, The*. Retrieved from https://www.nytimes.com/1993/09/08/nyregion/youth-receives-maximum-prison-term-in-2-students-killings.html

Crews, G. A. (2016). *Critical Examinations of School Violence and Disturbance in K-12 Education*, p. 6 & 7. Hershey, PA: Information Science Reference.

1150 - Robert Fulton Junior High School (Middle school)

Fernandes, L., & Chu, H. (1992, February 29). Gunfire hits 2 students at junior high in Van Nuys. *Los Angeles Times*, p. B14. Retrieved from https://www.newspapers.com/image/177460380/?terms=Robert%2BFulton%2BJunior%2BHigh%2BSchool%2C

Man, 18, charged in campus shooting. (1992, March 4). *Los Angeles Times*, B2. Retrieved from https://www.newspapers.com/image/177278864/?terms=Robert%2BFulton%2BJunior%2BHigh%2BSchool%2C

1149 - Hamilton Middle School

Shooting an 'isolated incident.' (1992, March 6). *Lancaster Eagle-Gazette*, p. 2. Retrieved from https://www.newspapers.com/image/296856537/?terms=Hamilton%2BMiddle%2BSchool%2C

Students pleads guilty in shooting. (1992, March 20). *Newark Advocate, The*, p. 7C. Retrieved from https://www.newspapers.com/image/289149520/?terms=Gordon%2BW.%2BDye

Boy gets probation in school shooting. (1992, April 18). *Lancaster Eagle-Gazette*, p. 2. Retrieved from https://www.newspapers.com/image/296880832/?terms=Gordon%2Bw.%2BDye%2C%2BJr%2C

1148 - Brandon High School

Incident reminds editor of life's thin thread. (1997, October 2). *Clarion-Ledger*, p. 12A. Retrieved from https://www.newspapers.com/image/185495695/?terms=Stacey%2BBuxton-Boyd

Wagster, E. (1992a, March 24). Student shot in Brandon High School classroom; 1 arrested. *Clarion-Ledger*, p. 1A. Retrieved from https://www.newspapers.com/image/183786090/?terms=Brandon%2BHigh%2BSchool%2C

Wagster, E. (1992b, April 22). Youth pleads guilty to 4 misdemeanors in shooting. *Clarion-Ledger*, p. 1A Retrieved from https://www.newspapers.com/image/182592880/?terms=Quintus%2BJohnson

School violence: metro area. (1997, October 2). *Clarion-Ledger*, p. 12A. Retrieved from https://www.newspapers.com/image/185495695/?terms=school%20violence&match=1

1147 - O. Perry Walker High School

Student, 15, dies after campus fight. (1992, April 1). *Times, The*, p. 13A. Retrieved from https://www.newspapers.com/image/220363673/?terms=Perry%2BWalker%2BHigh%2BSchool%2C

Alexander: school's safety reflects area. (1992, April 1). *Alexandria Daily Town Talk*, p. D-3. Retrieved from https://www.newspapers.com/image/218310392/?match=1&terms=Jamo%20Joseph

Daley, K. (2017, September 6). 25 years after Algiers student's slaying, victim's family not inclined to see killer paroled. *Nola*. Retrieved from https://www.nola.com/crime/index.ssf/2017/09/25_years_after_walker_students.html

1146 - Zia Middle School

Seventh-grader in custody following school shooting. (1992, April 12). *Carlsbad Current-Argus*, p. A-3. Retrieved from https://www.newspapers.com/image/506474448/?terms=Zia%2BMiddle%2BSchool%2C

Shock of Zia school shooting lingers. (1992, April 13). *El Paso Times*, p. 1B & 2B. Retrieved from https://www.newspapers.com/image/430099922/?terms=Zia%2BMiddle%2BSchool%2C

Lopez, S. (1992, April 16). Pair allegedly brought gun onto middle school grounds. *Albuquerque Journal*, p. D3. Retrieved from https://www.newspapers.com/image/156848936/?terms=zia%2Bmiddle%2Bschool%2C%2BJoe%2BRodriguez

1145 - Lincoln High School

Leffall v. Dallas Indep. Sch. Dist., 28 F.3d 521, 1994 U.S. App. LEXIS 21778 (United States Court of Appeals for the Fifth Circuit August 15, 1994, Decided). Retrieved from https://edb.pbclibrary.org:2306/api/document?collection=cases&id=urn:contentItem:3S4X-3HC0-003B-P2HS-00000-00&context=1516831

Lewis, M. (1992, April 19). Man, 18, shot at school dies Murder charge may be filed. *Dallas Morning News, The*, p. 33A. Retrieved from NewsBank: Access World News: https://infoweb-newsbank-com.ezproxy.lib.usf.edu/apps/news/document-view?p=AWNB&docref=news/0ED3D2338F502BED

Nagorka, J. (1992, April 18). Man shot after dance at school Incident may have been accidental, police say. *Dallas Morning News, The*, p. 25A. Retrieved from NewsBank: Access World News: https://infoweb-newsbank-com.ezproxy.lib.usf.edu/apps/news/document-view?p=AWNB&docref=news/0ED3D233620A802E

1144 - Lindhurst High School

Klein, J. (2012). *The bully society: school shootings and the crisis of bullying in America's schools*, p. 153. New York, NY: New York University Press.

Crews, G. A. (2016). *Critical Examinations of School Violence and Disturbance in K-12 Education*, p. 6 & 7. Hershey, PA: Information Science Reference.

Lebrun, M. (2009). *Books, Blackboards, and Bullets: School Shootings and Violence in America*, p. 173-177. Lanham, MD: Rowman & Littlefield Education.

State supreme court upholds death penalty for Houston in Lindhurst High rampage. (2012, August 2). *CBS Sacramento*. Retrieved from https://sacramento.cbslocal.com/2012/08/02/state-supreme-court-upholds-death-penalty-for-houston-in-lindhurst-high-rampage/

Locke, C. (2018, March 1). What happened to suspect in 1992 shooting at high school in Olivehurst? *Sacramento Bee, The*. Retrieved from https://www.sacbee.com/news/local/crime/article203031444.html

4 slain, 10 wounded in school hostage standoff. (1992, May 2). *Press Democrat, The*, p. A1. Retrieved from https://www.newspapers.com/image/311747905/

Hunt, K. (1993, July 21). Prosecutor: defendant plotted rampage. *Press-Tribune, The*, p. A2. Retrieved from https://www.newspapers.com/image/384245096/?terms=Eric%2BHouston%2C%2BLindhurst%2BHigh%2BSchool

People v. Houston, 54 Cal. 4th 1186, 281 P.3d 799, 144 Cal. Rptr. 3d 716. (2012, August 2). *SCOCAL*. Retrieved from https://scocal.stanford.edu/opinion/people-v-houston-34117

Harding, D., Fox, C., & Mehta, J. (2002). Studying rare events through qualitative case studies. *Sociological Methods & Research - SOCIOL METHOD RES*. 31. 174-217. 10.1177/0049124102031002003

Morain, D., & Ingram, C. (1992, May 3). School dropout questioned as town agonizes: Murders: The suspect tells police of his rage against a history teacher, one of the four who died in Olivehurst. Nine people were wounded. *Los Angeles Times*. Retrieved from https://www.latimes.com/archives/la-xpm-1992-05-03-mn-1981-story.html

1143 - Silverado Middle School

Rossman, R. (1992, May 15). Teen opens fire in class, hits 2. *Press Democrat, The*, p. A1 & A12. Retrieved from https://www.newspapers.com/image/311751656/?terms=Silverado%2BMiddle%2BSchool%2C

Flinn, J. (1992, May 14). 'Bullied' boy, 14, shoots 2 in Napa school. *San Francisco Examiner, The*, p. A-1 & A-12. Retrieved from https://www.newspapers.com/image/462021996/?terms=Silverado%2BMiddle%2BSchool%2C

1142 - Huntsville Junior High School (Middle school)

Youth acquitted. (1992, July 12). *De Rio Times*. Retrieved from https://www.newspapers.com/image/6320494/?terms=Huntsville%2BJunior%2BHigh%2BSchool%2C

Student who shot 'bully' is cleared. (1992, July 12). *St. Louis Post Dispatch*, p. 3D. Retrieved from NewsBank: Access World News: https://infoweb-newsbank-com.ezproxy.lib.usf.edu/apps/news/document-view?p=AWNB&docref=news/0EB04DB8A8764BDC

Junior high boy critical after shooting. (1992, May 15). *Victoria Advocate (Victoria, Texas)*, p. 9A. Retrieved from https://www.newspapers.com/image/432631309/?terms=%22Quinn%2BAshworth%22%2C

1141 - Venice High School

Banks, S. & Sengupta, S. (1993, January 22). Student Shot to Death in Fairfax High Class: Violence: Classmate was handling a .357 magnum in his backpack, officials say. Another youth is wounded. *Los Angeles Times*. Retrieved from http://articles.latimes.com/1993-01-22/news/mn-1693_1_fairfax-high-school

Timnick, L. (1992, May 30). Drive-by shots wound 3 outside Venice High School. *Los Angeles Times*, p. B9. Retrieved from https://www.newspapers.com/image/177464609/?terms=Venice%2BHigh%2BSchool%2C

3 teens shot. (1992, May 30). *San Bernardino County Sun, The*, p. A3. Retrieved from https://www.newspapers.com/image/83550739/?terms=Venice%2BHigh%2BSchool%2C

1140 - Merced High School

Washington, D. (1992, June 9). Boy held in school shooting. *Modesto Bee, The*, p. B1

1139 - Palo Duro High School

Parents confess fears over school shootings. (1992, September 13). *Victoria Advocate*, p. 3A. Retrieved from https://www.newspapers.com/image/433089734/?terms=Palo%2BDuro%2BHigh%2BSchool%2C

After shooting, fear may rule at Amarillo school. (1992, September 13). *Austin American-Statesman*, p. B6. Retrieved from https://www.newspapers.com/image/364125303/?terms=Palo%2BDuro%2BHigh%2BSchool%2C

Distraught father enters elementary school, opens fire. (1992, September 19). *Monitor, The*, p. 1B & 2B. Retrieved from https://www.newspapers.com/image/330808265

Mayer, J. (2012, September 12). Witnesses recall 1992 Palo Duro school shooting. *Monitor, The*, p. 5B. Retrieved from https://www.newspapers.com/image/286124106/?terms=Palo%2BDuro%2BHigh%2BSchool%2C%2BRandy%2BEarl%2BMatthews

Teen-ager shoots 6 in school after fight; 2 seriously hurt. (1992, September 12). *Los Angeles Times*, p. A12. Retrieved from https://www.newspapers.com/image/177322678/?terms=Palo%2BDuro%2BHigh%2BSchool%2C%2BRandy%2BEarl%2BMatthews

Brown, C. (1992, September 12). 7 students hurt in Amarillo school shooting. *Austin American-Statesman*, p. B12. Retrieved from https://www.newspapers.com/image/364122047/?terms=Donyel%2BAustin

1138 - Piney Point Elementary School

Distraught father enters elementary school, opens fire. (1992, September 19). *Monitor, The*, p. 1B & 2B. Retrieved from https://www.newspapers.com/image/330808265

Son's grades may be tied to gunman's school attack. (1992, September 19). *Indianapolis Star, The*, p. A-3. Retrieved from https://www.newspapers.com/image/106927210/?terms=Calvin%2BCharles%2BBell

Mental facility frees schoolyard gunman. (1994, June 30). *Monitor, The*, p. 5D. Retrieved from https://www.newspapers.com/image/332644722/?terms=Calvin%2BCharles%2BBell

Man who opened fire at school in '92 released from facility. (1994, June 30). *Odessa American, The*, p. 7B. Retrieved from https://www.newspapers.com/image/300826271/?terms=Calvin%2BCharles%2BBell

1137 - Hiram Johnson High School

Two Hiram Johnson students shot. (1992, September 29). *Press-Tribune, The*, p. A2. Retrieved from https://www.newspapers.com/image/384174219/?terms=Hiram%2BJohnson%2BHigh%2BSchool%2C

Four arrested in high school shootings. (1992, October 1). *Press Tribune, The*, p. A2. Retrieved from https://www.newspapers.com/image/384151217/?terms=Hiram%2BJohnson%2BHigh%2BSchool%2Band%2BTuan%2BDo%2C%2Bbinh%2Btran

1136 - John Marshall High School

Teen pleads guilty in school shooting. (1993, February 2). *Democrat and Chronicle*, p. 2B. Retrieved from https://www.newspapers.com/image/136026259/?terms=David%2BMoore%2C%2Bshooting

Wertheimer, L. K. (1992, October 1). Marshall edgy after shooting. *Democrat and Chronicle*, p. 1A. Retrieved from https://www.newspapers.com/image/138282076/?terms=John%2BMarshall%2BHigh%2BSchool%2C

Mills, S., & Morrell, A. (1992, October 6). Suspect held in school shooting. *Democrat and Chronicle*, p. 1B. Retrieved from https://www.newspapers.com/image/138288200/?terms=John%2BMarshall%2BHigh%2BSchool%2C

1135 - Hollibrook Elementary School

National School Safety Center. (2010, March 3). *School Associated Violent Deaths* [PDF file], p. 2-46. Retrieved from https://files.eric.ed.gov/fulltext/ED519244.pdf

Roll Call of the Dead. (1993, June 14). *People*. Retrieved from https://people.com/archive/roll-call-of-the-dead-vol-39-no-23/

Congress of the U.S. (1999). *Understanding violent children. Hearing before the Subcommittee on Early Childhood, Youth and Families of the Committee on Education and the Workforce: ISBN-0-16-057973-2* [PDF File], p. 69-89. Retrieved from https://files.eric.ed.gov/fulltext/ED435940.pdf

1134 - Desert View High School

National School Safety Center. (2010, March 3). *School Associated Violent Deaths* [PDF file], p. 2-46. Retrieved from https://files.eric.ed.gov/fulltext/ED519244.pdf

Corella, H. (1992, October 15). Teen knows the violence hand signs can evoke. *Arizona Daily Star*, p. 1A & 4A. Retrieved from https://www.newspapers.com/image/169151413/?terms=Desert%2BView%2BHigh%2BSchool%2C

O'Connell, M. (1992, October 15). Parents Chastise officials. *Arizona Daily Star*, p. 1A & 4A. Retrieved from https://www.newspapers.com/image/169151413/?terms=Desert%2BView%2BHigh%2BSchool%2C

Salkowski, J. (1993a, June 17). Self-defense asserted in Desert View slaying. *Arizona Daily Star*, p. 1B. Retrieved from https://www.newspapers.com/image/165243036/?terms=Antonio%2BRedondo%2C

Salkowski, J. (1993b, August 4). Man gets 32 years to life in Desert View High killing. *Arizona Daily Star*, p. 1A & 2A. Retrieved from https://www.newspapers.com/image/166186906

Congress of the U.S. (1999). *Understanding violent children. Hearing before the Subcommittee on Early Childhood, Youth and Families of the Committee on Education and the Workforce: ISBN-0-16-057973-2* [PDF File], p. 69-89. Retrieved from https://files.eric.ed.gov/fulltext/ED435940.pdf

1133 - Finney High School

Security tightens after 11 Detroit students are shot. (1992, November 6). *Ludington Daily News*, p. 1. Retrieved from https://news.google.com/newspapers?id=PRtQAAAAIBAJ&pg=4905,2601500

Johnson, L. A. (1992, November 5). Shootings at 3 schools leave 11 students hurt. *Detroit Free Press*, p. 1A & 11A. Retrieved from https://www.newspapers.com/image/99197503/?terms=Finney%2BHigh%2BSchool%2C

Kresnak, J. (1992, November 11). 7 youths held in shootings at schools. *Detroit Free Press*, p. 1B. Retrieved from https://www.newspapers.com/image/99204597/?terms=Finney%2BHigh%2BSchool%2C

Alexander, J. (1992, November 24). Violence in schools becomes business as usual. *Detroit Free Press*. Retrieved from https://www.newspapers.com/image/99199257

Charges dropped in school shooting. (1992, December 11). *Detroit Free Press*, p. 3B. Retrieved from https://www.newspapers.com/image/99220954/?terms=Finney%2BHigh%2BSchool%2C

'I saw everybody running and I felt all these bullets go past me.' (1993, February 7). *Detroit Free Press*, p. 5F & 6F. Retrieved from https://www.newspapers.com/image/97524856

1132 - Mumford High School

Security tightens after 11 Detroit students are shot. (1992, November 6). *Ludington Daily News*, p. 1. Retrieved from https://news.google.com/newspapers?id=PRtQAAAAIBAJ&pg=4905,2601500

Johnson, L. A. (1992, November 5). Shootings at 3 schools leave 11 students hurt. *Detroit Free Press*, p. 1A & 11A. Retrieved from https://www.newspapers.com/image/99197503/?terms=Finney%2BHigh%2BSchool%2C

Alexander, J. (1992, November 24). Violence in schools becomes business as usual. *Detroit Free Press*. Retrieved from https://www.newspapers.com/image/99199257

'I saw everybody running and I felt all these bullets go past me.' (1993, February 7). *Detroit Free Press*, p. 5F & 6F. Retrieved from https://www.newspapers.com/image/97524856

1131 - Sherman Elementary School

National School Safety Center. (2010, March 3). *School Associated Violent Deaths* [PDF file], p. 2-46. Retrieved from https://files.eric.ed.gov/fulltext/ED519244.pdf

Hawes, C. & Gottesman, A. (1992, November 12). Where gun is way of life, it becomes way of death. *Chicago Tribune*, p. 1 & 10. Retrieved from https://www.newspapers.com/image/389751681/

Classmates watch boy's fatal shot. (1992, November 12). *Pantagraph, The*, p.A6. Retrieved from https://www.newspapers.com/image/73319955/?terms=Sherman%2BElementary%2BSchool%2C

Congress of the U.S. (1999). *Understanding violent children. Hearing before the Subcommittee on Early Childhood, Youth and Families of the Committee on Education and the Workforce: ISBN-0-16-057973-2* [PDF File], p. 69-89. Retrieved from https://files.eric.ed.gov/fulltext/ED435940.pdf

1130 - Langham Creek Senior High School

National School Safety Center. (2010, March 3). *School Associated Violent Deaths* [PDF file], p. 2-46. Retrieved from https://files.eric.ed.gov/fulltext/ED519244.pdf

Obituaries. (1992, November 17). Stephen P. Wenzel. *Galveston Daily News, The*, p. 4-A. Retrieved from https://www.newspapers.com/image/14596040/?terms=Steve%2BWenzel%2C

Roll Call of the Dead. (1993, June 14). *People*. Retrieved from https://people.com/archive/roll-call-of-the-dead-vol-39-no-23/

Fernandez, B. S. & Roth, J. C. (2018, May 2). *Perspectives on School Crisis Response*. New York: Routledge.

Congress of the U.S. (1999). *Understanding violent children. Hearing before the Subcommittee on Early Childhood, Youth and Families of the Committee on Education and the Workforce: ISBN-0-16-057973-2* [PDF File], p. 69-89. Retrieved from https://files.eric.ed.gov/fulltext/ED435940.pdf

Man fatally shoots estranged wife, self in school parking lot. (1992, November 14). *Bryan-College Station Eagle*, p. A9. Retrieved from https://www.newspapers.com/image/1003347058/?match=1&terms=%22Langham%20Creek%20High%20School%22

1129 - Fairfield High School

National School Safety Center. (2010, March 3). *School Associated Violent Deaths* [PDF file], p. 2-46. Retrieved from https://files.eric.ed.gov/fulltext/ED519244.pdf

A murder in Alabama. (1992, November 18). *Atlanta Constitution, The*, p. A3. Retrieved from https://www.newspapers.com/image/402799825/?terms=Michael%2BL.%2BJackson%2BJr.

Student killed near school board room. (1992, November 17). *Anniston Star, The*, p. 6A. Retrieved from https://www.newspapers.com/image/106561686/?terms=Michael%2BL.%2BJackson%2BJr.

Suspects indicted in jacket slaying. (1993, April 9). *Anniston Star, The*, p. 8A. Retrieved from https://www.newspapers.com/image/106699508/

Congress of the U.S. (1999). *Understanding violent children. Hearing before the Subcommittee on Early Childhood, Youth and Families of the Committee on Education and the Workforce:*

ISBN-0-16-057973-2 [PDF File], p. 69-89. Retrieved from https://files.eric.ed.gov/fulltext/ED435940.pdf

1128 - Edward Tilden High School

Moore, M. H., Petrie, C. V., Braga, A. A., & McLaughlin, B. L. (2013). *Deadly lessons: understanding lethal school violence*. Washington, D.C.: The National Academy Press.

Wilson, T. (1994, January 22). Teen guilty of slaying in Tilden High hallway. *Chicago Tribune*. Retrieved from https://www.chicagotribune.com/news/ct-xpm-1994-01-22-9401220160-story.html

National School Safety Center. (2010, March 3). *School Associated Violent Deaths* [PDF file], p. 2-46. Retrieved from https://files.eric.ed.gov/fulltext/ED519244.pdf

Thompson, C. W. (1992a, November 28). Teen slain at Tilden is mourned. *Chicago Tribune*, p. 1-5. Retrieved from https://www.newspapers.com/image/389772604/?terms=Joseph%2BWhite

Prison term in school shooting. (1994, March 15). *Chicago Tribune*, p. 2-3. Retrieved from https://www.newspapers.com/image/241019330/?terms=Joseph%2BWhite%2C

Congress of the U.S. (1999). *Understanding violent children. Hearing before the Subcommittee on Early Childhood, Youth and Families of the Committee on Education and the Workforce: ISBN-0-16-057973-2* [PDF File], p. 69-89. Retrieved from https://files.eric.ed.gov/fulltext/ED435940.pdf

1127 - South Park High School

Bookbags banned in Buffalo after shooting of school guard. (1992, December 9). *Journal News, The*, p. B8. Retrieved from https://www.newspapers.com/image/163439635/?terms=South%2BPark%2BHigh%2BSchool

Gryta, M. (1993, May 12). Student who shot guard is sentenced. *Buffalo News, The*, p. C1. Retrieved from https://www.newspapers.com/image/877440019/?match=1&terms=%22George%20Steele%22

Hammersley, M., & Gryta, M. (1992, November 25). School suspect gets house arrest. *Buffalo News, The*, p. B1. Retrieved from https://www.newspapers.com/image/875244462/

Hammersley, M. (1992, November 23). Shot wounds South Park guard trying to break up school fight. *Buffalo News, The*, p. A1 & A7   . Retrieved from https://www.newspapers.com/image/875244252/?terms=South%20Park%20High%20School

1126 - Robert E. Lee High School

Smith, M. (1992, November 25). Student injures self in school bathroom shooting. *Montgomery Advertiser, The*, p. 1B & 2B. Retrieved from https://www.newspapers.com/image/258702514/?terms=Robert%2BE.%2BLee%2BHigh%2BSchool%2C

Student shot at school. (1992, November 25). *Alabama Journal*, p. 2A. Retrieved from https://www.newspapers.com/image/467095682/?terms=Robert%2BE.%2BLee%2BHigh%2BSchool%2C

Student charged in shooting incident. (1992, December 3). *Montgomery Adviser, The*, p.1B. Retrieved from https://www.newspapers.com/image/258728811/?terms=Robert%2BE.%2BLee%2BHigh%2BSchool%2C

Teen gets 20 years in shooting. (1993, October 6). *Montgomery Advertiser, The*, p.2C. Retrieved from https://www.newspapers.com/image/258758738/?terms=Candy%2BCogman%2C

1125 - Carter G. Woodson School (PreK - 8)

National School Safety Center. (2010, March 3). *School Associated Violent Deaths* [PDF file], p. 2-46. Retrieved from https://files.eric.ed.gov/fulltext/ED519244.pdf

Roll Call of the Dead. (1993, June 14). *People*. Retrieved from https://people.com/archive/roll-call-of-the-dead-vol-39-no-23/

Thompson, C. W. (1992b, December 5). Bullets rip school's illusion of safety. *Chicago Tribune*, p. 1-1 & 1-14. Retrieved from https://www.newspapers.com/image/389832828/?terms=Woodson%2BSchool%2C

Thompson, C. W., & Kiernan, L. (1992, December 5). Bullets rip school's illusion of safety. *Chicago Tribune*, p. 1-1 & 1-14. Retrieved from https://www.newspapers.com/image/389832828

Suspect denied bond in school shooting. (1992, December 15). *Chicago Tribune*, p. 2-3. Retrieved from https://www.newspapers.com/image/389864993/?terms=Woodson%2BSchool%2C

Congress of the U.S. (1999). *Understanding violent children. Hearing before the Subcommittee on Early Childhood, Youth and Families of the Committee on Education and the Workforce: ISBN-0-16-057973-2* [PDF File], p. 69-89. Retrieved from https://files.eric.ed.gov/fulltext/ED435940.pdf

1124 - Bard College of Simon's Rock

National School Safety Center. (2010, March 3). *School Associated Violent Deaths* [PDF file], p. 2-46. Retrieved from https://files.eric.ed.gov/fulltext/ED519244.pdf

Bernstein, M., Renner, G., Venema, S. (1992, December 20). The night Wayne Lo began shooting. *Hartford Courant*, p. A1, A12, & A13. Retrieved from https://www.newspapers.com/image/242416184

Wayne Lo convicted of murders. (1994, February 4). *Great Falls Tribune*, p. 2A. Retrieved from https://www.newspapers.com/image/244064941/?terms=Wayne%2BLo%2C

Pratt, A. (1992, December 17). At Simon's Rock, question is: why? *Berkshire Eagle, The*, p. A1 & A4. Retrieved from https://www.newspapers.com/image/532100541/?terms=Nacunan%2BSaez%2C

Newman, K.S., Fox, C., Harding, D., Mehta, J., & Roth, W. (2004). *Rampage: the social roots of school shootings*, p. 47-263. New York, NY: Basic Books.

1123 - Walton's O'Neil High School

Fullerton, F., & Jump, L. (1992, December 16). 'It was a message, "I need help."' *Press and Sun-Bulletini*, p. 1B & 3B. Retrieved from https://www.newspapers.com/image/257172973/?terms=Walton%2BHigh%2BSchool%2C

Student shoots teacher. (1992, December 16). *Post-Star, The*, p. B12. Retrieved from https://www.newspapers.com/image/347388588/?terms=Walton%2BHigh%2BSchool%2C

Jump, L. (1993, June 2). Walton teen avoids trial in attack on teacher. *Press and Sun-Bulletin*, p. 1A & 6A. Retrieved from https://www.newspapers.com/image/257403396/?terms=Jason%2BHodge%2C

1122 - Brentwood High School

McQuiston, J. T. (1993a, January 7). School upset by shooting of teen-ager during game. *New York Times, The*, p. B8 Retrieved from https://www.nytimes.com/1993/01/07/nyregion/school-upset-by-shooting-of-teen-ager-during-game.html

Held in shooting at hoop contest. (1993, January 8). *Daily News*, p. 15. Retrieved from https://www.newspapers.com/image/469962624/?terms=Brentwood%2BHigh%2BSchool%2Bshooting%2C

1121 - Norland Senior High School

National School Safety Center. (2010, March 3). *School Associated Violent Deaths* [PDF file], p. 2-46. Retrieved from https://files.eric.ed.gov/fulltext/ED519244.pdf

Yanez, L., & Smith, L. E. (1993, January 13). High school student killed in gun battle outside campus gym. *South Florida Sun-Sentinel*, p. 4B. Retrieved from https://www.newspapers.com/image/238949781/?terms=Norland%2BSenior%2BHigh%2BSchool%2C

Yanez, L. (1993, January 14). Student's slaying evokes memory of earlier victim. *South Florida Sun-Sentinel*, p. 1B & 5B. Retrieved from https://www.newspapers.com/image/238950794/?terms=Norland%2BSenior%2BHigh%2BSchool%2C

Congress of the U.S. (1999). *Understanding violent children. Hearing before the Subcommittee on Early Childhood, Youth and Families of the Committee on Education and the Workforce: ISBN-0-16-057973-2* [PDF File], p. 69-89. Retrieved from https://files.eric.ed.gov/fulltext/ED435940.pdf

1120 - East Carter High School

National School Safety Center. (2010, March 3). *School Associated Violent Deaths* [PDF file], p. 2-46. Retrieved from https://files.eric.ed.gov/fulltext/ED519244.pdf

Crews, G. A. (2016). *Critical Examinations of School Violence and Disturbance in K-12 Education*, p. 6 & 7. Hershey, PA: Information Science Reference.

Lebrun, M. (2009). *Books, Blackboards, and Bullets: School Shootings and Violence in America*, p. 173-177. Lanham, MD: Rowman & Littlefield Education.

Mother says boy, teacher had confrontation. (1993, January 21). *Messenger-Inquirer*, p. 7C. Retrieved from https://www.newspapers.com/image/379349676/?terms=East%2BCarter%2BHigh%2BSchool%2C

Voskuhl, J. (1993, April 28). 17-year-old held in two slayings at Carter schoolto be tried as adult. *Courier-Journal, The*, p. B-2. Retrieved from https://www.newspapers.com/image/111026866/?terms=Gary%2BScott%2BPennington%2C

Teenage boy indicted in Carter County school shootings. (1993, June 16). *Advocate-Messenger, The*, p. A3. Retrieved from https://www.newspapers.com/image/137958367/?terms=Gary%2BScott%2BPennington%2C

Congress of the U.S. (1999). *Understanding violent children. Hearing before the Subcommittee on Early Childhood, Youth and Families of the Committee on Education and the Workforce: ISBN-0-16-057973-2* [PDF File], p. 69-89. Retrieved from https://files.eric.ed.gov/fulltext/ED435940.pdf

Newman, K.S., Fox, C., Harding, D., Mehta, J., & Roth, W. (2004). *Rampage: the social roots of school shootings*, p. 47-263. New York, NY: Basic Books.

Hart, K. (2013, January 13). 20 years later: East Carter school shooting. *Daily Independent, The*. Retrieved from https://www.dailyindependent.com/news/local_news/years-later-east-carter-school-shooting/article_d98213db-dedb-5edc-9bf9-efa47c2e7d7b.html

1119 - Fairfax High School

Banks, S. & Sengupta, S. (1993, January 22). Student Shot to Death in Fairfax High Class: Violence: Classmate was handling a .357 magnum in his backpack, officials say. Another youth is wounded. *Los Angeles Times*. Retrieved from http://articles.latimes.com/1993-01-22/news/mn-1693_1_fairfax-high-school

Lara, J. (2011, January 19). Grieving mother recalls Fairfax High shooting. *KABC-TV*. Retrieved from https://abc7.com/archive/7908518/

One student killed, one wounded at Fairfax High School. (1993, January 21). *United Press International*. Retrieved from https://www.upi.com/Archives/1993/01/21/One-student-killed-one-wounded-at-Fairfax-High-School/9641727592400/

National School Safety Center. (2010, March 3). *School Associated Violent Deaths* [PDF file], p. 2-46. Retrieved from https://files.eric.ed.gov/fulltext/ED519244.pdf

Moran, J. (1993, June 3). Youth Found Guilty in Fairfax High Shooting : Courts: the teen-ager is convicted of involuntary manslaughter with a gun. He faces up to nine years in a state juvenile facility. *Los Angeles Times*. Retrieved from http://articles.latimes.com/1993-06-03/local/me-42677_1_fairfax-high-school

Mejia, B., & Vives, R. (2018, February 2). Gun in Westlake school shooting may have gone off inside a backpack, LAPD says. *Los Angeles Times*. Retrieved from https://www.latimes.com/local/lanow/la-me-ln-sal-castro-middle-20180202-story.html

Congress of the U.S. (1999). *Understanding violent children. Hearing before the Subcommittee on Early Childhood, Youth and Families of the Committee on Education and the Workforce: ISBN-0-16-057973-2* [PDF File], p. 69-89. Retrieved from https://files.eric.ed.gov/fulltext/ED435940.pdf

1118 - Patricia Roberts Harris Educational Center (PreK - 10)

Greene, M. S. (1993, February 9). D.C. student is shot dead at school. *Washington Post, The*. Retrieved from https://www.washingtonpost.com/archive/local/1993/02/09/dc-student-is-shot-dead-at-school/8a27d9f5-d6b1-4f82-86a9-a2b5c8b17072/

Gun in Washington traced to Va. (1993, January 31). *Daily Press*, p. B3. Retrieved from https://www.newspapers.com/image/236169519/?terms=Patricia%2BHarris%2BEducational%2BCenter%2C

Agents seek purchasers of weapons. (1993, February 3). *News Leader, The*, p. A3. Retrieved from https://www.newspapers.com/image/288655948/?terms=dave%27s%2Bhouse%2Bof%2Bguns%2C

1117 - Amityville High School

National School Safety Center. (2010, March 3). *School Associated Violent Deaths* [PDF file], p. 2-46. Retrieved from https://files.eric.ed.gov/fulltext/ED519244.pdf

Held in 2 shootings. (1993, February 3). *Daily News*, p. 1. Retrieved from https://www.newspapers.com/image/470548597/?terms=Amityville%2BHigh%2BSchool%2C

Teen shot to death during high school spat. (1993, February 2). *Ithaca Journal, The*, p. 5A. Retrieved from https://www.newspapers.com/image/255754296/?terms=Amityville%2BHigh%2BSchool%2C

Congress of the U.S. (1999). *Understanding violent children. Hearing before the Subcommittee on Early Childhood, Youth and Families of the Committee on Education and the Workforce: ISBN-0-16-057973-2* [PDF File], p. 69-89. Retrieved from https://files.eric.ed.gov/fulltext/ED435940.pdf

McQuiston, J. T. (1993b, February 3). Youth arraigned in killing at Amityville high school. *New York Times, The*. Retrieved from https://www.nytimes.com/1993/02/03/nyregion/youth-arraigned-in-killing-at-amityville-high-school.html

1116 - Redmond Junior High School (Middle school)

National School Safety Center. (2010, March 3). *School Associated Violent Deaths* [PDF file], p. 2-46. Retrieved from https://files.eric.ed.gov/fulltext/ED519244.pdf

Lobos, I. (1993, February 3). Teen suicides prompt education bill -- schools would be required to teach prevention. *Seattle Times, The*. Retrieved from http://community.seattletimes.nwsource.com/archive/?date=19930203&slug=1683509

Scattarella, C. (1993, February, 2). Redmond Teen Left No Clear Clues In Suicide -- Questions, Grief Flow From Death Of Boy, 14. *Seattle Times, The*, p. C5. Retrieved from http://community.seattletimes.nwsource.com/archive/?date=19930202&slug=1683288

Congress of the U.S. (1999). *Understanding violent children. Hearing before the Subcommittee on Early Childhood, Youth and Families of the Committee on Education and the Workforce: ISBN-0-16-057973-2* [PDF File], p. 69-89. Retrieved from https://files.eric.ed.gov/fulltext/ED435940.pdf

1115 - North Clayton High School

National School Safety Center. (2010, March 3). *School Associated Violent Deaths* [PDF file], p. 2-46. Retrieved from https://files.eric.ed.gov/fulltext/ED519244.pdf

Roll Call of the Dead. (1993, June 14). *People*. Retrieved from https://people.com/archive/roll-call-of-the-dead-vol-39-no-23/

Minter, R. (1993, February 5). Student, 18, killed after parking lot shooting at school. *Atlanta Constitution, The*, p. G2. Retrieved from https://www.newspapers.com/image/402779742/?terms=North%2BClayton%2BHigh%2BSchool%2C

Mistrial is declared in case of slain high school student. (1994, October 24). *Atlanta Constitution, The*, p. JI-13. Retrieved from https://www.newspapers.com/image/403712831/?terms=Damon%2BSinkfield%2C

Montgomery, B. (1995, September 25). 20-year-old convicted in Riverdale slaying. *Atlanta Constitution, The*, p. C11. Retrieved from https://www.newspapers.com/image/403626823/?terms=Damon%2BSinkfield%2C

Congress of the U.S. (1999). *Understanding violent children. Hearing before the Subcommittee on Early Childhood, Youth and Families of the Committee on Education and the Workforce: ISBN-0-16-057973-2* [PDF File], p. 69-89. Retrieved from https://files.eric.ed.gov/fulltext/ED435940.pdf

1114 - Washington-Dix Street Academy (High school)

National School Safety Center. (2010, March 3). *School Associated Violent Deaths* [PDF file], p. 2-46. Retrieved from https://files.eric.ed.gov/fulltext/ED519244.pdf

Greene, M. S. (1993, February 9). D.C. student is shot dead at school. *Washington Post, The*. Retrieved from https://www.washingtonpost.com/archive/local/1993/02/09/dc-student-is-shot-dead-at-school/8a27d9f5-d6b1-4f82-86a9-a2b5c8b17072/

Congress of the U.S. (1999). *Understanding violent children. Hearing before the Subcommittee on Early Childhood, Youth and Families of the Committee on Education and the Workforce: ISBN-0-16-057973-2* [PDF File], p. 69-89. Retrieved from https://files.eric.ed.gov/fulltext/ED435940.pdf

1113 - Middle River Elementary School (Grades K - 8)

National School Safety Center. (2010, March 3). *School Associated Violent Deaths* [PDF file], p. 2-46. Retrieved from https://files.eric.ed.gov/fulltext/ED519244.pdf

Roll Call of the Dead. (1993, June 14). *People*. Retrieved from https://people.com/archive/roll-call-of-the-dead-vol-39-no-23/

Boy kills himself in Middle River School. (1993, February 13). *Star Tribune*. P. 9B. Retrieved from https://www.newspapers.com/image/193108575/?terms=Middle%2BRiver%2BMiddle%2BSchool%2C

Congress of the U.S. (1999). *Understanding violent children. Hearing before the Subcommittee on Early Childhood, Youth and Families of the Committee on Education and the Workforce: ISBN-0-16-057973-2* [PDF File], p. 69-89. Retrieved from https://files.eric.ed.gov/fulltext/ED435940.pdf

Eighth-grader kills himself in school's music room. (1993, February 10). *Argus-Leader (Sioux Falls, South Dakota)*, p. 4B. Retrieved from https://www.newspapers.com/image/239907399/?terms=%22eric%20melby%22&match=1

1112 - Kimball High School

National School Safety Center. (2010, March 3). *School Associated Violent Deaths* [PDF file], p. 2-46. Retrieved from https://files.eric.ed.gov/fulltext/ED519244.pdf

Dallas. (1993, February 19). *El Paso Times*, p. 8A. Retrieved from https://www.newspapers.com/image/431534249/?terms=Kimball%2BHigh%2BSchool%2C

Congress of the U.S. (1999). *Understanding violent children. Hearing before the Subcommittee on Early Childhood, Youth and Families of the Committee on Education and the Workforce: ISBN-0-16-057973-2* [PDF File], p. 69-89. Retrieved from https://files.eric.ed.gov/fulltext/ED435940.pdf

Brumley, A. (1993, February 19). Student, 17, slain outside Kimball High - victim, suspect had fought over girlfriend, police say. *Dallas Morning News, The*, p. 1A. Retrieved from NewsBank: Access World News: https://infoweb-newsbank-com.ezproxy.lib.usf.edu/apps/news/document-view?p=AWNB&docref=news/0ED3D36BDB44CC3F

1111 - Reseda High School

Student shot in school corridor. (1993, February 22). *United Press International*. Retrieved from https://www.upi.com/Archives/1993/02/22/Student-shot-in-school-corridor/7126730357200/

Meyer, J., & Watson, C. (1993, February 24). Troubling Portrait of Suspect in Slaying: Reseda High: Officials say Robert Heard is a vandal with a criminal record. He allegedly tried to rob another student at gunpoint as he fled. *Los Angeles Times*. Retrieved from http://articles.latimes.com/1993-02-24/local/me-483_1_reseda-high-school

Colker, D., & Enriquez, S. (1993, February 23). Student Shot, Dies at Reseda High: Violence: Boy is the second killed in the L.A. district in a month. A school football player is arrested. Officials will step up metal detector searches on campuses. *Los Angeles Times*. Retrieved from http://articles.latimes.com/1993-02-23/news/mn-453_1_reseda-high-school

National School Safety Center. (2010, March 3). *School Associated Violent Deaths* [PDF file], p. 2-46. Retrieved from https://files.eric.ed.gov/fulltext/ED519244.pdf

Roll Call of the Dead. (1993, June 14). *People*. Retrieved from https://people.com/archive/roll-call-of-the-dead-vol-39-no-23/

Congress of the U.S. (1999). *Understanding violent children. Hearing before the Subcommittee on Early Childhood, Youth and Families of the Committee on Education and the Workforce: ISBN-0-16-057973-2* [PDF File], p. 69-89. Retrieved from https://files.eric.ed.gov/fulltext/ED435940.pdf

1110 - Gloucester High School

National School Safety Center. (2010, March 3). *School Associated Violent Deaths* [PDF file], p. 2-46. Retrieved from https://files.eric.ed.gov/fulltext/ED519244.pdf

McGeary, P. (1993, March 21). Gloucester sees sorrow, kindness, and joy. *Boston Globe, The*, p. 1 & 22. Retrieved from Gloucester sees sorrow, kindness, joy. Retrieved from https://www.newspapers.com/image/440243888/?terms=Gloucester%2Bsees%2Bsorrow%2C%2Bkindness%2C%2Bjoy%2C

Congress of the U.S. (1999). *Understanding violent children. Hearing before the Subcommittee on Early Childhood, Youth and Families of the Committee on Education and the Workforce: ISBN-0-16-057973-2* [PDF File], p. 69-89. Retrieved from https://files.eric.ed.gov/fulltext/ED435940.pdf

1109 - Harlem High School

National School Safety Center. (2010, March 3). *School Associated Violent Deaths* [PDF file], p. 2-46. Retrieved from https://files.eric.ed.gov/fulltext/ED519244.pdf

Roll Call of the Dead. (1993, June 14). *People*. Retrieved from https://people.com/archive/roll-call-of-the-dead-vol-39-no-23/

One student killed in Harlem high school shooting. (1993, March 19). *Times and Democrat, The*, p. 2A. Retrieved from https://www.newspapers.com/image/345513958/?terms=Harlem%2BHigh%2BSchool%2C

One killed, one injured in high school shooting. (1993, March 19). *Monitor, The*, p. 4A. Retrieved from https://www.newspapers.com/image/330672662/?terms=Harlem%2BHigh%2BSchool%2C

Harlem: shooting suspect formally charged. (1993, March 20). *Atlanta Constitution, The* , p B10. Retrieved from https://www.newspapers.com/image/402745866/?terms=Edward%2BGillom%2C

Congress of the U.S. (1999). *Understanding violent children. Hearing before the Subcommittee on Early Childhood, Youth and Families of the Committee on Education and the Workforce: ISBN-0-16-057973-2* [PDF File], p. 69-89. Retrieved from https://files.eric.ed.gov/fulltext/ED435940.pdf

School violence: metro area. (1997, October 2). *Clarion-Ledger*, p. 12A. Retrieved from https://www.newspapers.com/image/185495695/?terms=school%20violence&match=1

1108 - Rider College (Now called "Rider University")

Kelley, B. J. (1995, October 13). Rider murder Students' deposits waived trail begins [PDF file]. *Rider News, The*, p. 2. Retrieved from https://cdm16471.contentdm.oclc.org/digital/api/collection/p16471coll3/id/13651/download

Man acquitted in fatal shooting at college. (1995, November 19). *Courier-Post (Camden, New Jersey)*, p. 15A. Retrieved from https://www.newspapers.com/image/183384991/

South Jersey news in brief. (1995, October 12). *Philadelphia Inquirer, The (PA)*, p. S02. Retrieved from NewsBank: Access World News: https://infoweb-newsbank-com.ezproxy.lib.usf.edu/apps/news/document-view?p=AWNB&docref=news/0EB32C7C026310A0

Teen-ager charged in slaying at Rider College. (1993, March 23). *New York Times, The.*, p. B4. Retrieved from https://edb.pbclibrary.org:2293/api/document?collection=news&id=urn:contentItem:3SC6-X4V0-0024-J40D-00000-00&context=1516831

Pearce, J. (2003, November 9). When campus violence flares. *New York Times, The*. Retrieved from https://www.nytimes.com/2003/11/09/nyregion/when-campus-violence-flares.html

1107 - Sumner High School

National School Safety Center. (2010, March 3). *School Associated Violent Deaths* [PDF file], p. 2-46. Retrieved from https://files.eric.ed.gov/fulltext/ED519244.pdf

Little, J. (1993, March 26). Shooting numbs girl's parents. *St. Louis Post Dispatch*, p. 10A. Retrieved from https://www.newspapers.com/image/141625741/?terms=Sumner%2BHigh%2BSchool%2C

Librach, P. B., & Little, J. (1993, March 27). Sumner High hikes security after slaying. *St. Louis Post-Dispatch*, p. 3A. Retrieved from https://www.newspapers.com/image/141626514/?terms=Sumner%2BHigh%2BSchool%2C

Bryant, T. (1994, November 29). Woman gets life in killing. *St. Louis Post-Dispatch*, p. 1C. Retrieved from https://www.newspapers.com/image/142360134/?terms=Lawanda%2BJackson%2C

Congress of the U.S. (1999). *Understanding violent children. Hearing before the Subcommittee on Early Childhood, Youth and Families of the Committee on Education and the Workforce: ISBN-0-16-057973-2* [PDF File], p. 69-89. Retrieved from https://files.eric.ed.gov/fulltext/ED435940.pdf

1106 - Albert Ford Middle School

National School Safety Center. (2010, March 3). *School Associated Violent Deaths* [PDF file], p. 2-46. Retrieved from https://files.eric.ed.gov/fulltext/ED519244.pdf

Crews, G. A. (2016). *Critical Examinations of School Violence and Disturbance in K-12 Education*, p. 6 & 7. Hershey, PA: Information Science Reference.

Gunman kills school nurse. (1993, April 15). *Missoulian, The*, p. A-2. Retrieved from https://www.newspapers.com/image/350780645/?terms=Ford%2BMiddle%2BSchool%2C

Coakley, T. (1993, April 17). Principal recalls moments of terror. *Boston Globe, The*, p. 17. Retrieved from https://www.newspapers.com/image/440355312/?terms=Ford%2BMiddle%2BSchool%2C

1105 - Grant High School

National School Safety Center. (2010, March 3). *School Associated Violent Deaths* [PDF file], p. 2-46. Retrieved from https://files.eric.ed.gov/fulltext/ED519244.pdf

Blenke, J. (1993, April 21). Terrible week ends for Broncos baseball. *Orangevale News, The*, p. 11. Retrieved from https://www.newspapers.com/image/387206432/?terms=Grant%2BHigh%2BSchool%2C

Fire damages unpopular liquor store. (1993, July 6). *Press-Tribune, The*, p. A2. Retrieved from https://www.newspapers.com/image/384229473/?terms=Fred%2BLawson

Suspect charged in murder of ll coach. (1993, May 4). *Press-Tribune, The*, p. A2. Retrieved from https://www.newspapers.com/image/384200603/?terms=Arthur%2BTyes

Congress of the U.S. (1999). *Understanding violent children. Hearing before the Subcommittee on Early Childhood, Youth and Families of the Committee on Education and the Workforce: ISBN-0-16-057973-2* [PDF File], p. 69-89. Retrieved from https://files.eric.ed.gov/fulltext/ED435940.pdf

1104 - Nimitz High School

Texas teen killed in school by classmate. (1993, May 16). *Deseret News*. Retrieved from https://www.deseretnews.com/article/290704/TEXAS-TEEN-KILLED-IN-SCHOOL-BY-CLASSMATE.html

Student killed in Texas school shooting. (1993, May 15). *Associated Press, The*. Retrieved from https://www.apnews.com/0aef75b1068eee2cf27e518eb97420a2

Student dies in shooting. (1993, May 16). *Carlsbad Current-Argus*, p. A-5. Retrieved from https://www.newspapers.com/image/504551347/?terms=Nimitz%2BHigh%2BSchool%2C

Congress of the U.S. (1999). *Understanding violent children. Hearing before the Subcommittee on Early Childhood, Youth and Families of the Committee on Education and the Workforce: ISBN-0-16-057973-2* [PDF File], p. 69-89. Retrieved from https://files.eric.ed.gov/fulltext/ED435940.pdf

1103 - Upper Perkiomen High School

National School Safety Center. (2010, March 3). *School Associated Violent Deaths* [PDF file], p. 2-46. Retrieved from https://files.eric.ed.gov/fulltext/ED519244.pdf

Roll Call of the Dead. (1993, June 14). *People*. Retrieved from https://people.com/archive/roll-call-of-the-dead-vol-39-no-23/

Crews, G. A. (2016). *Critical Examinations of School Violence and Disturbance in K-12 Education*, p. 6 & 7. Hershey, PA: Information Science Reference.

Landry, P. (1993, May 25). Teen slain in class; schoolmate, 15, held. *Philadelphia Inquirer, The*, p. A1 & A8. Retrieved from https://www.newspapers.com/image/177755496/?terms=Upper%2BPerkiomen%2BHigh%2BSchool%2C

Funk, L. K. (1994, March 17). Judge rejects suit against teen killer's mom. *Morning Call, The*, p. B4. Retrieved from https://www.newspapers.com/image/276695292/?terms=Jason%2BMichael%2BSmith%2C

Congress of the U.S. (1999). *Understanding violent children. Hearing before the Subcommittee on Early Childhood, Youth and Families of the Committee on Education and the Workforce: ISBN-0-16-057973-2* [PDF File], p. 69-89. Retrieved from https://files.eric.ed.gov/fulltext/ED435940.pdf

1102 - Francis T. Nicholls High School (Renamed KIPP Renaissance High School)

National School Safety Center. (2010, March 3). *School Associated Violent Deaths* [PDF file], p. 2-46. Retrieved from https://files.eric.ed.gov/fulltext/ED519244.pdf

Roll Call of the Dead. (1993, June 14). *People*. Retrieved from https://people.com/archive/roll-call-of-the-dead-vol-39-no-23/

Dropout killed in shooting. (1993, May 28). *Hattiesburg American*, p. 2A. Retrieved from https://www.newspapers.com/image/278618494/?terms=Francis%2BT.%2BNicholls%2BHigh%2BSchool%2C

Ex-high school student shot to death at school. (1993, May 28). *Town Talk, The*, p. D-4. Retrieved from https://www.newspapers.com/image/218281711/?terms=Francis%2BT.%2BNicholls%2BHigh%2BSchool%2C

High school quarrel ends in fatal shooting. (1993, May 28). *Daily Review, The*, p. 5. Retrieved from https://www.newspapers.com/image/469895877/?terms=Shon%2BWilliams%2C

Congress of the U.S. (1999). *Understanding violent children. Hearing before the Subcommittee on Early Childhood, Youth and Families of the Committee on Education and the Workforce: ISBN-0-16-057973-2* [PDF File], p. 69-89. Retrieved from https://files.eric.ed.gov/fulltext/ED435940.pdf

1101 - Wichita State University (Cessna Stadium)

Finger, S. (2015, August 10). Man, woman arrested in death of Wichita State student in dorm parking lot. *Wichita Eagle, The*. Retrieved from https://www.kansas.com/news/local/crime/article30610167.html

Roy, J. C., & Dorsey, R. (1993, July 5). *Wichita Eagle, The (KS)*, p. 1A. Retrieved from NewsBank: Access World News: https://infoweb-newsbank-com.ezproxy.lib.usf.edu/apps/news/document-view?p=AWNB&docref=news/0EADB5836B39EFCF

Thomas, J. L. (1993, November 21). Juvenile prison getting a hard look legislators want system overhauled. *Wichita Eagle, The (KS)*, p. 1A. Retrieved from NewsBank: Access World News: https://infoweb-newsbank-com.ezproxy.lib.usf.edu/apps/news/document-view?p=AWNB&docref=news/0EADB5B8E9386381

Gragg v. Wichita State Univ., 261 Kan. 1037, 934 P.2d 121, 1997 Kan. LEXIS 80 (Supreme Court of KansasMarch 14, 1997, Opinion filed). https://edb.pbclibrary.org:2293/api/document?collection=cases&id=urn:contentItem:3RX4-2XT0-003F-D08B-00000-00&context=1516831

Laviana, H. (1994, June 10). Probe wasn't 'sloppy', WSU police chief says. *Wichita Eagle, The (KS)*, p. 1D. Retrieved from NewsBank: Access World News: https://infoweb-newsbank-com.ezproxy.lib.usf.edu/apps/news/document-view?p=AWNB&docref=news/0EADB60F7A993602

1100 - Weber State University

Carter, M. (1993, July 9). Harassment hearing ends in shootout, 1 dead. *Paducah Sun, The*, p. 6A. Retrieved from https://www.newspapers.com/image/427321486/?terms=Weber%2BState%2BUniversity%2C&match=2

Student shoots 3 at hearing, is killed by officer. (1993, July 9). *Springfield News-Leader, The*, p.9A. Retrieved from https://www.newspapers.com/image/207806684/?terms=Mark%2BDuong%2C

Student opens fire in hearing, dies. (1993, July 9). *Press-Tribune, The*, p. A7. Retrieved from https://www.newspapers.com/image/384233930/?terms=Mark%2BDuong%2C

WSU releases partial transcript of tape at grievance hearing. (1993, August 4). *Daily Spectrum, The*, p. A2. Retrieved from https://www.newspapers.com/image/285592675/?terms=Mark%2BDuong%2C

1099 - Theodore Roosevelt High School

Bronx student is shot. (1993, August 3). *Daily News*, p. 22. Retrieved from https://www.newspapers.com/image/471449642/?terms=Theodore%2BRoosevelt%2BHigh%2BSchool%2C

Hernandez, R. (1993, August 3). Student shot during class in Bronx high school. *New York Times, The*. Retrieved from https://www.nytimes.com/1993/08/03/nyregion/student-shot-during-class-in-bronx-high-school.html

1098 - Harper High School

National School Safety Center. (2010, March 3). *School Associated Violent Deaths* [PDF file], p. 2-46. Retrieved from https://files.eric.ed.gov/fulltext/ED519244.pdf

Kelly, M. L. (1993, September 2). Aftermath: tension, grief. *Atlanta Constitution, The*, p. C1. Retrieved from https://www.newspapers.com/image/402927282/?terms=Harper%2BHigh%2BSchool%2C

Harper High slaying was lesson for change. (1994, April 3). *Atlanta Constitution, The*, p. G2. Retrieved from https://www.newspapers.com/image/403865496/?terms=Shooting%2Bdeath%2Bof%2BHarper%2BHigh%2Bstudent%2BMarcus%2BTaylor%2C

Congress of the U.S. (1999). *Understanding violent children. Hearing before the Subcommittee on Early Childhood, Youth and Families of the Committee on Education and the Workforce: ISBN-0-16-057973-2* [PDF File], p. 69-89. Retrieved from https://files.eric.ed.gov/fulltext/ED435940.pdf

1097 - Junction City High School

Fort Riley teen charged with attempted murder in shooting. (1993, September 4). *Salina Journal, The*, p. 3. Retrieved from https://www.newspapers.com/image/1006387/?terms=Junction%2BCity%2BHigh%2BSchool%2C

Teen will be held by state. (1994, March 16). *Manhattan Mercury, The* , p. B8. Retrieved from https://www.newspapers.com/image/425018911/?terms=Russell%2BWilliams%2C

Authorities name youth held in shooting. (1993, September 5). *Manhattan Mercury, The*, p. A3. Retrieved from https://www.newspapers.com/image/424942247/?terms=Russell%2BWilliams%2C

1096 - Roosevelt High School

National School Safety Center. (2010, March 3). *School Associated Violent Deaths* [PDF file], p. 2-46. Retrieved from https://files.eric.ed.gov/fulltext/ED519244.pdf

Teen-ager dies after shooting at Dallas high school. (1993, September 3). *Austin American-Statesman*, p. B3. Retrieved from https://www.newspapers.com/image/356740507/?terms=%22Roosevelt%2BHigh%22

Student dies after shooting. (1993, September 3). *Paris News, The*, p. 2A. Retrieved from https://www.newspapers.com/image/6395287/?terms=%22Roosevelt%2BHigh%22

Teen-ager dies in shooting at school. (1993, September 3). *Odessa American, The*, p. 3B. Retrieved from https://www.newspapers.com/image/300633688/?terms=%22Roosevelt%2BHigh%22

Congress of the U.S. (1999). *Understanding violent children. Hearing before the Subcommittee on Early Childhood, Youth and Families of the Committee on Education and the Workforce: ISBN-0-16-057973-2* [PDF File], p. 69-89. Retrieved from https://files.eric.ed.gov/fulltext/ED435940.pdf

1095 - Dorsey High School

Teenage boy shot on first school day. (1993, September 8). *San Bernardino County Sun, The*, p. A1. Retrieved from https://www.newspapers.com/image/81873501/?terms=Dorsey%2BHigh%2BSchool%2C

L.A. shooting mars 1st day of school. (1993, September 8). *Press Democrat, The*, p. B3. Retrieved from https://www.newspapers.com/image/311844223/?terms=Dorsey%2BHigh%2BSchool%2C

Man gets 14 years for shooting boy. (1995, March 12). *Los Angeles Times*, p. 8. Retrieved from https://www.newspapers.com/image/159239522/?terms=%22Bryant%2BBoyd%2C%22

1094 - Central Middle School

National School Safety Center. (2010, March 3). *School Associated Violent Deaths* [PDF file], p. 2-46. Retrieved from https://files.eric.ed.gov/fulltext/ED519244.pdf

4 students shot; motive is unclear. (1993, September 19). *New York Times, The*. Retrieved from https://www.nytimes.com/1993/09/19/us/4-students-shot-motive-is-unclear.html

Ehli, N., & Blair, P. (1993, September 18). Gunman shoots 4 children. *Billings Gazette, The*, p. 1A &14A. Retrieved from https://www.newspapers.com/image/412019144

Congress of the U.S. (1999). *Understanding violent children. Hearing before the Subcommittee on Early Childhood, Youth and Families of the Committee on Education and the Workforce: ISBN-0-16-057973-2* [PDF File], p. 69-89. Retrieved from https://files.eric.ed.gov/fulltext/ED435940.pdf

Forster, J. (1993, September 18). Victim shouted, 'help me!' after being shot on field, p. 1A. *Billings Gazette, The*. Retrieved from https://www.newspapers.com/image/412019144/

1093 - Downers Grove South High School

Babwin, D. (1993, September 20). Teen shot after game dies; classmate held. *Chicago Tribune*. Retrieved from https://www.chicagotribune.com/news/ct-xpm-1993-09-20-9309200089-story.html

Sjostrom, J. (1994, April 27). Powell bought gun just before killing, trial told. *Chicago Tribune*. Retrieved from https://www.chicagotribune.com/news/ct-xpm-1994-04-27-9404270213-story.html

1092 - Weatherless Elementary School

National School Safety Center. (2010, March 3). *School Associated Violent Deaths* [PDF file], p. 2-46. Retrieved from https://files.eric.ed.gov/fulltext/ED519244.pdf

Cockburn, P. (1993, October 23). Semi-automatic weapons fuel D.C. way of death. *Ottawa Citizen, The*, p. A3. Retrieved from https://www.newspapers.com/image/464870353/?terms=Weatherless%2BElementary%2BSchool%2C

Two wounded at football game. (1993, September 26). *Daily Times, The*, p. A2. Retrieved from https://www.newspapers.com/image/281338583/?terms=Weatherless%2BElementary%2BSchool%2C

2nd murder suspect arrested. (1993, October 11). *Star-Democrat, The*, p. 5A. Retrieved from https://www.newspapers.com/image/91898609/?terms=Steven%2BChadwick

Lewis, N. (1995b, September 12). Man received 15 to life in slaying of 4-year old. *Washington Post, The*. Retrieved from https://www.washingtonpost.com/archive/local/1995/09/12/man-receives-15-to-life-in-slaying-of-4-year-old/76e4cc24-c4d0-4de8-99d7-98b2b4fdc6f4/?noredirect=on

Congress of the U.S. (1999). *Understanding violent children. Hearing before the Subcommittee on Early Childhood, Youth and Families of the Committee on Education and the Workforce: ISBN-0-16-057973-2* [PDF File], p. 69-89. Retrieved from https://files.eric.ed.gov/fulltext/ED435940.pdf

1091 - Dover High School

National School Safety Center. (2010, March 3). *School Associated Violent Deaths* [PDF file], p. 2-46. Retrieved from https://files.eric.ed.gov/fulltext/ED519244.pdf

Obituaries. (1993, October 14). *News Journal, The*, p. B4. Retrieved from https://www.newspapers.com/image/158898181/?terms=Dover%2BHigh%2BSchool%2C

Svetvilas, K. (1993a, October 13). Suicide try rocks school. *News Journal, The*, p. A1. Retrieved from https://www.newspapers.com/image/158897842/?terms=Dover%2BHigh%2BSchool%2C

Svetvilas, K. (1993b, October 14). Dover High tries to cope with a suicide. *News Journal, The*, p. A1. Retrieved from https://www.newspapers.com/image/158897994

Congress of the U.S. (1999). *Understanding violent children. Hearing before the Subcommittee on Early Childhood, Youth and Families of the Committee on Education and the Workforce: ISBN-0-16-057973-2* [PDF File], p. 69-89. Retrieved from https://files.eric.ed.gov/fulltext/ED435940.pdf

1090 - J.H. Johnson Junior High School (Middle school)

Horwitz, S. (1994, March 10). Student shot in eastern high school. *Washington Post, The*. Retrieved from https://www.washingtonpost.com/archive/politics/1994/03/10/student-shot-in-eastern-high-school/41194b25-2aa1-49e0-8f9d-29281dbc554e/

Castaneda, R. (1993, October 19). Student, 13, is shot inside SE Junior High. *Washington Post, The*. Retrieved from https://www.washingtonpost.com/archive/local/1993/10/19/student-13-is-shot-inside-se-junior-high/67d7efc1-5f5a-4140-9b2e-44d0de8f49f3/?noredirect=on

1089 - Neshoba Central High School

Incident reminds editor of life's thin thread. (1997, October 2). *Clarion-Ledger*, p. 12A. Retrieved from https://www.newspapers.com/image/185495695/?terms=Stacey%2BBuxton-Boyd

Philadelphia student shot outside school. (1993, October 20). *Greenwood Commonwealth, The*, p. 5. Retrieved from https://www.newspapers.com/image/237827151/?terms=Neshoba%2BCentral%2BHigh%2BSchool%2C

1 Neshoba student shot, 1 in jail after argument. (1993, October 20). *Hattiesburg American*, p. 10A. Retrieved from https://www.newspapers.com/image/279654202/?terms=Trevone%2BStribling

School violence: metro area. (1997, October 2). *Clarion-Ledger*, p. 12A. Retrieved from https://www.newspapers.com/image/185495695/?terms=school%20violence&match=1

1088 - Bay Springs High School

National School Safety Center. (2010, March 3). *School Associated Violent Deaths* [PDF file], p. 2-46. Retrieved from https://files.eric.ed.gov/fulltext/ED519244.pdf

James, E. N. (1993a, November 6). Dad tells of attempt to save son. *Hattiesburg American*. Retrieved from https://www.newspapers.com/image/278601565/?terms=Bay%2BSprings%2BHigh%2BSchool%2C

James, E. N. (1993b, November 6). Police question students in death of classmate. *Hattiesburg American*. Retrieved from https://www.newspapers.com/image/278601565/?terms=Bay%2BSprings%2BHigh%2BSchool%2C

James, E. N. (1993c, November 16). Jasper approves metal detectors at high school. *Hattiesburg American*. Retrieved from https://www.newspapers.com/image/278605451/?terms=Bay%2BSprings%2BHigh%2BSchool%2C

1087 - Terry Parker High School

National School Safety Center. (2010, March 3). *School Associated Violent Deaths* [PDF file], p. 2-46. Retrieved from https://files.eric.ed.gov/fulltext/ED519244.pdf

Grand jury indicts nine teens as adults. (1993, November 19). *Florida Today*, p. 1B & 5B. Retrieved from https://www.newspapers.com/image/179150239/?terms=Terry%2BParker%2BHigh%2BSchool%2C

9 Duval teens indicted as adults. (1993, November 19). *Palm Beach Post, The*, p. p. 8A. Retrieved from https://www.newspapers.com/image/133060976/?terms=Terry%2BParker%2BHigh%2BSchool%2C

Duval County grand jury indicts 9 teens in attacks. (1993, November 19). *Tampa Tribune, The*, p. Metro-3. Retrieved from https://www.newspapers.com/image/339524595/?terms=Terry%2BParker%2BHigh%2BSchool%2C

Slaying settlement reached. (1997, May 8). *Florida Today*, p. 1B. Retrieved from https://www.newspapers.com/image/175171231/?terms=Omar%2BShareef%2BJones%2C

Court reverses death sentence. (1998, January 16). *News-Press*, p. 5B. Retrieved from https://www.newspapers.com/image/217449193/?terms=omar%2Bjones%2C

Congress of the U.S. (1999). *Understanding violent children. Hearing before the Subcommittee on Early Childhood, Youth and Families of the Committee on Education and the Workforce: ISBN-0-16-057973-2* [PDF File], p. 69-89. Retrieved from https://files.eric.ed.gov/fulltext/ED435940.pdf

1086 - New Britain High School

Student shot at a school; gang war is suspected. (1993, November 5). *New York Times, The*, p. B5.

Springer, J. (1995, July 21). Man, 20, charged in shooting outside New Britain High. *Hartford Courant*. Retrieved from http://articles.courant.com/1995-07-21/news/9507210401_1_latin-king-rival-gang-gang-war

National School Safety Center. (2010, March 3). *School Associated Violent Deaths* [PDF file], p. 2-46. Retrieved from https://files.eric.ed.gov/fulltext/ED519244.pdf

Carlson, M (1993, November 10). New Guards, new cameras may beef up high school security. *Hartford Courant*, p. C3. Retrieved from https://www.newspapers.com/image/175876853/?terms=New%2BBritain%2BHigh%2BSchool%2C

Kauffman, M. (1994, November 15). Ex-leader tells origins of gang war. *Hartford Courant*, p. A7. Retrieved from https://www.newspapers.com/image/175935086/?terms=Maurice%2BFlanagan

Man charged in killing outside high school. (1995, July 21). *Hartford Courant*, p. B1. Retrieved from https://www.newspapers.com/image/176543500/?terms=Thomas%2BMejia

Williams, T. (1994, December 1). Judge finds probable cause 2 plotted slaying. *Hartford Courant*, p. B11. Retrieved from https://www.newspapers.com/image/176515611/?terms=Thomas%2BMejia

Congress of the U.S. (1999). *Understanding violent children. Hearing before the Subcommittee on Early Childhood, Youth and Families of the Committee on Education and the Workforce: ISBN-0-16-057973-2* [PDF File], p. 69-89. Retrieved from https://files.eric.ed.gov/fulltext/ED435940.pdf

1085 - Center High School

National School Safety Center. (2010, March 3). *School Associated Violent Deaths* [PDF file], p. 2-46. Retrieved from https://files.eric.ed.gov/fulltext/ED519244.pdf

Congress of the U.S. (1999). *Understanding violent children. Hearing before the Subcommittee on Early Childhood, Youth and Families of the Committee on Education and the Workforce: ISBN-0-16-057973-2* [PDF File], p. 69-89. Retrieved from https://files.eric.ed.gov/fulltext/ED435940.pdf

Montgomeryleslie, R., & Dillon, T. (1993, December 2). Man fearful of street violence dies victim of it. *Kansas City Star, The*, p. A1. Retrieved from NewsBank: Access World News: https://infoweb-newsbank-com.ezproxy.lib.usf.edu/apps/news/document-view?p=AWNB&docref=news/0EAF3FD799207B21

Lozano, C. (1993, December 1). Man shot, killed near Center High. *Kansas City Star, The*, p. C1. Retrieved from NewsBank: Access World News: https://infoweb-newsbank-com.ezproxy.lib.usf.edu/apps/news/document-view?p=AWNB&docref=news/0EAF3FD5A99777E6

1084 - Wauwatosa West High School

National School Safety Center. (2010, March 3). *School Associated Violent Deaths* [PDF file], p. 2-46. Retrieved from https://files.eric.ed.gov/fulltext/ED519244.pdf

Crews, G. A. (2016). *Critical Examinations of School Violence and Disturbance in K-12 Education*, p. 6 & 7. Hershey, PA: Information Science Reference.

Suspect arrested in high school shooting. (1993, December 2). *Post-Crescent, The*, p. A-1. Retrieved from https://www.newspapers.com/image/290330525/?terms=Wauwatosa%2BWest%2BHigh%2BSchool%2C

Finkel, G. E. (1993, December 3). Police search for gun used in Wauwatosa school shooting. *Green Bay Press-Gazette*, p. B-1. Retrieved from https://www.newspapers.com/image/189953944/?terms=Wauwatosa%2BWest%2BHigh%2BSchool%2C

School killing spurs calls for state help. (1993, December 3). *Green Bay Press-Gazette*, p. B-1. Retrieved from https://www.newspapers.com/image/189953944/?terms=Wauwatosa%2BWest%2BHigh%2BSchool%2C

Jury must decide killer's sanity. (1994, April 28). *Post-Crescent, The*, p. B-2. Retrieved from https://www.newspapers.com/image/290447027/?terms=Leonard%2BMcDowell%2C

Congress of the U.S. (1999). *Understanding violent children. Hearing before the Subcommittee on Early Childhood, Youth and Families of the Committee on Education and the Workforce: ISBN-0-16-057973-2* [PDF File], p. 69-89. Retrieved from https://files.eric.ed.gov/fulltext/ED435940.pdf

1083 - Alfred E. Beach High School

National School Safety Center. (2010, March 3). *School Associated Violent Deaths* [PDF file], p. 2-46. Retrieved from https://files.eric.ed.gov/fulltext/ED519244.pdf

Savannah: teen to serve 18 months for shooting. (1993, December 24). *Atlanta Constitution, The*, p. C4. Retrieved from https://www.newspapers.com/image/403544801/?terms=Beach%2BHigh%2BSchool%2C

Portner, J. (1998, September 23). In the Hands of Children. *Education Week*. Retrieved from https://www.edweek.org/ew/articles/1998/09/23/07gun.h18.html

Congress of the U.S. (1999). *Understanding violent children. Hearing before the Subcommittee on Early Childhood, Youth and Families of the Committee on Education and the Workforce: ISBN-0-16-057973-2* [PDF File], p. 69-89. Retrieved from https://files.eric.ed.gov/fulltext/ED435940.pdf

1082 - Chatsworth High School

Police arrested two youths. (1993, December 22). *Desert Sun, The*, p. A2. Retrieved from https://www.newspapers.com/image/248807268/?terms=Chatsworth%2BHigh%2BSchool

Moran, J. (1994, April 8). Wounded youth tells of shooting in Chatsworth. *Los Angeles Times*, p. A1 & A18. Retrieved from https://www.newspapers.com/image/158685434

Shuster, B. (1994, February 20). Officials find no easy solution to violence in schools. *Los Angeles Times*, p. B13. Retrieved from https://www.newspapers.com/image/158430799/?terms=Gabriel%2BGettleson%2C

1081 - Chelsea High School

National School Safety Center. (2010, March 3). *School Associated Violent Deaths* [PDF file], p. 2-46. Retrieved from https://files.eric.ed.gov/fulltext/ED519244.pdf

George, M., Trimer-Hartley, M., & Adams, D. (1993, December 18). Chelsea mourns school leader; suspect charged. *Detroit Free Press*, p. 1A & 10A. Retrieved from https://www.newspapers.com/image/97637471/

Kageyama, Y. (1993, December 17). Terror at Chelsea High. *Herald Times, The*, p. 14A. Retrieved from https://www.newspapers.com/image/211241823/?terms=Chelsea%2BHigh%2BSchool%2C

Lawyer blames Prozac. (1994, August 3). *Herald-Palladium, The*, p. 5B. Retrieved from https://www.newspapers.com/image/366558378/?terms=Stephen%2BLeith%2C

George, M. (1994, September 8). Teacher offers apology, receives life in prison. *Detroit Free Press*, p. 3B. Retrieved from https://www.newspapers.com/image/97390850/?terms=Stephen%2BLeith%2C

Congress of the U.S. (1999). *Understanding violent children. Hearing before the Subcommittee on Early Childhood, Youth and Families of the Committee on Education and the Workforce: ISBN-0-16-057973-2* [PDF File], p. 69-89. Retrieved from https://files.eric.ed.gov/fulltext/ED435940.pdf

1993 Chelsea school shooter on gun control: 'These are man-made efforts to try to correct what can't be corrected.' (2013, April 11). *MLive*. Retrieved from https://www.mlive.com/politics/2013/04/chelsea_school_shooter_gun_con.html

1080 - Los Altos High School

National School Safety Center. (2010, March 3). *School Associated Violent Deaths* [PDF file], p. 2-46. Retrieved from https://files.eric.ed.gov/fulltext/ED519244.pdf

Carlson, M. (1994, January 27). Shooting deaths of 2 teen-agers linked to Asian gangs. *Los Angeles Times*, p. 8. Retrieved from https://www.newspapers.com/image/159190089/?terms=Los%2BAltos%2BHigh%2BSchool%2C

Torres, V. (1994, January 21). Teen-ager killed in shooting at high school. *Los Angeles Times*, B4. Retrieved from https://www.newspapers.com/image/158418970/?terms=Los%2BAltos%2BHigh%2BSchool%2C

Congress of the U.S. (1999). *Understanding violent children. Hearing before the Subcommittee on Early Childhood, Youth and Families of the Committee on Education and the Workforce: ISBN-0-16-057973-2* [PDF File], p. 69-89. Retrieved from https://files.eric.ed.gov/fulltext/ED435940.pdf

1079 - Kennard High School

National School Safety Center. (2010, March 3). *School Associated Violent Deaths* [PDF file], p. 2-46. Retrieved from https://files.eric.ed.gov/fulltext/ED519244.pdf

Student commits suicide at Houston County high school. (1994, January 23). *Longview-News-Journal*, p. p. 14-A. Retrieved from https://www.newspapers.com/image/219396903/?terms=Kennard%2BHigh%2BSchool%2C

Items of interest from the week: Kennard. (1994, January 24). *Austin American-Statesman*, p.B4. Retrieved from https://www.newspapers.com/image/356033457/?terms=Kennard%2BHigh%2BSchool%2C

District news roundup. (1994, February 2). *Education Week*. Retrieved from https://www.edweek.org/ew/articles/1994/02/02/19dists.h13.html

Congress of the U.S. (1999). *Understanding violent children. Hearing before the Subcommittee on Early Childhood, Youth and Families of the Committee on Education and the Workforce: ISBN-0-16-057973-2* [PDF File], p. 69-89. Retrieved from https://files.eric.ed.gov/fulltext/ED435940.pdf

1078 - Voorhees College

More info: school shootings in South Carolina. (2010, September 21). *WISTV*, p. 12. Retrieved from http://www.wistv.com/story/23589594/school-shootings-in-south-carolina

Milkie, J. W. (1994, January 27). Voorhees campus calm after shooting incidents; classes to resume today. *Times and Democrat, The*, p. 1A & 4A. Retrieved from https://www.newspapers.com/image/345380586/

Hendren, L. (1994a, January 28). Student arrested, charged in shooting at Voorhees. *Times and Democrat, The*, p. 1B. Retrieved from https://www.newspapers.com/image/345381013/?terms=Voorhees%2BCollege%2C

Second man under arrest in Voorhees shooting case. (1994, February 2). *Times and Democrat, The*, p. 1B. Retrieved from https://www.newspapers.com/image/345692494/?terms=Voorhees%2BCollege%2C

Suspect jailed in shooting at Bamberg County college. (1994, January 28). *Greenville News, The*, p. 2C. Retrieved from https://www.newspapers.com/image/199704741/?terms=Marcus%2BBlakely

1077 - Eau Claire High School

Jones, J. (1994, January 26). Fatal shooting at Columbia school leaves parents, students, officials pondering security. *Times and Democrat, The (Orangeburg, South Carolina)*, p. 1A & 4A. Retrieved from https://www.newspapers.com/image/345380321/?terms=%22Eau%2BClaire%2BHigh%22

Jury: Brown innocent of shooting Floyd Brown. (1995, October 29). *Times and Democrat, The*. Retrieved from https://www.newspapers.com/image/345475032/?terms=Floyd%2BBrown

1076 - Washington Elementary School

National School Safety Center. (2010, March 3). *School Associated Violent Deaths* [PDF file], p. 2-46. Retrieved from https://files.eric.ed.gov/fulltext/ED519244.pdf

Court of Appeal, Sixth District, California. (1997, October 15). *The people, plaintiff and respondent, v. Francisco Valdez, defendant and appellant: H014664*. Retrieved from https://caselaw.findlaw.com/ca-court-of-appeal/1122045.html

Congress of the U.S. (1999). *Understanding violent children. Hearing before the Subcommittee on Early Childhood, Youth and Families of the Committee on Education and the Workforce: ISBN-0-16-057973-2* [PDF File], p. 69-89. Retrieved from https://files.eric.ed.gov/fulltext/ED435940.pdf

Fischer, J., & Guido, M. (1994, January 29). A prisoner in her own home - shooting shatters Gardner District. *Mercury News, The*, p. 1B. Retrieved from NewsBank: Access World News: https://infoweb-newsbank-com.ezproxy.lib.usf.edu/apps/news/document-view?p=AWNB&docref=news/0EB71C71549927A7

Boubion, G. (1994, December 24). Three convicted of killing man at S.J. school. *Mercury News, The*, p. 1B. Retrieved from NewsBank: Access World News: https://infoweb-newsbank-com.ezproxy.lib.usf.edu/apps/news/document-view?p=AWNB&docref=news/0EB71DEE60344A03

South Bay - arrest in killing of man in parked car. (1994, January 29). *San Francisco Chronicle*, p. A21. Retrieved from NewsBank: Access World News: https://infoweb-newsbank-com.ezproxy.lib.usf.edu/apps/news/document-view?p=AWNB&docref=news/0EB4F5AD1E757FC2

Barnacle, B. (1994, April 18). 4 adults, 9 teens held in slaying. *San Jose Mercury News (CA)*, p. 1B. Retrieved from NewsBank: Access World News: https://infoweb-newsbank-com.ezproxy.lib.usf.edu/apps/news/document-view?p=AWNB&docref=news/0EB71CDD03C3A7C8

1075 - Marcus Whitman Middle School

Angelos, C., Birkland, D., Guillen, T., Henderson, D., Nalder, E., Pols, M.F., Rockne, D., Whitely, P., Wilson, D., Wittenmyer, G., & Gillman, J. (1994, February 2). Sex a part of murder case -- suspect, slain teacher had a relationship for years, Seattle Police say after arrest. *Seattle Times, The*. Retrieved from http://community.seattletimes.nwsource.com/archive/?date=19940202&slug=1892986#_ga=2.196697711.293148091.1534538235-484006350.1534538235

Jury convicts man of killing teacher ex-student says sex abuse by victim cause of shooting. (1995, March 31). *Spokesman-Review, The*. Retrieved from http://www.spokesman.com/stories/1995/mar/31/jury-convicts-man-of-killing-teacher-ex-student/

National School Safety Center. (2010, March 3). *School Associated Violent Deaths* [PDF file], p. 2-46. Retrieved from https://files.eric.ed.gov/fulltext/ED519244.pdf

Police arrest man in shooting of teacher. (1994, February 2). *Statesman Journal*, p. 5B. Retrieved from https://www.newspapers.com/image/200197527/?terms=Marcus%2BWhitman%2BMiddle%2BSchool%2C

Man is convicted of killing teacher who molested him. (1995, March 31). *Statesman Journal*, p. 7B. Retrieved from https://www.newspapers.com/image/202431165/?terms=Darrell%2BCloud%2C

Seattle man who killed teacher sues estate. (1994, April 16). *Kipsap Sun*. Retrieved from https://products.kitsapsun.com/archive/1994/04-16/292327_seattle_man_who_killed_teacher_.html

Teacher in Seattle shot at school. (1994, February 1). *Statesman Journal*, p. 3B. Retrieved from https://www.newspapers.com/image/200194070/?terms=Whitman%2BMiddle%2BSchool%2C

Congress of the U.S. (1999). *Understanding violent children. Hearing before the Subcommittee on Early Childhood, Youth and Families of the Committee on Education and the Workforce: ISBN-0-16-057973-2* [PDF File], p. 69-89. Retrieved from https://files.eric.ed.gov/fulltext/ED435940.pdf

School shootings in Washington state. (2012, December 16). *Seattle Times*. Retrieved from https://www.seattletimes.com/seattle-news/history-of-school-shootings-in-washington-state/

1074 - South Carolina State University

More info: school shootings in South Carolina. (2010, September 21). *WISTV*, p. 12. Retrieved from http://www.wistv.com/story/23589594/school-shootings-in-south-carolina

In wake of shooting, SCSU seeks ways to prevent crime on campus. (1994, February 13). *Times and Democrat, The*, p. 10B. Retrieved from https://www.newspapers.com/image/345696328/?terms=South%2BCarolina%2BState%2BUniversity%2C

York, K. E. (1994, February 8). 'We will not provide havens for fools,' Hatton tells SCSU. *Times and Democrat, The*, p. 1A & 7A. Retrieved from https://www.newspapers.com/image/345694807/

Hendren, L. (1994a, January 28). Student arrested, charged in shooting at Voorhees. *Times and Democrat, The*, p. 1B. Retrieved from https://www.newspapers.com/image/345381013/?terms=Voorhees%2BCollege%2C

S.C. State shooting suspects to see judge. (1994, February 7). *Greenville News, The*, p. 2A. Retrieved from https://www.newspapers.com/image/199608181/?terms=Marcus%2BWhite

1073 - Lee County School Services Building

National School Safety Center. (2010, March 3). *School Associated Violent Deaths* [PDF file], p. 2-46. Retrieved from https://files.eric.ed.gov/fulltext/ED519244.pdf

Francheschina, P., & Melsek, L. (1994, February 9). Gunman suffered hard times. *News-Press*, p. 1A & 4A. Retrieved from https://www.newspapers.com/image/216612656/

Congress of the U.S. (1999). *Understanding violent children. Hearing before the Subcommittee on Early Childhood, Youth and Families of the Committee on Education and the Workforce: ISBN-0-16-057973-2* [PDF File], p. 69-89. Retrieved from https://files.eric.ed.gov/fulltext/ED435940.pdf

1072 - Osborn High School

National School Safety Center. (2010, March 3). *School Associated Violent Deaths* [PDF file], p. 2-46. Retrieved from https://files.eric.ed.gov/fulltext/ED519244.pdf

2nd slaying from gunfire renews grief for family. (1994, February 9). *Detroit Free Press*, p. 8B. Retrieved from https://www.newspapers.com/image/98007492/?terms=Osborn%2BHigh%2BSchool%2C

Collier, N. (1994, March 8). Violence fuels teens' feelings of insecurity. *Detroit Free Press*, p. 4E. Retrieved from https://www.newspapers.com/image/97831665/?terms=Steven%2BWatkins

1071 - Kemper Military School and College (Private military high school and college)

Defendant unrestrained in courthouse. (1994, March 16). *Springfield News-Leader, The*, p. 5B. Retrieved from https://www.newspapers.com/image/207842765/?terms=Kemper%2BMilitary%2BSchool%2B%26%2BCollege%2C

Man surrendered after two killed at military academy. (1994, March 2). *Springfield News-Leader, The*, p. 1B. Retrieved from https://www.newspapers.com/image/207742565/?terms=Kemper%2BMilitary%2BSchool%2B%26%2BCollege%2C

Life sentences for academy shooting. (1994, May 24). *Daily Journal, The*, p. 4. Retrieved from https://www.newspapers.com/image/418300801/?terms=%22Dante%2BHayes%22

1070 - Eastern High School

Frazier, L. (1996, January 7). After shooting, parents force changes at Oxon High. *Washington Post, The*. Retrieved from https://www.washingtonpost.com/archive/local/1996/01/07/after-shooting-parents-force-changes-at-oxon-hill-high/375a84f1-6115-4a95-8f3e-e6b2972bb797/

Horwitz, S. (1994, March 10). Student shot in eastern high school. *Washington Post, The*. Retrieved from https://www.washingtonpost.com/archive/politics/1994/03/10/student-shot-in-eastern-high-school/41194b25-2aa1-49e0-8f9d-29281dbc554e/

Castaneda, R., & Lewis, N. (1994, March 11). D.C. Police will talk tough in bid to discourage retaliation. *Washington Post, The*. Retrieved from https://www.washingtonpost.com/archive/politics/1994/03/11/dc-police-will-talk-tough-in-bid-to-discourage-retaliation/4e2abb16-2f5f-4dc4-a5b4-fe57f19308d1/?noredirect=on

1069 - Goose Creek High School

National School Safety Center. (2010, March 3). *School Associated Violent Deaths* [PDF file], p. 2-46. Retrieved from https://files.eric.ed.gov/fulltext/ED519244.pdf

More info: school shootings in South Carolina. (2010, September 21). *WISTV*, p. 12. Retrieved from http://www.wistv.com/story/23589594/school-shootings-in-south-carolina

School shooting in Goose Creek leaves one dead, two injured. (1994, March 16). *Times and Democrat, The*, p. 2B. Retrieved from https://www.newspapers.com/image/345694372/?terms=Goose%2BCreek%2BHigh%2BSchool

Patrols requested. (1994, March 17). *Index-Journal, The*, p. 12. Retrieved from https://www.newspapers.com/image/71413383/?terms=Goose%2BCreek%2BHigh%2BSchool

Goose Creek school shooting leaves one dead, two injured. (1994, March 17). *Times and Democrat, The*, p. 1A & 7A. Retrieved from https://www.newspapers.com/image/345694553/?terms=Goose%2BCreek%2BHigh%2BSchool

Bond set for four implicated in school shooting death. (1994, March 18). *Times and Democrat, The*, p. 2B. Retrieved from https://www.newspapers.com/image/345695071/?terms=%22Lang%2BWolfe%22

Man sentenced to life for school murder. (1994, October 21). *Times and Democrat, The*, p. 2B. Retrieved from https://www.newspapers.com/image/345748048/?terms=Randolph%2BJohnson

Congress of the U.S. (1999). *Understanding violent children. Hearing before the Subcommittee on Early Childhood, Youth and Families of the Committee on Education and the Workforce: ISBN-0-16-057973-2* [PDF File], p. 69-89. Retrieved from https://files.eric.ed.gov/fulltext/ED435940.pdf

1068 - Ballard High School

National School Safety Center. (2010, March 3). *School Associated Violent Deaths* [PDF file], p. 2-46. Retrieved from https://files.eric.ed.gov/fulltext/ED519244.pdf

Seattle teen turns himself in. (1994, March 28). *Statesman Journal*, p. 3B. Retrieved from https://www.newspapers.com/image/200801708/?terms=Ballard%2BHigh%2BSchool%2C

Girl wounded in drive-by shooting dies. (1994, March 25). *Corvallis Gazette-Times*, p. A4. Retrieved from https://www.newspapers.com/image/387394967/?terms=Ballard%2BHigh%2BSchool%2C

Congress of the U.S. (1999). *Understanding violent children. Hearing before the Subcommittee on Early Childhood, Youth and Families of the Committee on Education and the Workforce: ISBN-0-16-057973-2* [PDF File], p. 69-89. Retrieved from https://files.eric.ed.gov/fulltext/ED435940.pdf

School shootings in Washington state. (2012, December 16). *Seattle Times*. Retrieved from https://www.seattletimes.com/seattle-news/history-of-school-shootings-in-washington-state/

1067 - Etowah High School

National School Safety Center. (2010, March 3). *School Associated Violent Deaths* [PDF file], p. 2-46. Retrieved from https://files.eric.ed.gov/fulltext/ED519244.pdf

Hendrick, B. (1994, March 26). Student's death underscores problem of teenage suicides. *Atlanta Constitution, The*, p. B1. Retrieved from https://www.newspapers.com/image/403913523/?terms=Etowah%2BHigh%2BSchool%2C

Jacobson, L. (1994, March 29). Teen's death no. 1 topic on 1st day back to school. *Atlanta Constitution, The*, p. C6. Retrieved from https://www.newspapers.com/image/403699966/?terms=Etowah%2BHigh%2BSchool%2C

Teen kills himself in front of class. (1994, March 26). *Reno Gazette-Journal*, p. 2A. Retrieved from https://www.newspapers.com/image/153280004/?terms=Etowah%2BHigh%2BSchool%2C

1066 - McNeil High School

Welch, L. L. (1994, April 14). Patrols at high schools to begin on Monday. *Austin American-Statesman*, p. 1. Retrieved from https://www.newspapers.com/image/366529638/?terms=McNeil%2BHigh%2BSchool%2C

Burgees, M. (1994, April 7). Students suspected in sale of stolen gun. *Austin American-Statesman*, p. A1 & A17. Retrieved from https://www.newspapers.com/image/366500478/

Burgess, M., & Vargas, D. J. (1994, April 6). 2 students shot at Round Rock school. *Austin American-Statesman*, p. A1 & A17. Retrieved from https://www.newspapers.com/image/366497591/?terms=McNeil%2BHigh%2BSchool%2C&match=4

1065 - Largo High School

Teacher shot with cop's gun. (1994, April 10). *Star-Democrat, The*, p. 6A. Retrieved from https://www.newspapers.com/image/93129213/?terms=Largo%2BHigh%2BSchool%2C

Bail set for officer's son held in teacher's shooting. (1994, April 12). *Baltimore Sun, The*, p. 2B. Retrieved from https://www.newspapers.com/image/373534114/?terms=Largo%2BHigh%2BSchool%2C

Official urges plan to stop school violence. (1994, April 12). *Indianapolis News, The*, p. B-5. Retrieved from https://www.newspapers.com/image/313016363/?terms=Warren%2BEmmanuel%2BGraham%2C

1064 - Margaret Leary Elementary School

National School Safety Center. (2010, March 3). *School Associated Violent Deaths* [PDF file], p. 2-46. Retrieved from https://files.eric.ed.gov/fulltext/ED519244.pdf

Crews, G. A. (2016). *Critical Examinations of School Violence and Disturbance in K-12 Education*, p. 6 & 7. Hershey, PA: Information Science Reference.

Anez, B. (1994, April 13). Butte 4th-grader shoots boy. *Great Falls Tribune*, p. 1A. Retrieved from https://www.newspapers.com/image/242817796/?terms=Margaret%2BLeary%2BElementary%2BSchool%2C

DelBonis, P. (1994a, May 13). In Butte school shooting. *Independent-Record, The*, p. 1A & 8A. Retrieved from https://www.newspapers.com/image/394106935/?terms=James%2BOsmanson%2C

DelBonis, P. (1994b, June 17). Youth sent for treatment. *Montana Standard, The*, p. A1 & A6. Retrieved from https://www.newspapers.com/image/351235895/?terms=James%2BOsmanson

Fenner, D. (1994, May 22). Guidance on AIDS urged at meeting. *Billings Gazette, The*, p. 1C. Retrieved from https://www.newspapers.com/image/410517301/?terms=James%2BOsmanson%2C

1063 - 49th Street Elementary School

National School Safety Center. (2010, March 3). *School Associated Violent Deaths* [PDF file], p. 2-46. Retrieved from https://files.eric.ed.gov/fulltext/ED519244.pdf

Kata, J. (1994, April 14). A school asks why. *Los Angeles Times*, p B12 & B17. Retrieved from https://www.newspapers.com/image/158907199/?terms=49th%2BStreet%2BElementary%2BSchool%2C

Klein, D. (1994, April 23). Grief, blame over Jorge's suicide can't be laid to rest. *Los Angeles Times*, p. A1 & A31. Retrieved from https://www.newspapers.com/image/159125080/

Congress of the U.S. (1999). *Understanding violent children. Hearing before the Subcommittee on Early Childhood, Youth and Families of the Committee on Education and the Workforce:*

ISBN-0-16-057973-2 [PDF File], p. 69-89. Retrieved from https://files.eric.ed.gov/fulltext/ED435940.pdf

1062 - William Smith Special School, a National Christian Academy affiliate (Private Christian high school)

Jeter, J. (1994a, April 19). Youth shot at church academy. *Washington Post, The*. Retrieved from https://www.washingtonpost.com/archive/politics/1994/04/19/youth-shot-at-church-academy/3930d678-4c54-41c7-ac9d-c105c39adbc6/?noredirect=on&utm_term=.118f37156755

Teen held without bond in shooting of student. (1994, April 20). *Baltimore Sun, The*. Retrieved from https://www.newspapers.com/image/170876335/?terms=%22Rodriguez%2BDurden%22

Jeter, J. (1994b, April 20). Public school had expelled student accused in shooting. *Washington Post, The*. Retrieved from https://www.washingtonpost.com/archive/local/1994/04/20/public-school-had-expelled-student-accused-in-shooting/99e9a8c7-4db4-49b3-8ea4-281f31246a6f/?utm_term=.51009973c0ab

1061 - East Norriton Middle School

Boy shoots girl who allegedly taunted him. (1994, April 21). *Standard-Speaker*, p.4. Retrieved from https://www.newspapers.com/image/59914910/?terms=East%2BNorriton%2BMiddle%2BSchool%2C

King, L., & Downs, J. (1994, April 22). Girl shot in face still on serious list. *Philadelphia Enquirer, The*, p. B1 & B10. Retrieved from https://www.newspapers.com/image/175851486/?terms=East%2BNorriton%2BMiddle%2BSchool%2C

King, L. (1994, May 25). Mother questions bus safety. *Philadelphia Inquirer, The*, p. B1 & B3. Retrieved from https://www.newspapers.com/image/177783261/?terms=Michael%2BAnthony%2BStenson

1060 - John Trotwood Moore Middle School

Seventh grader shot, killed in class. (1994, April 21). *Associated Press*. Retrieved from https://www.apnews.com/172912f2506448cb13c91367c5ef9dd3

7th-grade boy shot to death while viewing video in class. (1994, April 22). *Orlando Sentinel*. Retrieved from https://www.orlandosentinel.com/1994/04/22/7th-grade-boy-shot-to-death-while-viewing-video-in-class/

National School Safety Center. (2010, March 3). *School Associated Violent Deaths* [PDF file], p. 2-46. Retrieved from https://files.eric.ed.gov/fulltext/ED519244.pdf

Congress of the U.S. (1999). *Understanding violent children. Hearing before the Subcommittee on Early Childhood, Youth and Families of the Committee on Education and the Workforce: ISBN-0-16-057973-2* [PDF File], p. 69-89. Retrieved from https://files.eric.ed.gov/fulltext/ED435940.pdf

1059 - North Miami High School

National School Safety Center. (2010, March 3). *School Associated Violent Deaths* [PDF file], p. 2-46. Retrieved from https://files.eric.ed.gov/fulltext/ED519244.pdf

Student in shooting dies. (1994, May 5). *South Florida Sun Sentinel*, p. 3B. Retrieved from https://www.newspapers.com/image/239009086/?terms=North%2BMiami%2BHigh%2BSchool%2C

Charges elevated. (1994, May 5). *Tampa Tribune, The*, p. 8. Retrieved from https://www.newspapers.com/image/339868326/?terms=North%2BMiami%2BHigh%2BSchool%2C

Congress of the U.S. (1999). *Understanding violent children. Hearing before the Subcommittee on Early Childhood, Youth and Families of the Committee on Education and the Workforce: ISBN-0-16-057973-2* [PDF File], p. 69-89. Retrieved from https://files.eric.ed.gov/fulltext/ED435940.pdf

1058 - Ottumwa High School

National School Safety Center. (2010, March 3). *School Associated Violent Deaths* [PDF file], p. 2-46. Retrieved from https://files.eric.ed.gov/fulltext/ED519244.pdf

Siebert, M. (1994, July 30). Friends fill church to mourn teen. *Des Moines Register, The*, p. 1M. Retrieved from https://www.newspapers.com/image/131987969/?terms=Ottumwa%2BHigh%2BSchool%2C

Santiago, F. (1995, August 10). Boy will spend life in prison. *Des Moines Register, The*, p. 2A. Retrieved from https://www.newspapers.com/image/132354405/?terms=Michael%2BP.%2BCoffman%2C

Congress of the U.S. (1999). *Understanding violent children. Hearing before the Subcommittee on Early Childhood, Youth and Families of the Committee on Education and the Workforce: ISBN-0-16-057973-2* [PDF File], p. 69-89. Retrieved from https://files.eric.ed.gov/fulltext/ED435940.pdf

1057 - Hollywood High School

National School Safety Center. (2010, March 3). *School Associated Violent Deaths* [PDF file], p. 2-46. Retrieved from https://files.eric.ed.gov/fulltext/ED519244.pdf

Teen fatally shot at Hollywood High. (1994, September 8). *San Bernardino County Sun, The*, p. A1. Retrieved from https://www.newspapers.com/image/92287538/?terms=Hollywood%2BHigh%2BSchool%2C

Riccardi, N., & Chavez, S. (1994, September 9). Students, teachers stunned by slaying. *Los Angeles Times*, p. B12. Retrieved from https://www.newspapers.com/image/158191566/?terms=Rolando%2BRuiz%2C

Congress of the U.S. (1999). *Understanding violent children. Hearing before the Subcommittee on Early Childhood, Youth and Families of the Committee on Education and the Workforce: ISBN-0-16-057973-2* [PDF File], p. 69-89. Retrieved from https://files.eric.ed.gov/fulltext/ED435940.pdf

1056 - South Florence High School

Two teens shot at South Florence High School; former student arrested. (1994, September 15). *Times and Democrat, The*, p. 3B. Retrieved from https://www.newspapers.com/image/345379214/?terms=South%2BFlorence%2BHigh%2BSchool%2C

Two teens shot at high school; student arrested. (1994, September 14). *Index-Journal, The*, p. 11 & 12. Retrieved from https://www.newspapers.com/image/71428359/?terms=South%2BFlorence%2BHigh%2BSchool%2C

Suspect in school shootings arraigned. (1994, September 16). *Greenville News, The*, p. 3C. Retrieved from https://www.newspapers.com/image/193613642/?terms=South%2BFlorence%2BHigh%2BSchool%2C

1055 - Sheepshead Bay High School

Mangan, P. (1994, September 18). School' daze after shooting of HS student. *Daily News*, p. C8. Retrieved from https://www.newspapers.com/image/474138277/?terms=Theodore%2BRoosevelt%2BHigh%2BSchool%2C

Student shot, wounded at Sheepshead Bay HS. (1994, September 15). *Daily News*, p. 5C. Retrieved from https://www.newspapers.com/image/474090477/?terms=David%2BEstrada%2C

Student critically injured in Brooklyn school shooting. (1994, September 15). *Journal News, The*, p. B4. Retrieved from https://www.newspapers.com/image/165389221/?terms=David%2BEstrada%2C

Chiang, S., Mangan, P., Marzuli, J., & Speyer, R. (1994, September 16). Probe hs shooting puzzle. *Daily News*, p. 20. Retrieved from https://www.newspapers.com/image/474084339/?terms=Maurice%2BFerguson

1054 - Grimsley High School

National School Safety Center. (2010, March 3). *School Associated Violent Deaths* [PDF file], p. 2-46. Retrieved from https://files.eric.ed.gov/fulltext/ED519244.pdf

Hunt visits school to promote end to violence. (1994, October 15). *Rocky Mount Telegram*, p.2A. Retrieved from https://www.newspapers.com/image/338238456/?terms=Grimsley%2BHigh%2BSchool%2C

Student kills self at school. (1994, October 13). *Asheville Citizen Times*, p. 2B. Retrieved from https://www.newspapers.com/image/200095726/?terms=Nicholas%2BAlexander%2BAtkinson

Swofford, S. (1994, November 5). Turmoil ends with tragedy. *News & Record*. Retrieved from https://www.greensboro.com/turmoil-ends-with-tragedy/article_8a983951-14c6-5b87-a82e-e972684a3481.html

Congress of the U.S. (1999). *Understanding violent children. Hearing before the Subcommittee on Early Childhood, Youth and Families of the Committee on Education and the Workforce: ISBN-0-16-057973-2* [PDF File], p. 69-89. Retrieved from https://files.eric.ed.gov/fulltext/ED435940.pdf

1053 - Wickliffe Middle School

National School Safety Center. (2010, March 3). *School Associated Violent Deaths* [PDF file], p. 2-46. Retrieved from https://files.eric.ed.gov/fulltext/ED519244.pdf

Crews, G. A. (2016). *Critical Examinations of School Violence and Disturbance in K-12 Education*, p. 6 & 7. Hershey, PA: Information Science Reference.

Motive sought for shooting. (1994, November 8). *News Herald*, p. A1. Retrieved from https://www.newspapers.com/image/293997064/?terms=Wickliffe%2BMiddle%2BSchool%2C

Community waits for justice, gunman stays in hospital. (1994, November 6). *Marysville Journal-Tribune*, p. 5. Retrieved from https://www.newspapers.com/image/330027277/?terms=Keith%2BA.%2BLedeger%2C

Gunman kills one, wounds three. (1994, November 8). *Marysville Journal-Tribune*, p. 6. Retrieved from https://www.newspapers.com/image/330236357/?terms=Keith%2BA.%2BLedeger%2C

Congress of the U.S. (1999). *Understanding violent children. Hearing before the Subcommittee on Early Childhood, Youth and Families of the Committee on Education and the Workforce: ISBN-0-16-057973-2* [PDF File], p. 69-89. Retrieved from https://files.eric.ed.gov/fulltext/ED435940.pdf

Reed, T. (2012, February 29). Remembering 1994: Wickliffe Middle School shooter has since died in prison. *News-Herald, The*. Retrieved from https://www.news-herald.com/news/remembering-wickliffe-middle-school-shooter-has-since-died-in-prison/article_d4adf987-a303-5152-bd70-699442051a1d.html

1052 - West Delaware High School

Teen charged after firing Teen charged as adult in shooting at Lawrence high school. (2016, January 26). *16 News Now WNDU*. Retrieved from https://www.wndu.com/content/news/Teen-charged-as-adult-in-shooting-at-Lawrence-high-school-366528881.html

Hovelson, J. (1994, November 10). School stunned by gunfire. *Des Moines Register, The*, p. 1M. Retrieved from https://www.newspapers.com/image/129110165/?terms=West%2BDelaware%2BHigh%2BSchool%2C

Swinton, V. (1994, November 11). Charges in school shooting - 2 felony counts for Manchester teen. *Gazette, The*, p. 1. Retrieved from NewsBank: Access World News: https://infoweb-newsbank-com.ezproxy.lib.usf.edu/apps/news/document-view?p=AWNB&docref=news/0EAFE7B26EC9CB74

1051 - Stadium High School

National School Safety Center. (2010, March 3). *School Associated Violent Deaths* [PDF file], p. 2-46. Retrieved from https://files.eric.ed.gov/fulltext/ED519244.pdf

Porterfield, E., Gordon, S., & Marchionni, D. (1994, November 17). 'You'd never think he was suicidal' amid grief, dead teen's family, friends ask themselves why. *News Tribune, The*, p. A1.

1050 - University of Albany

Bauder, D. (1994, December 28). 'Snap judgment' ended hostage crisis. *Times, The*, p. A-2. Retrieved from https://www.newspapers.com/image/309239113/?terms=University%2Bof%2BAlbany%2C

Hughes, K. (1994, December 15). SUNY classroom held hostage. *Democrat and Chronicle*, p. 4A. Retrieved from https://www.newspapers.com/image/138506573/?terms=Ralph%2BJ.%2BTortorici

Gunman found to be incompetent. (1995, January 8). *Post-Star, The*, p. A6. Retrieved from https://www.newspapers.com/image/347107078/?terms=Ralph%2BJ.%2BTortorici%2C

1049 - Cardozo Senior High School (Cardozo Education Campus)

National School Safety Center. (2010, March 3). *School Associated Violent Deaths* [PDF file], p. 2-46. Retrieved from https://files.eric.ed.gov/fulltext/ED519244.pdf

Murder suspect, 14, pleads innocent. (1995, January 8). *News Journal, The*, p. A7. Retrieved from https://www.newspapers.com/image/157238311/?terms=Cardozo%2BHigh%2BSchool

Duggan, P., & Melillo, W. (1995, January 6). Student fatally shot at Cardozo High. *Washington Post, The*. Retrieved from https://www.washingtonpost.com/archive/politics/1995/01/06/student-fatally-shot-at-cardozo-high/5005c413-044e-42fb-adcc-8faf629c9994/?noredirect=on&utm_term=.ce4bddc0806a

Lewis, N. (1995a, March 17). Teen pleads guilty as juvenile to slaying of student at Cardozo High School. *Washington Post, The*. Retrieved from https://www.washingtonpost.com/archive/local/1995/03/17/teen-pleads-guilty-as-juvenile-to-slaying-of-student-at-cardozo-high-school/e88a8130-dbf4-42ff-a0cf-1d3a339d5ac8/?utm_term=.238746950092

Congress of the U.S. (1999). *Understanding violent children. Hearing before the Subcommittee on Early Childhood, Youth and Families of the Committee on Education and the Workforce: ISBN-0-16-057973-2* [PDF File], p. 69-89. Retrieved from https://files.eric.ed.gov/fulltext/ED435940.pdf

Cardozo High School III Three shootings since 1995 speak to lessons ignored. (2006, September 26). *Washington Post, The*. Retrieved from https://www.washingtonpost.com/archive/opinions/2006/09/23/cardozo-high-school-iii-span-classbankheadthree-shootings-since-1995-speak-to-lessons-ignoredspan/53fbca09-c4c7-4259-9555-1cebab1d2af7/

1048 - Palm Beach Gardens High School

National School Safety Center. (2010, March 3). *School Associated Violent Deaths* [PDF file], p. 2-46. Retrieved from https://files.eric.ed.gov/fulltext/ED519244.pdf

Nealy, J. L. (1995, January 11). Boy shoots himself at school. *Palm Beach Post, The*, p. 2B. Retrieved from https://www.newspapers.com/image/134212274/?terms=Palm%2BBeach%2BGardens%2BHigh%2BSchool%2C

Athans, M. (1995, January 13). Withdrawn teen's friends, family ask: what went wrong? *South Florida Sun Sentinel*, p. 3B. Retrieved from https://www.newspapers.com/image/239023302/?terms=Robert%2Bwarthen%2C

Congress of the U.S. (1999). *Understanding violent children. Hearing before the Subcommittee on Early Childhood, Youth and Families of the Committee on Education and the Workforce:*

ISBN-0-16-057973-2 [PDF File], p. 69-89. Retrieved from https://files.eric.ed.gov/fulltext/ED435940.pdf

1047 - Garfield High School

Henderson, D., & Lilly, D. (1995, January 24). Shooting at Garfield wounded student body. *Seattle Times, The*. Retrieved from http://community.seattletimes.nwsource.com/archive/?date=19950124&slug=2101183

Gruenwald, R., & Smith, J. (2018, March 23). I was hit by a ricochet bullet in high school. *Vice*. Retrieved from https://www.vice.com/en_us/article/wj75x4/i-was-hit-by-a-ricochet-bullet-in-high-school

2 wounded in school shooting. (1995, January 13). *Statesman Journal*, p. 4B. Retrieved from https://www.newspapers.com/image/202339113/?terms=garfield%2Bhigh

Haines, T.W., Birkland, D., Lilly, D., & Simon, J. (1995, January 13). Garfield shooting spurs talk of metal detectors. *Seattle Times, The*. Retrieved from http://community.seattletimes.nwsource.com/archive/?date=19950113&slug=2099324

1046 - Sacred Heart School (Private Catholic Christian PreK - 8 school)

National School Safety Center. (2010, March 3). *School Associated Violent Deaths* [PDF file], p. 2-46. Retrieved from https://files.eric.ed.gov/fulltext/ED519244.pdf

Montano, R. (1995, January 25). Police look to gun for clues to boy's motive. *San Bernardino Sun, The*, p. B1. Retrieved from https://www.newspapers.com/image/81306078/?terms=Sacred%2BHeart%2BSchool%2C

Hanna, G. (1995, January 29). Family, friends mourn Redlands teen. *San Bernardino Sun, The*, p. B1. Retrieved from https://www.newspapers.com/image/81307142/?terms=John%2BSirola

Gorman, T. (1995, January 25). School shooting leaves a mystery. *Los Angeles Times*, p. A3 & A18. Retrieved from https://www.newspapers.com/image/158975816/?terms=John%2BSirola

Congress of the U.S. (1999). *Understanding violent children. Hearing before the Subcommittee on Early Childhood, Youth and Families of the Committee on Education and the Workforce: ISBN-0-16-057973-2* [PDF File], p. 69-89. Retrieved from https://files.eric.ed.gov/fulltext/ED435940.pdf

Church, S., & Valenzuela, C. A. (1995, January 24). Teen dead, principal hurt. *San Bernardino Sun, The*, p. A1 & A6. Retrieved from https://www.newspapers.com/image/81305875/?terms=Richard%2BFacciolo%2C

1045 - University of North Carolina

Shooting victim was exemplary athlete, student. (1995, January 28). *Asheville Citizen-Times*, p. 2B. Retrieved from https://www.newspapers.com/image/200527988/?terms=University%2Bof%2BNorth%2BCarolina%2C

North Carolina gunman kills two. (1995, January 27). *Journal News, The*, p. A3. Retrieved from https://www.newspapers.com/image/166153113/?terms=University%2Bof%2BNorth%2BCarolina%2C

Victim of shooting rampage remembered at N.C. funeral. (1995, January 31). *Daily Press*, p. C5. Retrieved from https://www.newspapers.com/image/230652621/?terms=Wendell%2BWilliamson%2C

M-1 Garland cuts a violent path. (1997, December 29). *Chicago Tribune*, p. 1-9. Retrieved from https://www.newspapers.com/image/168708056/?terms=Wendell%2BWilliamson%2C

Terzian, P. (1998, October 16). Killer blames his psychiatrist; jury agrees. *Tallahassee Democrat*, p.13A. Retrieved from https://www.newspapers.com/image/248320926/?terms=Wendell%2BWilliamson

'I just did it.' (1995, January 28). *Asheville Citizen-Times*, p. 2B. Retrieved from https://www.newspapers.com/image/200527988/?terms=Bill%2BLeone%2C

1044 - Chadron Middle School

Coach shot at Nebraska school. (1995, February 9). *SFGATE*. Retrieved from https://www.sfgate.com/news/article/Coach-Shot-at-Nebraska-School-3046056.php

Among worst U.S. school shooting incidents. (2011, January 5). *Lincoln Journal Star*. Retrieved from https://journalstar.com/among-worst-u-s-school-shooting-incidents/article_8612b28d-a1a8-5283-98d0-dce443a6ecd8.html

1043 - Lake Worth High School

Paola, J. D. (1995, June 15). One critically wounded at Lake Worth High; suspect charged. *South Florida Sun Sentinel*, p. 1A & 19A. Retrieved from https://www.newspapers.com/image/238628483/?terms=Lake%2BWorth%2BHigh%2BSchool%2C

Staletovich, J. (1995a, June 15). 2 hurt in school shooting. *Palm Beach Post, The*, p. 1A. Retrieved from https://www.newspapers.com/image/134485692/?terms=Lake%2BWorth%2BHigh%2BSchool%2C

Staletovich, J. (1995b, June 16). Shooting suspect, victim middle school rivals, police say. *Palm Beach Post, The*, p. 4B. Retrieved from https://www.newspapers.com/image/134214095/?terms=Alexander%2BKucer%2C

1042 - Memorial Middle School

National School Safety Center. (2010, March 3). *School Associated Violent Deaths* [PDF file], p. 2-46. Retrieved from https://files.eric.ed.gov/fulltext/ED519244.pdf

Congress of the U.S. (1999). *Understanding violent children. Hearing before the Subcommittee on Early Childhood, Youth and Families of the Committee on Education and the Workforce: ISBN-0-16-057973-2* [PDF File], p. 69-89. Retrieved from https://files.eric.ed.gov/fulltext/ED435940.pdf

Reddick, C. (2005). A decade later, many still in pain schoolyard death of Lizzy Rivera evokes sad memories. *Laredo Morning News*. Retrieved from https://archive.fo/ZYV6#selection-11.1-13.53

1041 - Cypress Junior High School (Middle School)

National School Safety Center. (2010, March 3). *School Associated Violent Deaths* [PDF file], p. 2-46. Retrieved from https://files.eric.ed.gov/fulltext/ED519244.pdf

Teen killed in junior high shooting. (1995, September 13). *Tennessean, The*, p. 2B. Retrieved from https://www.newspapers.com/image/113196655/?terms=Cypress%2BJunior%2BHigh%2BSchool%2C

Congress of the U.S. (1999). *Understanding violent children. Hearing before the Subcommittee on Early Childhood, Youth and Families of the Committee on Education and the Workforce: ISBN-0-16-057973-2* [PDF File], p. 69-89. Retrieved from https://files.eric.ed.gov/fulltext/ED435940.pdf

1040 - Olathe North High School

National School Safety Center. (2010, March 3). *School Associated Violent Deaths* [PDF file], p. 2-46. Retrieved from https://files.eric.ed.gov/fulltext/ED519244.pdf

Congress of the U.S. (1999). *Understanding violent children. Hearing before the Subcommittee on Early Childhood, Youth and Families of the Committee on Education and the Workforce: ISBN-0-16-057973-2* [PDF File], p. 69-89. Retrieved from https://files.eric.ed.gov/fulltext/ED435940.pdf

Bad blood between schools. (1995, September 27). *Daily Tribune, The*, p. 12B. Retrieved from https://www.newspapers.com/image/244773135/?terms=Jerrell%2BFrazier%2C

Teen charged in killings. (1995, September 27). *Salina Journal, The*, p. A3. Retrieved from https://www.newspapers.com/image/13017250/?terms=Jerrell%2BFrazier%2C

Teen-ager charged in fatal shootings. (1995, September 27). *Springfield News-Leader, The*, p. 13A. Retrieved from https://www.newspapers.com/image/207677156/?terms=Ryan%2BSpornitz

Hay, G. (2002, November 21). Judge puts down his gavel. *Olathe News, The*, p. 3A. Retrieved from https://www.newspapers.com/image/818268261/?terms=Alfred%20Williams

1039 - Tavares Middle School

Hayes, C. (2015, September 29). 20 years later, Lake County remembers fatal school shooting. *Orlando Sentinel*. Retrieved from http://www.orlandosentinel.com/news/lake/os-tavares-school-shooting-20th-anniversary-20150928-story.html#

Murphy, M., & Weber, D. (1995, September 30). Horror at Tavares school: teen guns down student. *Orlando Sentinel*. Retrieved from http://articles.orlandosentinel.com/1995-09-30/news/9509300197_1_keith-tavares-joey

Shaw, G. K. (1995, October 1). Student warned before shooting. *Sun Sentinel*. Retrieved from http://articles.sun-sentinel.com/1995-10-01/news/9509300345_1_joey-summerall-tavares-youth-football-gun

National School Safety Center. (2010, March 3). *School Associated Violent Deaths* [PDF file], p. 2-46. Retrieved from https://files.eric.ed.gov/fulltext/ED519244.pdf

Congress of the U.S. (1999). *Understanding violent children. Hearing before the Subcommittee on Early Childhood, Youth and Families of the Committee on Education and the Workforce:*

ISBN-0-16-057973-2 [PDF File], p. 69-89. Retrieved from https://files.eric.ed.gov/fulltext/ED435940.pdf

1038 - Blackville-Hilda High School

More info: school shootings in South Carolina. (2010, September 21). *WISTV*, p. 12. Retrieved from http://www.wistv.com/story/23589594/school-shootings-in-south-carolina

National School Safety Center. (2010, March 3). *School Associated Violent Deaths* [PDF file], p. 2-46. Retrieved from https://files.eric.ed.gov/fulltext/ED519244.pdf

Crews, G. A. (2016). *Critical Examinations of School Violence and Disturbance in K-12 Education*, p. 6 & 7. Hershey, PA: Information Science Reference.

Congress of the U.S. (1999). *Understanding violent children. Hearing before the Subcommittee on Early Childhood, Youth and Families of the Committee on Education and the Workforce: ISBN-0-16-057973-2* [PDF File], p. 69-89. Retrieved from https://files.eric.ed.gov/fulltext/ED435940.pdf

Smith, B. (1995, October 13). Teen wounds teacher, kills self; second teacher collapses, dies. *Times and Democrat, The*, p. 1A & 7A. Retrieved from https://www.newspapers.com/image/345458100/?terms=Blackville-Hilda%2BHigh%2BSchool%2C

Burgdorf, K. (1995, October 13). Shootings shock neighbors in North, Bamberg communities. *Times and Democrat, The*, p. 1A. Retrieved from https://www.newspapers.com/image/345458100/?terms=Blackville-Hilda%2BHigh%2BSchool%2C

Newman, K.S., Fox, C., Harding, D., Mehta, J., & Roth, W. (2004). *Rampage: the social roots of school shootings*, p. 47-263. New York, NY: Basic Books.

1037 - Lindbergh High School

Student held after school bus shooting. (1995, October 14). *St. Louis Post-Dispatch*, p. 4A. Retrieved from https://www.newspapers.com/image/142515364/?terms=lindbergh%2Bhigh%2Bschool%2C

Yaqub, R. M. (1995, October 14). Schools' rough week spurs action. *St. Louis Post-Dispatch*, p. 1A & 4A. Retrieved from https://www.newspapers.com/image/142515341/?terms=Schools%27%2Brough%2Bweek%2Bspurs%2Baction

1036 - Lake Howell High School

Taylor, B. (1995, November 15). Student faces trial as adult. *Orlando Sentinel, The*, p. D-3. Retrieved from https://www.newspapers.com/image/233564601/?terms=Expeditas%2B%22Odette%22%2BReyes%2C

McBreen, S. (1995, October 24). Shot student faces many questions. *Orlando Sentinel, The*, p. A-1. Retrieved from https://www.newspapers.com/image/233221705/?terms=Expeditas%2B%22Odette%22%2BReyes%2C

1035 - Richland High School

Leung, R. (2018, April 12). *The mind of a school shooter.* CBS News. Retrieved from https://www.cbsnews.com/news/the-mind-of-a-school-shooter/

National School Safety Center. (2010, March 3). *School Associated Violent Deaths* [PDF file], p. 2-46. Retrieved from https://files.eric.ed.gov/fulltext/ED519244.pdf

Crews, G. A. (2016). *Critical Examinations of School Violence and Disturbance in K-12 Education*, p. 6 & 7. Hershey, PA: Information Science Reference.

Congress of the U.S. (1999). *Understanding violent children. Hearing before the Subcommittee on Early Childhood, Youth and Families of the Committee on Education and the Workforce: ISBN-0-16-057973-2* [PDF File], p. 69-89. Retrieved from https://files.eric.ed.gov/fulltext/ED435940.pdf

Newman, K.S., Fox, C., Harding, D., Mehta, J., & Roth, W. (2004). *Rampage: the social roots of school shootings*, p. 47-263. New York, NY: Basic Books.

School violence: metro area. (1997, October 2). *Clarion-Ledger*, p. 12A. Retrieved from https://www.newspapers.com/image/185495695/?terms=school%20violence&match=1

U.S. Supreme Court rules on juvenile offenders. (2016, January 25). *The Daily Herald*. Retrieved from https://www.columbiadailyherald.com/story/news/local/2016/01/25/u-s-supreme-court-rules/25686578007/

1034 - Oxon Hill High School

National School Safety Center. (2010, March 3). *School Associated Violent Deaths* [PDF file], p. 2-46. Retrieved from https://files.eric.ed.gov/fulltext/ED519244.pdf

Frazier, L. (1996, January 7). After shooting, parents force changes at Oxon High. *Washington Post, The*. Retrieved from https://www.washingtonpost.com/archive/local/1996/01/07/after-shooting-parents-force-changes-at-oxon-hill-high/375a84f1-6115-4a95-8f3e-e6b2972bb797/

Congress of the U.S. (1999). *Understanding violent children. Hearing before the Subcommittee on Early Childhood, Youth and Families of the Committee on Education and the Workforce: ISBN-0-16-057973-2* [PDF File], p. 69-89. Retrieved from https://files.eric.ed.gov/fulltext/ED435940.pdf

1033 - Girard High School

National School Safety Center. (2010, March 3). *School Associated Violent Deaths* [PDF file], p. 2-46. Retrieved from https://files.eric.ed.gov/fulltext/ED519244.pdf

Congress of the U.S. (1999). *Understanding violent children. Hearing before the Subcommittee on Early Childhood, Youth and Families of the Committee on Education and the Workforce: ISBN-0-16-057973-2* [PDF File], p. 69-89. Retrieved from https://files.eric.ed.gov/fulltext/ED435940.pdf

Teen shoots himself. (1996, January 3). *Tyrone Daily Herald*, p. 2. Retrieved from https://www.newspapers.com/image/25574907/?terms=Girard%2BHigh%2BSchool

Suicide at Erie school. (1996, January 3). *Pittsburg Post-Gazette*, p. B-3. Retrieved from https://www.newspapers.com/image/95090329/?terms=Girard%2BHigh%2BSchool%2C

1032 - Winston Education Center (Martha H. Winston Community School, Grades PreK - 8)

Miller, B. (1997, June 25). Teen convicted of fatality shooting boy at D.C. school. *Washington Post, The*. Retrieved from https://www.washingtonpost.com/archive/local/1997/06/25/teen-convicted-of-fatally-shooting-boy-at-dc-school/097c0f6e-0e54-42ef-93b4-64c4c8a8cbbd/?utm_term=.8f154a72ce8a

National School Safety Center. (2010, March 3). *School Associated Violent Deaths* [PDF file], p. 2-46. Retrieved from https://files.eric.ed.gov/fulltext/ED519244.pdf

Crews, G. A. (2016). *Critical Examinations of School Violence and Disturbance in K-12 Education*, p. 6 & 7. Hershey, PA: Information Science Reference.

Congress of the U.S. (1999). *Understanding violent children. Hearing before the Subcommittee on Early Childhood, Youth and Families of the Committee on Education and the Workforce: ISBN-0-16-057973-2* [PDF File], p. 69-89. Retrieved from https://files.eric.ed.gov/fulltext/ED435940.pdf

Death in the schools. (1997, December 17). *Baltimore Sun, The*, p 2E. Retrieved from https://www.newspapers.com/image/172881844/?terms=%22Damion%2BBlocker%22

Brown, D. L., & Kyriakos, M. (1996, January 20). Masked teens slay youth, 14, in D.C. school. *Washington Post, The*. Retrieved from https://www.washingtonpost.com/archive/politics/1996/01/20/masked-teens-slay-youth-14-in-dc-school/d7bb516a-44aa-4c3c-97bb-d48612bf86cf/

1031 - East High School

National School Safety Center. (2010, March 3). *School Associated Violent Deaths* [PDF file], p. 2-46. Retrieved from https://files.eric.ed.gov/fulltext/ED519244.pdf

Congress of the U.S. (1999). *Understanding violent children. Hearing before the Subcommittee on Early Childhood, Youth and Families of the Committee on Education and the Workforce: ISBN-0-16-057973-2* [PDF File], p. 69-89. Retrieved from https://files.eric.ed.gov/fulltext/ED435940.pdf

State v. Maria Maclin, Tenn. Crim. Ap. LEXIS 877. (1998) Retrieved from www.lexisnexis.com/us/lnlib

1030 - Frontier Junior High School (Middle School)

National School Safety Center. (2010, March 3). *School Associated Violent Deaths* [PDF file], p. 2-46. Retrieved from https://files.eric.ed.gov/fulltext/ED519244.pdf

Crews, G. A. (2016). *Critical Examinations of School Violence and Disturbance in K-12 Education*, p. 6 & 7. Hershey, PA: Information Science Reference.

Lebrun, M. (2009). *Books, Blackboards, and Bullets: School Shootings and Violence in America*, p. 173-177. Lanham, MD: Rowman & Littlefield Education.

Congress of the U.S. (1999). *Understanding violent children. Hearing before the Subcommittee on Early Childhood, Youth and Families of the Committee on Education and the Workforce: ISBN-0-16-057973-2* [PDF File], p. 69-89. Retrieved from https://files.eric.ed.gov/fulltext/ED435940.pdf

Young student kills teacher, 2 classmates. (1996, February 4). *Berkshire Eagle, The*, p. A3. Retrieved from https://www.newspapers.com/image/533404504/?terms=Frontier%2BJunior%2BHigh%2BSchool%2C

Honors student arrested in killing of teacher, 2 students. (1996, February 4). *La Crosse Tribune, The*, p. A-6. Retrieved from https://www.newspapers.com/image/513788153/?terms=Frontier%2BJunior%2BHigh%2BSchool%2C

Geranios, N. K. (2017a, April 14). Barry Loukaitis, Moses Lake school shooter, breaks silence with apology. *Seattle Times, The*. Retrieved from https://www.seattletimes.com/seattle-news/barry-loukaitis-moses-lake-school-shooter-apologizes-in-1st-remarks/

Newman, K.S., Fox, C., Harding, D., Mehta, J., & Roth, W. (2004). *Rampage: the social roots of school shootings*, p. 47-263. New York, NY: Basic Books.

School shootings in Washington state. (2012, December 16). *Seattle Times*. Retrieved from https://www.seattletimes.com/seattle-news/history-of-school-shootings-in-washington-state/

School violence: metro area. (1997, October 2). *Clarion-Ledger*, p. 12A. Retrieved from https://www.newspapers.com/image/185495695/?terms=school%20violence&match=1

1029 - Mid-Peninsula High School

National School Safety Center. (2010, March 3). *School Associated Violent Deaths* [PDF file], p. 2-46. Retrieved from https://files.eric.ed.gov/fulltext/ED519244.pdf

Congress of the U.S. (1999). *Understanding violent children. Hearing before the Subcommittee on Early Childhood, Youth and Families of the Committee on Education and the Workforce: ISBN-0-16-057973-2* [PDF File], p. 69-89. Retrieved from https://files.eric.ed.gov/fulltext/ED435940.pdf

Mitchell, E. (1996, February 9). Teen shoots fellow student, self at school in Palo Alto. *San Francisco Examiner, The*, p. A-3. Retrieved from https://www.newspapers.com/image/462149555/?terms=Mid-Peninsula%2BHigh%2BSchool

Boy in high school shooting spree dies. (1996, February 11). *Santa Cruz Sentinel*, p. C-8. Retrieved from https://www.newspapers.com/image/184463609/?terms=Mid-Peninsula%2BHigh%2BSchool%2C

1028 - West Philadelphia High School

Bello, M. (1996, February 21). Teen held in school shooting. *Philadelphia Daily News*, p. 23. Retrieved from https://www.newspapers.com/image/187172266/?terms=West%2BPhiladelphia%2BHigh%2BSchool

Woodall, M. (1996, February 21). Request for change led to a shooting at W. Phila. High. *Philadelphia Inquirer, The*, p. B2. Retrieved from https://www.newspapers.com/image/178286043/?terms=Rojah%2BMorris%2C

1027 - Jenkins High School

National School Safety Center. (2010, March 3). *School Associated Violent Deaths* [PDF file], p. 2-46. Retrieved from https://files.eric.ed.gov/fulltext/ED519244.pdf

Congress of the U.S. (1999). *Understanding violent children. Hearing before the Subcommittee on Early Childhood, Youth and Families of the Committee on Education and the Workforce: ISBN-0-16-057973-2* [PDF File], p. 69-89. Retrieved from https://files.eric.ed.gov/fulltext/ED435940.pdf

2 deaths stun students at Savannah school. (1996, February 26). *Atlanta Constitution, The*, p. B5. Retrieved from https://www.newspapers.com/image/402875808/?terms=Dwayne%2BMartin%2C

Death suit. (1996, July 11). *Atlanta Constitution, The*, p. C9. Retrieved from https://www.newspapers.com/image/403274495/?terms=Dwayne%2BMartin%2C

1026 - Beaumont High School

National School Safety Center. (2010, March 3). *School Associated Violent Deaths* [PDF file], p. 2-46. Retrieved from https://files.eric.ed.gov/fulltext/ED519244.pdf

Congress of the U.S. (1999). *Understanding violent children. Hearing before the Subcommittee on Early Childhood, Youth and Families of the Committee on Education and the Workforce: ISBN-0-16-057973-2* [PDF File], p. 69-89. Retrieved from https://files.eric.ed.gov/fulltext/ED435940.pdf

Bryan, B. (1996a, March 27). Reward fund grows to $7,000 in killing of pregnant student. *St. Louis Post-Dispatch*, p. 10A. Retrieved from https://www.newspapers.com/image/142539243/?terms=Kyunia%2BTaylor%2C

Bryant, T. (1998, January 10). Killer of pregnant teen gets 23 years. *St. Louis Post-Dispatch*, p. 15. Retrieved from https://www.newspapers.com/image/141863840/?terms=Mark%2BBoyd%2C

Bower, C. (1996, June 2). 2nd arrest in school bus killing took sweat. *St. Louis Post-Dispatch*, p. 1D & 12D. Retrieved from https://www.newspapers.com/image/142534929/?terms=Mark%2BBoyd%2C

Grand jury indicts man, 29, in murder-for-hire scheme. (1996, June 2). *Springfield News-Leader, The*, p. 5B. Retrieved from https://www.newspapers.com/image/208143249/?terms=Mark%2BBoyd%2C

Chronology in killing. (1996, June 1). *St. Louis Post-Dispatch*, p. 7A. Retrieved from https://www.newspapers.com/image/142524981/?terms=Kyunia%2BTaylor%2C

1025 - North Stanly High School

National School Safety Center. (2010, March 3). *School Associated Violent Deaths* [PDF file], p. 2-46. Retrieved from https://files.eric.ed.gov/fulltext/ED519244.pdf

Congress of the U.S. (1999). *Understanding violent children. Hearing before the Subcommittee on Early Childhood, Youth and Families of the Committee on Education and the Workforce: ISBN-0-16-057973-2* [PDF File], p. 69-89. Retrieved from https://files.eric.ed.gov/fulltext/ED435940.pdf

Troubled teen's in-school suicide raises questions. (1996, March 13). *Rocky Mount Telegram*, p. 2A. Retrieved from https://www.newspapers.com/image/338230111/?terms=Jamie%2BHurley%2C

1024 - Talladega High School

National School Safety Center. (2010, March 3). *School Associated Violent Deaths* [PDF file], p. 2-46. Retrieved from https://files.eric.ed.gov/fulltext/ED519244.pdf

Congress of the U.S. (1999). *Understanding violent children. Hearing before the Subcommittee on Early Childhood, Youth and Families of the Committee on Education and the Workforce: ISBN-0-16-057973-2* [PDF File], p. 69-89. Retrieved from https://files.eric.ed.gov/fulltext/ED435940.pdf

Teen charged in classmate's death released on bond; placed in house arrest. (1996, May 8). *Anniston Star, The*, p. 12A. Retrieved from https://www.newspapers.com/image/106479424/?terms=Steven%2BCurry%2C

1023 - Alexander Junior High School (Middle School)

School violence: metro area. (1997, October 2). *Clarion-Ledger*, p. 12A. Retrieved from https://www.newspapers.com/image/185495695/?terms=school%20violence&match=1

Student feud ends with Lincoln school shooting. (1996, April 16). *Enterprise-Journal*, p. 1. Retrieved from https://www.newspapers.com/image/319465106/?terms=Alexander%2BJunior%2BHigh%2C

Brookhaven teen facing possible 20-year term in student shooting. (1996, August 24). *Clarion-Ledger*, p. 4B. Retrieved from https://www.newspapers.com/image/183018621/?terms=Travis%2BPendelton

1022 - Bingham Middle School

National School Safety Center. (2010, March 3). *School Associated Violent Deaths* [PDF file], p. 2-46. Retrieved from https://files.eric.ed.gov/fulltext/ED519244.pdf

Congress of the U.S. (1999). *Understanding violent children. Hearing before the Subcommittee on Early Childhood, Youth and Families of the Committee on Education and the Workforce: ISBN-0-16-057973-2* [PDF File], p. 69-89. Retrieved from https://files.eric.ed.gov/fulltext/ED435940.pdf

High schooler crashes hijacked bus; kills himself. (1996, May 15). *Courier, The*, p. A2. Retrieved from https://www.newspapers.com/image/358256878/?terms=Bingham%2BMiddle%2BSchool%2C

1021 - West Valley High School

National School Safety Center. (2010, March 3). *School Associated Violent Deaths* [PDF file], p. 2-46. Retrieved from https://files.eric.ed.gov/fulltext/ED519244.pdf

Arballo, J., Jr., & Moore, S. (1996, June 5). Student found dead at West Valley High. *Press-Enterprise, The*, p. B01. Retrieved from NewsBank: Access World News – Historical and Current: https://infoweb.newsbank.com/apps/news/document-view?p=WORLDNEWS&docref=news/0EB0424BD4B8B1B8

Moore, S., & Arballo, J., Jr. (1996, June 6). Campus mourns student's death. *Press-Enterprise, The*, p. B01. Retrieved from NewsBank: Access World News – Historical and Current: https://infoweb.newsbank.com/apps/news/document-view?p=WORLDNEWS&docref=news/0EB0424C15D1CC2C

1020 - John Marshall High School

Pyle, A. (1996a, July 30). Student is charged in Marshall High shootings. *Los Angeles Times*. Retrieved from https://www.newspapers.com/image/158760954/?terms=Yohao%2BAlbert%2BRivas%2C

Pyle, A. (1996b, July 31). Another gun found at high school. *Los Angeles Times*. Retrieved from https://www.newspapers.com/image/158764206/?terms=Yohao%2BRivas

Violent death in our schools. (1998, June 1). *Jackson Sun, The*, p. 8A. Retrieved from https://www.newspapers.com/image/282415675/?terms=Yohao%2BAlbert%2BRivas

1019 - San Diego State University

Slain professors called tough, but popular. (1996, August 17). *Signal, The*, p. A6. Retrieved from https://www.newspapers.com/image/333266366/?terms=San%2BDiego%2BState%2BUniversity%2C

Police: grad student hid gun in room. (1996, August 17). *Signal, The*, p. A6. Retrieved from https://www.newspapers.com/image/333266366/?terms=San%2BDiego%2BState%2BUniversity%2C

San Diego professors' slayer gets 3 life terms. (1997, July 19). *San Francisco Examiner, The*, p. A6. Retrieved from https://www.newspapers.com/image/462118858/?terms=Frederick%2BMartin%2BDavidson%2C

Student charged in fatal shootings of three professors in San Diego. (1996, August 16). *Courier, The (Waterloo, Iowa)*, p. A1 & A8. Retrieved from https://www.newspapers.com/image/357794575/?terms=Frederick%2BMartin%2BDavidson%2C

Graduate gunman was methodical. (1996, August 17). *Berkshire Eagle, The*, p. A3. Retrieved from https://www.newspapers.com/image/533402755/?terms=Frederick%2BMartin%2BDavidson%2C

1018 - University of Texas

Murder-suicide likely in death of 2. (1996, August 28). *Arizona Republic*, p. A10. Retrieved from https://www.newspapers.com/image/123657437/?terms=Gregory%2BHeath%2BTidwell%2C

Police say shootings a murder-suicide. (1996, August 28). *Victoria Advocate*, p. 3A. Retrieved from https://www.newspapers.com/image/432833399/?terms=Stephen%2BSorenson

1017 - Penn State University

Ivey, D. (1996a, September 22). Suspect suffered emotional conflict. *Sunday News (Lancaster, Pennsylvania)*. Retrieved from https://www.newspapers.com/image/565438177/?terms=Jillian%2BRobbins%2C

Ivey, D. (1996b, September 24). Slain Penn St. student honored. *York Daily Record (York, Pennsylvania)*. Retrieved from https://www.newspapers.com/image/554906080/?terms=Melanie%2BSpalla

Ivey, D. (1996c, September 27). Shooting suspect's tape played in court. *Morning Call, The*. Retrieved from https://www.newspapers.com/image/277528651/?terms=Jillian%2BRobbins%2C

Friends, family remember victim of college shooting. (1996, September 23). *Sentinel, The (Carlisle, Pennsylvania)*, p. A2. Retrieved from https://www.newspapers.com/image/346025609/?terms=Melanie%2BSpalla%2C

1016 - DeKalb Alternative School (Grades 6-12)

National School Safety Center. (2010, March 3). *School Associated Violent Deaths* [PDF file], p. 2-46. Retrieved from https://files.eric.ed.gov/fulltext/ED519244.pdf

Crews, G. A. (2016). *Critical Examinations of School Violence and Disturbance in K-12 Education*, p. 6 & 7. Hershey, PA: Information Science Reference.

Congress of the U.S. (1999). *Understanding violent children. Hearing before the Subcommittee on Early Childhood, Youth and Families of the Committee on Education and the Workforce: ISBN-0-16-057973-2* [PDF File], p. 69-89. Retrieved from https://files.eric.ed.gov/fulltext/ED435940.pdf

Oglesby, C. (1996, September 26). Learning life's tragic lessons. *Atlanta Constitution, The*, p. C8. Retrieved from https://www.newspapers.com/image/403234606/?terms=David%2BDubose%2BJr.%2C

1015 - Crestview Middle School

Bryan, B. (1996b, September 27). Stray bullet hits girl, 13, riding on school bus. *St. Louis Post-Dispatch*. Retrieved from https://www.newspapers.com/image/142567622/

Girl riding bus caught in crossfire of shootout. (1996, September 28). *Springfield News-Leader, The*. Retrieved from https://www.newspapers.com/image/208187544/?terms=Crestview%2BSchool

O'Neil, T. (1996, September 28). Wounded girl may not gain full vision. *St. Louis Post-Dispatch*, p. 4C. Retrieved from https://www.newspapers.com/image/142569122/?terms=Jodi%2BHenry%2C

1014 - Smedley Elementary School

National School Safety Center. (2010, March 3). *School Associated Violent Deaths* [PDF file], p. 2-46. Retrieved from https://files.eric.ed.gov/fulltext/ED519244.pdf

Congress of the U.S. (1999). *Understanding violent children. Hearing before the Subcommittee on Early Childhood, Youth and Families of the Committee on Education and the Workforce: ISBN-0-16-057973-2* [PDF File], p. 69-89. Retrieved from https://files.eric.ed.gov/fulltext/ED435940.pdf

Angeles, M. (1996, October 3). In front of grade school. *Philadelphia Daily Newsi*, p. 5. Retrieved from https://www.newspapers.com/image/187199896/?terms=Smedley%2BElementary%2BSchool%2C

Gibbons, T. J., Jr. (1996, October 4). Police hunt for suspect in 2 killings. *Philadelphia Inquirer, The*, p. B2. Retrieved from https://www.newspapers.com/image/179555392/?terms=Steven%2BBoyd%2C%2BPennsylvania%2C

School violence: metro area. (1997, October 2). *Clarion-Ledger*, p. 12A. Retrieved from https://www.newspapers.com/image/185495695/?terms=school%20violence&match=1

1013 - St. Bernard High School (Private Catholic Christian school)

National School Safety Center. (2010, March 3). *School Associated Violent Deaths* [PDF file], p. 2-46. Retrieved from https://files.eric.ed.gov/fulltext/ED519244.pdf

Congress of the U.S. (1999). *Understanding violent children. Hearing before the Subcommittee on Early Childhood, Youth and Families of the Committee on Education and the Workforce: ISBN-0-16-057973-2* [PDF File], p. 69-89. Retrieved from https://files.eric.ed.gov/fulltext/ED435940.pdf

High school player charged in fatal shooting. (1996, October 11). *Los Angeles Times*, p. B4. Retrieved from https://www.newspapers.com/image/160103496/?terms=St.%2BBernard%2BHigh%2BSchool%2C

Yarborough, S. (1996, October 10). Jordan student charged. *Long Beach Press-Telegram*, p. B1. Retrieved from NewsBank: Access World News: https://infoweb-newsbank-com.ezproxy.lib.usf.edu/apps/news/document-view?p=AWNB&docref=news/0EAE91056E7AEF91

Beck, H. (1998, September 3). Sad brush with mortality for Abercrombie - CSUN player lives with reminders of lost friend. *Daily News of Los Angeles*, p. SS6. Retrieved from NewsBank: Access World News: https://infoweb-newsbank-com.ezproxy.lib.usf.edu/apps/news/document-view?p=AWNB&docref=news/0EF80B2E01B39BDF

1012 - Jacksonville Senior High School

National School Safety Center. (2010, March 3). *School Associated Violent Deaths* [PDF file], p. 2-46. Retrieved from https://files.eric.ed.gov/fulltext/ED519244.pdf

Congress of the U.S. (1999). *Understanding violent children. Hearing before the Subcommittee on Early Childhood, Youth and Families of the Committee on Education and the Workforce: ISBN-0-16-057973-2* [PDF File], p. 69-89. Retrieved from https://files.eric.ed.gov/fulltext/ED435940.pdf

Student killed on school bus. (1996, October 10). *Daily News-Journal, The*, p. 7A. Retrieved from https://www.newspapers.com/image/422850018/?terms=Earl%2BRoutt

1011 - Purdue University

Gerrety, J., & Rahner, M. (1996, October 17). Shooter lived, played hard. *Journal and Courier*, p. B1. Retrieved from https://www.newspapers.com/image/265151290/?terms=Purdue%2BUniversity%2C

Fleming, M. (1996, October 18). Anguish touches parents at home, too. *Indianapolis Star, The*, p. A6. Retrieved from https://www.newspapers.com/image/106428747/?terms=Jarrod%2BAllen%2BEskew%2C

Calm back but not normalcy. (1996, October 18). *Indianapolis News, The*, p. G-1. Retrieved from https://www.newspapers.com/image/313272039/?terms=Jarrod%2BEskew%2C

1010 - Sumner High School

National School Safety Center. (2010, March 3). *School Associated Violent Deaths* [PDF file], p. 2-46. Retrieved from https://files.eric.ed.gov/fulltext/ED519244.pdf

Holleman, J. (1996, December 22). Suspect in killing at Sumner certified to be tried as adult: Five star Life edition. *St. Louis Post – Dispatch*, p. 11D. Retrieved from https://www.newspapers.com/image/141747938/?terms=Kembert%20Thomas&match=1

Congress of the U.S. (1999). *Understanding violent children. Hearing before the Subcommittee on Early Childhood, Youth and Families of the Committee on Education and the Workforce: ISBN-0-16-057973-2* [PDF File], p. 69-89. Retrieved from https://files.eric.ed.gov/fulltext/ED435940.pdf

Bryan, B., & Autman, S. (1996, November 1). Shooting injures student. *St. Louis Post-Dispatch*, p. 1A & 12A. Retrieved from https://www.newspapers.com/image/141687530/

1009 - George W. Wingate High School

National School Safety Center. (2010, March 3). *School Associated Violent Deaths* [PDF file], p. 2-46. Retrieved from https://files.eric.ed.gov/fulltext/ED519244.pdf

Congress of the U.S. (1999). *Understanding violent children. Hearing before the Subcommittee on Early Childhood, Youth and Families of the Committee on Education and the Workforce: ISBN-0-16-057973-2* [PDF File], p. 69-89. Retrieved from https://files.eric.ed.gov/fulltext/ED435940.pdf

Farrell, B., & Jamieson, W. (1997, January 9). Gunplay at b'ball court. *Daily News*, p. 3C. Retrieved from https://www.newspapers.com/image/476610889/?terms=Crown%2BHeights%2Bshooting

Fenner, A. E., & Claffey, M. (1997, January 10). Brothers held in HS shooting. *Daily News*, p. 19. Retrieved from https://www.newspapers.com/image/476768763/?terms=Crown%2BHeights%2Bshooting

South Shore student dies after shooting near Wingate. (1997, January 16). *Canarsie Courier*, p. 5. Retrieved from https://www.newspapers.com/image/556121826/?terms=Dwight%2BArcher%2C

1008 - Conniston Middle School

Ragland, S., Patrick, K., & Barszewski, L. (1997, January 28). Student dies in school shooting. *Sun Sentinel*. Retrieved from http://articles.sun-sentinel.com/1997-01-28/news/9701280066_1_school-day-conniston-middle-school-police

Sweeney, D. (2017, August 4). Parents of South Florida boy shot and killed at school 20 years ago await settlement from state. *Sun Sentinel*. Retrieved from http://www.sun-sentinel.com/news/florida/fl-reg-claims-bills-2018-story.html#

National School Safety Center. (2010, March 3). *School Associated Violent Deaths* [PDF file], p. 2-46. Retrieved from https://files.eric.ed.gov/fulltext/ED519244.pdf

Congress of the U.S. (1999). *Understanding violent children. Hearing before the Subcommittee on Early Childhood, Youth and Families of the Committee on Education and the Workforce: ISBN-0-16-057973-2* [PDF File], p. 69-89. Retrieved from https://files.eric.ed.gov/fulltext/ED435940.pdf

Sterghos, N. (1998, Jan 16). Boy, 15, gets life for killing classmate. *South Florida Sun Sentinel*, p. 1A & 18A. Retrieved from https://www.newspapers.com/image/238635729/?terms=Boy%2C%2B15%2C%2BGets%2BLife%2BFor%2BKilling%2BClassmate%2C

1007 - Bunche Early Childhood Development Center (PreK - Kindergarten)

Gun carrier faces shooting charge. (1997, February 12). *Daily Oklahoman, The*. Retrieved from https://www.newspapers.com/image/454709538/?terms=Bunche%2BEarly%2BChildhood%2BDevelopment%2BCenter%2C

Jury acquits Tulsa man in shooting. (1999, February 12). *Daily Oklahoman, The*. Retrieved from https://www.newspapers.com/image/454083814/?terms=Harold%2BGlover%2C

1006 - Wingfield High School

Wingfield teen moved from intensive care. (1997, February 18). *Clarion-Ledger*, p. 3B. Retrieved from https://www.newspapers.com/image/184078193/?terms=Wingfield%2BHigh%2BSchool%2C

Bland, T. (1997, February 12). High school shooting victim still critical; suspect at large. *Clarion-Ledger*, p. 3B. Retrieved from https://www.newspapers.com/image/183853957/?terms=Wingfield%2BHigh%2BSchool%2C

Oeth, A. (1997, February 15). Wingfield suspect in trouble quickly. *Clarion-Ledger*, p. 1A & 13A. Retrieved from https://www.newspapers.com/image/183855292/?terms=Elliot%2BCrosby

School violence: metro area. (1997, October 2). *Clarion-Ledger*, p. 12A. Retrieved from https://www.newspapers.com/image/185495695/?terms=school%20violence&match=1

1005 - Ohio State University-Wexner Center for the Arts

Police ID former Ohio State employee who committed suicide in Wexner Center. (2015, November 30). *Columbia Dispatch, The*. Retrieved from https://www.dispatch.com/story/news/crime/2015/11/29/police-id-former-ohio-state/24139534007/

Suspect in killing found dead. (1997, February 14). *Tribune, The*, p . 3. Retrieved from https://www.newspapers.com/image/322587311/?terms=Mark%2BEdgerton%2C

Seewer, J. (1997, February 15). Suicide appears to be killer of Ohio State police officer. *Cincinnati Enquirer, The*, p. C8. Retrieved from https://www.newspapers.com/image/102250272/?terms=Mark%2BEdgerton%2C

1004 - Bethel Regional High School

Demer, L. (2017, February 18). Evan Ramsey's tattered life filled him with rage. Then he brought a shotgun to school. *Anchorage Daily News*. Retrieved from https://www.adn.com/alaska-news/2017/02/18/evan-ramseys-tattered-life-filled-him-with-rage-then-he-brought-a-shotgun-to-school/

McBride, R. (2017, February 22). Twenty years after the Bethel School shooting. *Alaska Public Media*. Retrieved from https://www.alaskapublic.org/2017/02/22/20-years-after-the-bethel-school-shooting/

National School Safety Center. (2010, March 3). *School Associated Violent Deaths* [PDF file], p. 2-46. Retrieved from https://files.eric.ed.gov/fulltext/ED519244.pdf

Crews, G. A. (2016). *Critical Examinations of School Violence and Disturbance in K-12 Education*, p. 6 & 7. Hershey, PA: Information Science Reference.

Lebrun, M. (2009). *Books, Blackboards, and Bullets: School Shootings and Violence in America*, p. 173-177. Lanham, MD: Rowman & Littlefield Education.

Congress of the U.S. (1999). *Understanding violent children. Hearing before the Subcommittee on Early Childhood, Youth and Families of the Committee on Education and the Workforce: ISBN-0-16-057973-2* [PDF File], p. 69-89. Retrieved from https://files.eric.ed.gov/fulltext/ED435940.pdf

Newman, K.S., Fox, C., Harding, D., Mehta, J., & Roth, W. (2004). *Rampage: the social roots of school shootings*, p. 47-263. New York, NY: Basic Books.

Fainaru, S. (1998, October 19). A tragedy was preceded by many overlooked signals. *Boston Globe, The*, p. A1, A10 & A11. Retrieved from https://www.newspapers.com/image/441992217/?terms=%2C%2Btragedy%2Bwas%2Bpreceded%2Bby%2Bmany%2Boverlooked%2Bsignals

1003 - First Coast High School

National School Safety Center. (2010, March 3). *School Associated Violent Deaths* [PDF file], p. 2-46. Retrieved from https://files.eric.ed.gov/fulltext/ED519244.pdf

Congress of the U.S. (1999). *Understanding violent children. Hearing before the Subcommittee on Early Childhood, Youth and Families of the Committee on Education and the Workforce: ISBN-0-16-057973-2* [PDF File], p. 69-89. Retrieved from https://files.eric.ed.gov/fulltext/ED435940.pdf

Softball player dies of gunshot wounds. (1997, February 24). *Tampa Bay Times*, p. 3B. Retrieved from https://www.newspapers.com/image/326783312/?terms=Melissa%2BChambliss%2C

Teen shoots herself over poor scholarship tryout. (1997, February 22). *Clarion-Ledger*, p. 10A. Retrieved from https://www.newspapers.com/image/184101377/?terms=Melissa%2BChambliss%2C

1002 - Rancho High School

Vegas schools. (1997, February 21). *Elko Daily Press*, p. 1. Retrieved from https://www.newspapers.com/image/477281152/?terms=Rancho%2BHigh%2BSchool%2C

Rancho High shootings brings beefed-up security. (1997, March 3). *Reno Gazette-Journal*, p. 2B. Retrieved from https://www.newspapers.com/image/154471034/?terms=Rancho%2BHigh%2BSchool%2C&match=2

Scott, C. (1997, April 9). Boy, 14, charged in Feb. drive-by. *Las Vegas Sun*. Retrieved from https://lasvegassun.com/news/1997/apr/09/boy-14-charged-in-feb-drive-by/

1001 - Pershing High School

National School Safety Center. (2010, March 3). *School Associated Violent Deaths* [PDF file], p. 2-46. Retrieved from https://files.eric.ed.gov/fulltext/ED519244.pdf

Congress of the U.S. (1999). *Understanding violent children. Hearing before the Subcommittee on Early Childhood, Youth and Families of the Committee on Education and the Workforce: ISBN-0-16-057973-2* [PDF File], p. 69-89. Retrieved from https://files.eric.ed.gov/fulltext/ED435940.pdf

Kresnak, J. (1997, March 22). In letter, teen sough gang's end. *Detroit Free Press*, p. 1A & 2A. Retrieved from https://www.newspapers.com/image/99453675/?terms=Pershing%2BHigh%2BSchool%2C

Kresnak, J., & Siegel, S. (1997, March 19). Shove inside school escalates into violent standoff, teen's killing. *Detroit Free Press*, p. 1A & 7A. Retrieved from https://www.newspapers.com/image/99392407/

1000 - McKinley Technical High School

Thompson, C. W., & Beamon, T. (1997, April 16). Former student shot in D.C. high school gym. *Washington Post, The*. Retrieved from https://www.washingtonpost.com/archive/local/1997/04/16/former-student-shot-in-dc-high-school-gym/d462ba3a-eb1c-4ab3-bb2d-9ebdc930aed4/?noredirect=on&utm_term=.34b9c97b0663

Student pleads not guilty in shooting. (1997, April 17). *Washington Post, The*. Retrieved from https://www.washingtonpost.com/archive/local/1997/04/17/student-pleads-not-guilty-in-shooting/5ed287a2-1a0e-421e-9141-058fb4b0f159/?noredirect=on&utm_term=.aec806711860

999 - City-as-School (High school)

Marzulli, J. (1997, May 1997). Student is shot in hs fight. *Daily News*, p. 24. Retrieved from https://www.newspapers.com/image/475661598/?terms=City-as-School%2C

School steps shooting. (1997, May 1). *Daily News*, p. 7C. Retrieved from https://www.newspapers.com/image/475670257/?terms=%22Cornelius%2BRay%22

998 - Pearl High School

Kimmel, M. S., & Mahler, M. (2003). Adolescent Masculinity, Homophobia, and Violence: Random School Shootings, 1982-2001. *American Behavioral Scientist*, (10). 9, 1447, 1454, 1455 & 1447.

National School Safety Center. (2010, March 3). *School Associated Violent Deaths* [PDF file], p. 2-46. Retrieved from https://files.eric.ed.gov/fulltext/ED519244.pdf

Crews, G. A. (2016). *Critical Examinations of School Violence and Disturbance in K-12 Education*, p. 6 & 7. Hershey, PA: Information Science Reference.

Lebrun, M. (2009). *Books, Blackboards, and Bullets: School Shootings and Violence in America*, p. 173-177. Lanham, MD: Rowman & Littlefield Education.

Congress of the U.S. (1999). *Understanding violent children. Hearing before the Subcommittee on Early Childhood, Youth and Families of the Committee on Education and the Workforce: ISBN-0-16-057973-2* [PDF File], p. 69-89. Retrieved from https://files.eric.ed.gov/fulltext/ED435940.pdf

Newman, K.S., Fox, C., Harding, D., Mehta, J., & Roth, W. (2004). *Rampage: the social roots of school shootings*, p. 47-263. New York, NY: Basic Books.

Boyette charged in death of Luke Woodham's mom. (1998, November 11). *Hattiesburg American*, p. 7A. Retrieved from https://www.newspapers.com/image/276939621/?terms=luke%2Bwoodham%2C%2Bmother

Pressley, S. A. (1997, October 22). A Bible belt town searches for answers. *Washington Post*. Retrieved from http://www.washingtonpost.com/wp-srv/national/longterm/juvmurders/stories/pearl.htm?noredirect=on

Rossilli, M. (1998, June 12). Woodham tells jury satanic spells changed his life. *Clarion-Ledger*, p. 1A & 8A. Retrieved from https://www.newspapers.com/image/184827422/

Butch, J. (1998, June 12). Woodham's courtroom demeanor detached, distant then explosive. *Clarion-Ledger*, p. 1A & 8A. Retrieved from https://www.newspapers.com/image/184827422/

Woodham v. State, 779 So. 2d 158, 2001 Miss. LEXIS 3 (Supreme Court of Mississippi January 18, 2001, Decided). https://advance-lexis-com.pbcls.idm.oclc.org/api/document?collection=cases&id=urn:contentItem:425N-VDS0-0039-43KS-00000-00&context=1516831

997 - Lew Wallace High School

Kiesling, M. (1997, October 22). Judge imposes gag order in shooting. *Times, The*, p. B-2. Retrieved from https://www.newspapers.com/image/305514357/?terms=Gustavo%2BMcQuay

Gary mayor bans nighttime football. (1997, October 12). *Kokomo Tribune, The*, p. B8. Retrieved from https://www.newspapers.com/image/2786990/?terms=Gustavo%2BMcQuay

996 - Lakeview Centennial High School

National School Safety Center. (2010, March 3). *School Associated Violent Deaths* [PDF file], p. 2-46. Retrieved from https://files.eric.ed.gov/fulltext/ED519244.pdf

News Clip: H.S. Suicide. (1997, October 14). *KXAS-TV* [Video file]. Retrieved from https://digital.library.unt.edu/ark:/67531/metadc849530/m1/#track/1

Congress of the U.S. (1999). *Understanding violent children. Hearing before the Subcommittee on Early Childhood, Youth and Families of the Committee on Education and the Workforce: ISBN-0-16-057973-2* [PDF File], p. 69-89. Retrieved from https://files.eric.ed.gov/fulltext/ED435940.pdf

Student shoots self in school restroom. (1997, October 15). *Paris News, The*, p. 2A. Retrieved from https://www.newspapers.com/image/6156093/?terms=Armando%2BMontiel%2C

995 - Lincoln Memorial Middle School

Authorities review possible charges against boy's mother. (1997, October 17). *Tampa Bay Times*, p. 5B. Retrieved from https://www.newspapers.com/image/326820842/?terms=Lincoln%2BMemorial%2BMiddle%2BSchool%2C

Teen, mother agree to plea in shooting. (1998, April 22). *Tampa Bay Times*, p. 4B. Retrieved from https://www.newspapers.com/image/327084165/?terms=Brandon%2BHartsoe%2C

Charges filed in school shooting. (1997, October 21). *Tampa Tribune, The*, p. 2. Retrieved from https://www.newspapers.com/image/340805361/?terms=Brandon%2BHartsoe%2C

Student charged in shooting. (1997, October 16). *Florida Today*, p. 1A. Retrieved from https://www.newspapers.com/image/174494775/?terms=Brandon%2BHartsoe%2C

994 - John Glenn High School

National School Safety Center. (2010, March 3). *School Associated Violent Deaths* [PDF file], p. 2-46. Retrieved from https://files.eric.ed.gov/fulltext/ED519244.pdf

Congress of the U.S. (1999). *Understanding violent children. Hearing before the Subcommittee on Early Childhood, Youth and Families of the Committee on Education and the Workforce: ISBN-0-16-057973-2* [PDF File], p. 69-89. Retrieved from https://files.eric.ed.gov/fulltext/ED435940.pdf

Counselors helping Norwalk students cope. (1997, October 24). *Signal, The*, p. A4. Retrieved from https://www.newspapers.com/image/333275725/?terms=John%2BGlenn%2BHigh%2BSchool%2C

Leeds, J. & Riccardo, N. (1997, October 23). Murder-suicide frenzy at high school. *Los Angeles Times*, p. A1 & A18. Retrieved from https://www.newspapers.com/image/158335063/?terms=Catherine%2BTran

993 - Ribault High School

Teen-age suspect surrenders in fatal shooting near school. (1997, November 11). *South Florida Sun Sentinel*, p. 6B. Retrieved from https://www.newspapers.com/image/238923371/?terms=Ribault%2BHigh%2BSchool%2C

Teen charged in student's killing. (1997, November 11). *Tampa Bay Times*, p. 5B. Retrieved from https://www.newspapers.com/image/327045070/?terms=James%2BDavid%2BCampbell

Teenager pleads guilty to shooting 2 at school. (1998, August 13). *Orlando Sentinel, The*, p. D-6. Retrieved from https://www.newspapers.com/image/235100504/?terms=James%2BDavid%2BCampbell

992 - Creekside Elementary School

National School Safety Center. (2010, March 3). *School Associated Violent Deaths* [PDF file], p. 2-46. Retrieved from https://files.eric.ed.gov/fulltext/ED519244.pdf

Congress of the U.S. (1999). *Understanding violent children. Hearing before the Subcommittee on Early Childhood, Youth and Families of the Committee on Education and the Workforce: ISBN-0-16-057973-2* [PDF File], p. 69-89. Retrieved from https://files.eric.ed.gov/fulltext/ED435940.pdf

Father shot to death picking up kids at school. (1997, November 15). *Santa Cruz Sentinel*, p. A-12. Retrieved from https://www.newspapers.com/image/90209517/?terms=Creekside%2BElementary%2BSchool%2C

Dad killed at school. (1997, November 15). *Californian, The*, p. C-2. Retrieved from https://www.newspapers.com/image/579987454/?terms=Jess%2BPerry%2BWest

991 - Heath High School

Adams, L. (2014, November 19). Survivors remember deadly Ky. school shooting 17 years later. *WLKY*. Retrieved from http://www.wlky.com/article/survivors-remember-deadly-ky-school-shooting-17-years-later/3753900

UPI Focus: boy indicted in Ky. school shooting. (1997, December 12). *United Press International*. Retrieved from https://www.upi.com/Archives/1997/12/12/UPI-Focus-Boy-indicted-in-Ky-school-shooting/1067881902800/

Braun, S., & Pasternak, J. (1997, December 2). Student Opens Fire on Prayer Group, Kills 3. *Los Angeles Times*. Retrieved from https://www.latimes.com/archives/la-xpm-1997-dec-02-mn-59759-story.html

Third student dies in Kentucky school shooting. (1997, December 2). *CNN*. Retrieved from http://www.cnn.com/US/9712/02/school.shooting.on/

Moore, M. H., Petrie, C. V., Braga, A. A., & McLaughlin, B. L. (2013). *Deadly lessons: understanding lethal school violence*. Washington, D.C.: The National Academy Press.

Landman, P. (2013) Psychiatric medications and school shooters [PDF file]. *School Shooters.Info*, p. 1-6. Retrieved from https://schoolshooters.info/sites/default/files/Psychiatric%20Medications.pdf

Newman, K.S., Fox, C., Harding, D., Mehta, J., & Roth, W. (2004). *Rampage: the social roots of school shootings*, p. 47-263. New York, NY: Basic Books.

Kimmel, M. S., & Mahler, M. (2003). Adolescent Masculinity, Homophobia, and Violence: Random School Shootings, 1982-2001. *American Behavioral Scientist*, (10). 9, 1447, 1454, 1455 & 1447.

National School Safety Center. (2010, March 3). *School Associated Violent Deaths* [PDF file], p. 2-46. Retrieved from https://files.eric.ed.gov/fulltext/ED519244.pdf

Crews, G. A. (2016). *Critical Examinations of School Violence and Disturbance in K-12 Education*, p. 6 & 7. Hershey, PA: Information Science Reference.

Lebrun, M. (2009). *Books, Blackboards, and Bullets: School Shootings and Violence in America*, p. 173-177. Lanham, MD: Rowman & Littlefield Education.

Congress of the U.S. (1999). *Understanding violent children. Hearing before the Subcommittee on Early Childhood, Youth and Families of the Committee on Education and the Workforce: ISBN-0-16-057973-2* [PDF File], p. 69-89. Retrieved from https://files.eric.ed.gov/fulltext/ED435940.pdf

Harding, D., Fox, C., & Mehta, J. (2002). Studying rare events through qualitative case studies. *Sociological Methods & Research - SOCIOL METHOD RES*. 31. 174-217. 10.1177/0049124102031002003

Fleshler, D., Chokey, A., Huriash, L. J., & Trischitta, L. (2018, February 15). A Horrific Day. *Sun Sentinel*, p. 1A & 9A. Retrieved from https://www.newspapers.com/image/392406586/?terms=%22A%20Horrific%20Day%22&match=1

Student indicted as adult in deaths of praying teens. (1997, December 13). *Orlando Sentinel, The*, p. A-4. Retrieved from https://www.newspapers.com/image/235034922/?terms=Melissa%2B%22Missy%22%2BJenkins%2C

990 - Stamps High School

Newman, K.S., Fox, C., Harding, D., Mehta, J., & Roth, W. (2004). *Rampage: the social roots of school shootings*, p. 47-263. New York, NY: Basic Books.

Two students wounded in Arkansas shooting. (1997, December 15). *CNN*. Retrieved from http://www.cnn.com/US/9712/15/briefs.am/arkansas.student.shooting/index.html

Stamps teen accused of shooting students may use bully defense. (1997, December 30). *Baxter Bulletin*. Retrieved from https://www.newspapers.com/image/413208860/?terms=Joseph%2B%22Colt%22%2BTodd

Attorney files appeal for teen in shooting case. (1998, October 14). *Baxter Bulletin*. Retrieved from https://www.newspapers.com/image/413159520/?terms=Joseph%2B%22Colt%22%2BTodd%2C

Teen arrested for shooting Arkansas classmates. (1997, December 19). *CNN*. Retrieved from http://www.cnn.com/US/9712/19/school.shooting/

989 - South Texas Community College

Sandoval, E. (1998, January 15). College security guard died doing a job he loved, widow says. *Monitor, The*, p. 1A & 4A. Retrieved from https://www.newspapers.com/image/330685265/

DeLeon, J. (1998, January 15). Family receives news in disbelief. *Monitor, The*, p. 4A. Retrieved from https://www.newspapers.com/image/330685281/

Smith, M. (2019, March 21). Suspect in 1998 STC fatal shooting extradited to McAllen. *Monitor, The*. Retrieved from https://www.themonitor.com/2019/03/21/suspect-1998-stc-fatal-shooting-extradited-mcallen/

Reegan, M. (2022, March 4). Accused shooter in '98 STC shooting not guilty of capital murder. *MyRGV.com*. Retrieved from https://myrgv.com/featured/2022/03/04/accused-stc-shooter-not-guilty-of-capital-murder/

988 - Joel Elias Spingarn High School

National School Safety Center. (2010, March 3). *School Associated Violent Deaths* [PDF file], p. 2-46. Retrieved from https://files.eric.ed.gov/fulltext/ED519244.pdf

Fern, M. E., & Mooar, B. (1998, January 15). Youth held in slaying of girl. *Washington Post, The*. Retrieved from https://www.washingtonpost.com/archive/local/1998/01/15/youth-held-in-slaying-of-girl-16/4cd521ad-4d21-4578-a42c-62d718905fb8/

Slevin, P. (1998, October 23). Youth gets prison term in death of D.C. girl. *Washington Post, The*. Retrieved from https://www.washingtonpost.com/archive/local/1998/10/23/youth-gets-prison-term-in-death-of-dc-girl/eba1413e-031f-47fd-89bd-b985803b3fe3/?noredirect=on

987 - Hoboken High School

National School Safety Center. (2010, March 3). *School Associated Violent Deaths* [PDF file], p. 2-46. Retrieved from https://files.eric.ed.gov/fulltext/ED519244.pdf

Congress of the U.S. (1999). *Understanding violent children. Hearing before the Subcommittee on Early Childhood, Youth and Families of the Committee on Education and the Workforce: ISBN-0-16-057973-2* [PDF File], p. 69-89. Retrieved from https://files.eric.ed.gov/fulltext/ED435940.pdf

Herszenhorn, D. M. (1998, February 15). Teacher's killer suspected an affair that never happened. *New York Times, The*. Retrieved from https://www.nytimes.com/1998/02/14/nyregion/teacher-s-killer-suspected-an-affair-that-never-happened.html

986 - Reed City Middle School

National School Safety Center. (2010, March 3). *School Associated Violent Deaths* [PDF file], p. 2-46. Retrieved from https://files.eric.ed.gov/fulltext/ED519244.pdf

Christoff, C. (1998, February 27). Suicide at school shocks small town. *Detroit Free Press*, p. 1B & 6B. Retrieved from https://www.newspapers.com/image/100151213

Eighth-grader kills himself in Osceola County middle school. (1998, February 27). *Central Michigan Life* [PDF file], p. 2. Retrieved from https://cmuhistory.cmich.edu/?a=d&d=IsabellaCML19980227&e=-------en-10--1--txt-txIN--------

Leith, S. (1998, February 26). Teen's likely suicide second in a week. *The Muskegon Chronicle*, p. 2B. Retrieved from https://www.newspapers.com/image/1088538105/?match=1&terms=Reed%20City%20High%20School

985 - George C. Marshall High School

National School Safety Center. (2010, March 3). *School Associated Violent Deaths* [PDF file], p. 2-46. Retrieved from https://files.eric.ed.gov/fulltext/ED519244.pdf

Congress of the U.S. (1999). *Understanding violent children. Hearing before the Subcommittee on Early Childhood, Youth and Families of the Committee on Education and the Workforce: ISBN-0-16-057973-2* [PDF File], p. 69-89. Retrieved from https://files.eric.ed.gov/fulltext/ED435940.pdf

Teen sentenced to 17 years for role in slaying. (1998, August 10). *Daily Press*, p. B3. Retrieved from https://www.newspapers.com/image/238256890/?terms=George%2BC.%2BMarshall%2BHigh%2BSchool

Teen pleads guilty to assault in killing. (1998, May 23). *Daily Press*, p. C6. Retrieved from https://www.newspapers.com/image/238210990/?terms=Michael%2BChuop%2C

984 - Westside Middle School

A school shooting in Jonesboro, Arkansas, kills five. (2018, August 21). *History*. Retrieved from https://www.history.com/this-day-in-history/a-school-shooting-in-jonesboro-arkansas-kills-five

Kifner, J., Bragg, R., Johnson, D., Verhovek, S. H. (1998, March 29). From wild talk and friendship to five deaths in a schoolyard. *New York Times, The*. Retrieved from https://www.nytimes.com/1998/03/29/us/from-wild-talk-and-friendship-to-five-deaths-in-a-schoolyard.html?sec=&spon=&pagewanted=all

Schwartz, J. (1998, March 25). Boys' ambush at ark. School leaves 5 dead. *Washington Post, The*. Retrieved from https://www.washingtonpost.com/archive/politics/1998/03/25/boys-ambush-at-ark-school-leaves-5-dead/9a255437-7ec1-4057-bb85-94ff78e397ca/

Moore, M. H., Petrie, C. V., Braga, A. A., & McLaughlin, B. L. (2013). *Deadly lessons: understanding lethal school violence*. Washington, D.C.: The National Academy Press.

Bragg, R. (1998, August 12). Judge punishes Arkansas boys who killed 5. *New York Times, The*. Retrieved from https://www.nytimes.com/1998/08/12/us/judge-punishes-arkansas-boys-who-killed-5.html?search-input-2=Judge+punishes+Arkansas+boys+who+killed+5

Roberts, J. (2005, August 11). 'No Justice In This Whatsoever.' *CBS News*. Retrieved from https://www.cbsnews.com/news/no-justice-in-this-whatsoever/

Brantley, M. (2017, August 17). Judge opens dispositions of shooters in Westside case in 1998. *Arkansas Times*. Retrieved from https://www.arktimes.com/ArkansasBlog/archives/2017/08/15/judge-opens-depositions-of-shooters-in-westside-case-in-1998

Landman, P. (2013) Psychiatric medications and school shooters [PDF file]. *School Shooters.Info*, p. 1-6. Retrieved from https://schoolshooters.info/sites/default/files/Psychiatric%20Medications.pdf

National School Safety Center. (2010, March 3). *School Associated Violent Deaths* [PDF file], p. 2-46. Retrieved from https://files.eric.ed.gov/fulltext/ED519244.pdf

Kellerman, J. (1999, May 18). *Savage spawn: reflections on violent children*, p. 2. New York, NY. The Ballantine Publishing Group.

Crews, G. A. (2016). *Critical Examinations of School Violence and Disturbance in K-12 Education*, p. 6 & 7. Hershey, PA: Information Science Reference.

Lebrun, M. (2009). *Books, Blackboards, and Bullets: School Shootings and Violence in America*, p. 173-177. Lanham, MD: Rowman & Littlefield Education.

Congress of the U.S. (1999). *Understanding violent children. Hearing before the Subcommittee on Early Childhood, Youth and Families of the Committee on Education and the Workforce: ISBN-0-16-057973-2* [PDF File], p. 69-89. Retrieved from https://files.eric.ed.gov/fulltext/ED435940.pdf

Newman, K.S., Fox, C., Harding, D., Mehta, J., & Roth, W. (2004). *Rampage: the social roots of school shootings*, p. 47-263. New York, NY: Basic Books.

Ford, J. (2019). Westside School Shooting. *Encyclopedia of Arkansas*. Retrieved from https://encyclopediaofarkansas.net/entries/westside-school-shooting-3717/

Children, parents work through grief. (1998, March 26). *Florida Today*, p. 14A. Retrieved from https://www.newspapers.com/image/174701349/?terms=Shannon%2BWright%2C

983 - Coldwater High School

National School Safety Center. (2010, March 3). *School Associated Violent Deaths* [PDF file], p. 2-46. Retrieved from https://files.eric.ed.gov/fulltext/ED519244.pdf

Motley, K. (1998, March 26). Death stuns Coldwater. *Battle Creek Enquirer*, p. 1A & 2A. Retrieved from https://www.newspapers.com/image/207255250/?terms=Coldwater%2BHigh%2BSchool%2C

982 - Grey Culbreth Middle School

National School Safety Center. (2010, March 3). *School Associated Violent Deaths* [PDF file], p. 2-46. Retrieved from https://files.eric.ed.gov/fulltext/ED519244.pdf

Congress of the U.S. (1999). *Understanding violent children. Hearing before the Subcommittee on Early Childhood, Youth and Families of the Committee on Education and the Workforce: ISBN-0-16-057973-2* [PDF File], p. 69-89. Retrieved from https://files.eric.ed.gov/fulltext/ED435940.pdf

Parsons, T. (1998, March 31). Reluctant Ark. students return. *Daily Record*. Retrieved from https://www.newspapers.com/image/255748929/?terms=Grey%2BCulbreth%2BMiddle%2BSchool%2C

Student kills self at school. (1998, March 31). *Southern Illinoisan*, p. 6B. Retrieved from https://www.newspapers.com/image/83621918/?terms=Grey%2BCulbreth%2BMiddle%2BSchool%2C

981 - Pardeeville Elementary School

Piper, G. (1998, April 15). Teen allegedly shoots Pardeeville school janitor. *Wisconsin State Journal*, p. 1A. Retrieved from https://www.newspapers.com/image/404516915/?terms=Pardeeville%2BElementary%2BSchool%2C

15-year old will be tried in adult court in shooting. (1998, October 3). *Wisconsin State Journal*, p. 5B. Retrieved from https://www.newspapers.com/image/406344516/?terms=Ralph%2BPulver%2C

Teen sentenced to 40 years. (1999, August 11). *Stevens Point Journal*, p. A12. Retrieved from https://www.newspapers.com/image/251621041/?terms=Ralph%2BPulver%2C

980 - Culver City High School

2 teenagers arrested in shooting at high school. (1998, April 28). *Los Angeles Times*, p. B4. Retrieved from https://www.newspapers.com/image/160491569/?terms=Culver%2BCity%2BHigh%2BSchool%2C

Goldman, A. (1998, April 24). Culver City calm in wake of shootings. *Los Angeles Times*, p. B12 & B13. Retrieved from https://www.newspapers.com/image/158773770/?terms=Culver%2BCity%2BHigh%2BSchool%2C

979 - James W. Parker Middle School

Moore, M. H., Petrie, C. V., Braga, A. A., & McLaughlin, B. L. (2013). *Deadly lessons: understanding lethal school violence.* Washington, D.C.: The National Academy Press.

National School Safety Center. (2010, March 3). *School Associated Violent Deaths* [PDF file], p. 2-46. Retrieved from https://files.eric.ed.gov/fulltext/ED519244.pdf

Crews, G. A. (2016). *Critical Examinations of School Violence and Disturbance in K-12 Education*, p. 6 & 7. Hershey, PA: Information Science Reference.

Congress of the U.S. (1999). *Understanding violent children. Hearing before the Subcommittee on Early Childhood, Youth and Families of the Committee on Education and the Workforce: ISBN-0-16-057973-2* [PDF File], p. 69-89. Retrieved from https://files.eric.ed.gov/fulltext/ED435940.pdf

Newman, K.S., Fox, C., Harding, D., Mehta, J., & Roth, W. (2004). *Rampage: the social roots of school shootings*, p. 47-263. New York, NY: Basic Books.

Pennsylvania students cope with shooting spree. (1998, April, 25). *CNN*. Retrieved from http://www.cnn.com/US/9804/25/school.shooting.pm/

978 - Philadelphia Elementary School

National School Safety Center. (2010, March 3). *School Associated Violent Deaths* [PDF file], p. 2-46. Retrieved from https://files.eric.ed.gov/fulltext/ED519244.pdf

Lebrun, M. (2009). *Books, Blackboards, and Bullets: School Shootings and Violence in America*, p. 173-177. Lanham, MD: Rowman & Littlefield Education.

14-year-old held in slayings of 2 teenagers. (1998, May 2). *Los Angeles Times*, p. B2. Retrieved from https://www.newspapers.com/image/160402308/?terms=Andres%2BAzocar%2C

Shooting arrest. (1998, May 1). *Elko Daily Free Press*, p. A10. Retrieved from https://www.newspapers.com/image/477322505/?terms=Philadelphia%2BElementary%2BSchool

977 - Dr. Antonia Pantoja Community School (Public School 18) (Grades PreK - 8)

National School Safety Center. (2010, March 3). *School Associated Violent Deaths* [PDF file], p. 2-46. Retrieved from https://files.eric.ed.gov/fulltext/ED519244.pdf

Police: man shoots, kills wife inside an elementary school. (1998, May 2). *Journal Times, The*, p. 5A. Retrieved from https://www.newspapers.com/image/342967441/?terms=Juan%2BA.%2BRoman%2C

Ex-jail guard admits schoolhouse slaying. (1998, December 9). *Democrat and Chronicle*, p. 2B. Retrieved from https://www.newspapers.com/image/136385695/?terms=%22Juan%2BRoman%22

Slay suspect was psychiatric patient. (1998, May 3). *Post-Star, The*, p. A7. Retrieved from https://www.newspapers.com/image/347679520/?terms=%22Juan%2BRoman%22

976 - Lincoln County High School

Another Fatal School Shooting. (1998, May 19). *CBS News*. Retrieved from https://www.cbsnews.com/news/another-fatal-school-shooting/

Student Dies in School Shooting National School Safety Center. (2010, March 3). *School Associated Violent Deaths* [PDF file], p. 2-46. Retrieved from https://files.eric.ed.gov/fulltext/ED519244.pdf

Lebrun, M. (2009). *Books, Blackboards, and Bullets: School Shootings and Violence in America*, p. 173-177. Lanham, MD: Rowman & Littlefield Education.

Tennessee high-school student kills another in parking lot. (1998, May 20). *Seattle Times, The*. Retrieved from https://archive.seattletimes.com/archive/?date=19980520&slug=2751712

Sharp, T. (1998, May 21). Student charged with killing his classmate. *Tallahassee Democrat*, p. 3A. Retrieved from https://www.newspapers.com/image/247432496/?terms=Jacob%2BDavis%2C

Tate v. Davis, 2001 Tenn. Crim. Ap. LEXIS 341, 2001 WL 487688 (Court of Criminal Appeals of Tennessee, Middle Section, At Nashville May 8, 2001, Filed). Retrieved from https://edb.pbclibrary.org:2306/api/document?collection=cases&id=urn:contentItem:4315-CTS0-0039-44H4-00000-00&context=1516831

975 - Thurston High School

Frontline: the killer at Thurston High. (1998, May 20-21). *PBS*. Retrieved from https://www.pbs.org/wgbh/pages/frontline/shows/kinkel/kip/cron.html

8 years later: Thurston and Kinkel revisited. (2006, October 1). *Daily Emerald*. Retrieved from https://www.dailyemerald.com/archives/years-later-thurston-and-kinkel-revisited/article_d898f051-9e58-5621-9417-3d21f4ec946a.html

Egan, T. (1998, May 22). Oregon Student Held in 3 Killings; One Dead, 23 Hurt at His School. *New York Times, The*. Retrieved from https://archive.nytimes.com/www.nytimes.com/library/national/052298ore-school-shooting.html

Kimmel, M. S., & Mahler, M. (2003). Adolescent Masculinity, Homophobia, and Violence: Random School Shootings, 1982-2001. *American Behavioral Scientist*, (10). 9, 1447, 1454, 1455 & 1447.

National School Safety Center. (2010, March 3). *School Associated Violent Deaths* [PDF file], p. 2-46. Retrieved from https://files.eric.ed.gov/fulltext/ED519244.pdf

Crews, G. A. (2016). *Critical Examinations of School Violence and Disturbance in K-12 Education*, p. 6 & 7. Hershey, PA: Information Science Reference.

Lebrun, M. (2009). *Books, Blackboards, and Bullets: School Shootings and Violence in America*, p. 173-177. Lanham, MD: Rowman & Littlefield Education.

Newman, K.S., Fox, C., Harding, D., Mehta, J., & Roth, W. (2004). *Rampage: the social roots of school shootings*, p. 47-263. New York, NY: Basic Books.

Brandon, K., & Haynes, V. D. (1998, May 25). Oregon parents may have died day before spree. Chicago Tribune, p. 1 & 16. Retrieved from https://www.newspapers.com/image/169389145/

Thurston High reopens after deadly rampage. (1998, May 27). *Berkshire Eagle, The*, p. A3. Retrieved from https://www.newspapers.com/image/534170984/?terms=Mikael%2BNickolauson%2C

Longman, J. (1998, May 23). 'It was just like Jake to go after him,' coach says. *Detroit Free Press*, p. 6A. Retrieved from https://www.newspapers.com/image/100149918/?terms=Jake%2BRyker%2C

974 - Jersey Village High School

Lebrun, M. (2009). *Books, Blackboards, and Bullets: School Shootings and Violence in America*, p. 173-177. Lanham, MD: Rowman & Littlefield Education.

Houston area teen shot at high school. (1998, May 22). *Longview News-Journal*, p. 7A. Retrieved from https://www.newspapers.com/image/219923225/?terms=Jersey%2BVillage%2BHigh%2BSchool%2C

Houston student suffers from gunshot wound to leg in class. (1998, May 22). *Victoria Advocate*, p. 2A. Retrieved from https://www.newspapers.com/image/434244022/?terms=Marko%2BAntonio%2BGuerrero%2C

973 - Rialto High School

National School Safety Center. (2010, March 3). *School Associated Violent Deaths* [PDF file], p. 2-46. Retrieved from https://files.eric.ed.gov/fulltext/ED519244.pdf

Teen shoots self at school. (1998, May 23). *Californian, The*, p. C-8. Retrieved from https://www.newspapers.com/image/579860194/?terms=Rialto%2BHigh%2BSchool%2C

Boy, 15 dies after shooting himself in head at school. (1998, May 25). *Los Angeles Times*, p. A23. Retrieved from https://www.newspapers.com/image/159064526/?terms=Ricardo%2BMartin%2C

972 - Washington Middle School

National School Safety Center. (2010, March 3). *School Associated Violent Deaths* [PDF file], p. 2-46. Retrieved from https://files.eric.ed.gov/fulltext/ED519244.pdf

Boy, 14, killed, man wounded in middle school. (1998, May 29). *Los Angeles Times*, p. B4. Retrieved from https://www.newspapers.com/image/158790488/?terms=Salvador%2BGabriel%2BDiaz

Suspect sought in slaying at school. (1998, June 6). *Los Angeles Times*, p. B2. Retrieved from https://www.newspapers.com/image/159260040/?terms=%22Salvador%2BDiaz%22

971 - Stranahan High School

National School Safety Center. (2010, March 3). *School Associated Violent Deaths* [PDF file], p. 2-46. Retrieved from https://files.eric.ed.gov/fulltext/ED519244.pdf

Huriash, L. J. (1998, May 30). Family unaware of abuse problem. *South Florida Sun Sentinel*, p. 6B. Retrieved from https://www.newspapers.com/image/239009048/?terms=Stranahan%2BHigh%2BSchool%2C

Ex-boyfriend kills teacher, self in school parking lot. (1998, May 30). *Gazette, The*. Retrieved from https://www.newspapers.com/image/550927537/?terms=Stranahan%2BHigh%2BSchool%2C

King, J., Borden, T., & Kelley, L. (1998, May 30). Former boyfriend kills teacher, self in school lot. *South Florida Sun Sentinel (Fort Lauderdale, Florida)*, p. 1B & 6B. Retrieved from https://www.newspapers.com/image/239008999/

970 - Armstrong High School

Lebrun, M. (2009). *Books, Blackboards, and Bullets: School Shootings and Violence in America*, p. 173-177. Lanham, MD: Rowman & Littlefield Education.

News: Teacher, employee shot at high school in Richmond, Va. 6/15/98. (1998, June 15). *Amarillo Globe News*. Retrieved from https://archive.ph/zlDPj#selection-1013.21-1013.89

Baskerville, B. (1998, June 16). Boy, 14, shoots coach, aide in Va. *Herald-News, The*, p. A1 & A4. Retrieved from https://www.newspapers.com/image/529613835/

No bail in school shootings. (1998, June 17). *Tampa Bay Times*, p. 6A. Retrieved from https://www.newspapers.com/image/327414758/?terms=Quinshawn%2BBooker%2C

969 - Herbert Hoover High School

National School Safety Center. (2010, March 3). *School Associated Violent Deaths* [PDF file], p. 2-46. Retrieved from https://files.eric.ed.gov/fulltext/ED519244.pdf

Blankstein, A., & Moore, S. (1998, September 11). Boy wounded in shooting outside Glendale school. *Los Angeles Times*. Retrieved from http://articles.latimes.com/1998/sep/11/local/me-21578

Helfand, D. (1998, September 14). Glendale student. 15, hurt in shooting, dies. *Los Angeles Times*, p. B3. Retrieved from https://www.newspapers.com/image/159947828/?terms=Avetis%2BDemirchyan

Moore, S. (1998, October 10). Suspect in fatal campus shooting turns self in. *Los Angeles Times*, p. B8. Retrieved from https://www.newspapers.com/image/158978315/?terms=Avetis%2BDemirchyan

Mother asks for no jail time for son's killer. (1999, December 19). *Manhattan Mercury, The*, p. E6. Retrieved from https://www.newspapers.com/image/425725764/?terms=Artiom%2BBadalyan

968 - North Miami Senior High School

Ramirez, D., & Cazares, D. (1998, September 30). Student, teacher wounded in N. Miami. *South Florida Sun Sentinel*, p. 8B. Retrieved from https://www.newspapers.com/image/238875352/?terms=North%2BMiami%2BSenior%2BHigh%2BSchool%2C

Shootings injure teacher, 3 students in state. (1998, October 1). *Tampa Bay Times*, p. 7B. Retrieved from https://www.newspapers.com/image/327348724/?terms=Felly%2BPetit-Frere%2C

Viega, A. (1998, October 1). Two teens arrested in North Miami school shooting. *Palm Beach Post, The*, p.5B. Retrieved from https://www.newspapers.com/image/133670924/?terms=Lesonie%2BWalker%2C

967 - Leesburg High School

Quigley, K., & Fernandez, D. (1998, October 1). Shooting shocks school. *Orlando Sentinel, The*, p. 1 & 6. Retrieved from https://www.newspapers.com/image/235592020/?terms=leesburg%2Bhigh%2Bschool%2C

Quigley, K. (1998, October 2). Teen: I'm a victim - not a gunman. *Orlando Sentinel, The*, p. 1 & 5. Retrieved from https://www.newspapers.com/image/235594264

966 - Central High School

National School Safety Center. (2010, March 3). *School Associated Violent Deaths* [PDF file], p. 2-46. Retrieved from https://files.eric.ed.gov/fulltext/ED519244.pdf

Cowles, A., & Ellis, R. (1999, January 9). Girlfriend dies in suicide pact. *Atlanta Constitution, The*, p. C1 & C2. Retrieved from https://www.newspapers.com/image/403120959/?terms=Central%2BHigh%2BSchool%2C

Warner, J. & Scott, P. (1999, January 10). Carroll County teen dies, fulfills 'nightmare' pact. *Atlanta Constitution, The*, p. F1. Retrieved from https://www.newspapers.com/image/403135851/?terms=Jeff%2BMiller%2C

965 - Harry S. Truman High School

Claffey, M., Olmeda, R. A., & Goldiner, D. (1999, January 15). Two hurt in school shooting. *Daily News*, p. 80. Retrieved from https://www.newspapers.com/image/434128870/?terms=Truman%2BHigh%2BSchool%2C

Roane, K. R. (1999, January 15). 2 students shot outside Bronx high school. *New York Times, The*. Retrieved from https://www.nytimes.com/1999/01/15/nyregion/2-students-shot-outside-bronx-high-school.html

964 - Richland High School

National School Safety Center. (2010, March 3). *School Associated Violent Deaths* [PDF file], p. 2-46. Retrieved from https://files.eric.ed.gov/fulltext/ED519244.pdf

Boy shoots himself in high school bathroom. (1999, January 22). *Galveston Daily News, The*, p. A8. Retrieved from https://www.newspapers.com/image/13671024/?terms=Richland%2BHills%2BHigh%2BSchool%2C

In other news. (1999, January 22). *El Paso Times*, p. 5B. Retrieved from https://www.newspapers.com/image/432253017/?terms=Richland%2BHills%2BHigh%2BSchool%2C

963 - Ombudsman Education Service Center (High School)

National School Safety Center. (2010, March 3). *School Associated Violent Deaths* [PDF file], p. 2-46. Retrieved from https://files.eric.ed.gov/fulltext/ED519244.pdf

Holt, D., & Karuhn, C. (1999, February 16). Slaying permanently closes Elgin school. *Chicago Tribune*, p. Section 2-5. Retrieved from https://www.newspapers.com/image/168866614/?terms=Ombudsman%2BEducation%2BService%2BCenter%2C

Krol, E. (1999, December 23). Judge hears tape of teen confessing to Elgin shooting. *Daily Herald, The*, p. Section 1-4. Retrieved from https://www.newspapers.com/image/14482480/?terms=Rickey%2BL.%2BQuezada

Ferkenhoff, E., & Quintanilla, R. (1999, February 18). School slaying linked to gang rivalry. *Chicago Tribune*, p. Section 2-1 & 6. Retrieved from https://www.newspapers.com/image/168877247/?terms=Rickey%2BQuezada

962 - Columbine High School

Columbine Shooting. (2018, August 21). *History*. Retrieved from https://www.history.com/topics/1990s/columbine-high-school-shootings

Landman, P. (2013) Psychiatric medications and school shooters [PDF file]. *School Shooters.Info*, p. 1-6. Retrieved from https://schoolshooters.info/sites/default/files/Psychiatric%20Medications.pdf

National School Safety Center. (2010, March 3). *School Associated Violent Deaths* [PDF file], p. 2-46. Retrieved from https://files.eric.ed.gov/fulltext/ED519244.pdf

Crews, G. A. (2016). *Critical Examinations of School Violence and Disturbance in K-12 Education*, p. 6 & 7. Hershey, PA: Information Science Reference.

Lebrun, M. (2009). *Books, Blackboards, and Bullets: School Shootings and Violence in America*, p. 173-177. Lanham, MD: Rowman & Littlefield Education.

Newman, K.S., Fox, C., Harding, D., Mehta, J., & Roth, W. (2004). *Rampage: the social roots of school shootings*, p. 47-263. New York, NY: Basic Books.

Fleshler, D., Chokey, A., Huriash, L. J., & Trischitta, L. (2018, February 15). A Horrific Day. *Sun Sentinel*, p. 1A & 9A. Retrieved from https://www.newspapers.com/image/392406586/?terms=%22A%20Horrific%20Day%22&match=1

Columbine High School shootings fast facts. (2019, May 1). *CNN*. Retrieved from https://www.cnn.com/2013/09/18/us/columbine-high-school-shootings-fast-facts/

Cullen, D. (2004, April 20). The depressive and the psychopath. *Slate*. Retrieved from https://slate.com/news-and-politics/2004/04/at-last-we-know-why-the-columbine-killers-did-it.html

Cabell: Columbine killers video released. (2003, October 22). *CNN*. Retrieved from http://www.cnn.com/2003/US/Central/10/22/otsc.cabell/

Levenson, M. (2025, March 11). Anne Marie Hochhalter, Paralyzed in Columbine Shooting, Dies at 43. *New York Times, The*. Retrieved from https://www.nytimes.com/2025/02/18/us/anne-marie-hochhalter-columbine-shooting-dies.html

Conditions of school shooting victims. (1999, April 27). *South Coast Today*. Retrieved from https://www.southcoasttoday.com/story/news/nation-world/1999/04/27/conditions-school-shooting-victims/50528547007/

Conditions of the wounded. (1999). *Denver Post, The*. Retrieved from https://extras.denverpost.com/news/shot0430g.htm

Obmascik, M. (2019, April 15). Columbine High School shooting leaves 15 dead, 28 hurt. *Denver Post, The*. Retrieved from https://www.denverpost.com/1999/04/21/columbine-high-school-shooting/

Ontiveroz, A. (2019, April 19). Voices from the Columbine High School shooting: Survivors, families of the fallen reflect 20 years later. *Denver Post, The*. Retrieved from https://www.denverpost.com/2019/04/17/columbine-high-school-shooting-survivors-families/

Langman Ph.D., P. (2014). Charles Andrew Williams: sorting out the contradictions [PDF file]. *SchoolShooters.info*. Retrieved from https://schoolshooters.info/sites/default/files/williams_contradictions_1.1.pdf

Jefferson County Sheriff's Office. (2017, June 25). Columbine documents [PDF file]. *Internet Archive*, pp. JC-001-026013 - JC-001-026015. Retrieved from https://archive.org/details/columbine_201706/mode/2up?view=theater

961 - Martin Luther King Jr. Middle School

Carter, R. (2000, November 23). Web site will help commemorate life of shooting victim. *Atlanta Journal-Constitution, The*, p. E17

National School Safety Center. (2010, March 3). *School Associated Violent Deaths* [PDF file], p. 2-46. Retrieved from https://files.eric.ed.gov/fulltext/ED519244.pdf

Carter, R., & Ffrench-Parker, J. (1999, April 24). Suspect arrested in teen's slaying. *Atlanta Journal-Constitution, The*, p. G1 & G6. Retrieved from https://www.newspapers.com/image/403220181/?terms=Martin%2BLuther%2BKing%2BJr.%2BMiddle%2BSchool%2C

Warner, J. (1999, April 25). Witnesses point way to suspect. *Atlanta Constitution, The*, p. F1. Retrieved from https://www.newspapers.com/image/403223066

960 - Scotlandville Middle School

Teen-age girl is wounded in shooting at La. school. (1999, April 23). *Baltimore Sun, The*, p. 17A. Retrieved from https://www.newspapers.com/image/173623273/?terms=Scotlandville%2BMiddle%2BSchool%2C

School incidents probed. (1999, April 23). *Crowley Post-Signal, The*, p. 2. Retrieved from https://www.newspapers.com/image/469910043/?terms=Murphy%2BYoung

959 - Heritage High School

Moore, M. H., Petrie, C. V., Braga, A. A., & McLaughlin, B. L. (2013). *Deadly lessons: understanding lethal school violence*. Washington, D.C.: The National Academy Press.

Queen, A. (2016, July 26). TJ Solomon, Heritage High School shooter, released after 17 years. *Rockdale Citizen, The*. Retrieved from http://www.rockdalenewtoncitizen.com/news/local/tj-solomon-heritage-high-school-shooter-released-after-years/article_66508783-e652-5f3c-94c3-acaa6164f3ee.html

Cloud, J. (1999, May 24). Just a routine school shooting. *CNN*. Retrieved from http://www.cnn.com/ALLPOLITICS/time/1999/05/24/school.shooting.html

Lebrun, M. (2009). *Books, Blackboards, and Bullets: School Shootings and Violence in America*, p. 173-177. Lanham, MD: Rowman & Littlefield Education.

Newman, K.S., Fox, C., Harding, D., Mehta, J., & Roth, W. (2004). *Rampage: the social roots of school shootings*, p. 47-263. New York, NY: Basic Books.

Stafford, L. (2000, October 5). Seeking closure in shooting case. *Atlanta Constitution, The*, p. JR5. Retrieved from https://www.newspapers.com/image/399869930/?terms=Anthony%2BSolomon%2C

Stafford, L. (1999, August 10). Lawyers: teen shooter needs psychiatric hospital. *Atlanta Journal-Constitution, The*, p. C1 & C6. Retrieved from https://www.newspapers.com/image/403482867/?terms=Anthony%2BB.%2B%22T.J.%22%2BSolomon%2C

Jones, R. (1999, May 21). Another attack has Americans asking why. *Anniston Star, The*, p. 1A & 2A. Retrieved from https://www.newspapers.com/image/106706469

Quinn, C. (2015, October 9). A history of school shootings in Georgia. *Atlanta Journal-Constitution, The*. Retrieved from https://www.ajc.com/news/local-education/history-school-shootings-georgia/YtSs7RTBgta8uou947QSgO/

958 - Jasper County Comprehensive High School

National School Safety Center. (2010, March 3). *School Associated Violent Deaths* [PDF file], p. 2-46. Retrieved from https://files.eric.ed.gov/fulltext/ED519244.pdf

Williams, C. (1999a, August 26). Suicide: 16-year-old girl shoots self at Ga. high school. *Town Talk, The*, p. A-8. Retrieved from https://www.newspapers.com/image/213264269/?terms=Jasper%2BCounty%2BHigh%2BSchool%2C

957 - Vines High School

National School Safety Center. (2010, March 3). *School Associated Violent Deaths* [PDF file], p. 2-46. Retrieved from https://files.eric.ed.gov/fulltext/ED519244.pdf

Muscanere, A. (1999a, September 8). Student's death shocks Vines. *Plano Star Courier*, p. 1A.

Muscanere, A. (1999b, November 9). Counselors ease Vines' grieving. Plano Star Courier, p. 1A.

956 - Santa Teresa High School

National School Safety Center. (2010, March 3). *School Associated Violent Deaths* [PDF file], p. 2-46. Retrieved from https://files.eric.ed.gov/fulltext/ED519244.pdf

Teen kills self in San Jose school. (1999, September 10). *San Francisco Examiner, The*, p. A-5. Retrieved from https://www.newspapers.com/image/462641916/?terms=Santa%2BTeresa%2BHigh%2BSchool%2C

Squatriglia, C., Lynem, J. N., & Gaura, M. A. (1999, September 10). San Jose boy, 16, fatally shoots himself at high school / Santa Teresa student sneaked gun into rest room. *SFGate*. Retrieved from https://www.sfgate.com/bayarea/article/San-Jose-Boy-16-Fatally-Shoots-Himself-at-High-2909269.php

955 - John Bartram High School

Rubinkam, M. (1999, October 5). Assistant principal shot at Philly school. *Tribune, The*, p. C7. Retrieved from https://www.newspapers.com/image/529104302/?terms=John%2BBartram%2BHigh%2BSchool%2C

Conroy, T. (1999, October 9). Attorney: Bartram shooting accidental. *Philadelphia Daily News*, p. 6. Retrieved from https://www.newspapers.com/image/184618551/?terms=Eric%2BCoxen%2C

Dean, M. M., & Kim, M. O. (1999, October 7). Offenders aren't bounced, they're kept in the system. *Philadelphia Daily News*, p. 3. Retrieved from https://www.newspapers.com/image/184616588/?terms=Eric%2BCoxen%2C

954 - Ed W. Clark High School

2 Vegas students wounded in shooting. (1999, October 12). *Reno Gazette-Journal*, p. 2B. Retrieved from https://www.newspapers.com/image/152518043/?terms=Clark%2BHigh%2BSchool%2C

School shooting. (1999, October 15). *Elko Daily Free Press*, p. A10. Retrieved from https://www.newspapers.com/image/477371519/?terms=Clark%2BHigh%2BSchool%2C

Man pleads guilty. (2000, April 12). *Elko Daily Free Press*, p. A3. Retrieved from https://www.newspapers.com/image/477380654/?terms=Maynor%2BVillanueva%2C

Villanueva v. State, 117 Nev. 664, 27 P.3d 443, 2001 Nev. LEXIS 52, 117 Nev. Adv. Rep. 53 (Supreme Court of Nevada July 25, 2001, Decided). Retrieved from https://edb.pbclibrary.org:2306/api/document?collection=cases&id=urn:contentItem:43KK-4N20-0039-44ND-00000-00&context=1516831

953 - San Fernando High School

Manzano, R. J., & Fox, S. (1999, October 23). *Los Angeles Times*, p. B1 & B8. Retrieved from https://www.newspapers.com/image/161272866/?terms=San%2BFernando%2BHigh%2BSchool%2C

Sauerwein, K. (1999, October 22). Student wounded outside high school campus. *Los Angeles Times*, p. B15. Retrieved from https://www.newspapers.com/image/161258730/?terms=San%2BFernando%2BHigh%2BSchool%2C

952 - Martin Luther King Jr. High School

National School Safety Center. (2010, March 3). *School Associated Violent Deaths* [PDF file], p. 2-46. Retrieved from https://files.eric.ed.gov/fulltext/ED519244.pdf

Snyder, S., & Moran, R. (1999, October 28). After shooting, a call for safety and nonviolence. *Philadelphia Inquirer, The*, p. B1 & B4. Retrieved from https://www.newspapers.com/image/167871274/?terms=Martin%2BLuther%2BKing%2BJr.%2BHigh%2BSchool%2C&match=2

Racher, D. (1999, November 26). Pair facing murder trial in shooting of student at MLK high. *Philadelphia Daily News*, p. 23. Retrieved from https://www.newspapers.com/image/181881535/?terms=Larry%2BBurton%2C

Haney, K., Brennan, C., & Silary, T. (1999, October 27). Student slain at MLK High. *Philadelphia Daily News*, p. 11. Retrieved from https://www.newspapers.com/image/184628077/?terms=Larry%2BBurton%2C

951 - Dorchester High School

Daley, B. (1999, November 4). Shooting adds to unease at school. *Boston Globe, The*, p. B1 & B6. Retrieved from https://www.newspapers.com/image/442142036/?terms=Dorchester%2BHigh%2BSchool%2C

Commonwealth v. Furr, 58 Mass. Ap. Ct. 155, 788 N.E.2d 592, 2003 Mass. Ap. LEXIS 551 (Appeals Court of Massachusetts May 16, 2003, Decided). Retrieved from https://edb.pbclibrary.org:2306/api/document?collection=cases&id=urn:contentItem:48M2-YDH0-0039-4060-00000-00&context=1516831

950 - Dickinson High School

Williams, S. E. (1999b, November 18). 15-year old critical in what police call accidental shooting. *Galveston Daily News, The*, p. A1 & A7. Retrieved from https://www.newspapers.com/image/13325920/?terms=Dickinson%2BHigh%2BSchool%2C

Falgoust, N. (1999, November 18). Students and parents say safety policies failed at high school. *Galveston Daily News, The*, p. A1 & A7. Retrieved from https://www.newspapers.com/image/13325920/

15-year old wounded in shooting. (1999, November 18). *Times, The*, p. 5B. Retrieved from https://www.newspapers.com/image/218850098/?terms=Dickinson%2BHigh%2BSchool%2C

949 - North High School

Robinson, M. (1999, November 20). Shooting of student self-inflicted, police say. *Denver Post, The*, p. B-02. Retrieved from https://infoweb.newsbank.com/apps/news/document-view?p=AWNB&docref=news/0EAF454F3460BB3A&f=basic

Weber, B., & Washington, A. (1999, November 19). North High student shot outside school boy, 15, wounded in arm. *Rocky Mountain News*, p. 5A. Retrieved from https://infoweb.newsbank.com/apps/news/document-view?p=AWNB&docref=news/0EB4EEB4E88C6223&f=basic

Gutierrez, H. (1999, November 20). Boy's gun wound self-inflicted. *Rocky Mountain News*, p. 28A. Retrieved from https://infoweb.newsbank.com/apps/news/document-view?p=AWNB&docref=news/0EB4EEB755178B91&f=basic

948 - Deming Middle School

National School Safety Center. (2010, March 3). *School Associated Violent Deaths* [PDF file], p. 2-46. Retrieved from https://files.eric.ed.gov/fulltext/ED519244.pdf

Crews, G. A. (2016). *Critical Examinations of School Violence and Disturbance in K-12 Education*, p. 6 & 7. Hershey, PA: Information Science Reference.

Lebrun, M. (2009). *Books, Blackboards, and Bullets: School Shootings and Violence in America*, p. 173-177. Lanham, MD: Rowman & Littlefield Education.

Boy held in shooting of girl at New Mexico middle school. (1999, November 20). *Los Angeles Times*. Retrieved from https://www.latimes.com/archives/la-xpm-1999-nov-20-mn-35594-story.html

Brenner, S. (2000, April 26). Cordova pleads guilty to killing. *Deming Headlight, The*, p. 1 & 2. Retrieved from https://www.newspapers.com/image/558314130/?terms=Victor%2BCordova%2BJr.%2C

Boy sent to prison for school shooting. (2000, December 18). *Standard-Speaker*, p. 17. Retrieved from https://www.newspapers.com/image/503345798/?terms=Victor%2BCordova%2BJr.%2C

Thompson, F. (2000, April 15). DA says boy to admit Deming school killing. *Albuquerque Journal*, p. A1 & A2. Retrieved from https://www.newspapers.com/image/344825806/

947 - Fort Gibson Middle School

Romano, L. (1999, December 7). 4 wounded in Oklahoma school shooting; Alleged Gunman Is Seventh- Grade Boy Described as Popular Honors Student. *Washington Post, The*, p. A03

Ruble, R. (1999, December 7). Boy shoots four at Okla. school. *Herald-News, The*, p. A1 & A4. Retrieved from https://www.newspapers.com/image/528977027/

Gun in school shooting was father's, police say. (1999, December 8). *Los Angeles Times*. Retrieved from http://articles.latimes.com/1999/dec/08/news/mn-41650

Jackson, D.Z. (1999, December 14). Shy, sweet and nearly deadly. *Chicago Tribune*. Retrieved from http://articles.chicagotribune.com/1999-12-14/news/9912140076_1_seth-trickey-thurston-high-school-kip-kinkel

Lebrun, M. (2009). *Books, Blackboards, and Bullets: School Shootings and Violence in America*, p. 173-177. Lanham, MD: Rowman & Littlefield Education.

Newman, K.S., Fox, C., Harding, D., Mehta, J., & Roth, W. (2004). *Rampage: the social roots of school shootings*, p. 47-263. New York, NY: Basic Books.

School shooter may end up in Lawrence. (2003, September 26). *Lawrence Journal-World*. Retrieved from https://www2.ljworld.com/news/2003/sep/26/school_shooter_may/

Hutchinson, M. A. (1999, December 7). 5 hurt in Fort Gibson school shooting. *Daily Oklahoman, The*, p. 12A. Retrieved from https://www.newspapers.com/image/454900554

www.ingramcontent.com/pod-product-compliance
Lightning Source LLC
Chambersburg PA
CBHW040003040426
42337CB00033B/5210